LEADING LADY

LEADING
LADY

SHERRY LANSING

and the Making of a

Hollywood Groundbreaker

STEPHEN GALLOWAY

**CROWN
ARCHETYPE**
NEW YORK

Published in the United States by Crown Archetype, an imprint of the
Crown Publishing Group, a division of Penguin Random House LLC, New York.
crownarchetype.com

Crown Archetype and colophon is a registered trademark
of Penguin Random House LLC.

Library of Congress Cataloging-in-Publication Data
Names: Galloway, Stephen author.
Title: Leading Lady : Sherry Lansing and the Making of a Hollywood
Groundbreaker / Stephen Galloway.
Description: First edition. | New York : Crown Archetype, 2017.
Identifiers: LCCN 2016035586| ISBN 9780307405937 (hardcover : alk. paper) |
ISBN 9781101904770 (tradepaper : alk. paper)
Subjects: LCSH: Lansing, Sherry, 1944– | Women motion picture producers and
directors—United States—Biography. | Women executives—United
States—Biography. | Motion picture industry—United States—History—20th
century. | Motion picture industry—United States—History—21st century.
| Women philanthropists—United States—Biography.
Classification: LCC PN1998.3.L383 S35 2017 | DDC 791.4302/33092 [B]—dc23
LC record available at *https://lccn.loc.gov/2016035586*

ISBN 978-0-307-40593-7
Ebook ISBN 978-0-307-45171-2

PRINTED IN THE UNITED STATES OF AMERICA

Insert credits can be found on pages 391–392.

Book design by Anna Thompson
Jacket design by Elena Giavaldi
Jacket photograph: Peden & Munk/Trunk Archive

10 9 8 7 6 5 4 3 2 1

First Edition

LEADING LADY

CHAPTER 1

On January 23, 2003, a black sedan pulled out of Paramount Pictures' historic sixty-five-acre lot at the southern edge of Hollywood and eased into the clogged traffic, heading toward Los Angeles International Airport.

For the security guards who manned the studio's Melrose Avenue gate, this was nothing new: taxis and limousines went back and forth dozens of times each hour, ferrying everyone who was anyone, from Tom Cruise to Mel Gibson to Angelina Jolie. The guards knew them well, and all their follies and foibles. Some were liked, some loathed; few were as revered as the woman sitting inside the car now, her blue eyes brilliant against her raven hair.

At fifty-eight years old, Sherry Lansing was Hollywood royalty. Tall and elegant in one of her trademark Armani suits, she had been chairman of Paramount's movie division since 1992 and had ruled it with an iron fist hidden inside the most velvet of gloves. With her regal presence and commanding five-foot-ten frame, she would have intimidated the guards if not for her palpable warmth; she liked to be liked, needed it even, and unsheathed the steel within only when absolutely necessary.

For a quarter century she had reigned as the most powerful woman in film, overseeing two separate studios at different stages of her career and producing such high-profile pictures as *Fatal Attraction* and *Indecent Pro-*

posal in between. She had weathered hits and misses, victories and defeats, enemies who masqueraded as friends, and friends who might as well have been enemies. She was as much a part of the entertainment landscape as the Hollywood sign, one of a rare breed of executives known by their first names alone. To almost everybody, she was simply Sherry.

In her present role, she oversaw a billion dollars in annual production and marketing expenses, and was responsible for green-lighting hundreds of movies, from *Mission: Impossible* to *Saving Private Ryan* to *Forrest Gump*. Some of these had become part of the cultural lexicon; others, less widely seen, had nonetheless filled Paramount's coffers, thanks to shrewd deals Lansing had hammered out with her business partner, Jonathan Dolgen, the blunt executive who played bad cop to her good, yin to her yang. Both were careful not to repeat the errors of the past, most famously those of 20th Century Fox, whose bloated 1963 epic *Cleopatra* had left the studio so broke it was forced to sell off much of its land, allowing developers to swoop in and create the labyrinthine office complex now known as Century City.

Lansing's unusual ability to pick winners and avoid too many losers had given Paramount a unique stability in a town where there was next to none, where writers, directors, producers and stars lived in dread that today's success was merely a prelude to tomorrow's failure. And that stability benefited not just the names that lit up the screen but also the thousands of workers, from secretaries to screenwriters, from accountants to attorneys, all linked in a golden chain leading to Lansing herself.

Because of this, she was rarely plagued by the fears that ravaged her peers, who at any moment could be toppled from their posts, losing assistants, expense accounts, fine tables at finer restaurants, trips on the corporate jet, seven-figure bonuses and above all the deference that was de rigueur in this most feudal of ecosystems, where everyone knew his place, where rich was rich and poor was poor and ne'er the twain did meet. Wealthy beyond her dreams thanks to a clever deal that had brought her millions of dollars when Paramount was sold to Viacom in 1994, she floated in a zone of her own, thirty thousand feet above the turbulence that buffeted almost everyone beneath her.

———

THAT, AT LEAST, was in normal circumstances. But over the past year, what had begun as a faint notion had gathered steam: that she would turn her back on Hollywood altogether.

At various moments in her long and storied career, she had contemplated weaning herself from the industry that had fed her. In her younger and less burdened days she had peeled herself free for weeks, voyaging down the Amazon, trekking across India and even living with the Maasai and Samburu tribes in rural Kenya. During those trips she had treasured life away from the rapacious rituals of Hollywood, but each time she had returned, ready to lock horns again.

Lately, however, the urge to escape had become overwhelming. Just three years earlier, she had declined to renew her contract, at a potential cost of millions in salary and bonuses, until her lawyer dissuaded her, promising there was nothing she could sign that he could not get her out of.

The past two years had been particularly taxing. Movies for which she cared passionately had stumbled at the box office—even one of her favorites, *K-19: The Widowmaker*, a rare Hollywood action-adventure film directed by a woman, Kathryn Bigelow. Others had succeeded almost in spite of themselves, such as *Lara Croft: Tomb Raider*, the picture that made Jolie a household name, whose troubled shoot proceeded amid allegations of drug use and sexual harassment, hardly the stuff to make Lansing proud.

Nor were most star vehicles any easier. Edward Norton, whose career she had helped launch with 1996's *Primal Fear*, had given her endless grief, turning down roles for years even though he owed Paramount two pictures according to his original deal. When Lansing tried to book him for *The Italian Job,* and again he declined, she had enough. She threatened to sue; he threatened to countersue; and even when Norton caved, he made his irritation clear, hiring an assistant to videotape his every move on set, as if defying Paramount to find him remiss.

Once this would have been water off Lansing's back. But she was drained by the petty squabbles and endless aggravation, the oversize egos and childish demands. She longed to get out.

IN THE YEARS since she had arrived in Los Angeles, she had seen the business break free from the wreckage of the factory system, when a handful of studios controlled every aspect of filmmaking, holding thousands of workers in their thrall. She had lived through the golden age of the 1970s, as America emerged from the shadow of Vietnam, and masterworks such as *The Godfather, Chinatown* and *Network* poured forth. And she had endured all the way to the present, when giant corporations held sway over these once-proud islands of independence, now look-alikes that churned out superheroes and special-effects films far removed from the human dramas she so adored.

She had come of age at a time when women were relegated to being secretaries or starlets, when breasts were fondled, bottoms pinched, and the casting couch was just another station of the cross for any young woman aspiring to be a star. She had carved a path for women who sought to break the shackles of the Eisenhower era and penetrate the studio citadels, never thinking she would end up running one herself. She had stamped her times through force of personality, molding herself to the world until the world was ready to mold itself to her.

"There've been those that have tested her," said her *Fatal Attraction* star Michael Douglas, "and if Sherry had to get tough, she'd get tough. 'You want to go eyeball to eyeball? You want to go that route? Fine. I'm from Chicago.'"

She had rocketed to power and held on to it with a firm grip, helped by the fact that the more power she got, the less she seemed to crave it. She made her bosses feel safe and her subordinates safer. She was, as one of her colleagues put it, "the best no in town," able to turn down projects day in, day out, dozens of times a week, hundreds each year—a crucial part of any studio chief's job—while making even those she rejected feel good.

"More times than I care to admit," said producer and former studio head Robert Evans, "while walking over to her presidential suite, I promised myself, 'This time [she] ain't going to seduce me,' and more times than I care to admit I walked out of the meeting feeling better at getting a no from her than a yes from anyone else."

She was part of a dazzling generation of women, bound together by their gender but separated by their distinct personalities, who had arrived in Hollywood within the span of a few years and assailed the boys' club they found there. They included the brassy Dawn Steel, who rose to become president of Columbia Pictures before Hollywood shut its gates on her, forcing her into the netherworld of independent production; Laura Ziskin, the erudite producer of the *Spider-Man* series, who had tried and failed as an executive before launching one of Hollywood's most successful franchises; and Lucy Fisher, the Harvard grad whom Jack Nicholson called "the sweetest, smartest girl in class," but who lacked the drive to take the bullet train to the top. These women were impressive by any standard, yet none had Lansing's particular blend of artistry and authority, of people skills and commercial savvy.

But now her passion was fading. She knew that life was not about a beginning and a middle and an end, but rather about constant beginnings and middles and ends, and she was ready to begin the cycle again.

A plan had begun to take shape in her mind: to create a new life when she turned sixty. All she needed was guidance. And so, without telling even her closest friends, she was traveling to Atlanta on a stealth mission to meet a statesman who had reinvented his life, in the hope he could help her reinvent her own.

FOR FOUR AND a half hours she sat in silence as she flew across the country, struggling to control her nerves, attempting on occasion to dip into her bag of scripts and failing each time. It was evening when her plane touched down and a waiting car whisked her toward the shimmering lights of the city.

As she drove through the half-lit streets, it struck her how different this world was from the one of her youth. A vital spirit seemed to pervade the place even on a bitingly cold night like this. Young interracial couples

wove through the sidewalks hand in hand, something that would have
been inconceivable when she was their age. She had grown up in a Chicago breaking free of the Depression and World War II, where segregation
was a given and a doorman had once tried to bar her from entering a club
because her companion was black. She had fought that fight and won, just
as she would win so many others. But she no longer had the stomach for
fighting, at least not the countless petty fights that made up her life in Los
Angeles.

Here she was free from the numerous obligations she knew back
home. There, call would follow call, dozens upon dozens each day, as her
assistant "rolled" them, keeping one caller on hold while Lansing wrapped
up with the other. No matter who phoned or when, she would call back
within hours. That was her mantra: clear the decks, wipe the slate clean,
never let anything linger from the past that could snap up and bite her in
the future.

In Atlanta there was no office and no secretary—no laptop, not even a
cell phone. She was curiously old-fashioned like that. For a woman who
operated in such a cutting-edge business, she rarely bothered with emails
and texts, because a call was better than both. Hollywood might be a
multibillion-dollar industry, but it was an industry driven by personal relationships, and no one understood them better than Lansing.

After checking into her hotel, she went quickly to her room. By seven
the next morning she was up and showered, and after a turn on the treadmill and a bran muffin for breakfast, she set on her way.

As her taxi drove east, through the narrow streets that took her just a
few hundred yards from the tiny Ebenezer Baptist Church where Martin
Luther King Jr., a hero of her youth, had made his mark, she thought of his
impact and wondered about her own. The lives of executives were ephem-
eral, their power transient; at best all she could hope for was the legacy of
her films.

For ten minutes she sat in silence, toying with a single white card on
which her schedule was typed out. Most days, many meetings would be
noted here, but now there was only one, and it was all she thought about
as her car slowed to a stop.

She waited in the lobby of the main building until an assistant came to greet her. The woman led her down a long hallway and into a plain office where a silver-haired man stood with his back toward her, gazing out the window at the rolling hills. He turned, and his soft blue eyes fell on her, and whatever anxiety she had been feeling melted away.

"I'm so happy to meet you, Sherry," said President Carter. "Let's sit down and talk."

CHAPTER 2

Six decades before Lansing's trip to Atlanta, a much younger woman set out on a voyage of her own.

The year was 1938, the place Mainz, Germany, and fear was in the air. It was in the shops, few of which would remain in Jewish hands for long. It was in the classrooms, where Jewish admissions had been severely curtailed, pushing hundreds of boys and girls into the city's synagogue schools. It was in the cinemas, where Jews had to sit through Nazi propaganda newsreels—most recently one about Hitler's visit to Rome—on the same program as musical comedies including *Pigskin Parade* and *Born to Dance*, two of the later Hollywood pictures to trickle through Mainz's theaters before the war.

Since the National Socialists' seizure of power in 1933, barely a month had gone by without their tightening the knot on the twenty-six hundred Jews in the city, a Jewish enclave since the tenth century and a center of learning ever since its most famous son, Johannes Gutenberg, had invented the printing press. Oppression was racing so fast that few could keep up. In one public school, before the Jews were forced out altogether, the students had elected a Jewish girl to lead a Nazi parade, never imagining the consequences. Confusion, misery and uncertainty were all around, not least in the heart of a seventeen-year-old named Margot Heimann.

Until the past few years, Margot had lived a life of relative ease thanks to the wealth of her parents, with whom she was housed in an apartment on the elegant Hindenburgstrasse, the tree-lined street that led straight to the domed Neue Synagogue, a vast edifice of marble and gold that was the center of communal life for Mainz's Jews. She was warm, charming and exceptionally pretty. Her nickname was "Muschi," meaning "kitty cat."

On Sabbath nights, when Jews thronged the streets on their way to temple, Margot would gaze down as they passed beneath her window, the men in stiff suits and starched collars, the women in long, modest dresses. Then she and her family would set out on the five-minute walk to the synagogue, where the women and children sat in the gallery, above a sea of stovepipe hats. A thousand members of the community would congregate here every Friday and would continue to do so until November 9, 1938—Kristallnacht—when the Nazis rampaged through the country, attacking anything and everything Jewish. That night, the synagogue would be leveled in an earsplitting explosion that shattered the neighbors' windows.

Sometimes the smell of matzo would waft from the Heimanns' second-floor kitchen, not far from a white placard propped in a window, proclaiming F. HEIMANN—TABAKGROSSHANDEL (tobacco wholesaler), and Margot would race for the red currant jelly that her mother, Hilda, lathered on black bread.

Fritz, her father, was a rigid man of fifty-five, bound up in a dark suit and forced to cope with his growing deafness as well as the vanishing income from his once-thriving business. Those who remembered him described him alternately as gruff and gregarious, in a salesman-like way; some liked him, none knew him well. He was a man of mystery, and secret upon secret piled up in his house, permeating its Persian rugs and mahogany tables. Nobody fully understood why he had left his native Impfingen years earlier; there were rumors of a minor scandal, though what it was people could not say. He had done well with his tobacco practice, though not as well as some of his family and friends who had factories of their own where tobacco was processed, packed into boxes of cigarettes or cigars, and shipped out by the thousand. Fritz had never achieved as much as his older brother Max, who had left Germany in the late nineteenth century and now owned a thriving clothing store in Chicago.

One of Fritz's secrets could be gleaned from a small black-and-white photograph that he kept in the apartment, which showed him arm in arm with a sweet young woman named Minna Rothschild, whom he had married while young, and who had died shortly after giving birth to their first child, Lora. Minna was twenty-seven years old when she left her thirty-five-year-old husband a widower with a baby girl, a single parent before the term had come into existence. With no other recourse, Fritz followed Jewish tradition and in 1920 took Minna's younger sister, Hilda, as his bride. That year she gave birth to Margot.

Now Margot was leaving for America. After an agonizing wait, her visa had been approved, and if all went well she would soon join Lora, who had departed for Chicago the previous year.

What must she have thought as she left the city of her birth? Did she ache for the friends she had known all her life, many destined to die? Did she fear for her parents, still waiting for their visas, and her grandmother Jette, later to be murdered in Theresienstadt? All this is unknown, as Margot never said a word—not of her departure, nor of Mainz, nor of her teenage life. She sealed it up deep inside, walling it off from all who knew her, and with it some part of herself.

On May 17 she boarded the SS *Washington* and embarked on the eight-day crossing to New York.

The ship was enormous and state-of-the-art, a 24,000-ton floating megalopolis that carried 1,100 passengers and 478 crew members, and dwarfed any of the boats Margot had seen on the Rhine. It had its own orchestra and was packed with travelers from around the world, according to others who made the voyage, their recollections vivid in interviews conducted by the USC Shoah Foundation.

If Margot wanted to talk, she had to be careful. Spies could relay word of anything that was hostile to the Nazis. Danger was in the very air.

On the morning of May 26, the ship's horn blasted loud and clear, and its passengers hurried on deck, hundreds cheering, others in tears as the

Statue of Liberty loomed before them and they beheld the New World, many for the first time.

Following a cross-country train ride, Margot arrived in Chicago and was reunited with her beloved Lora.

IT WAS HARDLY the most auspicious of times. Weeks earlier, a banner headline in the *Chicago Tribune* had touted the arrest of three German spies, and the hunt was on for other members of their ring. A serial killer had just been caught after bludgeoning his latest victim with a brick. But normal life was at last returning to the city after the Great Depression had cost half its residents their jobs and spawned a crime wave that fueled the city's reputation as a mob magnet, and for Margot, all that mattered was that she was safe.

As spring gave way to a stifling summer, hotter and stickier than any she had known, she found work as a seamstress and then switched to sales at the Marshall Field & Co. department store. She embraced her new environment and lost all but a trace of her German accent.

Whatever fears she had about her parents ended in September, when they, too, arrived in America. Now the family was under one roof, at first with Max and then in a place of their own, as Fritz eked out a living going door-to-door selling ties.

At nineteen, Margot became engaged, though nothing is known of her fiancé except his name, Alan Joseph. Their betrothal was announced in the *Tribune*, but like so many youthful romances, it fizzled, and Margot remained single until her early twenties, when she met a young man named David Duhl.

David was Jewish, like her, a blue-eyed Chicagoan ten years her senior. He was warm and funny and so loving that Margot could almost become Muschi again with him. He liked ballet and classical music, and when he was not running his family's residential hotel, he would play her excerpts from the operas that always moved him to tears. Everyone remembered his brilliance: he had started buying apartments in the poorer parts of the city as soon as Chicago broke free of the Depression, building on a tiny business left him by his father, and had made enough money to put his siblings through the University of Chicago. But he was an artist by nature, a businessman by necessity.

On February 8, 1942, the couple married, and on July 31, 1944, Margot gave birth to a girl. Her name was Sherry Lee Duhl.

THE BABY WAS willful and would throw tantrums in her crib, but she and her father were inseparable. Each time someone came to the house, he would put his arm around her and say, "Isn't she the most beautiful child you've ever seen?" As she grew older, he would take her into the yard of their South Side house and toss a ball back and forth, always patient, never bored. Playing ball with her father would become one of the girl's fondest memories.

On Saturdays, he would drive her to the Museum of Science and Industry. "It was a magical palace with a huge lagoon in the back," she recalled. "The steps to the middle pavilion were the widest I'd ever seen, and inside was like something from *Alice in Wonderland*. There was a reproduction coal mine, and a cage where chicks hatched before my eyes, and a TV screen where I could watch myself, which felt like a miracle."

There was even an adult-size dollhouse resembling a fairy-tale castle, with the tiniest Bible in the world and a reproduction nickelodeon that played reruns of Charlie Chaplin and Harold Lloyd. It was here that Sherry Lee fell in love with film. Sitting at her father's side, gazing at the screen in the dark, she laughed when he laughed and cried when he cried. "Watching my father, I saw the joy the movies gave him and experienced that joy myself," she said.

Their relationship continued unimpeded even after Margot gave birth to a second daughter, Judy, in 1949. Rather than be jealous, Sherry Lee took the baby in hand. For years, Judy would be her sister's playmate, but it was David who was closest to her heart.

"Listen," he'd urge, tears running down his cheeks as *Madama Butterfly* crackled from his record player and he tried to explain the tale of a geisha abandoned by the man she loves. "He's not coming back. Do you understand? He's not coming back again."

SIX YEARS AFTER Sherry Lee's birth, David felt short of breath. Concerned, Margot drove him to the local hospital, where a doctor told her he had bacterial endocarditis, an inflammation of the heart, likely caused by an earlier infection. He had been unwell as a child, and his mother had taken him to Texas, where they remained a year as he recuperated from rheumatic fever, which may have weakened his heart. What neither he nor Margot knew was that his illness was fatal.

Much to his daughter's confusion, David began to decline. His illness upset her. Why were all the other fathers so strong, when he was so weak? How come those other fathers ran around with their children, when he could barely move? She was embarrassed and ashamed, much to her later regret. Once, coming home, she saw him sitting on the ground, catching his breath, and was terrified her friends would recognize him. A storm of conflicting feelings welled up inside her: adoration for this man who meant everything to her and horror at his illness.

Soon he could no longer go to work and had to run his business from a basement office. His breathing grew weaker, his skin pale, and eventually Margot set up a bed for him on the ground floor, because he could not manage the steep stairs alone. He clung to life, hoping against hope for a few more years. "I just want to stay alive long enough to be at my daughters' weddings," he told his wife.

For months he slept in the living room. A breeze wafted through the open window and cooled him as winter gave way to a warm spring. Then on June 20, 1953, he died. He was forty-two years old.

HOURS BEFORE HER father's death, Sherry Lee woke from a deep sleep, startled to see him pass through her room, heading toward the outside porch.

"Dad!" she shouted. "Be quiet! You woke me up!"

They were the last words she would remember saying to him, and for years they filled her with guilt—though her mother insisted she could never have said them, because David could not climb the stairs.

The next day, oblivious to the anguished sounds, the muffled voices and ambulance sirens that had wailed through the night, Sherry Lee rose from bed, pushed aside her dolls and bounded downstairs. Strange—there were people here at this ungodly hour, all looking so sad when she was in a mood for fun. A woman whispered that her father was in the hospital, but he had been to the hospital many times before and Sherry Lee thought no more about it. Out she went into the street, her bicycle arcing from side to side. Then she turned around and spotted two Siamese cats staring from a window, and they filled her with dread. For the rest of her life she had a morbid aversion to cats.

Hurrying back, she ran into the yard and climbed onto a swing, until she overheard her grandmother say: "What's wrong with her? Doesn't she care?"

She slowed, jumped off the swing and ran inside, clambering up the stairs until she reached Margot in the bathroom with Lora, leaning over the tub, scrubbing and scrubbing at a ring of dirt.

"Mother, why's Grandma Yetta being so mean?" asked the girl.

"Your father's sick," said Margot.

"But he'll come home soon, won't he?"

"No, sweetie," said Margot. "He's not coming home."

"I don't understand," said the girl.

"Sweetie," said Margot. "He's dead."

The girl began to scream.

"It's not true! It's not true!" she yelled.

"Be good, Sherry Lee," said Lora, "or the same thing will happen to your mother."

DAYS LATER, OVERWHELMED with grief, Margot packed the eight-year-old off to Elgin, a town forty miles from Chicago, where Lora lived with her husband, Harold Seigle, and their two children in a house with a tennis court and a lawn that led down to a pond.

The house dwarfed the girl, adding to her feeling of isolation, and Margot's decision to keep three-year-old Judy at home while sending the older child away only compounded her pain. It was because she was bad, she believed. She had shouted at her father and therefore he had died. "Everything was my fault," she reasoned. From now on, she told herself, she would never be bad again. She would be better than good: she would be perfect.

Her cousin Marsha shared her dolls, but dolls meant nothing to the lost girl. Nor did the big cake with nine candles that Marsha's family baked for her birthday, trying to make her feel as if she belonged. But she did not—not here, not anywhere, not now and perhaps not ever. "I was lonely," she said. "I felt abandoned."

Weeks passed before Margot came to fetch her home and normal life resumed, or something bordering on the normal, because a new reality set in of long hours filled with anguish and nights haunted by recurrent dreams. In one, Sherry Lee would walk down a narrow hallway and slow as she beheld a cold slab with her father's body. In another, fire would sweep through her home while she watched from the street, unable to do anything as the flames licked around her mother, who stood as still as the Statue of Liberty that had once beckoned her, with Judy in her arms. There were no therapists or fairy godmothers to take the young girl by the hand and assure her none of this was her fault—that life and death, her father's or anyone else's, were not hers to control.

At temple on Mother's Day, Sherry Lee sat frozen beside Margot as the rabbi delivered a muddled but terrifying sermon about a badly behaved girl whose parents gave her a dollhouse for her birthday. "Every time you're bad, we'll drill a hole in it," the girl was told. But she did not change and the parents kept drilling their holes until there was nothing left of the dollhouse, when the mother dropped dead from disappointment. Only then did the girl repent, throwing herself on her mother's grave, screaming, "Mommy! I'm so sorry."

"Too late," the rabbi intoned. "And I say to you, girls, be good to your mothers. Do whatever they ask."

"See?" said Margot, poking her daughter in the ribs.

Nor did the young girl get any closure with David's funeral. The rabbi warned that it would be too traumatic for her to attend. And so she never saw her father's dead body, and instead, in an extraordinary leap of imagination, she came to believe he was alive and had simply abandoned her for a better child. Desperate to find him, she peered into neighboring houses and through restaurant doors, and craned to see inside the home of a hermit she had once glimpsed down the street as he peeked from behind his curtains. She gazed through shop windows and stared into abandoned lots, longing to discover her father, though of course she never did. And each time she drove with her mother she strained to see the passengers in the passing cars, hidden from her by the reflections in the windows, always searching, searching, for the father she never could find.

MARGOT WAS THIRTY-TWO years old, still so very young and struggling to survive. She had lost her country, many of her family members and friends, and now her husband.

One evening, shortly after David's death, there was a knock at her door and two of his employees appeared in fedoras and dark suits. They shook her hand, and Margot ushered them into the basement office while Sherry Lee snuck downstairs and hid behind the door. After giving their condolences, the men got to the point.

"We don't want you to worry, Mrs. Duhl," one said. "You won't have to trouble yourself about a thing. We'll take over the business."

"No, you won't," Margot shot back. "You'll teach me how to run it myself."

Surprised, the men took their leave and Sherry Lee scurried away, only to creep back down when they had gone. She found her mother in tears.

"Mom, what is it?" she asked.

"It's nothing, sweetie," said her mother. "Just dust."

MARGOT IMMERSED HERSELF in her husband's work, learning about the tenants, the buildings, the law—each and every stitch in the thick tapestry of David's professional life. Much had been hidden from her, just as it was from so many wives of her generation. Locked away in the basement, deep into night, she pored over the ledgers, determined to succeed.

"Watching my mother had a profound effect on me," said her daughter. "She was my first role model. She took over my father's business and refused to be a victim."

No matter how tempting it was to turn to David's employees, Margot soldiered on alone, and if she had to visit one of her properties, she would bundle the girls in the car, driving to the poorest parts of the South Side, where she would encounter other women whose troubles often seemed worse than her own, though she was heartbroken when a resident manager ran off with the rent.

"She loved this woman who betrayed her," said Lansing. "But when the woman wrote and begged for forgiveness, my mother forgave her. Her dignity had been taken from her in Germany, and she didn't want to take anyone else's dignity away here."

Margot encouraged her daughters to help others, even if it meant spending hours outside a local grocery store, holding out a can to passersby and soliciting funds for Hull House, a neighborhood community center that provided social services for the needy. Sherry Lee raised so much money that the local paper ran a photo of her—all of which deepened the bond between mother and daughter, even as the pressures on each one tugged them apart.

"Our relationship was complicated," said Lansing. "I never doubted her love, but she couldn't express it. She couldn't say 'I love you' and she couldn't hug me. She never told me I was attractive or intelligent, but she demonstrated her love. One night when she was dressed up for a party and I was sick, she said, 'I'm not going. I would never leave you.'"

She struggled to understand her mother's contradictions: how her passion for life could co-exist with her deep anxiety, how her innate optimism could live in tandem with a learned pessimism. "She used to say over and over again, 'Sing before breakfast, cry before dinner,'" said Lansing. "That's just the way she was raised."

Once, when Sherry Lee was distraught at having no father to join her in a three-legged race, Margot insisted on racing with her, though the race was intended for fathers and daughters alone. She bound her daughter's leg to her own, and they tore across the field and won. "I felt she could do anything," said Lansing, "and that meant a woman could do anything, too."

ONE SUMMER EVENING, Sherry Lee was playing outdoors when an air-blue Cadillac pulled into her driveway, its horn tinkling like the Good Humor van.

Sherry Lee hopped and skipped toward the house, praying that one of her mother's many suitors had returned—the men who would court her, bestowing gifts on her daughters, only to vanish once it became clear she would never be theirs—then bounded into the living room and stopped in her tracks. A stranger was sitting there, immaculate in his sharp suit, with monogrammed cuffs and polished black shoes. He dangled a scotch in one hand, a cigarette in the other.

"Sherry, this is Mr. Norton Lansing," said her mother, flushed.

The man raised his dark eyes to the girl.

"Hello, Sherry," he said, without moving.

The girl shrank back. Why didn't he behave like the others? Why didn't he tease her or joke around? He was tough and radiated power, and she knew she must never cross him.

Over the following months, Margot began to see Norton more. He was forty-five years old, Chicago born and bred, a salesman and furniture maker. But this wasn't any furniture: he sold only top-of-the-line products, including a reclining chair his company had invented called a Strato-lounger; and he had two clients, but they were the giants Sears, Roebuck and Montgomery Ward. His wife had recently died, following an allergic reaction to anesthesia during an otherwise routine operation. He had few friends, and the ones he had were as disposable as his cigarettes. He disliked most people and only had eyes for Margot. He was David's antithesis, which made perfect sense: Margot had married an artist and he had died; this time she would marry a rock.

IN JANUARY 1956, the couple wed in their rabbi's study. Margot was thirty-five, Norton ten years older. The children were not invited.

Richard, nine, and Andrea, sixteen—both from Norton's first marriage—moved into Margot's house as the families merged into one and Margot sold off her properties, never to work again because a working woman was one who had failed. She came from the Old World, not the New; the professional life was for a husband, not his wife. The woman who had stamped the importance of work on her children now turned her back on it altogether.

Little by little, all traces of David disappeared. The ledgers, vinyl records, clothes and photographs were given away until there was no sign he had ever lived in the house. Sherry Lee had to go to her grandmother Yetta's to look at a photo of him on her piano. She was not even allowed to mention his name in front of Norton, nor was she permitted to attend Yom Kippur services in his honor because that would have hurt Norton's feelings—though she went, no matter what she was told.

"My father was very narcissistic, very charismatic," said Andrea. "He was very self-centered, very handsome, very good in business. Was he tough? Yes. He was not a warm person."

But Sherry Lee grew accustomed to Norton and he to her, and she was glad, "because now I was normal and had a father."

When she was twelve, Margot asked her to take her new father's last name, and she agreed. Sherry Lee Duhl had ceased to exist. She would be Sherry Lansing from now on.

———

THE ADULTS' LOVE affair was all-consuming. Each day, when Norton returned from work, the children would be banished while he and Margot sat over cocktails, absorbed in one another's company. "They'd snuggle up, and Norton would wrap his arm around my mother, when none of the other parents ever seemed to touch each other," said Lansing. "All the neighborhood kids were shocked."

They lived in their own private bubble, and as much as they cared for their children, none was allowed to penetrate their holy of holies. The couple would even take vacations alone, to exotic-sounding places such as the Bahamas, the children pining to go with them. Their bond was unassailable. Margot had had happiness and lost it; she would do whatever she could to maintain that happiness now.

True, there were times when Norton's armor cracked open, revealing an unexpected tenderness inside. Once, when he took his daughter shopping and she was unable to choose a dress, he let her buy every one she liked—eight in all—until her mother, horrified, made her take all but one back.

Sherry watched how her mother charmed her father, but did not know how to do so herself. Secretly, she was afraid of him and never dared to confront him. Instead, she stuffed her anger deep down inside, burying it so profoundly that it was hidden even from herself.

Unable to enter her parents' enchanted circle, the girl attempted to create one of her own. She performed plays with Judy (always taking the leading role) and on Saturdays would lose herself in the neoclassical Hamilton and Jeffery movie palaces, where she would stare up at the faces of her idols, longing to be as charming as Audrey Hepburn in *Sabrina* or as glamorous as Lana Turner in *Imitation of Life*, and aching to experience the passion of Susan Hayward in *I Want to Live!*

Each year she sat with her mother on the family couch, having begged to stay up late for the Academy Awards. When Hayward was named Best Actress for playing a real-life woman sent to death row, Sherry wept with longing and frustration, burning with the desire to be on that stage, too.

The seeds of her ambition were sown here, the first impulse to reinvent herself as something other than an ordinary girl living thousands of miles from the epicenters of glamour and power. But try as she might, she could never find a link between her humdrum existence and that over-the-rainbow place called Hollywood, and when she confided her dreams to a friend, he just laughed.

"I want to be in the movies," she said.

"What are you talking about?" he scoffed. "You're from the South Side of Chicago."

HER PARENTS INSISTED she attend a private high school for girls, and the teenager insisted she would not.

She had set her sights on the prestigious University of Chicago Laboratory Schools, a hub for gifted children. Grudgingly, Margot and Norton allowed her to sit for the exam, and despite having chicken pox when she took it, she passed.

Founded in 1896, the Lab School (as it was known) was famous for its academic rigor and liberalism, and the teenage girl flourished there, rubbing shoulders with some of the brightest minds she had encountered. If her home life lacked intellectual stimulus, her school was awash in it. Each day she was bombarded with analysis, debate and instruction on everything from the history of communism, fascism and democracy to advanced math, at which she excelled.

She fell in love with the school, which "was totally nonjudgmental," she said. "There was no prejudice, and there was interracial dating long before other schools considered it. But the pressures were different. Intellect was all that mattered. Some of the students were so brilliant, one who was three grades below me started crying because students from the university forced him to do their homework."

The school was the perfect incubator for the career woman she would become, and here she honed her work ethic and social grace, her intellect and drive. In this pre-feminist, "pre-revolution" world (in the words of her school friend Laurie Marshall), "I had confidence in my intellect," said Lansing, "even if I had no self-confidence in anything else."

She was plagued by insecurity. Tall and gawky, she felt that her looks paled beside those of her mother, who was still so stunning teenagers would wolf-whistle when she passed, reinforcing the teenager's sense of inadequacy.

Nor did Margot value her daughter's intelligence. How would that help her land a husband? Looks were what mattered, not brains. So she focused on Sherry's appearance, anxious that she was all skin and bone.

"Oh my God, she's grown another inch!" she yelled at the doctor. "Can't you give her some kind of medicine?"

"I felt like a freak," said Lansing.

She failed to notice she was changing, and so did her mother. Almost imperceptibly, the once-gangly girl's figure was filling out and she was emerging as a beauty. The stick-thin twelve-year-old began to disappear, replaced by an attractive teen. At sixteen, she was stunning.

Reading that the Carson Pirie Scott department store was searching for models in its bridal division, Margot decided Sherry should apply. For days on end, she taught her how to walk like a model, balance books on her head and twirl around. This was her way of boosting her daughter's confidence, and she was determined the girl would succeed.

"I was so scared when we arrived for my walk-through, but I kept going because my mother convinced me," said Lansing. "I was just happy she had faith in my looks. And then I was hired."

The ugly duckling had become a swan, and men took note. Even her brother was impressed when she brought home a University of Chicago basketball star—though when the two went out, the young woman could never think of anything to say, and after a few dates her would-be boyfriend lost all patience.

"I could take out a piece of paper and write down exactly what's going to happen to you," he groused. "You'll be a fat housewife, living in the suburbs with nothing to do."

"You're wrong," she said fiercely. "I'm going to Hollywood and I'm going to be a star!"

———

Five years later, a university graduate and new wife, she did just that.

She had spent the past years excelling at the Lab School and then working on her degree. Norton had wanted her to go to Tulane University in New Orleans, but when Northwestern accepted her as a speech major (with a minor in drama) she chose to remain in Chicago alongside her boyfriend and soon-to-be husband.

Lansing was seventeen and still in high school when she met Michael Brownstein at a University of Chicago fraternity house party. She had reached her full height of five feet ten inches, not as tall as her mother had feared, but enough to give her an aura of being older and considerably wiser than she was. She was warm, intelligent and beautiful—especially in the eyes of the young man she met this evening, sitting in one of the frat house rooms, strumming his guitar.

Michael was nineteen years old, a medical student and the son of a doctor, and Jewish like her. In his jeans and cowboy hat, he seemed to be the spitting image of James Garner, and academically gifted to boot. (He would become a leading sex-reassignment surgeon.) He excelled without trying, though he was also a maverick who showed little interest in doing what he was told. Rather than study, he would tear through the city on his old motorbike or spend his hard-earned cash taking flying lessons, once scaring Lansing stiff when he flew her to dinner in Detroit.

"He was very, very intelligent and good-looking and a little crazy in a positive sense," said his best friend, John Stiefel. "We drank a lot and laughed a lot and we would fight for fun. I don't think that was well received at the fraternity dorm."

Michael was as smitten with the young woman as she was with him. She was sparkling and fun, always the first on the dance floor and ready to run off at a moment's notice just to get a hamburger in Milwaukee, ninety miles away.

"Even then, she was kind of a prize," he said. "She was gorgeous. She was smart—I caught that right away—and funny. She came in with a fraternity brother of mine, and we hit it off and he wasn't too happy about it."

Michael was dangerous enough to be exciting, but wholesome enough to be safe. He was a good girl's idea of a bad boy, perfect for a woman seeking a rebel, not a revolutionary. He had a part-time job, an unusual one given his background: he drove a city bus, and Lansing would accompany him for long stretches, happy to sit behind him for his entire eight-hour shift.

For the first time since she was a child, she truly felt loved. With no money to buy flowers, Michael would cut up crepe paper and staple the petals on stems. He would discuss her longings and dreams without once laughing at their absurdity. "He listened," she said. "And I badly needed to be heard."

On July 5, 1964, the couple wed at the Continental Hotel and Town Club, in a ceremony attended by some 180 guests. After a honeymoon in New York, they took in their first Broadway musical, *Hello, Dolly!*, and Lansing tried out for the TV game show *Password* before they returned to a small apartment on the North Side of Chicago, where they remained until Lansing's graduation in June 1966.

Only one blot stained these years: her disappointment with Northwestern.

"I wasn't happy there," she acknowledged. "The Lab School was such a glorious place—it was all about intellect and not how you looked, and wasn't judgmental, and Northwestern just couldn't live up to that." She was disturbed by the anti-Semitism there. "It was huge at the time. There was a girl who didn't look Jewish, and she wanted to join one of the non-Jewish sororities, and I said, 'We can't pledge there, we're Jews.' She did it anyway. I said, 'They'll turn against you.' And in the second year, they did."

Lansing started to act, but while she loved rehearsals, fear kicked in as soon as she was cast, and her teacher terrified the students. "There was a girl he broke down in a horrible way, and she never came back," she recalled. "He was very hard on us."

Now this was drawing to an end.

On the last day of her school year, in the sweltering heat of an un-air-conditioned hall, Lansing waited until her name was called out and then went onstage, proud to be graduating cum laude. She scanned the crowd for her parents, but to her disappointment they were nowhere to be seen. Afterward, she found them outside.

When she asked what had happened, Norton shrugged.

"It was too goddamn hot," he said.

CHAPTER 3

On a hot and dusty afternoon in the summer of 1966, Sherry and Michael Brownstein's green-and-white Mustang clattered over the Cahuenga Pass, caked with mud and dirt after four days on the road. Lansing looked up from the tiny TV set she had stowed in the car, which would crackle into life and then die as they passed from one state to another, and glimpsed Los Angeles for the first time.

Her initial view was not of the ocean or the palm trees that swayed along the manicured boulevards of Beverly Hills, nor of the Hollywood sign that had fallen into disrepair, but rather of a city enveloped in smog. She could barely make out the skyscrapers that towered above downtown L.A., which resembled New York and Chicago more than the paradise of her dreams. A thick morass of smoke and fumes from the oil refineries and industrial plants enveloped buildings that climbed ever upward in their struggle for air, dwarfing the men and women who moved like figurines through the heavily trafficked streets.

If Lansing had had even an iota of cynicism, she might have regarded this as an omen: not everything was going to be quite the way she had imagined in the City of Angels. But she was wide-eyed and innocent, and knew nothing of herself or the world, let alone the mecca of entertainment she was about to confront.

Here she was soon to be discovered, she was sure, heedless of the thousands of others fleeing their adolescence, just like her, all streaming into

Los Angeles, swelling its population from almost two million in 1950 to twice that three decades later, each thinking he was bigger and better than the rest, each perfect prey for the hucksters and charlatans who masqueraded as producers, managers and agents.

She was dangerously naive, like Michael. Both were so oblivious to the reality of Hollywood that they had seriously contemplated moving to San Francisco instead of Los Angeles, by mistake; after all, that was California, too, wasn't it, so how far from Hollywood could it be?

The freeway whisked them through an avenue of skyscrapers and along a collection of urban arteries before spitting them into the streets of the city, where Lansing still believed unknowns such as Lana Turner had been spotted at a soda fountain, and where Schwab's Pharmacy was a real place, not just a metaphor for every hopeful waiting to be made a star.

Down Sunset Boulevard the Mustang rolled, along the very street she had seen in the movie that bore its name, with its haunting opening of a man floating facedown in a pool—dead, even as he narrated his story— though the real-life Sunset appeared to have nothing in common with the film, not this eastern section anyway. Where were the mansions and their celebrities, the lofty palaces where the rich and famous moved among liveried servants, hosting parties for the privileged few? One- and two-story stucco buildings lined the wide, straight street, with its car washes and drugstores and massive billboards, parading the wonders of everything from king-size Coke to the Marlboro Man.

Worn out from their marathon drive, the couple checked in to one of the hundreds of motels that had sprouted like refugee camps, providing shelter for the thousands of immigrants who flooded into the city, and plopped down on a king-size bed. But Lansing was in no mood to rest. She was hungry for each nugget of information she could wolf down about her new hometown, knowing that every day she dawdled she was one step further from stardom. The two went out almost immediately, back in their car, cruising alongside the immense, boat-like convertibles that floated along the highway, their smiling owners never honking or changing lanes, either dazed by the sun or on a perpetual, laid-back high, until they reached the center of Hollywood and found a run-down, squalid township that seemed light-years removed from the Shangri-la Lansing had envisioned.

Strip clubs and seedy bars popped up at intervals, sprinkled with the occasional hotspot whose name she vaguely recognized—from the Musso and Frank Grill to Frederick's of Hollywood, the lingerie store whose revealing outfits a proper girl like herself would never be caught buying. Hollywood was a dump, the magic behind its mythical name either hidden behind these walls or in some other secret place that had yet to be located.

None of this, however, was enough to dampen her excitement, which burned brightest when she reached the site she most craved to see, Grauman's Chinese Theatre. Built in the 1920s by the industry's best-known exhibitor, with the kind of baroque excess that made a mockery of understatement, it maintained an oriental splendor, with pagoda-like towers hovering over a concrete apron flecked with the hand- and footprints of stars. Lansing darted from Shirley Temple to Bette Davis to Marilyn Monroe and prayed that one day her name might be stamped beside theirs.

The streets were exploding with life. Hippies in bell-bottoms and Afghan coats weaved between the tourists; shady characters tried to sell her marijuana; peaceniks held up signs proclaiming MAKE LOVE, NOT WAR, the slogan that was just beginning to filter through the culture. These men and women belonged to a raw, anti-establishment breed hailing from a universe galaxies removed from Lansing's own. But their antiwar banners were warnings of the dark cloud that hovered alongside her dreams, reminders that Michael might soon be summoned to serve. The United States had launched a sustained aerial bombing campaign against the North Vietnamese, with the first heavy fighting involving American troops in the Ia Drang Valley. Lyndon B. Johnson had escalated the military's presence in Asia, with regular combat units deployed to Vietnam. Almost 400,000 troops were stationed there by the end of 1966, with talk that the president would ratchet up the war even more.

Lansing knew this. But here, as she gazed in awe at the splendor of the Chinese Theatre and its link to the Hollywood of old, that was far from her thoughts. Michael had signed up for the Berry Plan, which allowed medical students to defer their military service until they had finished their training, and his had not even begun. He still had his freedom, and— God willing—the war would be over before his hospital stint ended. And so Lansing pushed her fears aside and allowed the revolution of the 1960s to carry on around her but not inside her.

"That all happened outside my life," she said. "I might as well have been on another planet."

THE COUPLE WERE strapped. After paying to pack their things and ship them to Los Angeles, their savings were almost gone. They had just a few hundred dollars left, barely enough to cover the obligatory first and last months' rent.

Michael was due to begin work at the Cedars of Lebanon hospital, which meant he would be gone for twelve hours or more each day. Money would start trickling in—$300 per month, nowhere near enough to pay for rent and food and gas, let alone the occasional night out.

Lansing used her last moments of unalloyed freedom to visit Universal Studios (where she tried to sneak away from the tour group, until a security guard dragged her back into the fold) and MGM (where she spotted her first real-life star, *Dr. Kildare*'s Richard Chamberlain, but failed to make contact). Then she searched for a place to live.

She found what she needed on North Kenmore Avenue, a quiet street in the eastern part of Hollywood, nestled between Sunset and Hollywood Boulevards, where she and Michael moved into a boxy two-story building wrapped around a courtyard and pool. The place was close enough to Michael's work that he could get there on foot. After signing a month-to-month rental agreement, Lansing devoted her time to reading Fitzgerald and Hemingway while waiting for her belongings to arrive.

A week later, she set out for her first job interview, driving downtown for a meeting with a harried official from the teachers' union who told her to call at 7:00 a.m. sharp the following day to find out if a substitute teacher was needed. The next morning she rose early and discovered she had a job.

That day, she set out for the forbidden zone of South Central L.A., not realizing as she drove south on Crenshaw Boulevard, passing Adams and Jefferson Boulevards, that she was crossing an invisible threshold beyond which most sheltered Caucasian girls feared to tread. It was well before the era when the Crips and the Bloods would run rampant and a crack epidemic would decimate the inner city, but South Central was still reeling from one of the most destructive upheavals of modern times, the Watts Riots of 1965, which had climaxed in a conflagration that lasted almost a week.

"The city burning is Los Angeles' deepest image of itself," Joan Didion wrote in her 1968 essay collection, *Slouching Towards Bethlehem*. "For days one could drive the Harbor Freeway and see the city on fire, just as we had always known it would be in the end."

Entering a high school in the Crenshaw district, Lansing was unfazed by the staring eyes and occasional titters from the boys and girls she hoped to transform. She went straight to the principal's office and introduced herself.

"He looked at me and wondered why they had sent me," she said. "Then I was led into a classroom that seemed a lot like the classrooms I knew in Chicago, with a blackboard and a box of chalk and high windows."

She was here to teach English and math, the subjects she knew best, which represented her unusual combination of left- and right-brain strengths. But she had other aspirations, too: as a student, she had loved the work of anthropologist Margaret Mead and in her private fantasies had often thought of venturing to faraway places to help those less privileged than herself. South Central was not quite the Third World, but it was poles apart from the environment she knew. To her delight, she discovered she had a natural aptitude for teaching, even though she was not much older than her students.

"They were great," she said. "I loved teaching, and I was never afraid. Maybe it was my naïveté, but I didn't feel any sense of danger."

Still, the challenges she faced were hard to ignore. Ten months had passed since the fires were extinguished, but the embers left from the riots were still smoldering, and Lansing could sense that as she moved from one school to another.

"I took the toughest assignments," she said. "I went into reform schools where they only had plastic knives and forks, because nobody ever trusted the kids with real ones."

WHILE LANSING TAUGHT—searching for work as a model and actress at the same time—Michael buried himself in medicine. Much as he cared for his wife, he did not fully connect with her aspirations, and failed to understand how deeply they possessed her. Like her, he still had one foot set in the belief system of the 1950s, an age when men were men and women were women, their roles separate and distinctly unequal. He was glad she was earning money, but in his heart he expected her to give up her plans for him.

"I was going to be an intern at Cedars," he said. "I never thought we were going to Los Angeles for what she wanted." Her acting was a hobby, he believed, and "then she got serious."

In these early days, when their adult personalities were still coalescing and well before their differences would cleave them apart, Michael spent all his free time with his wife.

"We used to go out to eat, though we had no money for anywhere grand," said Lansing. "We went to Denny's and other simple places, but they were fun. We were used to Chicago, where you could buy a steak for $1.19. Michael was always working, six days a week, so a lot of the time we just stayed in and watched TV. And at night, whenever he was at the hospital, I'd go to see him and eat with him there, because it was only two blocks away. Without him, I read a lot and went to the movies, sometimes with a friend and often alone."

She felt sure her relationship would remain the same here as it was before. But strains were beginning to show. Michael, like every intern, was exhausted to the breaking point. At the same time, his interests were changing. He was increasingly drawn to plastic surgery, which puzzled his wife, though she never told him; she had imagined he was her own Dr. Kildare, a future heart surgeon or neurologist. But plastic surgery? Wasn't that all about fixing noses and enlarging breasts?

Her husband, in turn, was surprised to find the seventeen-year-old girl he had fallen for transforming into an ambitious woman. She had cast off the last vestiges of her awkward adolescence with the help of a surgeon friend of his who removed a small bump on her nose. Even if she did not realize it, Michael did: men were all over her. He could hardly turn his back without some stranger pouncing. In a city built on the belief that looks were everything—where Raquel Welch, wearing a fur bikini in the soon-to-be-released *One Million Years B.C.*, was the epitome of sexuality— she was a valuable commodity, and Michael hated it.

"I was jealous," he admitted.

While her husband paced the hallways of the old Cedars, Lansing soaked up everything Los Angeles had to offer. Clubs from the Troubador to the Whisky a Go Go were beginning to make their names, breathing life into new bands such as Buffalo Springfield and The Doors and redefining Sunset, the street where the Brownsteins had first stayed, as the center of all that was hip. Women were abandoning their twinsets and pearls in favor of low-cut dresses and the miniskirts that designer Mary Quant had popularized in London. Big boots were trampling all over demure heels (Nancy Sinatra's "These Boots Are Made for Walkin'" hit number one on the charts just before the Brownsteins moved to L.A.). It was a brave new world, irresistible to any starry-eyed immigrant, especially one harboring dreams of glory. She began to make new friends, several of them young women newly arrived like herself, few known to Michael. One day he snapped.

"I remember—this isn't nice—when she was out and was coming back late, I was just livid," he said. "She was coming up the street and I ran in front of the car. She stopped, and I opened the door and pulled her out. I was in a rage."

———

As time progressed, Lansing's job proved more demanding than she had expected.

It was tolerable when she found a stack of pornography on her desk. That she could handle with aplomb. "I suggested we make it into a bulletin board," she said, and followed that up with a lesson on human reproduction. But she got a bitter dose of reality when a student threw a shoe at her without repercussions. And fear kicked in when "a gang came in and started to beat up one of the students." The gang members were on a quest for vengeance—why, she never learned—and began to pound one of her pupils as he screamed for help and his classmates stared at him, frozen. "I tried to get them off," said Lansing, "then they tried to hit me. I went to find the principal, but he wasn't there because they'd thrown a Molotov cocktail in his office. He was sitting in the courtyard."

When the gang members rampaged through the school and even tied up some teachers before the police arrived, Lansing had enough. "I said, 'I can't do this anymore,'" she remembered. "I called my parents and begged them for help. I asked for money to leave my job. But they refused. My father had never liked the idea of my leaving Chicago, and perhaps he wanted me to come back. All he said was, 'Be careful.' And my mother handled it the same way."

It was tough love.

"I was really angry," Lansing admitted.

Throughout, she was living on hope.

Leaving work in East Los Angeles for an audition one afternoon, she pulled into a gas station to slip out of her drab clothes and into something more enticing. She did not get the job, but she saw the effect, and from then on that became her routine.

"It was always the same," she said. "I'd leave school and stop off somewhere to change my clothes. I owned one dress, a sexy pink number with a scooped neckline that showed a little cleavage, and I wore it over and over because I didn't have the money to buy anything else."

At her first audition, she discovered she was not alone. It was a cattle call, as she saw when she stepped into a hall packed with young women like herself. Each had migrated here from another city or state; each had come with the same goal of becoming a star. Few were serious actresses or appeared all that interested in their craft; riches and celebrity were the treasures they sought, the pots of gold they hoped to find at the end of the Los Angeles rainbow. This was the epicenter of fame and fortune, and a magnet for those who craved one or both.

After waiting for hours, Lansing had the briefest of meetings, then handed over an eight-by-ten photo of herself, just like all the other girls— they were always "girls," not women—and left without getting to show what she could do. This became a pattern.

"We were thrown into rejection early on," said Linda Gray, one of the young actresses who bonded with Lansing and who would later star in *Dallas*. "You would mop the floor or hold up a box of soap powder. It wasn't very creative, but it was what we did. And [some jobs] were lucrative. There was a standard fee. When I did still photography, it was $25 an hour, which was fantastic."

Such jobs were rare, and if one actress got them, that meant others did not. This was eat-or-be-eaten, Hollywood at its most naked and raw, and perhaps because of that, when Lansing tried to befriend her rivals, they often rebuffed her and she retreated into her shell. It never occurred to her that they might be as vulnerable as she, or that they might be even lonelier and more afraid. All she saw was their perfection and her lack of it.

"I'd wait in line for hours with a hundred girls," she said. "They were all five foot ten, with blue eyes and long, flowing hair. When my turn came, I'd show my pictures, toss my hair, and wait anxiously to see if I'd made the final round. Everyone was in competition and nobody talked to anyone else. It was horrible."

Even worse was the reality of the "casting couch," the sexual license exercised by the powers-that-be. "Many people made a move on me," said Lansing. "The worst was this agent, who was very well known, who I thought was going to represent me. He said he wanted to meet, and I was really excited. This sounds so stupid: he wanted to meet and talk in an apartment of his in the middle of the day. I went there, and he came out in his boxer shorts. It was so bad it was funny. I just said, 'This is ridiculous,' and walked out."

Knowing she needed to lift her game artistically, she began taking acting lessons twice a week and stuck to the work no matter what other obligations got in the way.

"She was very intellectual and very quick at analyzing," said her acting coach, Richard Brander, "but it took her longer to get to the emotion. There was a scene adapted from an Irwin Shaw short story, 'The Girls in Their Summer Dresses.' She had to argue with the man who played her husband, and she couldn't let go. So I took [the husband] aside and said, 'Give her a little shove'—and when he did, there was fire in her eyes. She got so angry, she started really falling into the scene. Afterward she went, 'Whoa!' I said, 'Now you're involved.' Then her real sensitivity started to come through."

Lansing had a brief taste of success when she landed a national shampoo commercial opposite the then-unknown Farrah Fawcett. Other modeling work followed, including commercials for Max Factor and Ivory Soap. But this was modeling, not acting. She was far from an overnight sensation, and as her first year bled into a second, her sense of conviction began to sag, only bouncing back when she was introduced to Gabriel Katzka, a producer who would later make 1974's *The Taking of Pelham One Two Three*.

"He was like an uncle to me," she recalled. "He said, 'What are you doing here? You're a nice Jewish girl. Go back to Chicago.' I said, 'I want to be an actress.' He said, 'But don't you know how terrible this place is?' I kept telling him how nice everyone was, and this elegant man walked in, in a beautiful suit. When he left, I said: 'Now that's a perfect gentleman. Why do you say everybody's so bad?' He said, 'You think that's a perfect gentleman?' and smiled."

The gentleman was producer Walter Wanger, known for making

Cleopatra, but even better known inside the gossip mill of Hollywood for shooting at a man's balls after he reportedly had an affair with Wanger's wife.

"Listen," said Katzka, "I'm going to protect you. I'm going to make some calls so nobody takes advantage." Whatever he did worked, and from that point on Lansing was inoculated, at least to some degree, against over-zealous admirers.

Through Katzka, she was led to a manager, Joe Wander. With some trepidation, she set out for Wander's house, afraid of what it meant that he was inviting her to his home, and even more worried when she laid eyes on his giant dog.

"Joe was a real 'dese, dems and dose' kind of guy who talked in mala-propisms, but he didn't do anything harmful, and he never made a pass at me," she said.

With his rough-hewn manner and great smile—another actress client called him "a sleazy looking version of Marcello Mastroianni . . . likable and engaging"—he turned out to be genuinely interested in her career. Shoving aside the debris that littered his sofa, he invited her to sit, then listened to her stories while he gave her every assurance of success, prom-ising that she would soon be catapulted to stardom. His willingness to take her on, his straightforward manner and lack of pretense made him instantly appealing. He laid out a strategy for his new client: he would send her to multiple auditions while spreading the word about this bril-liant unknown.

"He was an operator who was always looking for an angle," said Lan-sing. "He would fudge my résumé and tell me, 'Don't worry, no one will check.'"

Some of his clients believed he had other sidelines, though they could never figure out what. "It was very mysterious," said Annabelle Weston, an actress. "We didn't know much about his background. But he was as nice as could be."

Wander was a cut above most managers Lansing met, many of them Los Angeles versions of Woody Allen's Broadway Danny Rose. He would spend hours boosting her self-esteem, reminding her she was both beautiful and talented. He may not have been Pygmalion to her Galatea, but for a rough-and-tumble man, he was kind, walking her through each audition before it took place and always returning her calls.

While his client was going to meetings, Wander served as a de facto press agent, mailing out news items that were fodder for the gossip columns. Lansing was a stunning ingenue, he proclaimed, whom he had first seen in a performance of *The Crucible* at Northwestern. It did not matter that he had never seen the production, let alone that no such production had taken place; the hype was what counted.

"Sherry was so outstanding that I just had to go backstage and make my pitch, corny as it sounds," he told the *Los Angeles Herald-Examiner*'s James Bacon, a veteran newsman who was likely wise to these falsehoods. When Lansing objected, Wander told her to be quiet, that this was the way things were done in Hollywood. The news might have been printed in black and white, he said, but show business was full of grays.

"For years, I thought that's just how things were done," said Lansing. "This was the old Hollywood, where myth became reality."

THE NEW HOLLYWOOD had its own version of reality that was fast moving away from the old one, though few realized it in the mid-1960s.

Blow-Up, the story of a London photographer who witnesses a murder, and *Alfie*, which made a star of its Cockney hero Michael Caine (both released in 1966), were harbingers of a new era, with their frank discussions of sex, their heightened realism and critique of contemporary mores, even if neither had the ground-shaking impact of Mike Nichols's *The Graduate* and Arthur Penn's *Bonnie and Clyde* (both from 1967).

It would be three years before the watershed of 1969, when a low-budget release named *Easy Rider* turned the old model on its head by proving that a picture made for less than $500,000, starring a bunch of longhairs and unknowns, could outearn most studio releases. That in turn heralded an outpouring of more sexual, psychological and socially probing pictures from the "kids with beards," in Billy Wilder's phrase—a host of young directors itching to remake film, among them Francis Ford Coppola (*The

Godfather), Peter Bogdanovich (*The Last Picture Show*), Hal Ashby (*The Last Detail*), Woody Allen (*Annie Hall*), Bob Rafelson (*Five Easy Pieces*), Stanley Kubrick (*2001: A Space Odyssey*), Robert Altman (*Nashville*), William Friedkin (*The French Connection*) and Martin Scorsese (*Taxi Driver*).

Their works were not the distant gunfire of European auteurs whose pictures had more impact on filmmakers than on mainstream America. Rather, they were grenades lobbed into the very territory to which the studios had laid claim: the thirteen thousand theaters sprinkled across the heartland, one-third of them drive-ins.

For now, the signal of a coming revolution was lost amid the noise of industrial moviemaking. The two top box office hits of 1966 were the distinctly old-school *The Bible: In the Beginning . . .* , a fictionalized version of the first part of Genesis (with Richard Harris as Cain, John Huston as Noah and Peter O'Toole as the Three Angels); and *Hawaii*, a nineteenth-century period piece based on the James Michener novel in which a devout missionary and his bride set out for the islands, where naked girls splashed in the ocean, waiting to be converted. This was the bread and butter of the majors.

Other films "were still anomalies in a world that had just made *The Sound of Music* the highest-grossing film in history," writes Mark Harris in *Pictures at a Revolution: Five Movies and the Birth of the New Hollywood*. "What paid studio bills in the mid-1960s were James Bond extravaganzas, John Wayne westerns, Elvis Presley quickies, Dean Martin action comedies, and a long-standing willingness on the part of moviegoers to suspend disbelief."

LANSING WAS MORE than willing to suspend her own.

"Each day, I'd sit waiting for the phone to ring," she said. "I had no control over when I auditioned or where. Whenever Joe called, I'd race across town for some casting assistant who probably didn't want to see me, then go home and wait by the phone again."

Lansing would head out to offices large and small, meet filmmakers legitimate and illegitimate, hope for the best and frequently experience the worst. She saw that actors, if not quite cattle—as Hitchcock had described them—were treated as such, and grew to resent this injustice. It bothered her to be kept waiting for hours, as if she had no feelings. It humiliated her when casting directors regarded her as interchangeable with a hundred others. Actors, with the exception of a few major stars, were second-class citizens, she discovered—and actresses were third-class.

Small roles began to come her way, eventually allowing her to leave teaching after three years of substitute work. She was a background player on *Rowan & Martin's Laugh-In*, the benchmark 1960s comedy series, in which she pranced on the set with a handful of other young women, yelling the show's catchphrase, "Sock it to me!"

"Each week we'd throw a cocktail party, and every Monday morning we'd audition girls for it," said executive producer George Schlatter. "[A casting associate] comes in, looks around, sees this girl, and says, 'You're perfect! You're tall, you're brunette, you have full lips, you have dark eyes—they'll love you.' It was Sherry."

She also appeared in ten episodes of Hugh Hefner's short-lived jazz show *Playboy After Dark*, where she could be seen hanging out with the Playmates and guests in the Playboy Mansion, in an attempt to convey what a party there was like. Michael tolerated this, perhaps uneasily; his wife was fully clothed and Hefner treated her with respect. Like all those who worked for him, he made sure she was well fed, if nothing else. "Rather than the usual slop, there was always a huge spread of food," said Lansing. "It was a great lesson to see a boss making sure that everyone was treated like a human being."

She got her first taste of a real role as a "safari club girl" in 1969's *The April Fools*, a romantic comedy starring Jack Lemmon and Catherine Deneuve, in which she played a partygoer hovering in the background through the long scene when the two leads meet.

"It took us almost three weeks to shoot that," said Dee Gardner, another of the safari club girls, who remembered the stifling heat on the set. "It was closed in, like a box, and it was hot, and when they'd shoot they'd turn off the air-conditioning. But money seemed to be unlimited."

So did the lavish treatment the safari club girls were given after the film wrapped, when Lansing, Gardner and a third actress, Poupée Bocar, were sent on a multicity promotional tour. "Most of the girls were real 'actress' types," said Gardner, "but Poupée and Sherry were very smart women, so it was a completely different kind of tour than you'd normally find. We went to Dallas, and New Orleans was unique. We were on a float throwing doubloons out to the crowd, in these skimpy costumes, and these young men were doing provocative dances up against it. And we went to see the mayor [Victor Schiro], who was about five feet tall. We're all these tall, striking women—and he greets us, gives us the key to the city, then pulls out a shelf and stands on it to take pictures."

Lansing got her biggest break yet when Wander told her to take the next plane to New York, where she would audition for a small role in *Loving*, a movie that had already started filming under director Irvin Kershner, about a few days in the life of an illustrator struggling with alcoholism and a foundering marriage. She raced to the airport and agonized for hours as her plane remained grounded due to hydraulic problems.

Upon her arrival, she went straight to the casting office, where, typically, twenty other actresses were waiting. Convinced that one of them must have won the role, she checked in to her hotel and then got a call telling her the job was hers. She screamed for joy.

"I was so happy I even told the maid," she said. "I started dancing with her, yelling: 'I got the part! I got the part!'"

Lansing had two scenes as an attractive young woman whose life bisects that of the illustrator (George Segal) and who becomes almost comically inebriated. It was a secondary role but nonetheless challenging, and as the shoot progressed so did her fears. She was sure Kershner disliked her high-pitched voice with its distinct Chicago twang, no matter how much one of the producers, Ray Wagner, denied it.

"She was very good," he said. "She hadn't had that much experience, so it was a bit of a gamble, but Kershner was not a director to just say, 'That's OK.' He was very stringent. We were all pleased."

Lansing was thrilled when the *Hollywood Reporter* described her as "impressive and shapely," while *Variety* praised her for being a "chic sexpot." At the time, that was flattering rather than demeaning.

THE SPECTER OF war had been looming ever larger since the Brownsteins arrived in Los Angeles. In June 1968, shortly before Lansing got *April Fools*, her fears came true when Michael learned he had to serve. To their relief, he was going not to Vietnam but rather to the demilitarized zone that separated North and South Korea, where he would be stationed for the next thirteen months.

A welter of conflicting emotions consumed the young couple. Michael was worried about whatever dangers lay ahead, even though active hostilities had ended in 1953, while Lansing was torn, grateful that her husband had been spared Vietnam but also relieved by their imposed separation. Weeks after receiving his notice, Michael said goodbye, left their Kenmore Avenue home, and set out for the airport on his own.

"It was a very tearful parting," he said. "I took a taxi to LAX, flew to Seattle, and I was stuck there for three days."

Later that week, he got to Seoul and was shaken by what he saw. Flies swarmed from the meat that hung on hooks out in the open. Outdoor ditches served as toilets. His surroundings were primitive, telephone communication next to impossible. It took hours to get a phone line, and when he did, he had trouble making out his wife's voice, so faint that it seemed to have been wafted to him by a breeze. "This wasn't satellite, it was microwave," he said. "You'd go into this facility and you might be there two or three hours until you got a connection, and the wave goes in and out, and it just disappears, and you're yelling back and forth."

Eventually he gave up calling; Lansing could not get through at all. And so for months they hardly spoke, communicating instead through letters. Michael was alone and bored. Here, in the middle of nowhere, with little to do and nobody from home, he grew increasingly distant from the wife he had left behind.

The DMZ marked him deeply. "I saw horrible injuries, most of them from friendly fire," he said. "People were stepping on mines from the original conflict. Guys [would get] drunk and on drugs, wander in the mess hall and pass a grenade around—which went off one time. When we were called in, there were five guys dead, with their intestines coming down the stairs." Fear was a constant, uncertainty a given. "We'd go into those villages and I was like, 'God, what's happening? Where am I?' We'd [drink] and sit up on a stone and think, 'Which way is America?' and shout, 'Help!' But no one was there."

Back home, Lansing's experience as a wife with a husband at war was far from unique. "Everybody was being drafted," she said. "It was part of life. I'd go out with girlfriends or couples, but I was working seven days a week, trying to get acting jobs and teaching modeling at the Caroline Leonetti agency."

Halfway through Michael's tour of duty, she flew to meet him in Japan, where he kept silent about the hardships he was facing. An invisible curtain was falling between them. In Tokyo, "we talked about getting a divorce," he said. "There was no precipitating event. We just drifted apart."

Lansing was crushed by the prospect of breaking up, and even more by the thought of telling her family. When she called her mother, "she blamed me for not making the marriage work. She said it was the wife's job to hold a marriage together, and I should be able to fix what was wrong. She said, 'If you were a better wife, you'd make it work.'"

Divorce was still frowned on, though the divorce rate would explode in the 1970s. Riddled with guilt, Lansing decided to hold off, letting her marriage grind along its bumpy path, helped by Michael's absence. But when he returned in October 1969, she knew it was over. He spent the briefest time with her before leaving for Fort Irwin in the Mojave Desert, his next posting. When he halfheartedly asked if she wanted to join him, she demurred. "We're getting a divorce by attrition," he quipped. She did not disagree.

"Our breakup had no fireworks and no fights," she said. "Things were so amicable that we even used the same lawyer. I didn't want any money, but the lawyer said it would be a problem if I didn't ask for alimony, because if Michael became a successful doctor, I could sue and claim coercion."

Michael agreed to pay her $100 a year; the judge signed and stamped their papers, and the divorce was official.

"My mother was so ashamed, she didn't tell anyone," said Lansing. "When my grandmother was in the hospital and asked why Michael never visited, she'd point to a random doctor and say, 'You just missed him.'"

Living in her Kenmore Avenue apartment, the young woman felt abandoned. She had come to Los Angeles desiring so much, and after four years had so little. Her closest friends were far away, her family emotionally farther. She had imagined by now that Michael would be a doctor and she would be a film star, living the kind of idealized life she had seen on television and in the movies; instead, she was scraping by, taking jobs low on the artistic totem pole.

She looked at the acting she had done and found it wanting. With one or two exceptions, "these were glorified modeling jobs," she said. "Landing them was all about looks and luck. No talent was required."

Alone in her apartment, she cried at the thought of Michael's loss and what her life had become. Then Norton called. He said he was coming to Los Angeles on business, but she knew he was really flying out just to see her. For four days he remained at her side, sleeping on her couch and tending to her with a gentleness he had never allowed himself to reveal. For the first time, they talked fully and openly.

"My father was able to accept what was unpleasant, whereas my mother couldn't," reflected Lansing. "He didn't shirk from it. It was then that I knew I truly loved him, and he truly loved me."

CHAPTER 4

Shortly after her divorce, Lansing learned that one of Hollywood's most celebrated directors, Howard Hawks, was about to make a new western.

The director had been hired by an independent company, Cinema Center Films, in the belief he could still deliver a hit, though a decade had elapsed since his last one, 1959's *Rio Bravo*. Looking to reteam with John Wayne, he turned to a story by Burton Wohl about a Union Army captain who joins forces with a Confederate officer on the trail of a gang of train robbers. He later added another writer to the mix, his trusted colleague Leigh Brackett, as they worked on the screenplay, then called *San Timoteo* and later retitled *Rio Lobo*.

At seventy-three years old, Hawks was a cold and patrician figure, a philanderer and compulsive gambler whom few liked and fewer loved, a man's man more comfortable with Wayne and his ilk than with the women he invariably sought to reshape. One of Hollywood's most admired artists, he was also one of its most inscrutable.

"Many people are conveniently called enigmas," writes his biographer, Todd McCarthy, in *Howard Hawks: The Grey Fox of Hollywood*, "but even Hawks's friends referred to him that way. He was Sphinxlike, remote, cold, private, intimidating, self-absorbed, a man with eyes like blue ice cubes."

Hawks had directed such seminal works as 1932's *Scarface* and 1938's

Bringing Up Baby, but Lansing above all knew that he had launched the career of Lauren Bacall in 1944's *To Have and Have Not*. Summoned to meet him, she was petrified.

"I showed up in my nicest clothes, with my hair straightened and light makeup on my face," she said. "He shook his head and told me to come back looking less put-together."

When she returned days later in jeans, with her hair mussed up and no visible makeup, Hawks was content. He had never liked his women to be too conventionally feminine; androgyny was his thing, even his obsession—indeed, on one occasion, when he went to meet his estranged daughter, he took as a gift two men's shirts wrapped in a paper bag. He intimidated Lansing, but nonetheless treated her better than many other women in his orbit. "He had a gruff manner, but he didn't yell," she said. "He was quiet, but forceful and strong. I don't remember gabbing a lot or laughing with him—he wasn't that kind of person. It was more business: 'I told you to walk there, didn't I? Now walk here, do this, do that.' He knew what he wanted."

There was a darker side to him, however, with a need for absolute and unquestioned control. As he and Lansing spent more time together, with only vague hints that she would have a part in his movie, but no contract and no promises, she saw he was trying to mold her into someone else. Over and over, as they rehearsed, she felt her innermost self being siphoned away. Hawks wished to alter her very being—not just the way she acted but the way she moved, talked, walked. Reminding her that he had discovered Bacall, he urged her to speak like the throaty-voiced star. "He thought I sounded too girly," said Lansing. "He told me that to turn my voice from shrill to husky, I needed to practice screaming at the top of my lungs until I developed calluses on my vocal cords."

Each day at dawn, she would drive to the top of Los Angeles' Griffith Park and yell. "My hair was tied back, and I was wrapped in an old coat that I had brought from Chicago," she said. "My throat was sore, my vocal cords ached. I'd take a deep breath and let out a primal scream."

One morning, a homeless man leaped from the bushes at the sound of her shrieking, more scared of Lansing than she was of him. "What are you doing?" he demanded. "I'm screaming!" she replied. That seemed to satisfy him, and he returned to his bushes.

Hawks began to squire Lansing around town, taking her to dinners with the rich and famous, turning her into the latest of the many human baubles to decorate his arm. She did not object, however uncomfortable she felt. It helped that Hawks never made a pass, although in some ways that seemed stranger than if he had. This once-virile man, with his baritone voice and authoritative manner, simply needed to prove he could summon a beautiful girl at will, regardless of whether he had any intention to take it further. "It was all for show," said Lansing. "You arrived for dinner, you went wherever he wanted, you were polite, he kissed you on the cheek and said good night, and you went home. He never tried anything."

Only once, when she was invited to Hawks's home in Palm Springs, did she sense something different, something sexual in the air. "That's the only time I was a little nervous," she said. "And I remember thinking, 'I'll just go home. I'll get up and go. I'm a big girl. I have a car.'" Her worries proved unfounded. "The illusion was all that was important."

She never thought of her effect on him or on others. Polly Platt, a production designer then married to director Peter Bogdanovich, recalled the humiliation she felt when the four went out to dinner. Halfway through the meal, "[Lansing] gets up, stands up, and she was gorgeous," said Platt. "And I was not." As the young actress left them to find a restroom, according to author Rachel Abramowitz, Hawks leaned over to Bogdanovich and whispered loud enough for Platt to hear, as if she were not even there, "Peter, now that is the kind of girl that you should be with."

WEEKS AFTER THEIR first meeting, Hawks screen-tested Lansing opposite Chris Mitchum, whom he was considering for one of the leading roles. She had to shoot one scene topless, though her arms were draped across her breasts and pasties covered her nipples.

"She was absolutely terrified," said Mitchum. "She didn't know how the scene was going to be done. We talked about it and I said, 'Take that nervousness and use it in the scene. Play with it.' She had a Valium. She said, 'I was thinking of taking it to calm my nerves.' Well, she dropped the Valium. Had it been me, I would have been out cold by the time they shot the scene. But she was very calm."

Lansing landed the role, but she was convinced she was going to become an addict and end up on Skid Row, a fear that would haunt her for years, no matter how successful she became.

"I panicked," she said. "I was a Jewish girl from Chicago who was not only divorced, but losing track of who I was." She thought of Jacqueline Susann's *Valley of the Dolls*, the 1966 bestseller about the temptations facing three young women in show business. "I was convinced I was headed for a life of depravity."

Hawks wanted to shoot in Durango, Mexico, but British director Michael Winner had snuck in ahead of him and booked a preexisting set he would have liked to use, so Hawks relocated to Cuernavaca, Mexico, where a two-week shoot was followed by a month and a half in Old Tucson, Arizona, before the shoot ended with studio work in Los Angeles.

It was in Old Tucson that Lansing met Wayne for the first time and found him "warm and accessible," not merely the right-wing nemesis of Hollywood liberals. "He talked to everybody and played cards with the guys," she said. "He'd sit around and tell stories. He wasn't intimidating. He wasn't snobbish. People adored him. And at the end of the shoot, he gave each of us a cup that said, 'The Duke. *Rio Lobo*.'"

In their few scenes together, Wayne was professional and encouraging, if distant. He did not discuss his craft with her, nor did he say anything about his private life. She did not know that the sixty-three-year-old actor was battling the cancer that eventually would kill him, as well as dealing with the death of his mother and the implosion of his marriage to Pilar Pallete.

"I was cast as Amelita, a girl who vows revenge on the sheriff for beating me up and scarring my face," said Lansing. "I loved the idea of playing a vigilante who kills the bad guy. My big line, delivered in my huskiest voice, was: 'Turn around, sheriff, I want you to see who's going to kill you.' I remember thinking, 'Oh my God! I'm in a movie with John Wayne. This is what I worked for my whole life. This is what I dreamed of, sitting in those movie theaters in Chicago.'"

Early in the shoot, Wayne left to attend the 42nd Academy Awards, where he had been nominated for his role as Rooster Cogburn in 1969's *True Grit*. When he returned, having finally won an Oscar as Best Actor, he was greeted by the entire cast and crew, all wearing black eye patches in honor of his *True Grit* character. Even his horse had one.

On set, it was Hawks who impressed Lansing even more than Wayne. Hundreds of miles from the studio, he ruled with absolute authority, and nothing anyone said could shift him to do anything he didn't like. When the studio dragged its feet over Mitchum's casting, she recalled how the director dawdled, slowing production to a crawl. "He complained that his ankle hurt, meaning he would have to stop work for the day," she said. "Then he told them he was coming down with the flu. Everything started to drag and got strung out for days. The bottom line was, he wasn't going to shoot until he got the actor he wanted. There was nothing the studio could do; if they fired him, they'd have to replace him immediately or risk losing all their money. So Chris was given the part."

Lansing feared she was not delivering what her director wanted. She looked with envy at the film's leading lady, Jennifer O'Neill, wishing she could be as beautiful and sophisticated as the twenty-two-year-old former model who was going through her own conflicts with Hawks.

O'Neill recalled meeting him before the shoot began. It bore unfortunate parallels to Lansing's experience. "He was sitting behind a giant mahogany desk and we spoke for a few minutes about the film," she remembered. "He said, 'I created Lauren Bacall, and you need to speak from the diaphragm [like her].' He said, 'Come here!' and I hesitantly got up, and he said, 'No, no, come here around the desk.' I thought, 'Oh no, what's going to happen?' I was very, very nervous, and as I rounded the desk slowly, inches at a time, he suddenly punched me in the diaphragm and said, 'That's where you have to speak from!'"

When O'Neill refused to sign a multipicture contract with the director, which would have allowed him to loan her out to other filmmakers for a fraction of what she felt she deserved, he was incensed. "We went down to the set, and in front of the whole crew he said he was going to blackball me from the business and that I would never work again," she noted. "It was very intimidating."

Lansing observed the growing rift between them as Hawks started taking scenes away from O'Neill and giving them to her, including the final sequence when Amelita shoots the bad guy, the last scene Hawks would ever film. But she never felt free to discuss it. Divide and conquer was the order of the day, and Lansing and O'Neill never became friends, to each woman's regret, said O'Neill, because "she was as lovely then as she is now."

Lansing followed Hawks's rules, which meant not fraternizing with anyone of whom he did not approve, least of all the lowly crew members, with whom she felt most at home. He was old-school and class-bound, locked in the hierarchy of the past at a time when all things past and hier-archical were coming under assault.

"One of the stuntmen, whom I liked, though not in a romantic way, said, 'Oh, I'd better not talk to you. I'll get in trouble,'" recalled Lansing. "Hawks didn't want anyone talking to his leading ladies, because that was the fantasy: they were there for him alone."

The fantasy continued off-camera as well as on. "He insisted that I talk in my throaty voice during the entire shoot," she said. "I'd go out to lunch or dinner with him and Wayne and speak as if I were Lauren Bacall. I was supposed to be a sex symbol, which was totally unnatural to me. I sounded fake and I felt fake. I was miserable."

On her last day of work, Hawks turned on her with some of the harsh-ness he had previously reserved for O'Neill. "I had to cry and shoot the bad guy, and he kept making me do it again and again and again," she said. "Wayne—Duke, as he was called—went over and said, 'Hey, you're being too hard on her.' But Hawks just dismissed it out of hand. He told me later, 'I knew you could take it.'"

He was wrong. She could handle his criticism, but not her growing awareness that she hated acting. She loathed the falseness, the pretense, the need to transform herself into someone she did not recognize, the push to become a manufactured being removed from any part of her own reality. If this was acting, she realized, it was not for her. Just as her dream was starting to come true, it was turning into a nightmare.

She began to suffer from psychosomatic pain. "I got this incredible tension in my arms and legs whenever I acted, just from being anyone other than myself," she said. "I almost couldn't function. Hawks was creating who I was, and I had to become that person. It was all fake, and the fakeness drove me crazy."

When *Rio Lobo* opened in December 1970, her reviews fell flat. She and another actress, Susana Dosamantes, were "somewhat sultrier than they are talented," noted the *Los Angeles Times*. Nor did the movie fare any better at the box office than it did with the critics: it earned less than its $5 million budget.

"However charitable one might care to be," writes McCarthy of Hawks, "the evidence of decline is too obvious to ignore. The film's lack of creative spark, of inspiration, of energy, of any driving force is palpable in every scene save for the train prologue. . . . Few great directors ever went out with a bang; like most of them, Hawks, at the estimable age of seventy-four, sort of faded away."

And so did Lansing's acting career. If she had thought this would lead to bigger parts, she was wrong. After *Rio Lobo*, she guest-starred as Joel Grey's wife in the NBC courtroom drama *Ironside*, and then appeared opposite Burt Reynolds in an episode of ABC's crime series *Dan August*.

"*Dan August* was a disaster," she said. "I remember the day it all went wrong. We were shooting a critical scene. The director wanted me to cry, but all I could do was blink. I thought, if I squeezed my eyes tight, I could make tears come, but it was no use. I kept blinking as hard as I could. After at least ten awful takes, the director called for a break. I knew he was stopping because I couldn't give him what he wanted."

Reynolds wandered over. "Hey, high pockets," he said, referring to her pantsuit. "You're really good. You just need to relax."

But she could not, no matter how hard she tried. The more she forced herself, the worse she became, until she felt as if she were sinking deeper into an artistic and psychological quagmire. "I was becoming more and more miserable," she said. "Instead of relaxing, I became more uptight. I kept telling myself, 'If I just get this next role, everything will be different.' But it never was."

After *Dan August*, she never acted again.

"Her heart wasn't in it," said Reynolds. But he remembered their conversations four decades later and recalled something unique about this young woman, a vitality and hunger, an energy still inchoate but searching for an outlet.

"I was struck by that drive, that enormous drive," he said. "It was very powerful. I felt whatever she tackled, if she gave it 100 percent she'd succeed."

CHAPTER 5

As her acting career collapsed, Lansing fell into a depression. She had failed at the two things that mattered to her most, her marriage and her career.

The young woman who a few years earlier had attacked Los Angeles with an almost reckless abandon felt rudderless and adrift. Again and again, she asked herself: Why had her luck changed? What should she have done differently? Was it other people's fault, or had she constructed her own dollhouse full of holes?

In her mid-twenties she began to see a psychoanalyst, but her first experience was a disaster. "He said if I didn't see him five times a week, I'd become even more depressed," she recalled. "He told me only he could help me. He made me think I was mentally ill and that I'd commit suicide if I didn't keep going to him. When I told him I could only afford to come twice a week, he said, 'Make sacrifices.' He wanted to take total control of my life. He told me, 'When I'm done with you, you won't even want a career. You'll be happy staying home and baking pies.'"

With no guide to steer her away from the analyst, Lansing remained with him for two years. "It didn't occur to me that he should probably lose his license," she said. "I was young and impressionable. It took every ounce of strength I had to break free. The thought lingered in me that I was seriously unstable. It was a secret I carried for years."

When a friend set her up on a blind date, she was certain the man would soon spot the fissures beneath her polished façade. "I kept thinking, 'He'd better not get to know me well or he'll discover I'm certifiable,'" she said.

Her date was another psychoanalyst, and when she finally opened up about her experience, "he said, 'I beg you to see another doctor so this isn't what you think therapy is like,'" she recalled. "Then he picked up the phone and called a friend, who introduced me to Dr. Joshua Hoffs."

Lansing went to meet Hoffs at his West Los Angeles office, where she found him surrounded by paintings, as warm as her last therapist had been cold.

"I was instantly comfortable," she said. "He had this approach where nothing seemed too serious. I came from parents who were highly critical, where everything was life and death, and he'd just smile and say, 'I won't judge you unless you're doing something that's seriously going to hurt you.'"

Lansing began to see him regularly, and over the next five years would visit him as often as three times a week. She discussed the seemingly contradictory messages her mother had sent—she was a woman of unquestionable strength, who nonetheless had submerged her strength when she married her second husband; a woman skilled enough to run a business, who had turned her back on all forms of business as soon as she could resume domestic life. "Work, in effect, was only a placeholder until she could find a husband," said Lansing.

All this she discussed with Hoffs, along with the loss of her father, in an intense and emotional exploration that continued for years. "Analysis is about re-parenting yourself and relearning the habits of a lifetime," she said. "I'm convinced I wouldn't have the life I have today if it weren't for that."

LANSING'S ACTING CAREER was over, but what would take its place?

The answer came through Ray Wagner, her *Loving* producer. Some fifteen years her senior, he was old enough to have experience but not so old as to be removed from her concerns. A former advertising executive, he had started in commercials before producing an early TV movie, 1964's *The Hanged Man*, and one of Lansing's favorite films, 1968's *Petulia* with Julie Christie. He was a man of unusual warmth and sensitivity, and had become close to her during their Connecticut shoot, where he found she possessed a rare combination of analytic and intuitive intelligence.

"I said, 'Why don't you come and be a reader?'" he remembered. "Her judgment was excellent, better than mine."

In 1971, she began her new career. The gangling girl who had remade herself as an actress would remake herself again, this time as a script reader and future executive. If being a director's puppet had not worked, she would instead become the puppet master.

With Wagner, she discovered the intricacies of how a screenplay was developed. She learned that the best writing used dialogue almost in counterpoint to the visuals, so that what was heard was different from what was seen; she found that a well-made scene could unfold over many pages, with a beginning, middle and end just like a self-contained story; and she observed that each of the best screenplays was driven by an underlying idea that the writer wanted to convey about life itself. It was this that touched her the most, because it meant films could have meaning and be just as effective in catalyzing change as her work in schools.

Over the following weeks and months, she plowed through dozens and dozens of scripts, noting her thoughts on each one.

"She kept a little wire-bound book," said Wagner, "and she'd write down exactly how much time she spent on that script, how many hours and minutes, and I would pay her accordingly. She could see what worked and what didn't, and knew how to fix things."

Through Wagner, Lansing discovered she could be emotionally open without feeling any less secure. He was proud of his emotions and did nothing to hide them. "If Ray saw a film that moved him, he'd cry," she said. "If he was hurt or upset, he'd share his feelings. He was the first person I met who hugged, and I was so needy for hugs."

At twenty-six years old, she was starting from scratch, joining the legions of struggling readers, writers and would-be producers who lived off the scripts that floated through the city like industrial plankton. Thousands circulated at any time: comedies and dramas, science fiction and thrillers, action-adventures and romances, all hammered out by eager writers hunched over their Olympias and Olivettis.

It was the bottom rung on a tall ladder, but a rung often used as a starting point by others who had gone on to become producers and executives. Script reading, along with working in an agency mailroom, was the best means to earn a modest living while soaking oneself in Hollywood's rituals and rules.

"It was one of the most interesting ways to begin a career," said Jeff Berg, who also started as a reader and later became chairman of the agency ICM. "You read everything that comes in: plays, novels, manuscripts, screenplays, pilots, treatments, outlines. You're reading every kind of material that's going to be marketed. What better training to hone your critical skills?"

Earning $5 per hour as a part-timer, Lansing had to work around the clock to make a fraction of her pay as an actress, but she had none of the anxiety that accompanied it. For the first time, she was content, burrowing through material stacked in neat piles in the cubbyhole of a room that Wagner had set aside for her in his Beverly Hills offices.

"I felt instantly comfortable as a reader," she said. "I felt qualified, I felt valued and I felt peaceful. I felt, if I never did anything else for the rest of my life, I'd be happy."

For days and weeks, she toiled in her tiny office, indifferent to the world around her, as she read hundreds of submissions, studying the intricacies of character and dialogue and learning the mechanics of effective plots. She approached each script the same way: she would take an hour and a half to read it, then thirty minutes to write a synopsis and comments. First came the "log line," a sentence or two that explained the script's premise, the hook that would tell a buyer whether this was worth pursuing; next came a one-page story summary; and finally a critical evaluation, in which she explained each script's strengths and weaknesses and potential for success. Good screenplays, then as now, were the rarest of gems.

She wrote all her reports by hand because she had never learned to type. "I didn't want to," she said. "That was my form of rebellion, because

I knew I'd end up becoming a secretary if ever I did, and I was scared I wouldn't go further."

Throughout, Wagner was her mentor. "He would let me come to story meetings, and we'd analyze the characters and their connection to the plot," she said. "And he showed me how you could handle things with grace. If he had to tell a writer his script wasn't great, the writer would always leave feeling good. He was honest, he was emotional, and he didn't lie. He was an impeccable producer and an idealist, who had a profound effect on my life."

Wagner watched with delight as Lansing "took on a maturity and a wisdom that can only come from being in the arena, and learned all the highways and byways of traveling in the business."

After six months, he hired her full-time. A year and a half later, with Wagner's support, Lansing was named story editor at Leonard Stern's Talent Associates, where she joined a major television producer whose credits included *Get Smart* and *McMillan and Wife*.

This was a period of transformation, a voyage of intellectual and artistic discovery that altered Lansing's thinking about herself and her career. Unformed before, she began to take shape now.

"I spent hours in story meetings, immersed in conversation about characters' motivations and actions," she said. "For the first time in my life, I felt authentic."

IF WAGNER WAS her better angel, she had a darker one, too.

At a dinner party hosted by Stern, Lansing was seated next to Dan Melnick, a famed executive who was the head of production at MGM. He was as cynical as Wagner was idealistic, as suspicious as Wagner was trusting.

"He sat next to me, perfectly dressed," said Lansing. "He had a three-piece suit—he always wore a vest and a suit. He was so sophisticated, and I was so unsophisticated. He talked about art and movies, and I guess he tried to impress me, though I didn't realize that's what he was trying to do."

At forty-two years old, with his world-weary manner and sardonic voice, Melnick bore something of a resemblance to Humphrey Bogart, if a more urbane version. He had grown up poor in Rego Park, New York, and spent a lifetime trying to escape it. His house was a treasure trove of paintings and sculpture, and he fought for the money to maintain them. Even his office was filled with artwork, most notably the sculpture of a vagina—"a kind of impressionistic art, which he described as being there to remind him of his ex-wife," said an executive who knew him well.

He was complicated and contradictory, a Machiavellian mover and shaker who nonetheless loved film with a genuine passion. He battled for the pictures he believed in, fighting to piece together the money and the stars that would allow them to be made. Bob Fosse's semi-autobiographical dance movie *All That Jazz* (1979) would never have been made without him; nor would such original pictures as Ken Russell's *Altered States* (1980) and Alan Parker's *Midnight Express* (1978), which created an international uproar with its depiction of brutality in a Turkish prison, but which also gave Oliver Stone his first big break as a writer.

"A lot of studio executives ride the fence between the creative element and the corporate investor," observed Steven Spielberg. "Few have bent over as far in the direction of the filmmaker as Dan Melnick."

Melnick and Wagner became the two polar forces that tugged at Lansing's soul, the light and the dark, the sweet and the sour. Repeatedly she would be drawn to tough, uncompromising and sometimes scary men like Melnick, even as she gravitated toward more gentle souls like Wagner—perhaps the same split she had found in her two fathers, Norton and David.

It was one of the central mysteries of Lansing's personality that she could tolerate men whom others often found intolerable. Some felt her affinity for them was off-putting, while others deemed it incomprehensible. And yet, paradoxically, in an era when women were often shoved aside and ignored, it was these macho men—Melnick and the others who would later take his place—who were willing to take a chance and give Lansing her most significant breaks.

She never forgot what Melnick taught her, though she developed more ambivalent feelings about him in the coming years, partly because she had dated him for a while, to her regret. "After that, I never wanted to go out with any other executive I'd have to work with, because I felt it tainted me unfairly," she said. "And then it dogged me, even though I owe Danny so much."

In 1975, a few months after their initial meeting, Melnick made Lansing an offer she could not refuse: to join him as executive story editor at MGM.

THE STUDIO SYSTEM was in turmoil. Half a century after most of the majors had come into being, all ruled as personal fiefdoms by despots such as Louis B. Mayer, Harry Cohn, Jack Warner and Darryl F. Zanuck, they had become faint shadows of their former selves. The men who had founded them were either dead or defanged, and the audiences that had flocked to their product were in a steady decline that had begun at the end of World War II and was only now bottoming out. Average weekly attendance had tumbled to 44 million in 1965, half of what it was just after the war, as returning veterans settled down to build their families, and as television captured their attention at the expense of local theaters—and nobody had a clue what to do.

Mayer was long gone, having died in 1957, years after being ousted from the company that bore his name; Cohn, the profanity-spewing chief of Columbia Pictures, had died a year later. While Zanuck had had a brief and glorious restoration, summoned back to Fox in the early 1960s after a protracted exile in Paris, he was forced out in 1971, the victim of a power struggle with Fox's board. He did not go down without a fight, firing his own son before he in turn was fired.

Jack Warner, the last of the four brothers who had built the Burbank studio, clung to power a while longer, having cheated one sibling out of his shares in order to do so. But he, too, had left at last, and Warner Bros., like almost all the other studios, now belonged to outsiders, corporate behemoths that knew nothing of film. This was part of a tectonic shift that would jolt the movie industry out of one era and send it spinning into another.

The studios were in their death throes as autonomous nation-states. Gulf + Western Industries, which had its roots in the sale of auto parts, had purchased Paramount in 1966; a year later Transamerica, which made its money through insurance, had bought United Artists—and these were only the first assaults on Hollywood by the conglomerates. Warner Bros. was bought by Kinney National, a company built on parking lots and funeral parlors, and while Fox and Disney retained their independence, MGM had fallen into the hands of Kirk Kerkorian, the most predatory of Las Vegas raiders, who proceeded to sell it off piecemeal, unloading much of its land and auctioning or trashing priceless memorabilia, until all that was left was the shell of a studio.

The corporate owners brought in "a new age of greed," said film historian Leonard Maltin. "Hollywood has always been about greed, but before that they at least knew how to go about their daily business. And in the late 1960s and '70s a lot of the components of that business underwent radical change."

Curiously, as the business went through this change—and as knowledgeable insiders were replaced by far-away accountants less able to make informed decisions—Hollywood entered a golden age, perhaps because the barriers that had kept young directors at bay were now removed. In the years following 1969's *Easy Rider*, their work flooded the market. In part this was a response to the convulsions of the Vietnam War and the social upheaval of the 1960s, and audience demands for something different from the tame work they had seen until now; in part it was a reaction to the groundbreaking filmmaking coming out of France and England; and in part it was because a new establishment was rising up and replacing the old. Lansing was in the vanguard.

On her first day at MGM, however, as she entered the Thalberg Building, where she had her office, it was the studio's history and tradition that affected her far more than any thoughts of change.

"This was the place I'd dreamed of," she said. "It was so exciting, going through that gate and having my own office, and a big office, too. Danny had decorated it with lithographs from his own collection. He said, 'Change anything you want.' But there was nothing to change."

MGM had been struggling since the late 1950s, and things were only beginning to look up thanks to an unexpected hit, 1974's *That's Entertainment!*, a compilation of classic moments from the greatest movie musicals, which had debuted in Cannes the previous year. The movie's success breathed life into the moribund empire; and for several staffers who still remembered how bad things had been, Lansing's vitality matched their rising optimism.

"She walked in wearing a green miniskirt and matching green sweater and white boots," said Susan Merzbach, then an MGM script reader. "That was our first glimpse of this gorgeous person, the most exotic beast I had ever seen."

Regardless of the damage Kerkorian had inflicted, "the studio had a library the likes of which I had never known—every script, every piece of material," said Merzbach. "The files were meticulously kept. There was a basement of file cabinets that went on for yards, with memos from Louis B. Mayer, Marx Brothers screenplays, and all of MGM's history."

The pictures were just lying there, waiting to be seen whenever Lansing could find a projectionist to screen them. She taught herself film history through these movies.

"She had to learn," said Merzbach. "So lunchtimes we spent in an MGM screening room, watching film after film—*Singin' in the Rain*, *Dark Victory*, everything we could get a print of. Sometimes she would turn and say, 'Who would mind if we speed through this?' because she had gotten what she needed."

Melnick gave her a list of one hundred pictures, from classics such as Hitchcock's *Vertigo* and *Rebecca* and Fred Astaire's *Top Hat* to more modern endeavors such as Sam Peckinpah's *The Wild Bunch* and François Truffaut's *The 400 Blows*. He expected her to watch them all. She must learn to love the past as well as the present, he said, and judge filmmakers by their greatest work, not merely their latest. He also instructed her to delve into every detail of a script and read draft after draft, just as he did. This was unusual for an executive of his stature, who would normally expect his staff to do the grunt work.

"Danny was obsessed with doing it right," said Lansing. "There were no half measures with him. He'd meet with all the writers and read all their drafts and brainstorm ways to make each screenplay better. He had a great love of film and a great respect for the audience. He believed audiences were smart and would understand the material you gave them, so there was no need to dumb it down."

Soon she was developing her own material, including a sequel to *Gone with the Wind* that had been in the works with producers David Brown and Richard Zanuck (Darryl's son). Scarlett O'Hara died in the first draft Lansing read, but she believed the story should conclude with Rhett Butler's death. She won that argument, though the movie was never made.

"Sherry would share the scripts with all the readers and ask for our comments," said Merzbach. "That had never been done before. She wanted to know what we thought. She was as democratic a presence as I have ever seen. You'd walk into a meeting with Melnick or [production executive] Dick Shepherd, and their faces were sort of closed; they're waiting to hear what you're going to say and whether they'll like it. You'd walk into a meeting with Sherry and it was, 'Whaddya got?' I was in heaven."

On one occasion, Kerkorian, MGM's owner, stopped by Lansing's office. She had admired him from a distance and noted the way he stood in line at the studio commissary, never cutting in, even though he owned the place.

"It was the end of the day and I had cleaned off my desk, as was my routine," she recalled. "Kerkorian peeked in and said, 'You've got nothing on your desk.' 'That's right,' I told him. That was my routine. I was worried he'd think I had nothing to do. But he said: 'Neither do I, and neither does Lew Wasserman [the head of MCA-Universal and the most powerful man in Hollywood]. That's why you're a good executive.'"

She approached her work as methodically as a math problem. Years before executives used spreadsheets, and decades before the Internet revolutionized information, "she figured out a system for tracking every single book that came from the publishers," said Merzbach, "and she was very good at it."

When one top literary agent refused to deal with the studio, now something of a backwater compared to the others, "Sherry called him every day until he finally met her," continued Merzbach. "Then she charmed him and got this huge advance information. It didn't matter what their reputation was; Sherry could turn them all."

Others could sometimes turn her, particularly the founders of Creative Artists Agency, which had opened its doors in the same year she joined MGM, under the leadership of five upstarts from the William Morris Agency. Their roots were in television, not film, at a time when the two businesses were discrete and unconnected.

One of the CAA leaders, Bill Haber, had been trying to win Lansing over, without success. "The first time he called me, he said, 'I'd like to come and see you and go over the projects on your list,'" she remembered. "I said, 'That would be great, but Susan does that.' He said, 'But I don't want Susan.' I said, 'That's the way we do it with everybody else.' He said, 'But I don't want to be treated like everybody else.'"

Haber told her he had a plan. "He said, 'You know what? I'm going to shower you with gifts so you won't treat me like everyone else,'" she noted. "Then he literally started showering us with gifts. The first time, he sent us fifty boxes of Morton salt, whose logo was a girl with an umbrella under a shower. I started to laugh and called him back. He wouldn't take my call. The next day, sixty bottles of soap came for each of us. I called him again, and he still wouldn't return my call. This goes on for days. Soap, shower caps, mops start arriving—my office is now like a store. I keep calling him, saying, 'OK, stop!'"

Lansing decided she had to one-up him. "So we hired an actor and told him, 'We want you to go to CAA dressed in a towel, as if you've just had a shower,'" she said. "'Then go to Bill Haber's office and say, 'The girls throw in the towel.'"

The actor (one of Merzbach's friends) did as instructed, but when he talked his way into the agent's office, shampooing his hair, he got carried away. "He says, 'The girls throw in the towel'—and he whips off the towel, and he's stark naked underneath," said Lansing. "They were sitting there with one of the biggest stars in Hollywood, Peter Sellers, trying to sign him. Sellers goes: 'Wow. This is the coolest place I've ever seen!' and signs with CAA."

Finally Haber called and they agreed to meet. "I'm taking you some-place very special, so you won't forget," he said. "Just be outside your of-fice."

Lansing and Merzbach were waiting in the lobby when "suddenly a limo arrives and this red carpet is thrown out," recalled Lansing. "I don't think I'd ever been in a limo, and it was enormous. This guy comes out with a violin, and starts playing it as we get into the car. There's a bottle of champagne, and Susan starts to laugh, and I start to laugh. I've never seen Bill Haber in my life. I say to the driver, 'Are you Bill Haber?' 'Nope. I'm just taking you to him, miss.' I said, 'Well, where are we going?' He says, 'I'm not allowed to tell you.' He starts driving in the pouring rain. We cannot believe the sheer brilliance of this. Finally, he pulls up to the airport. We get out and a guy in a suit says, 'Hi, I'm Bill Haber.' I say, 'Wow. How clever. We're eating at the airport?' He says, 'No.' Then a guy with a blue badge that says PILOT MIKE comes out. I say, 'Oh. Do you work for the airline?' He says, 'No. I work for CAA.'"

The pilot was Mike Rosenfeld, another senior agent, whose hobby was flying. He and Haber flew the two women all of ten minutes to dinner. There they sat trading tales.

"[One of the men] said, 'Let's all tell stories of some strange tryst we've had,'" Merzbach remembered. "I won't tell you what Sherry said, but it had to do with a nooner at a motel not far from MGM, where she used her real name and her real credit card. We were all on a high. It was magic."

EVEN AS LANSING was becoming more entrenched in Hollywood, part of her was pulling away. The young woman who, like Huck Finn, had lit out for the territory was showing a dawning awareness that there were other territories beyond even this one.

She began to carve out time, taking three weeks each summer when she would travel the world, sometimes with her sister Judy, sometimes alone. The first such trip took her to Israel.

"I met my sister there," she said. "We had backpacks and no money, and did the whole trip on $125. We stayed in youth hostels and visited a kibbutz. Then I went to Italy, my first trip on my own. And later I went all through India, again with my sister. At the time, the trains were on strike and we were stuck in Calcutta. We'd go to the station every day, where there were many homeless who'd maimed themselves. One woman had two dead babies in her hands. I sat there thinking, 'This can't be happening.' Later, we went to Delhi and Kashmir and Mumbai, and finally stayed in a hotel, and when I took a bath, dirt was covering me all over because I'd been traveling so long."

Having read Mirella Ricciardi's *Vanishing Africa*, Lansing was keen to see Kenya. She flew to Nairobi, where she spent days living in a tent, first with the Maasai and then the Samburu tribe.

"A guide left me there," she said. "Nobody could speak to me, except by gestures, but I loved it. The kids would all gather outside, and when I woke up they'd be touching my hair, touching my skin. Everything comes into balance because you know the world is a big place and you're very small, and the things that bother you at home no longer seem like life or death. I wanted to live a simpler life. Travel was my salvation."

After voyaging down the Amazon, her last major expedition was to Australia. "I got permission to live with the Aborigines," she said. "It was sad because the culture, which had been so beautiful, had been bastardized. They had boom boxes. Everything had changed."

These were Lansing's happiest years, Merzbach believed, before the pressure of high office and her increasing visibility began to weigh her down. "She was fun and funny and real," said Merzbach. "The celebrity hadn't begun."

Despite her newfound success, Lansing could still feel like a country mouse. She recalled being humiliated when a hatcheck girl brought out her coat after a formal dinner with director Herbert Ross, and Ross's wife asked, "Whose is this fake vicuña thing?"

Snobbism was rampant, sexism raging. "I was promoted to vice president at the same time as one of my male colleagues," she said. "He was given more money, and I wasn't. So I went in and asked for a raise. The head of business affairs said, 'Well, I understand why you feel you deserve it, but you're single and he's married and has kids, so he deserves a raise and you don't.' The terrible thing is, I accepted it. I was so conditioned to think I was worth less money that I actually went, 'Oh. OK.'"

Still, she was gaining both confidence and skill, and Melnick soon asked her to meet with one of the industry's greatest writers, Paddy Chayefsky, in New York. Chayefsky had won Oscars for 1955's *Marty* and 1971's *The Hospital*, but he was notoriously hostile to executives and had even poured a bowl of soup over one who'd had the temerity to question him.

"He was at his best when he was angry," writes Dave Itzkoff in *Mad as Hell: The Making of* Network *and the Fateful Vision of the Angriest Man in Movies*. "It wasn't simply that so many things bothered him, or that when they did, they irritated him to the fullest possible degree. But where others avoided conflict, he cultivated it and embraced it. His fury nourished him."

After a falling-out with Columbia, Chayefsky had turned to MGM to make *Network*, the story of an aging news anchor who is about to be fired when he announces he will commit suicide on the air, sending ratings skyrocketing and the anchor, Howard Beale, on a downward spiral into madness.

Lansing read the 160-page black comedy in July 1975, when it was first submitted to MGM's story department. She was impressed with Chayefsky's dialogue and his deft interweaving of Beale's story with that of an ambitious young woman and an older, morally conflicted newsman. She was equally taken with the cast: Peter Finch as Beale, William Holden as the older newsman and Faye Dunaway as the young network executive with whom Holden has an affair.

"I loved the fact that this career woman is shaking when the older man leaves her," said Lansing, "and the cautionary tale that presents of building your whole life around your career, when you also need love."

"It was one of the most astonishing things I'd ever read," added Merzbach. "It read on the page the way you saw it on the screen. It was daring.

It was heartbreaking. It was gutsy. It was sentimental and 'fuck you' at the same time. There was concern about Holden: he was an alcoholic, and how would that work? And Faye was not easy. But we knew we were going to explode with it."

Entrusted to deliver MGM's script notes, Lansing arrived at Chayefsky's eleventh-floor office in midtown Manhattan to find him sitting near a piano and a pile of *National Geographics*, rumpled and weathered, but surprisingly sweet. He listened calmly and politely as she spoke, and never objected to any of her notes, though few—if any—made it into the finished film.

"I sat in a chair, and he sat in a chair," recalled Lansing. "He hunched forward and said, 'Who sent you?' I said, 'Well, Danny Melnick.' He listened, and went 'Hm-hmm.' When Danny told me to fly to New York, I didn't think twice. Here I was, a 'female' story editor, giving notes to one of the greatest writers of our time. Obviously, he was thinking: 'Melnick sent a story editor to give notes to Paddy Chayefsky? You sent a sacrificial lamb, because you ain't got the balls to do it yourself!'"

NOR DID HE have the balls to stand up to Don Siegel when the director confronted Lansing in a story meeting with Melnick and other executives.

Tough and anti-authoritarian, Siegel had made the original *Invasion of the Body Snatchers* in 1956, and had worked frequently with Clint Eastwood on films including 1971's *The Beguiled* and *Dirty Harry*. He was blunt and unpretentious, but became threatening when he met with MGM to discuss the Charles Bronson thriller *Telefon*.

"Sherry Lansing was a most attractive girl in her late twenties," he recounted in his autobiography, *A Siegel Film*. "She was very enthusiastic about a sequence in one of the earlier scripts, which took place in the lady's [sic] restroom at a train station. The scene showed our leading lady combing her hair. While looking in the mirror, she notices one of the toilet doors slowly opening, revealing a filthy derelict holding a knife. As he tries to rape our leading lady, she badly beats him up."

Siegel outlined their conversation:

ME: It's difficult to shoot leading ladies in any type of physical encounter. Bronson could and should take care of all the physical encounters. I know he'll want to. Also, we don't need the scene.

LANSING: (*Voice filled with emotion*) When she is attacked by this bum and fights him off, the audience will stand up and cheer!

ME: Sherry, the script is very long now and this scene should be the first one to be cut out.

LANSING: I feel very strongly that it should be left in.

ME: When it comes to rape, you unquestionably know more than I do. I'm also quite sure that in karate you are much better than I. (*Very businesslike, standing up.*) Perhaps the committee might like to witness what would happen if I tried to rape you—without a knife, of course. (*Walking towards her.*) I think you should get to your feet with your back towards me. Don't worry about hurting me."

Lansing did not move.

After that, Siegel wrote: "Her face turned beet-red. She was glued to her chair. Having made my point, Dick [Shepherd] asked me to take my seat. Sherry's face no longer looked flushed. Hatred filled it instead."

"I remember the final line he uttered as he returned to his seat," said Lansing. "He looked at me and condescendingly remarked, 'The point is, my child, I don't have to take your notes.' But I wasn't afraid to argue with him or anyone else."

And yet neither was she prepared to blame him for his flagrant sexism, any more than she blamed other Hollywood men.

"I dealt with sexism by denying it," she said. "Did I hold grudges? Absolutely. But I felt I had two choices. Either I was going to quit my job, stand on a picket line and burn my bra, or I was going to have to find a way to navigate the system until I reached a position where my opinions would be heard."

CHAPTER 6

In early 1977, Melnick left MGM to become Columbia's head of production and spent the next few months urging his protégée to follow him.

"I wouldn't go," said Lansing, "and he was furious, even though it was a much better position. I'd be overseeing films from beginning to end and not just working on scripts. But people thought I was attached to him, that I had no identity of my own. I had to break that tie."

"It was a problem for her, and it continued to be a problem," said one Columbia executive. "She was perceived as Danny's person, and Danny was very polarizing. He had such a sense of himself. He was so narcissistic and had such an overweening sense of his own power that it blinded him [to other things]. It was hard for her to create an identity away from that."

For months Melnick wooed Lansing, dangling his most coveted projects before her and convincing her she needed to ascend to the next level as a production executive.

"You've learned how to work with writers, but you need to know how everything fits together," he told her. "That means working on the casting, getting on the set, sitting through the editing." The worst kind of executive, he believed, "was one who simply stayed in his office without ever getting closer to the movie than his phone. The best was one who knew how to roll up his sleeves and plunge in during the myriad crises that would rock a movie, from the script all the way to the release."

In November 1977, she succumbed to Melnick's pleas and assumed her new post as vice president of production at Columbia.

SHE WAS NOW one of a tiny cadre of women to hold executive positions at the studios, including Marcia Nasatir at United Artists, Roz Heller at Columbia and Nessa Hyams and Paula Weinstein at Warner Bros. Soon there would be one fewer, when Heller was pushed out, partly to make room for Lansing. She blamed the sexism of the time, believing Melnick bought into the conventional wisdom that "it was inconvenient to have two women executives."

If he was guilty of such thinking, that would hardly have been unusual. Such attitudes toward women were omnipresent in Hollywood, which was still at a remove from the waves of feminist thought that were roiling the East Coast.

"There was no feminism in Hollywood," said Paula Weinstein, whose mother, Hannah, a pioneering producer, had fled to Europe to avoid the blacklist of the 1950s. "It had a half-asleep feeling. When they talked about 'women's pictures,' it was as if each film starring a woman had to be some kind of deep meditation or a depressing, menopausal story. They didn't see women in any complex, heroic way. And because we were competitive with each other, there wasn't the atmosphere that I saw in New York, where you could draw women from other businesses to be in your support group."

Women had always had a voice in Hollywood, from the silent era on, but had never banded together to fight for equal rights. Individuals had made their mark—from Mary Pickford, an early star and powerful executive who co-founded United Artists; to Virginia Van Upp, a producer who supervised dozens of productions in the 1940s; to Dorothy Arzner, a prominent director from the 1920s on; to Frances Marion, who for years was Hollywood's highest-paid screenwriter—but neither they nor the less prominent women in the studios had ever coalesced to demand change.

Few women dared to challenge the system head-on. Those that did often paid a steep price—witness actresses Olivia de Havilland and Bette Davis, who chafed under the studios' suffocating grip, and then were forbidden to work when they rebelled. (De Havilland took Warners to court when it tried to extend her contract illegally, and won a landmark ruling.) Most women were too focused on their own careers to worry about anything else and thought of their female peers as rivals rather than friends.

Lansing was no exception, and her contemporaries were as suspicious of her as she was of them, leaving little room for détente.

"The truth is, I didn't seek the friendship of the other women who'd reached my level, and they didn't seek mine," she said. "My only close woman friend in the industry was [ICM agent] Martha Luttrell. My mother's generation always said that women couldn't trust women, and I accepted that. We believed there was only room for one woman to succeed. It was only as I got older that I realized we could all succeed."

Among the few high-profile women whom she might have sought out, Julia Phillips, the first female producer to win an Oscar (for 1973's *The Sting*), "was so tough she intimidated me." There was also Sue Mengers, a formidable agent who represented everyone from Barbra Streisand to Tatum O'Neal and gave star-packed parties. "But I wasn't invited."

Nasatir, the most senior of the women executives, was eighteen years older than Lansing, and their relationship was never warm, though they worked in the same building when Nasatir was a vice president at United Artists. She was bright and pugnacious, but her philosophy was diametrically opposed to the younger woman's, and she was convinced the men around her saw women primarily as sexual objects. "Sexism doesn't have to be about making a pass, but just an attitude about women," she said. "Everyone is sexual prey."

Lansing's point of view was different. No matter how the men behaved, she believed, ultimately she would be judged by her work. Later, she reconsidered that stance as she gradually came to embrace feminism—particularly through the writings of Betty Friedan and Gloria Steinem—but for now she gave the notion of institutional bias short shrift.

"I should have spent more time thinking about that," she said. "But instead I chose to do the job."

————

AFTER YEARS IN the doldrums, Columbia was enjoying a renaissance following the arrival of Alan J. Hirschfield as CEO in 1973.

An émigré from Wall Street whose extroverted style and gregarious personality were well suited to the entertainment industry, he had hired David Begelman, a prominent agent, to run the film division, and together they had green-lit such hits as the Streisand movie *Funny Lady*, the rock musical *Tommy*, and the Warren Beatty satire *Shampoo* (all from 1975), along with the Martin Scorsese drama *Taxi Driver* (1976) and the ocean-bound thriller *The Deep* (1977).

A sense of exhilaration filled the hallways when Lansing got down to work days after the mid-November opening of *Close Encounters of the Third Kind*, a colossus for Columbia, which had bet the house on it. Originally titled *Watch the Skies* and then retitled *Kingdom Come* before assuming its eventual name, the picture had cost $19.4 million at a time when the average studio release was around $3 million. It would earn a spectacular $300 million around the world—though not enough to dethrone the year's biggest hit, *Star Wars*.

These were not the kinds of pictures Lansing identified with the most—"I liked characters and people, and stories about real relationships and human dilemmas," she said—but she recognized their importance.

A sea change was taking place. Spielberg and his friend George Lucas were reforming the industry with huge, special-effects-driven films that were sucking up audiences in droves and pushing out the cutting-edge dramas that had ridden in with the 1970s, before they had time to lodge in America's consciousness.

These new movies did not just have bigger budgets and bigger ideas; they also had quite different marketing campaigns. Whereas studios had traditionally opened their films in a few theaters and then gradually unfurled them across the country—a process that could take months and often more than a year—pictures were beginning to open at the same time throughout the United States. That meant studios could no longer rely on critical buzz and word of mouth but had to think nationally, making a massive number of prints and investing heavily in TV advertising.

Television ads in turn encouraged simple scripts and simple ideas that could be sold in thirty seconds.

1975's *Jaws* was among the first blockbusters to be marketed like this. Its success was a lightning bolt that prompted other studios to follow suit.

"We were still years away from the time when a movie would open on three thousand or four thousand screens," said Lansing, "but this was unmistakably different. I was coming in at the end of one era, just as another was beginning."

The China Syndrome, her first film at Columbia, straddled both.

A DRAMA STARRING Jane Fonda and Michael Douglas, its title referred to what might happen in the event of a nuclear catastrophe, when a reactor could hypothetically burrow through the earth and all the way to China. It had been developed by Douglas, who did not yet have enough clout to get it off the ground on his name alone. At the same time, Fonda had been preparing her own nuclear project at Columbia about the life of activist Karen Silkwood, but had been struggling to obtain the rights. When the studio made it clear that only one of these two stories would reach the screen, the stars merged their projects, and the lead role, originally written for a man, was reworked for Fonda.

The daughter of Henry Fonda, at her peak as one of the greatest stars of the screen, Jane was a serious "get" for the studio and carried the most clout on the film. But Douglas, another child of an industry icon, was the picture's producer as well as its co-star.

At thirty-three years old, he burned with the desire to escape the shadow of his father, Kirk. He had just won an Oscar for producing 1975's *One Flew Over the Cuckoo's Nest*, having obtained the rights to the Ken Kesey novel on which it was based from his father, on the understanding that Kirk would star. In the end, Jack Nicholson played the part, much to Kirk's disappointment.

Douglas had the glow of success but was still trying to use his producing acumen to further his stardom when Lansing strolled down the hallway and into his office.

"I poked my head in and said, 'Hi, I'm Sherry,'" she recalled. "He was standing behind his desk, looking over some papers. His hair was combed back and he was wearing a dress shirt and slacks. He was unpretentious and just adorable, but he took one look at me and said, 'Honey, casting doesn't start until next week.'"

When Lansing explained that she was the executive in charge of his movie and not some aspiring actress, "the color drained from his face," she said.

"We didn't know anything about a woman named Sherry Lansing," said Douglas, "and quite honestly, my jaw dropped. There was this absolutely stunning woman, in her high heels definitely over six feet tall. I had all these sexist thoughts and was ready to dismiss her simply based on how beautiful she looked."

The two were the same age, but Douglas was very much the senior in terms of experience. Still, if he expected to lord it over Lansing, he was wrong. He soon learned that she had strong convictions and great confidence in her judgment.

A meeting was convened at Melnick's home to discuss the script, and Lansing went over her notes with Douglas, Fonda, associate producer Bruce Gilbert and writer-director James Bridges. If she felt the slightest bit uncomfortable, it was only because Bridges remembered her from an audition a few years earlier, when he had been characteristically gracious, though he had not given her the role.

"Jim was a very calm man with a rumpled look and a soft-spoken, almost academic demeanor," she said, "but he must have wondered what I was doing there. I'd auditioned for 1970's *The Baby Maker*. In fact, I'd had two auditions, and I wasn't nervous in either one—they were two of the few where I wasn't terrible. He was so kind and had such an open, gentle face and treated people with such respect that I knew I'd never forget him."

The others in the room were less welcoming. Gilbert, who was beginning his career as Fonda's partner, seemed skeptical. "He just assumed I was Melnick's spy," said Lansing. "Maybe the others did, too. I could feel their eyes rolling."

"I was the young punk with one credit," said Gilbert. "The truth is, David Begelman [the movie division president] had tried to kill our movie. My best guess is it had been green-lit by [former studio executive] Stanley Jaffe, and Begelman wanted to kill anything Stanley laid his hands on. But Sherry really listened, and when she brought notes to the table they were clearly thought out."

With the script running at 160 pages, or forty pages longer than average, Lansing suggested trimming the first act by fifteen pages, pointing to scenes that could be eliminated and others that could be consolidated. She also pushed hard for the screenplay's dense thicket of nuclear information to be made simple and clear, allowing an audience to understand what was going on.

"All of them were well versed in the nuclear debate, and I had only a layman's knowledge," she said. "In many ways, I was the best and worst person to work on that script, because I knew enough to care but not so much that it would clutter the story. They were so obsessed with the issue, they couldn't comprehend that another person might not be. I'd say, 'I don't understand. Help me.' I wanted the underlying science to be clear to me, so that it would be clear to anybody."

Bridges and Douglas were impressed, and it helped that Lansing strongly connected with Fonda's character, a frustrated local TV news reporter whose bosses refuse to give her any meaningful assignments. "I identified with her," said Lansing. "To avoid being seen as a token, she has to work twice as hard and dig three times as deep."

Douglas found an ally in her, not least when she badgered Melnick to raise the budget from $4.8 million to $5.9 million. (Fonda received $500,000 of that, Jack Lemmon $250,000, and Douglas $262,000, which included his producing and acting services, according to documents in the Columbia archive.)

"In those days, Sherry was smoking these black Sherman cigarettes, and she sat down with us on the script," said Douglas. "I was, I would say, pretty defensive, but smart enough to realize she knew what she was talking about. She was a real structuralist."

Lansing sided with him when Melnick demanded he shave off the beard he had grown for the part. "I remember her coming in with a gift she brought in a little wrapped box from Melnick," said Douglas. "In it were a comb and some scissors, and a note from Dan saying, 'I trust you know what to do with this.' I was stubborn on that one and I ignored it. She had very mixed feelings about being the messenger. She handled it diplomatically but ultimately supported me."

Lansing knew from her experience with Hawks that no matter how rational and well-argued an executive's point, ultimately it would mean nothing once the shoot began, when the director and stars alone would determine what was done. "An executive has to build trust," she said. "Otherwise the talent isn't going to do a thing."

This was reinforced the hard way when Fonda called her one day, livid after learning that the studio wanted to change the picture's title. Its marketing executives thought nobody would understand what *The China Syndrome* meant, and did not want to spend a fortune to explain it. Among the alternative titles were *Misuse of Power, Event at Ventana, An Element of Risk, What Price Power, The Power Syndrome, Power Hungry, Chain Reaction* and *Scramm*. Many early production documents referred to the movie as *Eyewitness*, but neither that nor any other title had been locked in when Lansing's assistant said Fonda was on the line. The executive was secretly intimidated by her.

"Sherry," said Fonda, "I hear some idiot wants to change the title. That's totally unacceptable."

"The marketing people are afraid the audience won't understand it," said Lansing.

"That's ridiculous," said Fonda. "We'll explain the title, and then of course they'll understand it, just like *Dog Day Afternoon*. Wasn't that a good title?"

"Y-yes," stammered Lansing.

"Great," said Fonda, hanging up the phone.

NOWHERE DID FONDA impress Lansing more than during the shoot, which got under way in January 1978. At various times on location, the actress was vilified by locals, still incensed by her activism to end the Vietnam War. There were screams of "Commie bitch," and on one site a man dropped a wrench that "would have cracked her skull," according to her co-star, Jack Lemmon. But Fonda refused to cave in to the pressure and kept working as if nothing had happened.

Despite getting off to a shaky start (both Fonda and Douglas had the flu), the shoot stuck to its schedule until Fonda was involved in an accident while filming a sequence in which she had to board a helicopter.

"I was wearing very elevated espadrilles, kind of three-inch platforms," she said. "I was stupid. It was a scene up in the mountains where there had been a car accident, and I was running and hit a pebble and it twisted my ankle and I went down [and broke] my right foot. I'd broken it three times already. No big deal."

She was rushed to the hospital with Bridges racing alongside the car, calling to her through the open window as she ripped off her blouse and threw it out, yelling for him to put it on her stand-in and keep filming.

Lansing was not there. By then she had been involved in a far graver accident of her own.

RAIN WAS BUCKETING down on the evening of March 4, 1978, as Lansing hurried through Beverly Hills with her date, James Aubrey.

The former CBS and MGM executive was another of the older, powerful men to whom the young woman gravitated, mystifying even those who felt they knew her the best. "He was an enormous protector of hers and he cared deeply about her, as crazy as he was—and he was crazy," said Columbia executive Robert Cort.

Known as "the Smiling Cobra," Aubrey was among the most vilified executives in Hollywood history, but Lansing seemed blind to his less pleasant traits—his willingness to fire others and indifference to what they felt—and saw in him a reflection of Howard Roark, the iconoclastic hero of Ayn Rand's The Fountainhead, one of the books that had marked her the most as a teenager.

"That was a landmark novel for me, and I fell in love with his character," she said. "He was an iconic figure, wonderfully self-possessed, and didn't need the approval of others, and neither did Jim. He was utterly self-contained, and that was alluring."

Men like this appealed to her because they had qualities she felt she lacked: strength, security and self-assurance. "They did not need approval, they did not need to be liked," she said. "And those were traits I admired and wished I had. But I also felt, like with my father, that underneath the tough front was a softness I could reach."

She and Aubrey were crossing Wilshire Boulevard, heading toward the Fine Arts Theatre, where they planned to see a new Alain Delon film, *Monsieur Klein*, when the driver of a passing car failed to spot them. Even though they were in the crosswalk and another car had stopped to let them walk on, the first car kept going at around 40 m.p.h. and struck Lansing head-on.

"The car plowed into my right leg and flipped me so high in the air that my head smashed down on its roof, cracking my skull," she said. "I was carried thirty feet and dropped at the curb. Jim was clipped by the car and spun around, and seriously hurt, too, but I took the brunt of the hit."

The driver, a young lawyer who had passed his bar exam that very day, pulled over, but there was nothing he could do. He was not drunk; he simply had not noticed them, and now stood by helplessly as the horror unfolded. Passers-by stopped to gape, the traffic came to a dead halt, and an ambulance arrived within minutes to whisk Aubrey and Lansing away to Cedars-Sinai Medical Center.

"My leg was shattered," said Lansing. "I needed immediate surgery or I was at risk of losing it."

Weeks earlier, she had sent a chocolate leg to the *China Syndrome* crew, jokingly telling them to "break a leg." Now it was her leg that was broken, and the situation was deadly serious. Lying in the emergency room, she floated in and out of consciousness, only vaguely aware of the peril she was in, when she overheard doctors murmuring among themselves, saying they might have to amputate the limb.

"As I was being rolled into the operating room, I mumbled that I was allergic to anesthesia, even though I wasn't," she said. "I knew Norton's first wife had died from it, but I was delirious."

The hospital staff scrambled to find somebody who could tell them the truth, and reached Melnick, who had just canceled a skiing trip with Spielberg because of the bad weather. He tried to contact Margot, but did not know how to reach her. Lansing's secretary was the only person he could think of who might have her phone number—and nobody knew the secretary's last name. "That's how sexist things were then," said Lansing.

Eventually Melnick got hold of the number, but not before calling Dr. Harvard Ellman, a leading orthopedic surgeon who had recently operated on his shoulder, and who fortuitously was at Cedars that evening. He came to see Lansing at once. She had to have the operation, he told her, and she would have it with anesthesia.

After an MRI revealed that her skull was fractured, a four-hour surgery ensued, with surgeons operating on her head and leg. It was touch and go whether Ellman would be able to save the leg. "Later he told me it was broken in so many places, he'd have had to amputate if I'd lost circulation anywhere," said Lansing. "Luckily, I didn't."

When she regained consciousness, she found Melnick and one of her best friends, writer David Z. Goodman, in her room in the intensive care unit.

"Was it my fault?" she asked over and over.

"Of course not," Goodman assured her, and then smiled. "You're carrying a lot of guilt."

After the accident, Margot and Norton rushed to Los Angeles. So many of Lansing's friends swarmed the hospital that the staff tried to have them banned; Melnick had to steal a stethoscope and pretend he was a doctor just to sneak in.

"We were really scared because it sounded at first as if she had some brain damage," said Lansing's friend Luttrell. "It was a really horrible accident."

"I was lucky to be alive," said Lansing. "I had a nineteen-and-a-half-pound plaster cast with two huge pins sticking out and bandages wrapped around my head."

The accident shook her out of her obsessive work mode and made her pause to consider everyday life. "A flamboyant nurse named Zane washed the blood from my hair," she said. "It felt like the kindest thing anyone could do."

Dr. Ellman told her the surgery had been a success. "He said, 'You'll get to dance again,'" she recalled.

For the following month, she was confined to the hospital. Once she knew she was better, she began to worry about having permanent scars, and "spending my life looking like I did after the sheriff slashed my face in *Rio Lobo*." But the scars healed, as did her body.

And so did her relationship with her mother. Whatever tension still lingered between them from the years following David's death slowly began to dissipate as Lansing witnessed the full extent of her mother's love. "Everyone told me how worried she was," said Lansing. "She cried every day."

Alone with her, once Norton had gone home, Lansing finally had her mother to herself, and in her vulnerability discovered the mother she had always wanted. "My mother was so loving and so present and so caring," she said. "She was there every single morning, noon and night until I had to go to sleep."

When the plaster cast on Lansing's leg was cut off at last, Margot wept—tears of relief and joy and sorrow, because she knew her daughter did not need her anymore and would soon return to the life she had known before, just as Margot would return to her own. It was a bittersweet parting—the inevitable separation of one generation from another—and Lansing was heartsick to see her go. "But she knew I was truly healing," she said.

She left the hospital and settled into a friend's guest house, unable to climb the stairs of her own home. Alone in the lushness of a magnificent garden, she discovered an inner peace that had eluded her through her twenties.

"I sat outside every day, reading books and talking to my friends," she said. "The conversations weren't the rushed ones I was used to, and I began to learn things about them that I'd never known, and about myself, too. I started to think about my life, and wondered what I really wanted, and whether I was on the right path."

Sitting in that garden, surrounded by trees and flowers and birds, she savored each minute of her freedom, for once living fully in the moment. Part of her wished to live like this, free of all burdens; another part of her was tugged back to the working life, and all the stresses that went with it. For the first time, there was the hint of a collision between the Lansing who so fully inhabited the world and the Lansing who rebelled against it.

But here, earthly concerns no longer seemed to matter. "I hadn't died," she said. "I felt reborn."

A YEAR AFTER Lansing's accident, *The China Syndrome* opened on March 16, 1979, to critical praise and strong box office, despite being savaged by conservative pundits such as *Newsweek*'s George F. Will.

"The film falsely suggests that nuclear-power companies carelessly risk destroying their billion-dollar investments," he wrote, "that exposing to air the top of a reactor's core would produce a meltdown; that there are no backup systems to prevent the magnification of small human or mechanical mishaps into meltdowns."

Two weeks later, he was proved wrong. On the morning of March 28, a valve malfunctioned inside a reactor at the Three Mile Island power plant near Harrisburg, Pennsylvania. In itself, the incident would have been minor, but it set off a series of responses that the plant's staff misunderstood, and therefore they failed to take appropriate action. As the reactor's core began to overheat, warning lights flashed and klaxons blared, while temperatures inside the core rose to 4,300 degrees, just a few hundred degrees short of a meltdown. Soon the international media heard about what was happening and swarmed to Pennsylvania as the entire world waited in fear that the meltdown would take place, possibly killing hundreds of thousands or even more.

Lansing was driving to work when she heard about the incident on her radio and pulled over to listen. She had wanted to make films that were relevant, but to have them wrapped up in a real-life tragedy was surreal. "It was all over the news, all day and night," she said, "and they kept taking a clip from the movie to explain what had happened, the very thing I'd wanted us to insert."

Fonda was shooting *The Electric Horseman* in St. George, Utah, when she learned what was going on, "which was interesting," she noted, "because that was where the big nuclear tests were made, out near Nevada, and the wind blew across that part of Utah, and big concentrations of cancer began to emerge around the area. I had been an activist against nuclear energy and nuclear power. I had been traveling the country, speaking out. I was terrified, but I also felt, 'I told you so.'"

For the rest of the week, America was held in the grip of fear.

"The world has never known a day quite like today," CBS news anchor Walter Cronkite declared on Friday, March 30, one and a half days after the inciting incident. "And the horror tonight is that it could get much worse. The potential is there for the ultimate risk of a meltdown."

Lansing was appalled at the catastrophe, but had to make rational decisions about its impact on her film. "You can't believe that on every newscast you're seeing excerpts from your movie," she said. "You're shaken by the reality and you feel guilty because you also wonder how it will affect the film."

She and her fellow executives conferred with the filmmakers to create a unified strategy while wondering if this would even matter, given what might occur. Bridges refused to capitalize on the news and declined to speak to Cronkite, despite the newsman's towering authority.

"No interviews—this whole thing is too serious," he wrote in an unpublished diary. "Referring all calls to Columbia."

There was talk of evacuating Pennsylvania, and speculation that even this would not save its residents. Frantic efforts got under way to find anyone, anywhere, who could repair the plant, and the danger was defused only when its original designers ordered technicians to flood the reactor with water, lowering temperatures and finally bringing the crisis under control.

"By Sunday, it was over," said Lansing. "President Carter visited the site four days after the accident, and the plant was safe."

The China Syndrome would forever be connected with that disaster, the most serious nuclear accident in American history. The film did well and earned $51.7 million in North America alone; while many observers believed the movie's box office was boosted by its proximity to reality, Lansing and marketing executive Robert Cort felt otherwise.

"Everybody thought, 'Oh my God, we're just going to have this runaway hit,'" said Cort, "and the next weekend, after Three Mile Island, the movie fell off the charts. It just dropped."

"People want to be scared at the movies, and they enjoy being scared when it isn't real," Lansing reflected. "Then suddenly it is real and you're hearing about that every day, and the last thing you want to do is see a movie about it."

THE PICTURE WAS Lansing's first close-up experience of the extraordinary interplay between movies and society.

"I believed films had the ability to change the world," she said. "They could alter public opinion and impact legislation and affect how you felt. Film and social change were wrapped up in my mind, not as interchangeable things but as interwoven forces. A wonderful piece of entertainment is great, but it's not where my heart lay."

Her heart lay in movies like *Kramer vs. Kramer,* the second major picture Melnick assigned her at Columbia. He had used the project as bait to draw her to the studio, knowing she loved it.

Based on a 1977 novel by Avery Corman, *Kramer* told the story of a New York advertising executive so preoccupied with his work that he fails to notice his marriage is on the rocks. When his wife leaves him, he has to bring up their young son alone, only for her to return fifteen months later and demand custody.

"It wasn't the man who interested me—it was the woman," said Lansing. "I was attracted to a woman who broke social conventions, and I identified with her. I was fascinated by the idea that a woman abandons her child. What behavior could be less acceptable than that?"

She had attempted to buy the rights while still at MGM, but Corman's agent had sold them to Stanley Jaffe, the former Columbia executive who was now a producer. Jaffe had asked Robert Benton to write the script, which he had agreed to do on the condition that François Truffaut direct. It was a reprise of Benton's dream for *Bonnie and Clyde*—the film he had co-written with David Newman that had put both of them on the map— which Truffaut had toyed with making before Arthur Penn directed it.

"Truffaut and I were friends," said Benton. "I'd always wanted to work with him as a writer, and at one point we had talked about doing *Mildred Pierce*, and then about [telling the story of] Howard Hughes as he got older, but we weren't able to work either one out. Truffaut was interested in this, but he couldn't do it right away."

When Truffaut pushed *Kramer* off to some unspecified date in the future, Benton realized his hopes were futile and agreed to direct as well as write. With Dustin Hoffman cast as Ted Kramer, the male lead, the problem of finding his wife, Joanna, became pressing.

"I remember talking to Benton endlessly about that," said Lansing. "The challenge was not to make her overly unsympathetic. Leaving a child is almost unforgivable for a woman, but I viewed it as her attempt to find her identity. She was always someone's wife or mother, and had never established who she really was. She didn't leave her son because she didn't love him; she left him because she had no sense of herself."

The filmmakers considered casting Kate Jackson, a star of the ABC TV series *Charlie's Angels*, and Benton met with her in New York. "She was a lovely woman, a really lovely woman," he said. "We were quite happy with her, and we talked and talked, and I was thrilled. Then the network began to play games. I knew with this picture, working with a child, availability had to have flexibility built in."

Jackson fell out and Benton's agent, Sam Cohn, mentioned another client, whom Lansing had noticed in the 1978 miniseries *Holocaust*. Her name was Meryl Streep.

Streep was still relatively unknown, and the two movies that would rocket her to fame, 1978's *The Deer Hunter* and 1979's *Manhattan*, had yet to be released (one of them had not even been made: she would spend three days shooting *Manhattan* in the middle of *Kramer*). When Benton brought her in to read, her audition was a disaster: she was cold and listless, and it was hard to see the spark of the soaring actress she would become, perhaps because she was still suffering from the death of her great love, actor John Cazale.

"It was a terrible meeting," said Benton. "It was just awkward. There was not a lot of energy. [But] Dustin and I turned to one another and said, 'That's Joanna.'"

Some executives felt Streep was neither pretty enough nor a commercial-enough name. But with Lansing's support, she was signed for $75,000 (compared to the $2 million Hoffman received).

"I was a young actress, for the most part unknown, when I was cast in *Kramer vs. Kramer,* which I believe encountered no small resistance in development," said Streep. "I was not aware how unusual it was that we had a woman executive in charge."

A sixty-six-day shoot commenced in New York in September 1978, on a $7.5 million budget, several hundred thousand dollars more than Melnick would have liked.

"I flew out to watch, and I loved it," said Lansing. "I'd just stand in a corner, out of the way. Benton knew I identified with Meryl's character, and he'd say: 'Why's she like this? Why's she like that?' I told him she had no identity of her own, and she needed to create it."

Because child labor laws limited the hours that seven-year-old Justin Henry was allowed to work, the filmmakers were under pressure to shoot quickly. Hoffman grew so irritated by the rapid pace that at one point he refused to come on set. "He felt we were rushing, which we weren't," said Jaffe. That was the culmination of a host of difficulties with the actor. He had initially turned the role down, then insisted on reworking the script, and now this. "I'd had it," said Jaffe. "I said, 'Go fuck yourself. How dare you talk to us like that?' Benton and I thought the picture was over at that point. We had some real blowups."

Hoffman's relationship with Streep could not have been worse. During a restaurant scene, without telling her what he was planning to do, he knocked a wineglass and sent it smashing against a wall, shards flying into her hair. She was livid. Even worse, at one point just before they shot a dramatic scene, out of the blue he hit her, perhaps believing her performance would be more authentic.

"He thought he'd give her a little motivation, so he slapped her off camera," said Jaffe. "Meryl is a consummate actress, and she was furious."

They never acted together again.

The film opened on December 19, 1979, eight months after *China Syndrome*, and became a touchstone in the debate on divorce. It earned a huge $106 million at the box office in the United States and the following year was named Best Picture at the Oscars, where it won statuettes for Benton, Hoffman and Streep.

But Lansing was not there to take part in the celebrations. Much to her disappointment, she had been banned from attending, following a battle that culminated in her departure from the studio.

LANSING'S EXIT FROM Columbia had its roots in the biggest financial scandal ever to rock Hollywood.

The problems began in February 1977, when Cliff Robertson, the star of such movies as *Charlie* and *Three Days of the Condor*, was asked to pay taxes on income of $10,000, which the IRS claimed he had been paid by Columbia. Puzzled, he contacted the studio's accounting department to say he had never received the money.

During a subsequent investigation, studio chairman Alan Hirschfield discovered that David Begelman—the suave former agent he had named president of the company—had been embezzling money by writing checks to men including Robertson then cashing them himself. It was simple, brazen and criminal.

Lansing was far down the chain of command from Begelman, but studios were smaller enterprises then, and some close contact was inevitable. Unlike many of those around her, she had always been suspicious of him.

"He carried himself like a gentleman," she said. "He dressed in tailored suits and drove a Rolls-Royce and lived by appearances. One day Danny Melnick and I went to a party and I sat next to him. Danny said, 'God, aren't you lucky? You have the best person to sit next to,' because everybody loved him. But I said, 'He has strange eyes.' There was something that made me nervous, something off."

Lansing had arrived at Columbia just as the scandal was unfolding, and Begelman was suspended soon thereafter. To her amazement, he was reinstated weeks later. She could not believe the studio's board would bring back a known felon. "It was such a mistake," she said. "It was obvious he had to go."

For the next few weeks, Columbia existed in a twilight zone, ping-ponging from extreme highs to extreme lows as it reveled in the success of *Close Encounters* while anticipating the indictment of a senior officer. Behind the scenes, the board was locked in a fight over whether he should remain, with Hirschfield arguing to get rid of him and Ray Stark, the most powerful producer of his era and a major holder of Columbia stock, insisting he remain.

"It was obviously a tremendous trauma for everyone," said Hirschfield. "None of us were prepared for it. It was a huge upset for the company. We were at a peak. We had really saved it from going under, thanks to the efforts of a lot of people. Begelman did a great job and everybody was doing a great job."

It was unrealistic, however, to think Begelman could survive. The *New York Times* and the *Wall Street Journal* were nipping at his heels. It would not be long before the full extent of his misdeeds was uncovered, and when David McClintick's *Indecent Exposure* was published in 1982, revealing every sordid detail of the crimes and the cover-up, the book became a sensation. Its galleys were passed by hand from one insider to another, from the very top executives all the way down to the mailroom assistants, and from them on through the industry and across the city.

In February 1978, Begelman resigned, setting in motion the chain of events that would lead to Lansing's departure two years later.

After wooing but failing to hire several prominent executives to replace Begelman, Hirschfield decided to promote Melnick in June 1978. It was a mistake: Melnick loathed the bureaucratic nitpicking, the endless minutiae and countless administrative chores for which he was now responsible as the studio's president, rather than just as its head of production. He began to show signs of stress, possibly exacerbated by his growing use of cocaine.

Lansing was ignorant of the degree to which drugs in general—and cocaine in particular—were taking their toll on Hollywood, though that would become more pronounced in the 1980s when careers were wrecked, families broken and lives lost. "I don't think I ever really knew the extent," she said. "Dan never offered drugs to me—nobody did. They're smart, addicts. They know who does drugs, and that wasn't my world. I never saw him take coke. But lots of people were doing drugs then."

She noticed that Melnick was erratic, but he was naturally a person of intense emotions, whose moods could swing up and down and all around; this was one of the traits that made him such an unusual executive.

"I knew he was doing drugs, but barely," said Hirschfield. "The drug culture in Hollywood really exploded in the early eighties, and that was when it was clear he was starting to have problems. Then in the nineties it cost him everything."

Drugs exacerbated Melnick's paranoia, which became clear when he walked into Lansing's office after learning she had turned down a job at a rival studio.

"I guess I can take the piece of paper out from under your desk," he said.

"What piece of paper?" asked Lansing.

"I taped a piece of paper there," he replied.

She reached under her desk and, sure enough, found a sheet of paper plastered there. On it, Melnick had written: *I knew you would betray me.*

Lansing laughed in disbelief. Throughout this time, she had thought he trusted her implicitly, when he was secretly living in fear that she would abandon him. "It's in situations like that that you really understand the depths of a person's pain and their lack of trust," she said. "He didn't trust anyone."

With Melnick's promotion, his old job as head of production became available. There was no chance Lansing would get it at this stage in her career, but she worried it might be filled by an executive who was hostile to her, and so she recommended one of her business acquaintances, Frank Price. Price had tried to persuade her to join him at Universal, where he was a top television executive. But she had declined because film was her passion, not TV. Now she was returning the favor.

In his late forties, Price was almost the same age as Melnick, but the two could not have been more different. A buttoned-up former military man and bottom-line corporate player, Price had an avowed goal to deliver hits, regardless of their artistic merit, not the kind of highfalutin material to which Melnick aspired. He despised the latter's pretensions, his pathetic attempts to elevate himself from the poor kid who had grown up in a suburban ghetto, dreaming of making it in Manhattan. Those pretensions colored his taste, Price believed.

"In the field I operated in—which was really about your judgment on story, script, picture and so on—Danny was not good," he reflected. "He didn't have good judgment about projects. He had good judgment with regard to what was current and hot, but not necessarily [with regard to] could we make any money out of it? Danny was also a person with a lot of conflict going on, which led to the cocaine."

Later, Price would become known as the man who said no to *E.T. the Extra-Terrestrial*, but he had a distinguished track record in television, where he had overseen such hits as *The Rockford Files* and *The Six Million Dollar Man*, and his strong history made him a valuable asset to a studio badly in need of more.

Still, television was very much a poor cousin to film, a shoddy medium whose best work paled beside the artistry of the movies, which it would not begin to rival until the explosion of cable unleashed a new wave of creativity in the 2000s. Price longed for the glamour of film, craved the vindication of the major leagues—even if that meant giving up the $3 million he would have received in stock options at Universal and accepting a job at the tarnished Columbia, still reeking from the stink of the Begelman affair.

"It was generally known that there was chaos at Columbia," he said. "There was a civil war going on [within the board]. When I met Danny, I said, 'I'm interested, but I don't want to come in the middle of that.'"

Melnick asked him to meet Hirschfield, without realizing he was sealing his own fate. Hirschfield, overeager to land this clever player and be unburdened by Melnick's demons, secretly made promises he could not keep, assuring Price that Melnick was not long for this job and that Price would succeed him. He introduced Price to several Columbia board members who threw their support his way, and so the Universal executive accepted the Columbia job, seeing it as a stepping-stone to a better one.

Friends had warned Price that when Melnick was feeling the heat, his left eye would start twitching, and this was already apparent. "Danny liked things to appear perfect," he said. "That creates great stress."

But when Price took up his post as production president, he was appalled at what he found. "Nothing was running smoothly," he said. "We were in trouble. The studio had no money. I found I had to operate on a six-month budget—usually you have yearlong budgets. We couldn't forecast out more than six months. The company was in the toilet."

Change was inevitable, and it came swiftly and brutally. In July 1978, Hirschfield was forced out and replaced by Francis T. "Fay" Vincent Jr., a lawyer who had previously served with the Securities and Exchange Commission. Then in March 1979, Melnick was fired, too, and Price was given his job.

"It was very hard work getting Danny to understand that Columbia was not MGM in the old days," explained Hirschfield. "We were a failed company, quite frankly. We were technically bankrupt and everybody had to give up the idea of 'This is the old Hollywood.' This was the new Hollywood and it was survival."

He and Melnick could only look on in wonder at the quiet revolution that had chewed them up and spat them out, and they blamed Price.

"When I make a mistake, it's a beaut," Melnick told the *Los Angeles Times*. "I felt he [Price] had no creative abilities, but he did have a reputation for being a good administrator. I thought he would free me to work with the filmmakers on such movies as *The China Syndrome* and *Kramer*. Price set out to destroy me."

———

LANSING WAS TORN. She had been close to Melnick but also liked his re-placement, who would go on to have his own distinguished career in film. She respected the level-headedness he showed when an assistant rushed into a meeting to say a major star was on the phone with a crisis, only for Price to wave him away, saying there was nothing that couldn't wait until the meeting was over. "It's his crisis, not mine," he shrugged. He was cool and calm, smart and imperturbable, and gave Lansing the space to do what she needed.

"Frank left me alone to work on the movies I cared about," she said.

With Price promoted to president of Columbia Pictures, the produc-tion presidency was again vacant. Given the success of *China Syndrome* and the promise of *Kramer*—both pictures Lansing had overseen—she seemed ripe for the job, and yet she never seriously thought of it.

"Why can't you have it?" asked Dr. Hoffs, her analyst.

"Are you out of your mind?" she replied.

A woman had never held such a high-level position and in all likeli-hood never would, she believed. Only eight months earlier, she had told *Life* magazine she doubted that "in my working lifetime, I'll see a woman as president of a movie company."

But now she began to weigh it as a possibility and pondered what it would mean for her career. Just five years earlier, she had been a reader, and then, in what felt like the blink of an eye, she had gone from MGM to Columbia, had overseen two dream movies, had nearly lost her life and had survived the ravages of the Begelman era. Now, eight years after aban-doning acting, she was within striking distance of becoming the highest-ranking woman in film.

She asked Price to consider her for the job, but he deflected her request with a vague promise to take it to the board.

Then she made a strategic blunder. Instead of telling him she would leave if she did not get the promotion—or at least letting that possibility float in the air—she backpedaled and gave him the perfect out. "I told him I was fine if it didn't happen, as long as I continued to report to him and nobody else," she said. "He assured me I'd only report to him and prom-ised to present the idea to the board with his full support."

That Sunday, she was at home, wading through her usual pile of screenplays, when Aubrey called. He had just heard that another Columbia executive, John Veitch, was being promoted to president of production. Lansing was in shock.

"I'd trusted Frank completely," she said, "and I was wrong."

The tall, silver-haired Veitch was a nuts-and-bolts guy whose background was physical production—that is, he oversaw the actual shoot of a film, approving which equipment was used, how many extras were hired and the thousand and one other day-to-day decisions that kept a film rolling. He had no knowledge of the creative aspects of moviemaking and little contact with the writers, actors and directors who were its beating heart.

Had Price favored Veitch over Lansing because she was a woman? "I'll never know," she said, "but they [the board] really didn't know me all that well, whereas Johnny Veitch had the board relationships. He'd been there a long time and was much older than me."

Price must have known he was going to promote Veitch even as he was promising to support Lansing. She had been royally outplayed.

"I was mad and I was hurt," she said. "I wasn't sure if I should storm into his office and quit or break down in tears."

Aubrey advised her to bottle up her feelings. There was nothing she could gain by being open, he said, and now she must consider her future, which was suddenly thrown into question. Given that Veitch had beaten her to the job and considered her a rival to boot, there was a real risk he might force her out, costing her her salary as well as her pride.

"Put on your nicest dress and best makeup," Aubrey told her. "Go in and smile, and don't let anyone know you care."

Overnight, the atmosphere at Columbia changed. Lansing's new boss blocked her at every turn. He questioned her judgment, interrupted her in meetings and even told her she was not welcome at the first test screening of *Kramer*. "He said only the president of production could attend," she recalled. "Frank overruled him, but the damage was done."

"John was a difficult character," acknowledged Price. "But he was a political calculation. He was very well regarded by [some of the board members]. He was not some creative type. The package was what appealed. I said I wanted to make Sherry head of production, and that it would take me about a year because of the political thing. Then I'd make Veitch a producer and I would move her into that job."

Lansing found this hard to believe. While she was quickly promoted to senior vice president, she knew what had happened to Melnick and feared the same would happen to her. She felt she had to leave, but until her contract lapsed at the end of the year, she was stuck, afraid to lose her paycheck and worried about her future.

"This was the first time in my career that I was involved in a political battle," she said. "And the truth is, I was too scared to quit."

ELEVEN MILES AWAY, on the other side of the hills that served as a modern-day Maginot Line between Los Angeles and the sprawling San Fernando Valley, 20th Century Fox was going through its own problems. After enjoying an extraordinary run, fueled by such pictures as 1977's *The Turning Point* and *Julia*, and revved into overdrive by *Star Wars*, the man most responsible for Fox's success was ready to call it quits.

Alan Ladd Jr., known to almost everyone as "Laddie," was an exceptional executive. The son of a movie star, he was a former agent and producer who indulged in none of the backslapping behavior that was routine for most executives, the easy camaraderie that served as an hors d'oeuvre to the main course of a business deal. He was as taciturn as a Trappist monk and so uncharismatic he might have passed for an accountant were it not for his astounding ability to pick pictures.

But Ladd's boss had never liked him. Dennis Stanfill, Fox's chairman and CEO, had establishment written all over him—in his clothes, his bearing, his Naval Academy education and his Rhodes Scholarship. He was a corporate player to the core.

"Dennis and I just didn't agree on anything," said Ladd. "He was a suit-and-tie man, and I was always very casual. We really couldn't get along. The film people, my side, were making all the profits with *Star Wars*, and yet he was paying the accountants and people like that the same salary and bonuses. I gave away most of my bonus to my team. He thought I was crazy. I said, 'I'm leaving.' He said, 'You can't.'" News reports at the time claimed the two got into a shoving match on the lot, but Ladd denied that. "He made me a very substantial offer to stay another year, but I said, 'No, thank you.'"

Ladd's exit was one of the ritual bloodlettings in which the studios indulged every few years, when one top executive would be bounced out only to be replaced by another, thrown out of his own studio, each one gathering up his loyalists and taking them to his next destination. But it left Stanfill with a gaping hole, especially as most of Fox's brightest talent had flowed out in a great exodus after Ladd. With no senior executive ready to take over, he had to look elsewhere, and thought of Hirschfield.

The former Columbia executive, after becoming collateral damage in the Begelman affair, had gone to Warners, where he had an office and a phone but essentially was in a holding pattern until he found something else to do.

"I had a couple of very good friends from my investment-banking days who were on the Fox board," he said. "When Ladd and his group walked out, my friends talked to Stanfill. They said, 'Hirschfield's at Warners. You should talk to him.'"

When Stanfill came calling, Hirschfield jumped at the chance to go to Fox as its vice chairman and chief operating officer, even though the former Wall Street player would have been better in Stanfill's job. Now it was up to him to find someone who could make the movies.

Melnick was an option, but Melnick preferred producing; besides, did Hirschfield really want to deal with a prima donna like that? He could not help thinking of Melnick's demands—like the time both went to a test screening on the other side of the country: when Melnick was nowhere to be found, Hirschfield called his assistant, who told him Melnick was at the local airport, refusing to budge until a limousine picked him up—and not just any limousine, but a white one specifically. "I said, 'Tell Mr. Melnick, as far as I'm concerned, he can stay at the airport all night,'" Hirschfield recalled, "'because there's not going to be any car—white, black or anything else.'"

What about Michael Ovitz, the gap-toothed Valley boy who was fast making a name for himself at CAA? "I thought he'd be perfect," said Hirschfield. "He had great credibility, knew everybody, and had access—and access is important. But Michael clearly had bigger things in mind. He said, 'I don't want to run a studio.'"

Unsure where to turn, Hirschfield consulted Melnick and Jaffe, both of whom had agreed to leave Columbia and join Fox as producers. Each sold him on the same name: Lansing.

"I knew she was experienced and I knew she was smart," said Hirschfield. "I needed someone who would reestablish our credibility as quickly as possible, because Ladd and his team were godlike in the industry. We needed something to stop the bleeding. We didn't even have a guy who worked in the mailroom. Everybody had left."

He mentioned the idea to Stanfill, unsure how his old-school boss would react, "because there were [almost] no female executives in that company. But he just loved the idea. 'It's an absolute stroke of genius,' he said."

"It was the first time a woman [would be] in a top role in a movie company, and that was one of the distinctions I was happy to make," said Stanfill. "I knew what she had done and thought she would be able to do more."

Hirschfield offered Lansing the job, only for her to hesitate.

After seeing what Douglas had done with *China Syndrome* and Jaffe with *Kramer*, she had developed a taste for producing and was planning to become a producer once her deal ran out at Columbia. Burned by the studio shenanigans she had just witnessed, she was no longer sure she had the appetite for the work.

"My first thought was I didn't want the job," she said. She had begun to date actor Wayne Rogers, one of the stars of the TV series M*A*S*H, "and I was concerned about how it would affect whatever personal life I had left. I knew the routine of a studio executive was all-consuming, and to be president of production would only increase the demands. It also seemed like a no-win proposition. As [executive] Peter Guber said, 'The best you can hope for is a tie.'"

"She was really worried about losing control of her life," said her friend

Luttrell, with whom she huddled to hash things out. "The conversation was about, 'Oh my God! What should I do? Do I want to take on this huge responsibility?'"

Lansing consulted Norman Garey, her attorney, a benevolent and paternal figure whose clients included such superstars as Marlon Brando; she spoke to Melnick and Jaffe and other executives who had made the move from Columbia to Fox, all of whom urged her to accept. And still she hesitated.

She firmly believed that no woman could have everything she wanted, at least not at once—not a husband, kids and a career. Maybe two of the three, but no more. "I never thought I could have it all," she said. "I thought, you have to make choices in life and it's important for the choices to be the ones that make you happy, not someone else. I felt I couldn't be a wife and a mother and run a studio—maybe sequentially, but not all together. That wasn't necessarily true for others, but it was true for me, and I knew I'd always feel guilty if I tried to do all three. I was afraid that being a mother would take over my identity, and at that point I wanted a career and a relationship more than I wanted children."

She vacillated. Each time she was about to say yes, she thought of everything she would have to give up; each time she was about to say no, she worried she would never have an opportunity like this again.

"When Sherry makes a decision, she tortures over it," said Luttrell. "That's just who she is. She spends a lot of time discussing it in detail and talking about the bad and the good. I questioned her: 'Do you want to have a family? Let's talk about it.' It's hard to do this job and have a full personal life, and none of us had much of one in those days. We all worked harder than anybody. But I don't think that was driving her so much as the fear of losing control."

After days of introspection, Lansing realized she would regret it if she did not take the job. She called Hirschfield to say yes.

Negotiations got under way between the studio and Garey, her lawyer, the latter insisting she get a substantial raise from the $75,000 she had earned at Columbia—more like $100,000, he suggested.

"That won't work," said Hirschfield.

"But this is a much bigger job," Garey hit back.

"Will you let me finish?" continued Hirschfield. "No one will take her seriously unless she gets the same salary as a man. The job pays $325,000."

The lawyer was silent.

"OK," he said. "That will be fine."

With the contract signed, all that remained was for Lansing to inform Price, who was unaware of the machinations going on behind his back. He had started to wonder why Lansing was taking so long to sign her new deal when she walked into his office, unannounced. The rage she had bottled up came pouring out.

"With righteous indignation I said, 'I'm leaving,'" she recalled. "This was a woman scorned, getting her revenge. It wasn't a good side of me. I said, 'You told me I'd never report to anyone but you, and you lied. And I'm gone.' I felt empowered. I felt morally justified, though I regret it today. I felt he hadn't told me the truth, and this was justice."

Price was furious.

"He threw me out," said Lansing. "He wouldn't even let me go to the *Kramer* premiere."

ON JANUARY 2, 1980, the front page of the *New York Times* broke the story: "Sherry Lansing, Former Model, Named Head of Fox Productions."

The news swept across the world. Other publications—in England, France, Italy, Germany, Israel, India, Kenya and even Zambia—followed with their own reports. The media frenzy caught Lansing unawares. "The coverage continued for months," she said. "There were magazine profiles and news analyses about what my promotion meant for women in the corporate world. *Time* ran a story, and that spring I made the cover of the *New York Times Magazine*. I was even in a *Doonesbury* comic strip."

Us used her name as an answer in a pop quiz, beneath a photo with the question: "This woman is smiling because (a) she no longer teaches high school math (b) she has just become head of 20th Century-Fox (c) she earns $300,000 a year." The answer: all of the above.

"The headlines were hilarious," said Lansing. "In the *New York Post* I was a 'Foxy Lady.' In *Variety*, a 'First Lady.' *Fortune* said, 'The Math Teacher Goes Hollywood.'"

The *Los Angeles Times* headlined its story "A Movie Mogul Eats Her Words," reminding readers that she had only recently predicted that no woman in her lifetime would become a studio president. When a reporter asked her to defend that remark, she explained: "I just thought there was too much prejudice [for it to happen now]. When people talked about possible heads of production, a woman's name was never considered— even if she was in line for the job. I was dealing with reality."

While she had not felt pressured to represent her gender—because she never imagined anyone would perceive her as its representative—that changed when Frances Lear, the wife of producer Norman Lear and future editor in chief of *Lear's* magazine, threw a dinner party in her honor. "It started nicely," said Lansing. "Someone got up to make a toast, saying, 'We're so excited—the first woman to head a studio, it's a big breakthrough.' Then a feisty little woman stood up, jabbing her finger at me, and said: 'You represent all of us. And if you fail, you fail for all of us. You have to succeed more than anybody's ever succeeded.' I was taken aback. [Actress] Marlo Thomas said, 'Jesus! Give her a break. If a guy lasts a year in that job, it's considered a miracle.'"

Reporters tracked down Lansing's ex-husband, Michael, now living in San Francisco, and he graciously said that if the couple had moved there instead of Los Angeles, "she would have become the president of Bank of America." Even Princess Grace of Monaco, a Fox board member, asked Lansing how she was coping and wondered if she could give her daughter some advice about handling pressure.

Only Margot seemed more concerned than happy. "Well," she said, "no one's going to marry you now."

But none of this mattered, because Lansing was glowing with the joy of success. The would-be star was part of Hollywood's most exclusive club. The failed actress had found the role of a lifetime.

CHAPTER 7

On the morning of January 2, 1980, Lansing rose early, did her usual hour of exercise, left the one-bedroom townhouse on the outskirts of Westwood where she had been living for several years after leaving her Kenmore apartment, and set out for 20th Century Fox.

Her nerves were tingling, her brain was on fire. She was agitated and exhilarated at the same time. She had just gone through the bone-crushing experience of discovering that a man she had deemed an ally, even a friend, had maneuvered behind her back to fill the job she felt should have been hers; she in turn had outmaneuvered him and gone to Fox. Was this what making movies was all about? Was this how you changed the world?

At age thirty-five, she had an income beyond anything she had ever imagined and a level of celebrity that had caught her unawares. Even Norton, who had thought little of her attempts to become an actress, was in awe of his daughter's salary, and at last had begun to acknowledge how capable she was. Part of her was thrilled, part wary. She was entering rocky terrain, without a dash of Melnick's manipulativeness or a hint of his cunning. She reflected on what he so often said: "Running a studio is like leading a cavalry charge. The position is prominent, but the mortality rate is uncomfortably high."

Melnick was a grandmaster compared to this novice, a strategist where she was still a tactician, but it was she who would be running things now and it would be her skills, not his, that would determine the outcome. Ten thousand industry eyes were watching as she took over a post hitherto reserved for men. She had no peers, no female predecessors to whom she could turn; only a sprinkling of women could address her as a professional equal, and most were scattered across the country in different industries and different time zones.

"Those were hard days for a woman to come in," said Hirschfield. "Women were always in tertiary roles. But she really didn't let that get in the way. She had a great way of getting on with people, and she was always very pragmatic about what the objective was."

If Lansing succeeded, she would open the door for other women to follow; if not, the door might close on them for years to come.

All this played through her mind as her car pulled off Pico Boulevard and into Fox's historic lot on the west side of Los Angeles, where she came to a dead halt, face-to-face with an implacable security guard. He scanned his list of employees and could not find her name. Word of her appointment had leapfrogged across the globe but had not reached him.

"Sorry, miss," he told her. "I can't let you in."

"But I'm the head of the studio," she insisted.

"You can't be," he said with a shrug.

No matter what she told him or how vehemently she did so, he refused to believe her. Finally, she gunned her engine, charged around the barrier with the guard on her heels, and made it all the way to her new office, as Hirschfield's secretary came running to the rescue.

BY 9:00 A.M. she had settled into her palatial office in the very building where Darryl Zanuck had ruled supreme. Ignoring the hundreds of flowers from admirers and rivals alike, she began to conduct an inventory of the material at hand.

Fox had deep pockets thanks to 1977's *Star Wars*, but perhaps less deep than people imagined. The Lucas film had provided 85 percent of Fox's earnings in 1978 and 62 percent in 1979, according to *Newsweek*; moving forward, however, projected earnings looked weak. Indeed, the magazine noted, "the company had to rely on its diverse subsidiary operations—everything from soft-drink bottling to the Aspen (Colo.) Skiing Corp.—to keep over-all profits from falling sharply."

The studio would soon have *The Empire Strikes Back*, the second release in the *Star Wars* franchise, which was due out in May, but only a small part of the money it made would come back to Fox. In closing his deal for the original *Star Wars*, Lucas had cleverly retained the rights to any sequels. It was a mistake that one of Lansing's colleagues called "the costliest decision in the history of motion pictures"—and one that became even costlier when Fox gave back the merchandising rights to Lucas in order for him to make *Empire*, rights that would bring in more than $20 billion over the coming years.

Star Wars and *Jaws* were ushering in a new era, and the corporations that were muscling in on the studios were looking for the sort of returns only movies like these could make. But their full impact was still a decade or two away.

"When big corporations saw the kind of money that could be made with blockbusters, they wanted to own them, and then nobody knew how to make anything except things that had already been made," said Amy Pascal, later chairman of Sony Pictures Entertainment. "When you know it's possible to get that kind of audience, that's what you want."

At Fox, where *Star Wars* was still regarded as a freak exception, other films were already in the pipeline, including the Jane Fonda–Lily Tomlin–Dolly Parton comedy *Nine to Five*, which would be released in December 1980 and give Fox a bona fide hit. But Lansing knew any credit would go to Laddie, not her. She needed new pictures and she needed them fast.

"We were starting from zero," said Hirschfield. "We went over some of the material. We had no films at all. The backlog Laddie had left was very problematic."

Two senior production executives remained in place, and Lansing kept both. Claire Townsend was a Princeton graduate in her late twenties who had worked for consumer advocate Ralph Nader before joining the studio, and whose nickname was "Blonde Ambition"—which said just as much about the antipathy women faced as it did about Townsend herself, whom Lansing found easy to work with. David Field, a former United Artists president of production, was different: distant at best, moody and aloof at worst.

"Everybody was loyal to Laddie—they didn't have anything against me, but that was where their loyalty was," said Lansing. "Still, I believed then, as I've always believed, that you give people a chance to prove themselves."

While searching for another senior executive, she did everything she could to solidify her relationships with Fox's in-house producers, who served as a de facto second bench of executives, culling story ideas and pushing them up the ladder. She had observed two masters at work: Douglas, as he fought for *The China Syndrome*, and Jaffe, who had used every trick in the book to persuade Hoffman to star in *Kramer*, even flying to England to convince him. Jaffe was now at Fox, and so was Melnick, appropriately ensconced in lavish, black-marble offices, and soon to savor victory at the Cannes film festival, where his cherished *All That Jazz* would share the Palme d'Or with Kurosawa's *Kagemusha*.

With these men at her side, along with three other major producers— Frank Yablans, and partners David Brown and Richard Zanuck—Lansing was confident in her team. But it would take months, if not years, for them to develop a steady stream of pictures, and Fox had a pipeline that needed to be filled.

Starting work, she began to read two dozen scripts a week, held countless meetings and fielded more than a hundred calls a day. During her lunch break she would watch the rushes of any movie in production. She was lucid and logical, never shouted or made unreasonable demands, and yet there was no mistaking who was in charge. She insisted her staff join her for mandatory Friday-night dinners, because the workweek was so packed there was little face time. None of them dared to refuse.

"Nobody was thrilled," she admitted. "I overworked, which I felt I had to do as a woman. I never missed meetings, dailies or screenings, and I saw virtually every movie that was released."

Despite her elevated position, she was kept at a remove from the studio's innermost circle, which remained a boys' club headed by the cool, reserved Stanfill—"the ultimate WASP," in Robert Cort's words—and the affable but slippery Hirschfield. All key decision-making centered on them, and even if they rarely saw eye to eye, Lansing was at best a high-level functionary, valuable but not irreplaceable.

"I wasn't angry about it," she said. "I was more anxious about what I didn't know, because I'd never done the job before. There was no handbook to show me how to do it."

Condescension was routine, derision a fact of life. One agent took pleasure in peppering his talk with abstruse terminology, purely to torment her. "You do know what a 'rolling break' is, don't you?" he asked, referring to the profit point of a movie, which recedes farther from view the longer a movie is in theaters, as a studio has to spend more and more money to keep the picture in circulation.

"I bluffed my way through," said Lansing. "There was no one to ask. If I called business affairs, some lawyer would inevitably spread the word that I didn't know what I was doing."

Sometimes she would catch faint squibs of conversation as her colleagues whispered about her behind her back—not just men, but women, too. "I often showed up at parties looking bedraggled from working all day," she said. "I never had time to shop for clothes, and I didn't care. Once I looked so bad that a woman pulled me aside and whispered, 'Darling, let me take you out to buy some clothes.'"

Reports of her nocturnal activities stung her to the quick, especially when she heard she was having an affair with a man she barely knew. There was always talk of women sleeping their way to the top, but the same was never true of men; a double standard was at play, and there was nothing to be done about it.

One producer, asked how he felt about submitting his projects to a woman, said it was a win-win situation: if she did not like his ideas, she might at least sleep with him.

"I'd have been happy to turn him down, and his movie with him," said Lansing.

———

OUTSIDERS USED HER inexperience to their benefit. When Lansing passed on a screenplay by Larry Gelbart, the distinguished writer of the TV series *M*A*S*H*, agency operatives began a whispering campaign about her mistake. *Neighbors* was a black comedy about an obnoxious couple that moves next door to a traditional family and wreaks havoc, "but I didn't think the script was funny," said Lansing, "so I put it in turnaround," the industry term for selling a project to another studio.

Weeks later, CAA's Ovitz called with the news that two top comedy stars had agreed to make the film, which, naturally, he represented. "I want you to be the first to know that John Belushi and Dan Aykroyd are doing it," he said. They were joined by John Avildsen, the Oscar-winning director of *Rocky*.

"For the next six months, I lived in fear that the movie would open to a huge number," said Lansing. She need not have worried: the picture fizzled when it debuted in December 1981 and was notable only for being Belushi's last film before his death from a drug overdose the following year.

If *Neighbors* was not in her wheelhouse, she nonetheless backed an impressive range of movies across the spectrum of both genre and sensibility, from the visually sumptuous *Quest for Fire* (which followed three Cro-Magnon warriors searching for the origins of fire) to the Burt Reynolds action comedy *Cannonball Run* to the George Hamilton spoof *Zorro: The Gay Blade* to the Al Pacino dramedy *Author! Author!*

Her job was to usher in a broad slate of pictures for all audiences, not just ones that reflected her personal taste. "That's what a production chief does," she said. "It's his or her role to keep the product flowing and make commercial movies, not to be the producer."

WEEKS INTO HER job, Lansing flew to New York for a screening of *Brubaker*, a prison drama starring Robert Redford that was due to come out in June 1980.

"Everybody was there except him," she said. "After waiting twenty-five minutes, I told the projectionist to start the movie. People were surprised, but I had a day full of meetings and had no time to lose." The picture screened, Lansing gave her notes to its producer and director, and all three were just stepping out of an elevator and into the building's lobby when Redford strolled in.

"I'm sorry I'm late," he said.

"No problem," said Lansing, unaware that the actor was notorious for his lack of punctuality. "Take a look at the movie and let me know what you think."

She left him to watch the film while she went about the rest of her day. She did not know that the movie, initiated before her arrival, had been riddled with problems, and that Redford was even more nervous about the result than most stars normally are. There had been fights during the drug-infested shoot, both verbal and physical: one of the studio's executives had gone to the set to sort out the mess and had gotten into a tussle with director Bob Rafelson, who was replaced by Stuart Rosenberg. Redford, shaken after Rafelson was fired, had grown still more concerned when Fox decided to position the picture as a summer blockbuster, though it was hardly obvious summer fare. "It wasn't a classic June movie," said one of the executives who worked on the film. "It was a dark prison drama."

As the picture headed toward its release, an article came out arguing that this was the end of the movie star era, lumping Redford with two other seemingly failed stars, Burt Reynolds and Clint Eastwood. Redford was furious. "He demanded we intervene to differentiate him from Eastwood and Reynolds," the executive continued. "He had a very thin skin."

When a studio publicist tried to counterbalance the previous article by planting a positive item about Redford's appeal, New York *Daily News* gossip columnist Liz Smith saw through the ruse. "What she went with was, 'Robert Redford is concerned about his image,'" said the executive. "Then Redford called the studio, insane, really just insane. He said, 'I want this guy fired. I'm never working at Fox again unless you fire him.' Sherry said, 'Let me handle Bob.' She was very good about it. But he was furious. He kept saying, 'I won't work at Fox.'"

The low-level publicist was shunted off to a different division, but Lansing was unable to mollify Redford further. It was her first taste of the limits to an executive's power, and especially to her power at Fox.

SOMETIME LATER, LANSING circled back to Redford with another project.

Zanuck and Brown had optioned Barry Reed's 1980 novel *The Verdict*—a drama about a washed-up, alcoholic lawyer and the medical malpractice case he brings to court—for a substantial $150,000, and attached Arthur Hiller (*Love Story*) to direct. David Mamet, the young playwright who had established his reputation as a major force in the theater with *Sexual Perversity in Chicago* and *American Buffalo*, was hired to adapt, and the producers were thrilled—until they read his script and found it ended with no verdict.

"They told me the script was so bad they wouldn't even show it to me," said Lansing.

Zanuck hired a new writer, Jay Presson Allen, while Hiller, stuck in a holding pattern, jumped ship to direct a different Fox picture, *Making Love*, a controversial gay-themed drama in which a husband leaves his wife for a man.

"When Dick [Zanuck] found out, he was furious," said Lansing. "He called me and read me the riot act. But I told him I couldn't control Hiller's creative choices. The life of a studio executive is all about putting out fires, and you rarely have time to handle individual problems, although I'd have done anything to keep *The Verdict* together."

While the group was trying to salvage the picture, which now had no director or script, Redford happened to visit Presson Allen at her Connecticut home, where he saw a draft of her screenplay lying around and asked if he could read it.

Out of the blue, Lansing got a call from the actor's agent, telling her Redford wished to play the leading role. Under normal circumstances, an executive would go through hoops to land a star of his stature; here the star was chasing her. "I couldn't believe it," she said.

But Redford had his own ideas for the script. Like most A-list stars, his commitment came with a string of contingencies, and he insisted on bringing in another writer. Lansing and the producers suggested *China Syndrome*'s Bridges, who had known Redford since their early acting days, and the star agreed.

The two sat down to talk and their initial meeting went well. Redford said he wanted this to be the darkest role he had ever played, and Bridges, who would also direct, embraced that notion. Neither he nor Lansing paid heed to Melnick's warning that, whatever Redford said, in the end he would only play safe.

A second meeting did not go so well. "He doesn't want to play a Southie or a man with wife + children or a drunk," Bridges wrote in his diary, referring to the character's South Boston roots. "My hard-on goes down."

The filmmaker was especially taken aback when Redford told him he could not possibly play someone whose wife had left him, because nobody would believe that a woman would leave Redford, according to Bridges's partner, Jack Larson. "Jim was stunned and didn't know what to do," he said.

Then Redford started to get cold feet, and Lansing watched with ever-increasing concern as her highest-profile project began to implode. The more Bridges struggled with the script, the more Redford resisted discussing it, until things reached a point where he would not even return Bridges's calls.

When the filmmaker flew to Boston to meet his star, having agreed that they would spend several days hunting for locations together, Redford never materialized. Bridges hung around, and Redford failed to appear.

"Redford's assistant would call and say, 'Bobby will be there in two days,' and 'Bobby will be there tomorrow,' and he never showed up," said Larson. "Jim waited. And [the assistant] called again and said, 'Bobby will be there on Thursday.' And Jim said, 'Well, I won't. I'm going back to Los Angeles.'"

After multiple conference calls were set up, only to be canceled by Redford at the last minute, Bridges had had it. A final meeting was arranged, only to turn sour when the star came armed with two separate, seemingly contradictory sets of notes, neither of which made the least sense to Bridges. He asked to be released from the picture.

Lansing refused and told him if he quit she would pull the plug on his dream project, *Manhattan Melody*, a biography of George Gershwin.

"Sherry said, 'If you don't do *The Verdict*, Redford won't either,'" recalled Larson. "She said, 'You are contractually committed to do the film.' She was very tough."

On August 26, 1981, an exasperated Bridges met with Zanuck over lunch and begged to leave the picture, bewildered that the producer—given all his years at his father's feet—would put up with the actor.

"I ask him how much [shit] will he eat?" Bridges wrote. "He says he'll eat it all."

Days later, Bridges withdrew, defying Fox to sue him. The studio never did.

Redford brought in his frequent collaborator Sydney Pollack (*The Way We Were*), with whom he holed up on a mountaintop to rework the script, according to press reports at the time, but Zanuck had reached the end of his rope. Lansing was scrambling to find another director when he blindsided her and fired Redford, an unheard-of move by a producer who had one of the world's top stars attached to his film. The firing was so unusual that the story made the local news and spread across the country.

"Robert Redford has been booted out of *The Verdict*, by producers Richard Zanuck and David Brown," gossip columnist Marilyn Beck reported in September 1981, adding that they had "accused the star of being difficult and high-handed—and more."

"Without Redford," Zanuck told Beck, "there's every chance *The Verdict* will never get made. But you reach a point where you've got to look in the mirror. My partner and I looked, and decided no star was worth the aggravation Redford was putting us through. He was kidnapping our property—and we had to regain control."

Lansing was horrified. "The biggest producer on our lot had just fired our biggest star," she said. "Dick didn't ask my opinion. He just called and gave me an update. Our movie had fallen apart. And there was nothing I could do."

She considered asking Fonda to star, repeating the *China Syndrome* strategy of casting a woman in a man's part; but before she could make a move, Zanuck called. *Network*'s Sidney Lumet wanted to direct, he said, and Paul Newman had agreed to play the lead role of the alcoholic lawyer, Frank Galvin.

This meant one of Lansing's favorite filmmakers, whose 1964 post-Holocaust drama *The Pawnbroker* had been a seminal movie for her as a young woman, had boarded her project, along with one of her screen idols. There was only one condition: Lumet wanted to go back to the original Mamet script—the one without an ending, which Lansing still had not read.

"I told Dick, 'I thought you hated it,'" she said. "'But I have to read it before I meet with Lumet.'"

When Zanuck gave it to her, she found the script excellent, though still lacking a jury's resolution. After flying to New York to meet Lumet, she said, "I sat there biting my lip for twenty minutes, thinking, 'Without an ending, I can't make this movie.' But I was afraid if I dictated to him, the whole thing would collapse. I said, 'Look, I don't know how we make this without a verdict.'"

"Of course there's going to be a verdict," Lumet assured her. "I'm working on it with Mamet right now."

WHILE LANSING WAS waging an external war over *The Verdict*, she was fighting an internal battle with a fellow executive, Norman Levy.

A large, red-faced man who had worked with her at Columbia before being named to his current position as Fox's head of marketing and distribution, he was as old-school as Lansing was new, "a man of appetites, a big man who demanded a certain fealty," said story editor Merzbach, who had joined them at Fox. "He'd been around a thousand years and this was his venue. He knew every distribution guy, every exhibition guy. I don't think he expected the adoration that accompanied Sherry to the top. He was jealous."

It was Levy's job to get movies out to theaters, the least glamorous part of the business but nonetheless crucial, given that landing the right venues could determine a film's success. It was also his job to oversee the marketing and make sure the posters, billboards, television commercials, radio ads and unpaid publicity were all functioning to maximum effect. But his opinion carried greater weight than his title suggested, because Lansing did not have the authority to overrule him; neither one had green-light authority, which rested with Hirschfield, their boss. This meant Lansing had to win over both men to make any movie she loved, effectively triangulating the green-light process, with its committee of three members all tugging in different directions.

Early in her tenure she had clashed with Levy over a small British period piece about two runners who enter the 1924 Olympics. The picture had been developed by David Puttnam, an independent-minded producer based in London, who had commissioned the script from actor-writer Colin Welland.

Welland had made a few TV movies, all small in scope but charming nonetheless; he had yet to become known as a film writer. Now he had written a drama about two real-life runners, Harold Abrahams and Eric Liddell, a Jew and a religious Scot. Both were played by unknowns (Ben Cross and Ian Charleson) under the guidance of a first-time feature filmmaker, Hugh Hudson.

The film appeared to have limited commercial prospects: it seemed jingoistic and locked into a plot that alternated uncomfortably between two protagonists whose storylines never meet. Its title, which was biblical in origin but better known as a line from William Blake's "Jerusalem," did not have anything to do with its subject. But Lansing loved everything about it. Its name was *Chariots of Fire*.

Prior to her arrival, Fox had paid $3 million for the foreign rights, half of the $6 million budget, though the deal had strings attached.

"There were a few 'conditions precedent,'" said Puttnam. "The key condition precedent was they wanted two marquee names [stars] and I had no money for marquee names at all. Then Brad Davis, who'd done *Midnight Express* with me, and Dennis Christopher, who'd done *Breaking Away*, agreed to do the film for free. All I did was pay their airfare and expenses. Without those two, the film would never have been made."

Scared that Fox would dismiss his movie as too small-scale, Puttnam shrewdly shot one of its biggest scenes, in which Cambridge students gather inside a hall, at the very beginning of production and quickly cut together shots of the runners racing on a beach, all designed to win over studio skeptics.

Once the film had wrapped, Lansing flew to London for a screening, where Puttnam met her, winded. He had gotten stuck in the subway when the train ground to a halt and had raced through the city's streets, lugging heavy film cans under his arms, terrified he'd be late. "It almost killed me," he said.

Lansing was enthralled by what she saw, even without the movie's celebrated Vangelis theme, which was added later. She fully expected Levy to love the movie as much as she did when Puttnam flew to Los Angeles to show them the completed version. But twenty minutes into the screening, the executive raised himself heavily from his seat and stumbled out of the room, never to return.

"Norman walks out, smokes a cigar and decides not to do the movie because he thinks it's not commercial," said Lansing. "I was so angry. I begged Hirschfield to pick up the U.S. rights, but he deferred to Norman, who refused to release it."

"Sherry was very, very embarrassed," said Puttnam. "We then had a series of extraordinary conversations [with Levy], who wanted to sell the picture to another company. He even showed it to ABC Sports to see if they'd buy it as a movie-of-the week. But they turned it down."

Instead, the film's North American rights went to Warner Bros. and the newly formed Ladd Company, which jointly paid a negligible $1.2 million, while Fox retained the foreign release. The following year, *Chariots* won the Oscar for Best Picture in an upset over the two favorites, *Reds* and *Atlantic City*, giving the Ladd Co. an Academy Award and rubbing salt in Lansing's wound.

At this point, even Levy realized he had made a mistake and openly acknowledged it.

"The wonderful thing," said Puttnam, "was that the morning after we won the Oscar, Norman walked into a staff meeting, rolled up *Daily*

Variety with the headline about it, did a [mock] hara-kiri on himself, and slumped over the table."

LANSING'S RELATIONSHIP WITH Levy took another hit when Fox was given the chance to pick up a low-budget comedy named *Porky's*, a raunchy coming-of-age story that had been financed independently, with just a little money from the studio. The movie—about a group of Florida high-school students who go to a nightclub in the hope of finding a prostitute to relieve them of their virginity—may have been crass, but it was also funny, and Lansing felt sure it would appeal to the audience she most needed to reach: the teenage boys and young men who were increasingly dominating ticket sales. *Porky's* seemed to fit neatly into the mold established by 1978's *National Lampoon's Animal House*, which had earned more than $142 million and made Belushi a movie star. But Levy was appalled.

"It's disgusting," he said. "It goes against everything Fox stands for."

"It's hysterical and it's sweet," Lansing maintained, "and it'll make a fortune."

Reluctantly, Levy agreed to give the picture a trial run in a few provincial theaters before going on to a wider release.

"I lobbied Norman like crazy to release the picture at Christmas," said one of its producers, Don Carmody, "which of course he refused to do. He was like, 'Get rid of this dirty movie!'"

Lansing waited to see how it performed. "I knew nothing about distribution or how theaters were booked," she said, "so I believed Norman was genuinely testing the marketplace. But all he was trying to do was bury the movie."

When *Porky's* debuted in two cities in 1981 without any promotion, it sold out every show. Local audiences somehow heard about it and flocked to see it, giving Lansing a huge boost, only for Levy to take the credit. "He told the press that his limited-release strategy had worked," she said. "It showed there was an audience for *Porky's*, and now he was going wide."

The picture opened across the nation in March 1982 and stayed number one for nine weeks, making a fortune in relation to its cost. But it laid bare a fundamental flaw at the top of the studio, apparent to all its staff: not only were the marketing and production heads at loggerheads, but neither was able to make any important decision without the other's agreement. King and queen were frozen in place, each checked by the other.

"If I'd known how important marketing and distribution were, and how little power I'd have if I couldn't control that," said Lansing, "I would never have accepted the job."

She soon found Levy angling to control production as well. Unknown to her, his contract stated that he would be promoted over Lansing within eighteen months, and he would be given the job of running the whole movie division. It was an agreement Hirschfield had arranged and kept secret, just as he had secretly agreed to promote Frank Price without telling Melnick. But this was in complete violation of Lansing's contract, which guaranteed that nobody could be promoted above her and that she would report to Hirschfield alone. It was the kind of contractual quagmire that could have led to a lawsuit.

For more than a year, Lansing and Levy worked together in ignorance of Hirschfield's duplicity, until the truth came out.

"I was in Norman's office," recalled Lansing. "We were arguing about a movie. He said, 'Why are you always so difficult? You know you're going to be reporting to me in a year.' I said, 'What? I'm going to be reporting to *you?*' He got it right away. He looked at me and said, 'Oh my God.' I said, 'I can't report to anybody but Alan. That's in my contract.' He was so angry. He went to his desk and picked up the phone. He said, 'Tell Alan Hirshfield to come into my office. It's urgent.' Alan walked in the door and we were both standing there. Norman said, 'You never told her that she was going to report to me?' Alan shrugged and smiled. He went, 'What do you want me to do?'"

Added Lansing: "My relationship with Norman was terrible, and the fact that Alan had lied to both of us, and signed two contracts giving each of us the same power—telling me I was the head of the studio and couldn't report to anyone but him, and telling Norman he'd have complete authority—was unethical beyond belief."

For once they were united in anger. "Norman was furious," she continued. "He said, 'What does her contract say? *What does it say?*' And Alan just grinned and said, 'So sue me.' We couldn't do anything except live with it—unless we really did sue, and then we'd be hurting ourselves."

Even as Hirschfield's subordinates were clamoring for more authority, he was fighting to gain authority of his own. Like Ladd, he bristled under Stanfill's leadership, and the tension between them was mounting.

"It was a sea of dysfunction," said John Davis, a young executive whose father would later buy the company. "Stanfill hated Hirschfield, and they all hated Stanfill."

As Stanfill struggled to maintain order, his troops chafed under his leadership. Then he had a brainwave: he would hire Theodore Levitt, a professor at the Harvard Business School, to develop a strategy for success. The economist had proved brilliant in many arenas, but "his ideas were amateurish," said Davis. "Basically, it all came down to 'Make more blockbusters.'"

After weeks of work and thousands spent on developing this economic theory, Levitt was dismissed and his suggestions tossed aside, useless to a group of executives whose every thought was about how to make blockbusters.

Then Stanfill drew howls of derision when he hired a therapist to broker the peace. "The psychologist would sit in everybody's office," said Davis. "They all thought he was an idiot. He'd talk to the executives and do sessions [with them] and try to figure out how to get these warring people to get along. It could never work and it never did. It was the Keystone Kops."

THE KEYSTONE KOPS ended their run when Davis's father, Marvin, bought the studio from its shareholders in June 1981.

He had purchased it for $725 million, along with financier Marc Rich, who would soon flee the country to avoid charges of tax evasion, leaving Davis on the hook for the fugitive's share of the money. (Rich was infamously pardoned by President Clinton many years later.) But Davis was nothing if not shrewd: he had spent only $50 million of his own money, the rest coming from bank loans.

A six-foot-four, three-hundred-pound Denver oilman whose country-boy bonhomie masked his toughness, he was an odd fit with Hollywood. He could be immune to social niceties: the *Los Angeles Times* reported that he once hired a group of African Americans to sit on cotton bales and eat watermelons at his birthday party, to enhance its Old South theme. He was also said to have added Rolls-Royce grilles to his two golf carts (one for himself, the other for his clubs). But he was as rich as he was large, and had amassed a fortune estimated at anything from $300 million to $1 billion, earning his money as a wildcatter who would gamble by digging for oil on untried land, operating on his "third for a quarter" rule: for every three investors, he would get one-fourth of the profits.

Days after Lansing's new boss arrived, he summoned his production chief to meet him for the first time. She walked down the hall to his cavernous office and his secretary motioned for her to enter. The man was immense, with a great booming voice to match his girth.

"Hi, I'm Sherry Lansing," she said.

"No, no, honey," he said. "I don't want any coffee."

"Excuse me, Mr. Davis," she replied. "I'm Sherry Lansing."

"I want *Jerry* Lansing," he said, "the person who's running the studio."

"I'm *Sherry* Lansing," she hit back, "and I'm the person running the studio."

"A girl?" he said.

"Yes," she replied. "A girl."

Despite his reaction, Davis raised no objection, though he called her "doll face" from then on. "Perhaps I should have been offended," said Lansing, "but it was a term of affection, and he seemed willing for me to do the job."

He was brash, but could be generous, too. When he gave his "doll face" a huge gold watch for Christmas, she thanked him politely, then left his office. "Because I don't know anything about jewelry, I just thought, 'Oh, it's really nice,'" she said. Then she ran into Hirschfield. "He said, 'Do you know what that is?' I said, 'Yes, it's a watch.' He said, 'No, It's a Piaget! And it's worth $20,000.'" Lansing went running back into Davis's office, almost tripping over herself in her hurry to thank him. "I said, 'Oh my God! I was so overwhelmed, I didn't know how to respond.'"

Davis wanted her to invest in his oil wells, but she had used all her extra cash to buy a small house in Beverly Hills' Benedict Canyon, and refused. She was financially risk-averse in the best of circumstances, and would have hidden what she earned in her mattress if not for the counsel of her boyfriend, Rogers.

"A guy was suing Marvin because he had taken his money and put it in what was already a dry hole," said Rogers. "I said, 'You don't need to do this, Sherry. Put the money in the goddamn bank.'"

"Marvin would call us in and say, 'Give me your money, and I'll invest it in my wells, and you'll double it,'" said Lansing. "And everyone invested with him, except for one other executive and me. He kept saying, 'Why won't you give me your money? I'll make you rich.' I'd say, 'Well, Marvin, I really don't want to lose it.' He'd say, 'Lose it? You'll never lose it!'" But many of her colleagues did.

Her relationship with her patron was warm, but professional differences soon emerged. Davis had his own ideas about the movies his studio should be making.

"Some of them were completely unrealistic," said Lansing. "He said, 'Let's make a sequel to *The Sound of Music*.' I tried to explain that the composers were dead. But he didn't want to hear a word."

On another occasion, he became incensed about changes he believed Lansing had made to the ending of *Taps*, her first Fox production. An antiwar tale about a group of cadets who seize control of their military academy to prevent its closure, the picture was produced by Jaffe and starred George C. Scott, Timothy Hutton, Sean Penn and a then-unknown Tom Cruise. Davis loved it, at least the first time he saw it.

"Norman was nervous about its commercial prospects and said we should sell off half to a third party," said Lansing, "but Marvin wouldn't think of it. He said, 'I'm a wildcatter. I dig holes in the ground. I put my money where my mouth is, and I hit gushers. I love this movie and I want all of it.'"

Then the first reviews came out and were scathing, particularly about the ending in which the cadets die. "They were terrible," said Lansing, "and Marvin calls me into his office with cold eyes and says, 'Why did you change the ending?' I said, 'What do you mean?' He said, 'When I saw the movie, the kids all lived.' 'I said, 'Marvin, they all died.' He said, 'Don't lie to me. You changed the ending.' I said, 'The kids were dead six weeks ago. They were dead then and they are still dead now.' But he refused to back down."

His anger continued to simmer during the film's glittering New York premiere. He was mortified that his first movie would be a flop, the very movie he had invited all his friends to see. In fact, it turned out to be a hit, but the experience soured him on Lansing, she believed. "I don't think he ever forgave me," she said. "I thought, 'Oh God, even a guy who's worth $1 billion can't stand being wrong.'"

Davis also blamed her for one of the riskier films she had backed: *Making Love*, the gay-themed story that starred Harry Hamlin, Kate Jackson and Michael Ontkean. When Lansing screened it for him, he reacted badly.

"He was this conservative oilman, just learning to deal with a female division head, and here he was in a Fox screening room having to watch two men kiss," she said. The movie tanked.

One failure alone could be forgiven, but Lansing was unable to make up for it with any blockbusters. Films such as *Monsignor* (a Vatican drama starring Christopher Reeve) and *Omen III: The Final Conflict* (a horror film) came and went without notice, while even successes such as *Taps* and *Cannonball Run* did less well than she might have hoped. She prayed for the kind of breakout hits that rival studios were enjoying—like Paramount, which was enjoying a storied run under the leadership of Barry Diller, Michael Eisner and Jeffrey Katzenberg, and which seemingly could do no wrong thanks to movies such as *Star Trek: The Motion Picture*, *Friday the 13th*, *Airplane!* and *Raiders of the Lost Ark*—just a few of the pictures it released between mid-1980 and mid-1981.

Perhaps her taste was too genteel, people whispered, or perhaps she was not strong enough to impose her will. Maybe a woman simply was not right for this job.

As Lansing entered her third year, the industry was awash in speculation that she would soon be gone, and that the whole Fox executive team was on its way out. When a publicity release of July 1982 announced that Lansing's contract was being extended "for an indefinite period," few believed it, and the New York Times leaped to the conclusion that "such wording is usually a tipoff in Hollywood not of strength but of weakness.... Miss Lansing has had to take the blame for making pictures that are considered too 'soft.'"

Compounding everything, on August 18, 1982, Lansing learned that Norman Garey, her lawyer, had committed suicide.

A wise counsel and father figure to his clients, he had been under strain after spending heavily to set up a new law firm, and had become obsessed with the idea that Melnick was going to sue him for malpractice over a minor mistake. In the days before his death, he had fretted about this and about his lack of money. Already under a doctor's care for depression, he was taking a prescription medication that later was found to have major negative side effects, and had begun to suffer from fainting spells. He blacked out twice within several weeks before shooting himself in the head.

"The day before he died, he phoned me to say that a client of mine owed his firm $5,000," an agent, Melinda Jason, said at the time. "He sounded distraught and terribly nervous. I checked and the bill was less than a week old. It hadn't even gotten to the accountant yet."

Garey discussed all this with his wife and casually mentioned that maybe "he should shoot himself." But nobody expected him to do so.

"We thought he had it all," Lansing told the New York Times. "When we heard how he died, we were sure someone must have killed him. Suicide would mean none of us knew Norman Garey. It would mean that our father, in a sense, [had] betrayed us. Why? Because none of us could accept not knowing the answer. We started looking for one."

Rumors began to spread that she and Garey had conspired with Melnick to embezzle money from Fox. "That led to talk that I was the 'bag lady' who was taking the money on my trips to Europe for work, and depositing it in a bank," said Lansing. "It was ludicrous, but it just grew."

"An inquiry by the Los Angeles District Attorney precipitated by the suicide of Norman Garey, a lawyer for Daniel Melnick, the movie producer, is focusing on a contract between Mr. Melnick and the 20th Century-Fox Film Corporation that was terminated last August," the *New York Times* reported in October 1982. "Mr. Garey shot himself Aug. 18, in the midst of negotiations to dissolve the contract. Shortly before, he had told his wife and others that he was concerned about a 'mistake' he had made during the negotiations, according to Robert K. Wrede, another of Mr. Melnick's attorneys. Both Mr. Melnick and Fox deny any financial irregularities or wrongdoing."

The article noted: "Investigations by members of the District Attorney's staff dealing with white-collar crime in the entertainment industry, who are handling the inquiry into the Melnick-Fox contract, had resulted in criminal cases in the past."

Even the usually circumspect trade press floated the rumors, as people began to whisper that Lansing had siphoned money from Fox and given it to Melnick, allegations later believed to have originated with a disgruntled former Melnick employee. Melnick, Lansing and Garey had allegedly been complicit in a deal to split $500,000, the difference between what Fox had authorized Melnick to pay one of his writers and the money the writer had received. When the *Hollywood Reporter* printed Melnick's denials, some fifty or sixty people called him to commiserate. "Probably half of them were secretly gloating," he said.

"The uglier the rumor, the more people relish it," quipped music mogul David Geffen.

"Watch for this story," wrote gossip columnist Liz Smith. "It could be bigger than Columbia and David Begelman!"

"It was so fantastic," said Steve Roth, a Fox executive. "You can't steal money from a studio during the development process. People can pad production budgets on a film, but not development money."

Soon, insiders were not just speculating about $500,000 going amiss but claiming that Lansing had purloined $1 million from Fox and given it to Melnick. Days later, the number was up to $50 million, all allegedly hidden in British banks.

"My God," quipped Melnick, "what are the Swiss going to say?"

Lansing became the subject of an official investigation by the city of Los Angeles' Task Force on White Collar Crime in the Entertainment Industry, created in the wake of the Begelman affair.

"At first I dismissed it as preposterous," she said. "I'd done nothing wrong, but I was powerless to correct it. The Fox lawyers knew the rumors couldn't be true, but even they were concerned. They were worried that all the negative press would affect the studio's reputation. Every expense had to be documented, and I could hardly get a pencil sharpened without a corporate sign-off."

When Davis's lawyer, Mickey Rudin, came to see her in private, she realized how serious things were. He advised her to have her own attorney present, but she declined. "I told him I had nothing to hide," she said. "By the end of our conversation, he was practically apologizing to me and he agreed how ridiculous the allegations were."

For three months this continued, and it was only at the end of that period—when Lansing's reputation had been shredded, along with her ability to concentrate on her job—that she was redeemed when the task force concluded its work in November 1982 and declared: "We have found no evidence to support any type of criminal investigation. No evidence has been found to support any of the rumors. Moreover, none of the key persons involved have made any allegations that criminal activity took place."

"What remains are bruised feelings and damaged reputations and a singular case history of how rumors feed on rumors in the insular world of movie-making in Hollywood," reported the *New York Times* in a story headlined "How a Hollywood Rumor Was Born, Flourished and Died." "The anatomy of this incident offers a crash course in the pathology of a community united chiefly by its fear of failure and its envy of success."

LANSING HAD NEVER expected this. Now, just as she hoped the worst was over, her conflict with Levy peaked as they argued about a new Scorsese film.

She had leaped at the chance to make *The King of Comedy*, the latest movie from one of America's most brilliant young directors, about a down-at-the-heels comedian (Robert De Niro) who kidnaps a TV star (Jerry Lewis). "I was behind it from the moment it was offered to me," she said. When the film was finished, she was flattered to have Scorsese ask her opinion. "I loved the way he was open to hearing what anybody thought, even the janitor. That was the mark of a truly confident artist. He was willing to get ideas from anywhere and had no ego about them."

Many have since damned the film as one of Scorsese's lesser works, with too much of a resemblance to the themes and characters of *Taxi Driver*. "[It is] one of the most arid, painful, wounded movies I've ever seen," wrote Roger Ebert in the *Chicago Sun-Times*. "It's hard to believe Scorsese made it; instead of the big-city life, the violence and sexuality of his movies like *Taxi Driver* and *Mean Streets*, what we have here is an agonizing portrait of lonely, angry people with their emotions all tightly bottled up. This is a movie that seems ready to explode—but somehow it never does."

Levy hated it. It was ugly, mean-spirited and morose, he believed, the very opposite of what audiences wanted to see. The country was going through the most serious recession since the Great Depression; unemployment was fast approaching 10.8 percent, and Ronald Reagan's "morning in America" was looking more like midnight. Even though conventional wisdom held that the movie business did well at such times, many insiders knew this notion dated to a time before ticket buyers could watch their free television instead, and at the height of the Great Depression ticket sales had in fact declined. The last thing people needed now, Levy argued, was something like this.

When a test screening confirmed his opinion, "Norman wrote it off," said Lansing. "In his mind, the movie wasn't going to be commercial, so he chose to open it in just a few theaters, with minimal advertising. He completely buried it, and there was nothing I could do."

Regardless of the film's merits, the idea of dumping any movie was anathema to Lansing's growing conviction that a studio must do everything to promote its pictures out of a moral obligation to the artists as well as bottom-line concerns. She felt she had personally let Scorsese down, especially when Levy told her he would not attend the film's premiere.

The director was appalled. "Basically, it was, Screw you, forget the picture," he said. "I realized at that point nobody cared, and that was when I really understood that the '70s were over for me, that the directors, the ones with the personal voices, had lost."

For Lansing, the movie marked a turning point when she realized she could no longer be part of the studio fold.

"I'd gone through not being able to buy *Chariots of Fire* and then the fight over *Porky's*, and I was even more crushed by *The King of Comedy*," she said. "I couldn't deliver on any of my promises, not the marketing or the advertising or the release. So what was the point of staying in the job? I knew I had to go."

Less than three years since news of her appointment had ricocheted around the world, the buoyant, almost giddy sensation Lansing had felt had melted away. She had savored success and found it wanting. All that was left was a bitter aftertaste, and the memories of her lost hopes and faded dreams.

"Ultimately, what did it mean?" asked Merzbach, the story editor. "Sherry became head of Fox, and it wasn't happy-making. I don't think it ever gave her enormous joy. She was powerless to do anything, and when things failed, she was the one who took the hit."

"We hadn't been really successful," said Hirschfield, "and Sherry wasn't happy. Toward the end, we both thought we were going to get terminated. There was a last party, where all the outcasts had a big celebration. We were in one corner and everybody else was in another, like we had leprosy."

The Verdict might have turned things around if it had come out a little sooner, but its December 1982 release was a case of too little, too late, especially from Davis's point of view.

"My dad loved Sherry," said his son John. "He just really, really got along with her, and after he sold the studio he remained close to her, personally. But he was an oilman trying to understand the business, and she had had a run of movies that didn't go well, and he knew he needed to shore the company up. In reality, he needed to get rid of Norman and Alan, and probably Sherry, too. She wasn't yet the great, seasoned executive she would become."

Lansing began to explore other options. Melnick wanted to partner with her as a producer, but he was not offering her a full 50 percent of their new venture; besides, she had grown distant from her former mentor, bothered by his braggadocio and endless claims that he was the queen-maker of Hollywood. "We had dinner downtown at the Omni Hotel, far from prying eyes," she recalled. "I told him it wasn't possible, that I'd always be in his shadow." A cooling took place in their relationship that would continue until his death in 2009.

Another executive, Ned Tanen, broached the idea of partnering, but Lansing declined, perhaps because his experience as Universal's production president was too close to her own, or perhaps, as one friend observed, because "Sherry never really felt he needed her, and she wanted someone who did."

Instead, she opted for Jaffe. They had come to know each other well, having worked on *Kramer* before going through the roller-coaster ride of *Taps*. She admired his taste, his ethics, his business skills and his knowledge of production. Besides, he wanted a true and equal partnership, which was remarkable given that he was already an Oscar winner with major releases to his credit.

"Stanley said we'd be fifty-fifty," Lansing noted. "Even though I wasn't his equal, he never let me feel that way."

"I said, 'If we're partners, we're partners,'" recalled Jaffe.

Now they dug in: Where would their company be based? What kind of films would it make? How many staff members would it need? They thought of returning to their old home at Columbia but decided against going back to the studio both had left with some bitterness. And any notion of remaining at Fox was squelched by Levy's ascendance.

"There was no legal impediment to either of us leaving Fox," said Lansing. "Stanley had a 'key man' clause, saying that if I left he could leave, too, and I had an out that allowed me to go after eighteen months."

Sherry Lee
Duhl as a child.

Margot Heimann, Lansing's mother.

David Duhl,
Lansing's father.

Modeling work came before Lansing began her career as an actress.

In her early acting days.

"These were glorified modeling jobs," said Lansing about her initial work as an actress. "Landing them was all about looks and luck."

Opposite Jack Lemmon (left) in 1969's *The April Fools*. Their relaxed manner belied the reality of being cooped up for weeks in a sweltering studio.

John Wayne was always gracious, but he kept silent about his cancer and marital problems.

Lansing would regularly escape Hollywood, traveling around the world. In her late twenties, she spent several days living with the Maasai and Samburu tribes in rural Kenya.

The New York Times Magazine

APRIL 27, 1980/SECTION 6

WHAT MAKES HOLLYWOOD RUN NOW?
By Budd Schulberg

Lansing's appointment as president of Fox made the cover of the
New York Times Magazine.

In her early days at Fox.

With her stepfather,
Norton, and her mother,
Margot, in the 1980s.

China Syndrome star Jane Fonda secretly intimidated Lansing, much as she admired the actress (bottom right).

Lansing (on the set of *Black Rain*) was devastated when her partner, Stanley Jaffe, left to become president of Paramount.

Anne Archer and Michael Douglas joined their *Fatal Attraction* producer Lansing for the motion picture academy's 1988 nominees' lunch.

On location with *Black Rain*.

With Michael
Douglas on the
set of *Black Rain*.

Robert Redford surprised everyone when he wanted to pull out of *Indecent Proposal*. "The kids [Demi and Woody] are wonderful, but I'm not," he said.

With director Adrian Lyne (center) on the set of *Indecent Proposal*.

In December 1982, after a period of talks that they managed to keep under wraps, the two closed a deal with Paramount, where Jaffe had deep ties, having served as the company's president several years earlier. When everything was in place, Lansing walked into Hirschfield's office to tell him she was resigning.

"He was shocked," she said. "He picked up the phone and called Marvin on his private jet, and Marvin went berserk. He lived by the credo that no one could leave until he fired them."

"Doll face, you can't quit!" he barked. "Nobody quits on me."

"I just did," replied Lansing.

CHAPTER 8

The man with whom Lansing would be joined at the hip was in many ways her opposite. Like her, Stanley Jaffe had lost a parent early (his mother died when he was five); like her, he had served as an executive before becoming a producer; and like her, his tastes veered toward the more thoughtful end of the motion picture spectrum. But unlike her, he was born into Hollywood royalty, or at least its East Coast aristocracy.

The son of Leo Jaffe, a former chairman of Columbia Pictures, he had grown up in New Rochelle, New York, in a home where kids traded movie gossip as others traded baseball cards. After graduating from the Wharton School of the University of Pennsylvania, he had risen quickly to become president of Paramount Pictures at age twenty-nine, making him the youngest studio chief in history. Then, in a burst of indignation, he walked out following a spat with his boss and friend Charles Bluhdorn, the founder of Paramount parent Gulf + Western Industries.

He was intelligent, elegant and refined, but he was also volatile, with a temper that was liable to get the better of him, just as it did when he blew up at Bluhdorn. "Stanley was very direct," said Karen Rosenfelt, a Paramount executive. "He took no prisoners. It would be, 'With all due respect, you're full of shit.'"

Like so many of the men to whom Lansing was drawn, he had echoes of Norton; his anger was familiar and even familial, his strength a reminder of the safety Norton had brought her following David's death.

The two had met in 1975 at a dinner party hosted by *Dynasty* producer Douglas Cramer and his gossip-columnist wife, Joyce Haber. There, during a game, they had bonded over a math problem, a five-line algebraic equation based on a false syllogism that they had solved with ease.

"Stanley had a lot of the traits that I like in men," said Lansing. "He was fearless, direct, loyal and honest to a fault. Our styles couldn't have been more different: he'd get upset if his coffee came without cream. But there was nobody better in a crisis and nobody I'd rather have at my side when things went wrong."

With Jaffe, she embarked on her new career as a producer, fulfilling the dream she had envisioned at Columbia. Whatever the surface similarities of the two jobs, being a producer was very different from being a studio executive.

"When you're running a studio you're largely reactive," she said. "You walk into the office. There are sixty calls. You have to read this script in five minutes, that one in the next hour. You have a screening in ten minutes. There are constant problems and fires to put out, but you're usually not creating anything from scratch. Whereas a producer has to come up with ideas and get them off the ground, find the money to pay for development, work with the writer, cast the actors and oversee everything from the first day of shooting on. If you're not active, nothing gets done."

While she had no producing experience, she knew from running Fox that she would need the full support of Paramount's executives, who ultimately would have the power to green-light her films.

Since the thirty-two-year-old Diller had been named Paramount's chairman in 1974 and hired the equally young Eisner to join him, the studio had become the hottest place in town, delivering an unparalleled succession of hits.

"Paramount has figured out, better than any other studio, how to make the right movies," wrote Tony Schwartz in *New York Magazine*. "This scarcely means flawless judgment, just that successes like *48 Hrs.* are big enough to overshadow failures like *The Keep*. The studio bases its choices less on the timeliness of subject matter or the ability to attract big-name stars than on the concept—the story itself, stripped of considerations."

Schwartz was referring to a new pattern of thinking that was beginning to dominate the studio system and would do so ever more markedly as it moved from the 1970s into the 1980s. Gone were the glory days of auteur directors and antihero stars; now what the studios wanted were stories that could sell themselves—"high-concept" movies, as they were called—where the basic idea was so compelling it could be expressed in a single sentence and bring in an audience, almost regardless of quality—from *Jaws* (killer shark must be stopped) to 1993's *Jurassic Park* (cloned dinosaurs rampage out of control).

This was a fundamental shift. It was given a significant boost by Don Simpson, a Paramount executive turned producer who had partnered with Jerry Bruckheimer to make such films as 1983's *Flashdance* and 1986's *Top Gun*. Other kinds of moviemaking were still tolerated, and indeed frequently found within Paramount's development slate, but this particular format was fundamental to the success of Diller, Eisner and their protégé Katzenberg.

Later, these movies and their spawn—the "franchise" films that would give brands precedence over one-off stories—would suffocate the adult-oriented films that Lansing most loved. But right now there was room for both, and she was eager to start developing the character-driven, richly thematic pictures she and Jaffe held dear.

On January 4, 1983, the industry's trade publications announced the formation of Jaffe-Lansing Productions. "Paramount, a unit of Gulf & Western Industries Inc., said it made a five-year exclusive production agreement with Jaffe-Lansing under which Mr. Jaffe, 43 years old, and Miss Lansing, 38, will co-produce their own films and acquire completed films for distribution," wrote the *Wall Street Journal*. "The company also will produce films that Mr. Jaffe will direct."

Eisner said he was counting on the producers to make at least three pictures per year, either a case of irrational exuberance or political spin, given that Jaffe had produced only seven films in his entire career, while Lansing was a neophyte. Most producers took years to stock their quivers, guiding their scripts through "development hell," when each one could pass through a dozen iterations or more, with just as many different writers, before it came close to being made.

"But," said Eisner, "I believed in them and believed they would do great. Stanley had done this a long time and Sherry had already proved she had great taste."

She and Jaffe established their own distinctive methodology when it came to finding and overseeing scripts. "We developed things separately," said Lansing. "Stanley was on the East Coast and I was on the West Coast, and we both had our own projects. It was only when we felt the screenplays were in shape that we'd give them to each other and then take careful notes, and eventually work together on the final drafts."

In early 1983, they settled into historic oak-paneled offices in Paramount's Lucille Ball Building, where Lansing was based full-time, while Jaffe traveled back and forth between Los Angeles and his main office in New York. It was in these Paramount offices that Lucy and Howard Hughes had once held court, in these very offices that some of the most talented people in Hollywood history had done their best work.

"I was beyond excited," said Lansing. "It was like entering a whole new world. I felt nothing could stop us."

IT WAS PERHAPS inevitable that the first Jaffe-Lansing film would flop.

Racing with the Moon was a poignant story about two friends preparing to leave home to fight in World War II; it was written by Steve Kloves, who would go on to write most of the *Harry Potter* films. Lansing had developed the script at Fox, where it had been a passion project, but that enthusiasm was not shared by her successor as Fox's president of production, Joe Wizan, who made his indifference plain.

Soon after Wizan took over, he reached an impasse with director Richard Benjamin, a longtime character actor who had won acclaim for his debut as a filmmaker, 1982's *My Favorite Year*. Fox would green-light the movie only if Benjamin agreed to make it for $5 million, rather than the $6 million he felt he needed.

"Things got very strained," Benjamin recalled. "Fox didn't see what we saw. I started having meetings with them, and they were questioning things where there were no questions before. They began to bring up the budget, then there were comic elements, and they wanted us to go more in that direction. I said, 'I can't have this conversation.' I gave back a third of my salary to keep it going. I was fighting to keep the picture alive."

A start date had been set for May 1983, even as the studio and film-makers bickered about the cost. A month before principal photography, Benjamin asked if he could take the movie elsewhere, and Fox agreed.

Lansing had observed all this from a distance, too preoccupied with setting up her company to pay much attention while the film remained at Fox. She had never expected Wizan to let the picture go, knowing the last thing an executive wanted was to see a small picture he had rejected become a hit for someone else. But when Benjamin asked Lansing to step in, she urged Paramount to buy it, aware that the clock was ticking and the shoot was about to begin.

Negotiations were not easy, as Fox wanted to keep a share of the profits in order to have some upside if the film did well. Paramount, in turn, expected a bargain. The talks came to a head one April afternoon.

"Dick [Benjamin] was en route to Northern California, where the crew was already at work," said Lansing. "He flew to San Francisco, then caught a twin-engine Cessna to Mendocino, and when he landed he wasn't sure which studio was backing his movie."

"The plane let me off at this tiny airport—no lights, nothing," added Benjamin. "They had to get animals off the runway before we could land. I arrived not knowing if this picture was going to be made, or with whom. So I got off the plane, and as the plane started to taxi away, somebody at this phone booth said, 'There's a phone call for you.' I picked up the phone and it was Stanley." Benjamin never found out how Jaffe had tracked him down. "He said, 'It's done—it's a Paramount movie.' It was Fox's before I landed, and after I got back on that plane it was Paramount's."

Weeks later the shoot got under way, and Lansing discovered the joy of being on a set full-time. She embraced the steep learning curve, even if she feared she was not on Jaffe's level.

"I knew nothing about the camera and about different angles and lenses, or the way a scene should be put together visually," she said. "I thought, 'If you're a producer, you need to know all of this.' And Stanley had such a mastery of detail that I expected as much from myself. He told me if I was going to be a good producer, I needed to be on the set when the crew arrived, and I couldn't leave until the last shot of the day was completed. His philosophy was, if the producers didn't show a 100 percent commitment, how could they expect it from the crew?"

Jaffe was the sorcerer, Lansing the apprentice. But from Benjamin's point of view, they worked in perfect tandem.

"There was no better team," he said. "Stanley knew everything about production, right down to how many lengths of cable you might need, and Sherry knew story and all the creative aspects. She had such wonderful taste that I could have her watch dailies without seeing them myself. At the same time, she could tell me anything she liked because of the way she presented it. She was strong—there's no question of that—but she got things done in such a lovely way that you wanted to do anything for her."

As the shoot progressed, Lansing grew concerned about a budding romance between two of the movie's stars, Sean Penn and Elizabeth McGovern. Penn had burst onto the scene with his role as the dim-witted Jeff Spicoli in 1982's *Fast Times at Ridgemont High* and had worked for both Lansing and Jaffe on *Taps*. He was gaining a reputation as one of the finest actors of his generation, but also as a hothead. As for McGovern, she had recently been Oscar-nominated for Milos Forman's 1981 drama *Ragtime* and was expected to become a big star. When Lansing observed them hand in hand, off camera as well as on, she told Benjamin she feared the romance might backfire.

"Don't worry," he assured her. "It will be good for their chemistry."

During the shoot, he was right. Filming continued without a hitch, and the genuineness of the emotion added an undercurrent of electricity to a picture that might otherwise have lacked it. But later, after the wrap, Penn refused to do publicity, in part because he did not want to answer questions about his relationship with McGovern, and his co-star followed suit.

Neither had any contractual obligation to do interviews, and even if they had, a recalcitrant star would have been worse than no star at all.

"They were a couple, and when he told Elizabeth not to do press, she obeyed," said Lansing. "He said, 'Bobby De Niro doesn't do it. That's hawking the movie. That's not what great actors do.' We begged him and begged her, but he had a great influence over her, and they wouldn't do a thing."

The situation became contentious. "We'd negotiated a cover story on Sean and Elizabeth with *People* magazine, a real bonanza for a small film like this," Lansing noted. "The interview would only have taken ten minutes on the phone, and we'd even arranged for questions to be sent to Sean in advance. But he still wouldn't do it."

She was furious, and so was Jaffe. But nothing they did could move Penn, McGovern and their co-star, Nicolas Cage. "We believed it was their responsibility to help the picture, and our cast disagreed," said Lansing. "But Stanley was rock solid. He said: 'We made a great movie. I'm really proud of it. We'll just do the best we can.'"

Instead of the stars, Paramount had to turn to its producers and director for a nationwide publicity tour, which lacked the sizzle it might have had with the three young actors. Despite Lansing and Jaffe's appearances on morning shows, and interviews with daily newspapers and magazines, the film made only $6 million at the box office.

"I remember going to a preview, when it was thought if you got [a test score] in the 80s, you were going to make a lot of money," said Jaffe. "We got an 85, and no one showed up."

Years later, Lansing and Penn ran into each other. She had long realized the importance of letting go of anger, and Penn had changed, too, she said. "He gave me a really warm hug and said, 'I've grown up a lot since then.'"

THE PARTNERS WERE no luckier with their second film, *Firstborn*, the story of a teenage boy whose life is disrupted when a sinister man takes up with his mother.

Paramount had asked Jaffe and Lansing to join the picture as executive producers (a notch down from full producers) in order to support producers Paul Junger Witt and Tony Thomas, both more experienced in television than film.

"Nothing went right," said Lansing. "We got Michael Apted to direct when he became available after another movie was canceled, and we tried to hire that movie's stars, Jon Voight and Jessica Lange, now that they were free. But Paramount wouldn't sign off on them."

The studio wanted Tom Berenger, who had just appeared in *Southern Comfort* to considerable acclaim. "We all thought Tom was going to be a big star, and so we agreed," said Lansing.

Right before shooting, however, Berenger was in a car crash and had to be replaced by Peter Weller. The movie tanked, earning only $6.2 million when it opened in October 1984, giving Jaffe-Lansing back-to-back failures.

BY THE TIME *Firstborn* opened, two years had passed since the partners had come to Paramount, an eternity in the motion picture business. Even though Eisner maintained that "our relationship was very good," the champagne had gone flat, the confetti had been vacuumed away. Nor were their movies dazzling: both were small in budget and scope, and "Paramount didn't hire us to make little movies," said Jaffe.

By late 1984, Lansing began to fear their production deal would not be renewed. After putting her Fox salary into her new house, she had a relatively meager cushion, and she had followed Jaffe's counsel to take little salary or up-front payment in exchange for a big share of the back end. "What a studio hates is when you make money and they don't," she explained. "Here, everyone was rewarded in success."

That was all well and good when success seemed within grasp, but now it was barely a blip on the radar, and Jaffe's prickliness did not help. "He was always threatening to break our deal," said Lansing. "Any time he disagreed with Paramount, he'd say, 'Forget it. We're out of here.' I kept telling him, if he broke the deal I'd be out of a job."

Jaffe began to explore raising outside money for their films, but Lansing balked. "Stanley was talking to bankers about giving us a fund," she said. "Instead of making a movie a year or two movies every eighteen months, we'd be making several at a time. I didn't want to do that because it would be going back to being an executive. I wanted to be deeply involved in one movie at a time."

She was also wary of investing her own money, and the deal would have required her to contribute $500,000. To Jaffe, that was more than manageable; to Lansing, it was unfathomable. "We could have raised $150 million," Jaffe mused. "That was a lot of money. But Sherry was afraid."

For years she had had a recurring dream, and now it came rushing back in force. In the dream, "an elegant man and a stunning blonde are in a Rolls, riding through Beverly Hills," she said. "They spot a homeless woman, and when the man does a double take, his wife says, 'Do you know who that is?' The man says, 'Yes. That used to be my wife.'"

The man in the dream was Lansing's ex-husband, Michael, "and the homeless woman was me."

WHILE LANSING WAS coping with nightmares, a different nightmare was consuming Paramount.

In February 1983, on his way home from a trip to the Dominican Republic, Gulf + Western's Bluhdorn had died of a massive heart attack. Its domino effect would reshape the leadership of three studios.

Bluhdorn's deputy, Martin Davis (no relation to Fox's Marvin Davis), was named to replace him and began to make radical changes, selling off many of G+W's subsidiaries, removing dozens of senior executives (even those who had considered themselves his allies) and ruthlessly slashing perks—so much that he refused to let Bluhdorn's widow retain a company car and driver.

A rift grew between the bullheaded Davis and the troika of Diller, Eisner and Katzenberg. Once, when Katzenberg dropped by Davis's New York office, expecting a pat on the back, Davis launched into a tirade, calling him "a little Sammy Glick" and accusing him of conspiring with his colleagues to get Davis removed.

"Marty Davis was elected year-in and year-out the worst boss in America," said Eisner. "Having a continued relationship with him was not easy."

Frustrated, the Paramount team began to look for opportunities elsewhere, and their timing could not have been better. Over at Fox, Marvin Davis had severed his ties to Dennis Stanfill and had had enough of Hirschfield. He asked Diller to run the studio, and the answer was yes. At the same time, the floundering Walt Disney Co. was looking for fresh blood to restore its battered name and zeroed in on Eisner, who learned he had the job days after Diller told him he was leaving for Fox.

"Barry had his opportunity at Fox, and out of the blue the opportunity came for me to be CEO of Disney," said Eisner. "It was a no-brainer."

Within weeks, the top layer of Paramount executives was gone (Katzenberg followed Eisner) and the map of the industry was redrawn. Disney's leadership was replaced; Fox was now headed by Diller (who would soon have a new boss of his own in Rupert Murdoch); and Paramount, which recently had seemed the very model of what a studio should be, was rudderless.

These changes were as seismic as any the industry had seen, and they left Lansing and Jaffe uncertain about their prospects as they entered their fourth year at Paramount. No matter how much Frank Mancuso, the gentlemanly executive who took over as studio chairman, tried to reassure them ("It was just a matter of a little bad luck," he said), Lansing was sure he was wrong.

"I knew, if you have two failed movies, you aren't long for the world," she said. "Stanley had had nothing but success before me. I felt like a curse."

WHILE GRAPPLING WITH uncertainty, Lansing was devastated to learn that her mother was seriously ill.

At first she did not appreciate the gravity of the situation: all her mother said was that her stomach was bothering her. Then Lansing went to Miami, where Margot and Norton had started spending their winters.

"The minute I saw her, I knew something was wrong," she said. "Her stomach was distended, and the pain was so severe it often left her doubled over."

The initial prognosis was diverticulitis, an intestinal disorder that can require surgery. But treatment proved ineffective, and Margot's condition deteriorated. "Her stomach kept swelling as though it were filling with helium," said Lansing. "She got to the point where she looked as if she were pregnant."

At her daughter's insistence, Margot returned to Chicago to see Arthur Herbst, a leading oncologist, who informed her she had ovarian cancer.

Lansing knew nothing about cancer, a subject regarded at the time with such unease that many victims would not acknowledge having it, let alone mention it in polite conversation.

"I was worried, but I didn't take in the full magnitude of what my mother was saying," she said. "Nobody I knew had cancer. It wasn't part of my life. All I heard was that my mother had a medical problem and it needed to be fixed. She'd have to be treated, and then she'd get well. I was relentlessly upbeat. I just knew she'd be cured."

But the news got progressively worse: Margot not only had cancer, it was at stage four, which meant she had merely a slim chance of recovering.

Lansing could not believe it. No matter how complicated their relationship, she could not imagine life without her mother. When an oncologist friend told her, "Your mother's going to die," she snapped: "Who do you think you are? God?"

Dr. Herbst outlined a course of treatment: Margot would have surgery to remove the bloating in her stomach, and after that she would undergo chemotherapy.

"And then she'll be fine?" asked Lansing.

"Maybe," the doctor replied.

Ignoring his ambivalence, Lansing put all her energy into helping her mother, as if energy alone could solve the problem. She blinded herself to the possibility that Margot's cancer was terminal.

"I never gave up hope," she said. "I was desperate to fix it. My only thought was, 'I'm going to figure out how to cure her.' I'd call the doctors to make sure she had the best care. I even called my ex-husband, Michael, to see that she was in the best possible hands at the University of Chicago Medical Center."

The prospect of losing her hair appalled Margot. "She was sitting on a bed at the doctor's, taking notes on a pad, and wrote BALD in capital letters and underlined it over and over," said Lansing. "She was so beautiful, and so full of pride, and couldn't get over the fact that she was going to lose her hair. I told her she could wear a wig until it grew back, and no one would notice." In fact, Margot's wig was so well made that when she went out to dinner one night, a stranger asked for her hairdresser's name.

Chemotherapy got under way, the sessions spaced a few weeks apart.

"That allowed my mother and father to travel back and forth to Miami, to take advantage of the warm weather," said Lansing. "My mother insisted on buying the cheapest plane tickets, and refused to spend money on herself. They could easily have afforded it, but she hated to be extravagant. That's what's so terrible: the inability to spend on yourself when you need to. She was so sick that she'd throw up during the layovers."

Lansing pretended the studio had given her some first-class tickets, which she gave to her mother. The ruse worked once or twice, "until she figured out I'd bought them myself, when she flatly refused to accept them."

Margot abhorred being a victim. "The greatest fear she had was that people would pity her," said Lansing. "She didn't want to be talked about when she had the disease. She didn't want people's pity."

Lansing longed to have her mother by her side and solder whatever rift remained between them. She wanted to talk about everything they had felt and experienced, but that was not in her mother's nature.

"She concentrated on becoming well, rather than looking back," said Lansing. "She never said, 'Come home. Let's have a long lunch.' None of that happened. There were no intimate conversations."

If her mother revealed any of her concerns, they were more about her family than herself. "She didn't say, 'Why me?'" said Lansing. "She worried about us. 'Can you really take all this time off work?' 'Are you OK?' I saw the comfort her girlfriends gave her—more than I could give her, because when you're a mother you still want to take care of your children. I would see her close girlfriends come to visit and I often thought they were able to give her more joy than I was."

A pall fell over the family as each of its members grappled with the situation and what it might mean, none able or willing to discuss it with the others. Margot and Norton preferred it that way: when they made their trips to Chicago, they did not even tell Lansing's siblings they were there, though both Andrea and Dick lived within driving distance of the hospital.

"Like every serious topic in my childhood," said Lansing, "it wasn't discussed at all."

Judy flew in from New York, where she was now married with two children and working as a psychotherapist, and spent the nights in Margot's hospital room during the chemotherapy; Lansing came almost every weekend, and was constantly on the phone.

Norton hardly ever left his wife's side. "He showed her absolute love," said Lansing. "He just kept reassuring her how beautiful she was. Each time he had to step away, he'd give her a thumbs-up and say, 'I love you, honey. You'll be OK.'"

At first it appeared he might be right. After the initial rounds of chemotherapy, Margot's hair grew back in all its luster, and soon she felt well enough to visit her daughter in Los Angeles, where one of Lansing's friends recalled being charmed by this woman with her faint foreign accent.

But months into her remission, she found a lump on her stomach. It was malignant. Rapidly and inexorably, she began to decline until she was so sick that, during one of Lansing's visits, she failed to notice a huge bandage wrapped around her daughter's face, from a brush with melanoma.

"She didn't even ask what happened," said Lansing. "That's how sick she was. I just said I'd had a skin irregularity removed, and she was ashamed she hadn't noticed."

Soon after, Margot forgot her daughter's fortieth birthday.

———

"I DREAMED I could put her cancer in my body and fight it off," said Lansing. "I was younger and stronger, and thought I could handle it better. I kept praying, 'Please, give me the disease so that I don't have to watch her suffer.'"

When she learned of an experimental vaccine being developed at the MD Anderson Cancer Center at the University of Texas in Houston, she cold-called the hospital, only to be told the next available appointment was three months away. "I don't have three months!" she insisted. "The cancer's eaten a hole in my mother's stomach!" She approached anyone and everyone for help, and eventually found a friend who led her to one of the hospital's benefactors, who in turn secured her an appointment.

Margot was too sick to travel, so Lansing flew to Houston and was introduced to an oncologist. In a testament to his graciousness and her perseverance, he flew to Chicago the next day and administered the vaccine. It was an extraordinary gesture that he repeated every other week for two months.

"After the first round of shots, my mother felt better," said Lansing. "One afternoon we took her out in the sun. She was tired and fragile, but she looked beautiful again. 'It's working,' she kept saying. But it wasn't working at all. I wanted her to live so badly, I couldn't see she was about to die."

As Margot grew more and more ill, Lansing became frantic. Time seemed to be cornering her, crushing her, and the more she fought, the less she seemed able to do.

Even now, Margot was unable to tell her daughter all the things she so needed to hear. "I desperately wanted her to tell me how much she loved me," said Lansing. "I longed to have that loving, hugging relationship with her. I told her, 'I love you so much.' But she never said it back."

In her anguish, she kept thinking how much her mother had wanted her to marry, but now, in her final days, Margot let that go. "I'd say, 'I'll get married. I'll find some nice Jewish guy,'" said Lansing. "And she said, 'No. I don't know that marriage is for you.' She liberated me. On her deathbed, she set me free."

The end came in September 1984, a year after Lansing first learned of her mother's illness. She was in New York City, taking a brief break over the Labor Day weekend to visit friends, when she received an urgent message to fly to Chicago. By the time she arrived, her mother was dead. She was sixty-three years old.

"I remember walking into her hospital room and seeing her lying there, motionless," said Lansing. "She was so beautiful, and she looked so much at peace, I didn't believe she was really dead. All the tubes were gone. Nothing was beeping. Her death didn't even register until my father entered the room and started sobbing hysterically. I'd never seen him cry. That's when I couldn't deny it. I just kept thinking, 'I didn't save her. I failed.' And my body went numb."

THE NUMBNESS LINGERED for months. Lansing longed to escape through work, but there was no work pressing enough to give her release. She was distraught and would cry at the mention of her mother's name.

"She was emotional, emotional, emotional," said her friend Luttrell. "She felt lost when her mother died. It took her a long time to get over it, and maybe she never did."

Going through Margot's possessions, Lansing discovered a secret: her mother had kept a scrapbook of her daughter's achievements over all these years. Photos and newspaper articles had been clipped and pasted with loving care, and yet Margot had never said a word. It was more than Lansing could bear.

"I was almost nonfunctional," she said. "For days and weeks and months, there were so many emotions swirling around my head, and I couldn't find a way to block them off or separate them from the other things I was meant to think about."

Margot's death was a watershed for her daughter. If the loss of her father David had fostered her insecurity and driven her to become an actress, so the loss of her mother would push her to help others.

Two deaths shaped her life—one the first half, the other the second.

Ashamed to realize how little she knew about cancer, she now began to familiarize herself with the latest medical advances. Over the next few years, that passion almost supplanted film as she filled her calendar with activities in the nonprofit world.

"I felt the only way I could honor my mother and make sense of her death was to fund research for a cure, so that no one would suffer like she did," said Lansing.

In the late 1980s, she approached industrialist Armand Hammer, a leading financier of cancer research, with a singular proposition. With his permission, she said, she would serve as his eyes and ears, going around the country and finding the most worthwhile young researchers for him to support. He agreed, and for several weeks each year, she would set out on her scouting expeditions.

"I'd get a list of scientists and learn about their work and directly call their labs," she said. "I'd say, 'Could I visit you and see what you're doing, with the goal of finding you funding?' And everybody said yes. And what I found was, scientists are very much like actors and directors. They're passionate, they never give up, they're quirky and idiosyncratic. If you said, 'We have no money, but you can have this tiny little space there, and you can work on your molecules or your mice,' they would do it. They're very much like people from the film business, with one difference: in the movie world, if something goes bad, we say, 'Well, we're not curing cancer,' but that's exactly what these scientists are doing."

When she introduced Hammer to one scientist, UCLA Medical Center's Judith Gasson—the key player behind GM-CSF, a drug used to ward off infections and increase patients' tolerance for chemotherapy—their meeting bore parallels to some of Lansing's earlier encounters.

"Honey, do you work with other doctors?" asked Hammer.

"Yes," said Gasson.

"So you helped them discover GM-CSF?" Hammer continued.

"No," said Gasson. "I purified it, and they helped me."

Hammer gave her a $50,000 grant and Lansing joined him to create Stop Cancer, a nonprofit organization dedicated to raising funds for young scientists, which she chaired after his death in 1990.

BY THE MID-1980S, Jaffe and Lansing still only had two pictures to show for their efforts. Perhaps they had erred in their approach. Rather than work on a diverse group of projects, all at various stages of development and liable to pop at any time—standard operating procedure for most producers, who would oversee thirty to forty screenplays at once—their development slate was limited to a few choice vehicles.

"We didn't have a lot, probably fewer than eight," said Lansing. "We didn't believe in developing anything we didn't love."

Only two of their scripts were ready to go a step further. One, *Diversion*, was adapted from a British short about a husband who commits adultery and pays the price; the other, *Reckless Endangerment*, was a rape drama based on a real-life case that had made headlines across the country. Nobody wanted to make either one. "The titles alone suggested our predicament," said Lansing.

With their professional life stalled, CAA's Ovitz stepped in. In his late thirties, he was at the peak of his power, and as the producers' agent, he was also responsible for directing good material their way and helping to close their deals.

Over the past decade, he had built CAA into the dominant force in Hollywood, signing almost all the big stars. Their attachment to him and his agency had given him enormous political capital, which he was willing to leverage. He was admired and feared, respected and reviled, but Jaffe and Lansing felt they should heed his advice.

"My goal as an agent was to create work for the clients before they ever got an offer, and to protect them," said Ovitz. "The whole look of the CAA building [a white fortress designed by architect I. M. Pei] was a protective façade for creative people. But now it was about saving [the Jaffe-Lansing company]."

In 1985, the three met for dinner at Spago, the industry's most prominent watering hole. "We sat in a prime booth in the corner, with a picture window that featured a full view of the Sunset Strip and its movie billboards," said Lansing. "Ovitz was showing the town that we were worthy of dinner."

He was also showing the two producers how ineffective they were. As he gestured toward the Strip, with its cascading billboards and parade of displays for upcoming movies, it was obvious none of these pictures was theirs. Nor was that likely to change with their current batch of apparently uncommercial screenplays, particularly the two they most cared to make.

"Put those things aside," Ovitz counseled. "Stop beating your heads against the wall. Let me get you guys back in the mainstream. Eddie Murphy's really hot, and comedies with him are in demand. I can put one of those together for you."

Ovitz knew artists, respected them, sometimes even liked them, but he also realized that they had to be steered away from their worst instincts. Art was all well and good, but it did not pay the bills. Some of his most gifted clients, of course, might have rebelled against that concept, but Ovitz was sure he was right. That's what had put him on top, and it was what would keep him there years longer.

"You have to realize," he said, "I handled Marty Scorsese, and Marty's penchant was not always to do commercial movies, and when he came to me I switched that around. I used Marty as an example. I said, 'I can help you.'"

"He was doing what an agent should," said Lansing, "because we were as cold as ice. He was saying, 'I can put you on one of these movies.' But that wasn't what we expected."

Had she opted to be a producer simply to make the vapid comedies Ovitz was recommending? Had she given up an executive's salary to oversee movies she would never pay to watch? True, a film like the one Ovitz was proposing would put her and Jaffe back in the game, but was that their real goal? Was it not possible to have success and still make the movies they cared for?

She listened and said nothing, and the more Ovitz spoke the more her heart sank. At last, the threesome said goodbye, as Jaffe and Lansing stepped out of the restaurant into the chill of the night. The city stretched before them, its lights gleaming with the promise they had held so many years earlier, when Lansing first came to Los Angeles, and the city held up a mirror to a future that would have no pain and no regrets. But at this moment, the world looked dark.

"I think I'm going to cut my throat," said Jaffe.

Lansing felt the same way.

"What do we do now?" she asked.

"Only movies we believe in," he replied.

CHAPTER 9

At forty, Lansing knew what it was to be obsessed.

Just a few years earlier, she had been jilted by a steady boyfriend who had told her, "I don't think I love you anymore" while both were in bed, and then got up and said goodbye, leaving her so deflated she could not drag herself out of her home for two full days. No matter what she had accomplished, it seemed like nothing compared to his love. And for the next few weeks, this woman who had been a pioneer in her field, who had risen to the summit of the most competitive industry in the world, kept circling his house deep into the night, searching for evidence of the thing she dreaded: another woman's presence. Each time she spotted a stranger's car, she would agonize that he had found someone else. She would call him at all hours, only to hang up as soon as he answered the phone. Her emotions were in turmoil; her life seemed unhinged. Wasn't wisdom supposed to kick in by now? "I felt he took part of me with him," she said.

This was the backdrop to the movie that would revitalize her career.

Fatal Attraction was based on a short film that Jaffe had discovered on a scouting trip to London. It was written and directed by James Dearden, the son of director Basil Dearden (*Khartoum*), one of the British film industry's elder statesmen. A graduate of Oxford University, James had three shorts to his name and was just beginning to get some feature projects off the ground when Jaffe met him and saw what he had done. He called Lansing at once, he recalled: "I said, 'What do you think? This guy's really talented.'"

Diversion, the short that Jaffe liked best, was the story of a writer who is left alone for a weekend when his family goes away, and then calls a woman whose number he has kept. That night, they sleep at her place, only for the woman to slash her wrists before he leaves. Shaken, the man nurses her through the night and returns home, believing the nightmare is over. But when he is sitting with his wife and kids, she calls. The film ends with him staring at the ringing phone as his wife asks, "Aren't you going to answer it?"

"I'm not going to say [the story] was autobiographical," said Dearden, "but everyone has been in situations where they've been harassed. I had an experience where somebody kept calling me, and I got very uncomfortable. And I had a girlfriend who cut her wrists, very theatrically and not to kill herself. Then a good friend of mine was pursued by this beautiful but crazy woman and it was destroying his marriage."

Not much had happened since his short was completed in 1980, and when Dearden met Jaffe he did not expect anything to change. "I thought I'd never hear from him again," he said. "That's usually the case."

Jaffe was intrigued, Lansing fascinated when she saw the film, not just because its sexual morality enthralled her, but also because it echoed her belief that each of us must bear responsibility for his or her actions.

The short came only a few years after she had been riveted by the trial of Jean Harris, the elegant principal of a girls' boarding school who made headlines when she shot and killed her lover and was found guilty of second-degree murder. Lansing could not get Harris out of her head, and the real-life woman's passions dovetailed with those of the movie's antiheroine. "How could a professional woman feel so scorned that she murdered her lover?" she asked. "What did he do to her psyche to make her snap?"

It was the rejected woman in *Diversion* who drew her far more than its male protagonist. She understood the pain of abandonment and knew men like him—successful and seemingly content, with loyal wives on whom they cheated without a shred of guilt. Once she had gone on a blind date with a former basketball star, only to learn after he picked her up that he was married. She told him to turn the car around. "I was furious," she said. "And I was even angrier with the friend who set me up for assuming I'd ever go out with him."

Lansing invited Dearden to meet her in Los Angeles. Initially they planned to discuss several story ideas, but they kept returning to the short film, debating ways to make it strong enough to sustain a feature. "I couldn't get it out of my mind," said Lansing.

No matter how hard they tried to find a twist that would propel the thin plot forward, they came up blank. Jaffe was skeptical. "What's the movie?" he kept asking. "The wife picks up the phone, the woman says, 'I had an affair with your husband,' and then the wife throws him out. Where's the drama?"

Lansing could not answer that just yet, but the story haunted her nonetheless. She fretted over it, engaging in marathon talks with Dearden, both in person and by phone once he had returned to London. "I couldn't get that relationship out of my mind," she said. "I couldn't forget this woman whose self-esteem is stripped away when her lover leaves. I thought of my own experience, and couldn't let it go."

She resumed work with Dearden in Los Angeles during a second lengthy session and then a third, hashing and rehashing his story, always in the hope of a breakthrough. "We'd meet all morning and all afternoon, and maybe all morning and all afternoon again," said the writer. "It was quite intense."

Just when both were about to give up, Lansing had an epiphany. She remembered an executive she had known who, to all appearances, seemed as conventional as a human being could be, until she discovered he was living a double life: a good family man, he was also a cheater living another existence altogether with his mistress. When the latter became pregnant, the executive was too scared to tell his wife, and the woman bore him a baby without his wife ever knowing.

"What if our woman got pregnant?" asked Lansing. "An affair can come and go, but a child is forever."

"That was the key to up the stakes and make it much more dynamic," said Dearden.

Locking himself in, over the course of a few hours Dearden created a new plot that pushed his story into deeper and darker terrain.

"We wanted to escalate Dan's problems and show that his actions had real consequences," said Lansing, referring to the hero, Dan Gallagher. "First, the woman tries to kill herself. Then she won't leave him alone. Then she tells him she's pregnant and wants to have the baby. When he insists that's her decision, she keeps calling his office. After he refuses to take her calls, she tracks him down at home and meets his wife. She even picks up his child from school."

As the story came into focus, so did the characters. The leading man would no longer be a writer, as he was in the short; instead, he became a lawyer who has a one-night stand with a book editor, initially named Sean Forrest, who places his family in jeopardy and forces him to take action.

Later the name Sean was changed to Alex. "There was a rumor that I'd based the character on [actress] Sean Young, with whom I'd had an affair—which wasn't true," said Dearden. "I didn't have an affair with her, and I didn't base the character on her."

Dearden's sympathies lay primarily with the husband, while Lansing's lay with Alex, and in this duality lay some of the film's power.

Alex's line "I'm not going to be *ignored*, Dan" resonated with her. "That was the essence of the movie for me," she said. "She was standing up for her rights, saying, 'You can't just discard me because it's convenient.' I always thought Alex was a successful career woman who became involved with one married man too many. That's what caused her to crack. I didn't think she was crazy to start with, but each of us has something that could put us over the tipping point."

ON A FLIGHT with Jaffe, Lansing ran into Michael Douglas, who agreed to read the script.

"It was the perfect what-if, the ultimate quickie nightmare," he said. "It was great how [it showed that] a little mistake can just poison your family and everything around you, to the point of being life-threatening."

Douglas was no longer the B-list star he had been when Lansing first met him. Since *The China Syndrome,* he had co-starred in two significant hits, 1984's *Romancing the Stone* and its sequel, 1985's *The Jewel of the Nile.* But he still did not have the heft to get a film green-lit on his name alone, and Paramount passed on the project, as did every other studio Lansing and Jaffe approached. Some questioned how anyone could ever sympathize with the lead; others did not like Douglas.

Paramount's new head of production, Dawn Steel, was so outraged by the story that she hurled the script across the room.

"She yelled, 'How can you give me this? I'm a newlywed!'" recalled Lansing. "She said, 'Why should we care about a guy who cheats on his wife, especially when he doesn't have a reason?' But in some ways the fact that there was no reason was the whole point. Things like that happen, and knowing it adds to the feeling of 'This could happen to me.'"

Lansing failed to persuade Steel, just as she failed to persuade numerous others to direct. "Everyone passed," she said. "I remember begging directors to do it. I begged John Carpenter [*Halloween*]. And it wasn't just him. I begged everyone."

The movie was in trouble. Studio readers were sick and tired of seeing the same old script recycled, making its way again and again through their story departments. And the agencies were bored with Lansing's repeated requests to show it to clients, knowing they would all say no.

Everything changed when Brian De Palma, the director of films such as 1976's *Carrie* and the 1983 remake of *Scarface,* said he wanted to do it. De Palma was hot and at the top of Hollywood's A-list, and Steel could not have been more excited. So what if she had thrown the screenplay across the room? Suddenly it became her favorite project.

"Dawn was very keen on him," said Lansing. "So we met, and it went great. He was intense, but this was exciting. We were going to make our movie."

Red flags might have been visible if Lansing had cared to look. For one thing, De Palma did not share her sympathy for Alex, the jilted woman; for another, he wanted to make changes that seemed awfully close to turning the story into a horror film, a genre he knew well, but one in which neither Lansing nor Dearden had any interest.

"We even had a Halloween scene, with Alex running around in a Kabuki mask, terrorizing the household," noted the writer.

This was business as usual with a top director, who almost always had the power to rework a script however he saw fit, and what counted was that he had Steel's support, along with an undeniable visual flair.

"We were thrilled," said Lansing. "We knew that, with him, Paramount would make the movie."

Gearing up for the shoot, she rented an apartment in New York, where the movie was going to be filmed; Dearden flew in to go over details with the director; and Jaffe set to work finding locations and staffing the picture. Then De Palma had second thoughts.

"He came to our New York office and said, 'I have a problem,'" Lansing explained. "We thought he was going to say 'I need a new set,' or something like that. We were just a few weeks away from the shoot, and he said, 'I can't make the movie with Michael Douglas.' We said, 'What?' There was no warning. Then he carried on, saying, 'Michael's completely unsympathetic. No one will ever like him.'"

As Lansing fumbled for a response, De Palma gave her and Jaffe an ultimatum: "It's either him or me."

"It was one of those come-to-Jesus moments," said Lansing. "De Palma was the reason the studio said yes. He was the element that got us a green light, and we knew the picture was over without him. But Michael had been on it for two years, all through the time when everybody else rejected us. We'd committed to him, and we couldn't drop him now. So we said, 'We're sticking with Michael,' and that was that."

With De Palma out, the film was dead. And it continued to be, even when Dustin Hoffman heard about the project and said he might like to do it—not an option, as far as Jaffe and Lansing were concerned, because that would mean abandoning Douglas. They had an actor nobody wanted and a script in which no one believed.

Then ICM agent Diane Cairns read the screenplay and sent it to her client, Adrian Lyne. The British director of such films as 1980's *Foxes* and 1983's *Flashdance* was at home in the south of France when he received the package and sat down on the stone steps of his farmhouse to read it. He finished the whole thing without moving.

"I went and woke my wife up," he remembered. "I fell in the bed and said, 'Listen, if I don't fuck this up, I know this is a huge movie.'"

Lyne arranged to meet with Jaffe on his next trip to New York. But the producer had just seen Lyne's latest film, *9½ Weeks*, an erotic drama about an art gallery employee and a Wall Street trader, and was appalled. He hated the subject, and loathed the look Lyne had given it, with staged smoke that wafted through each room.

"This could be the shortest meeting in the history of this business," Jaffe told him when they met. "Adrian said, 'Why?' I said, 'Number one, I don't want the smoke alarm to go off in the theater. Number two, we're not doing a sneaker commercial.' Then he looked at me and grinned, and we spent about two hours talking."

At the end of the meeting, Jaffe called Lansing, ecstatic.

"He said, 'I can't wait for you to meet him,'" she recalled. "He said Adrian was everything we'd talked about. And our film came back to life."

A KEY PIECE of the puzzle remained: casting Alex. "The role was critical, because she had to be sexy but vulnerable, a career woman who had her act together but could still completely collapse," said Lansing.

At the beginning, she had felt that Gallagher, the male lead, would be the hardest role to fill; after all, finding someone who would remain sympathetic after cheating on his wife was no mean feat. But now she realized that casting his mistress was equally challenging.

Her first choice, Barbara Hershey, was unavailable. Another possibility, French actress Isabelle Adjani, did not speak enough English. Debra Winger, Susan Sarandon, Michelle Pfeiffer and Jessica Lange were all considered or turned the role down. One actress did so with a vengeance. "Judy Davis flew in from Australia to test, and then tried to talk Adrian out of doing the movie," said Lansing. "Adrian called me to meet her, and she said, 'This is the worst piece of shit I've ever read.'" Melanie Griffith was also in contention, newly a sensation thanks to the 1986 comedy *Something Wild*. But the filmmakers feared that what she had in sexuality, she might lack in gravitas.

Cheers star Kirstie Alley read for the role, and while she was not cast, she contributed a unique element to the finished film. "Her husband [actor Parker Stevenson] had been stalked by a woman who camped outside their house and made their lives hell," said Lansing. "Kirstie had saved a tape of the woman's calls and gave it to Adrian. You could hear the woman crying, and you could hear people talking downstairs as she begged to be part of this man's life. Adrian ended up using it verbatim in the scene where Dan listens to Alex's tape."

The options were fast running out when agent Fred Specktor urged the filmmakers to meet one of his clients, Glenn Close.

The actress was in her mid-thirties and therefore the right age for the part, but she was not known for her sex appeal, and Hollywood still thought of her as Robin Williams's earth mother in her debut feature, 1982's *The World According to Garp*.

"There was a debate about her sexiness," said Douglas. "They gave me the most beautiful wife you could imagine [Anne Archer], and the whole thing was, how could you leave this gorgeous woman for Glenn Close?"

Lansing dreaded the idea of bringing in anyone to whom she would have to say no, and for some time resisted all of Specktor's entreaties to meet with his client.

"I overcompensated for how poorly I'd been treated as an actress," she said. "I often felt so bad during auditions that I'd pop my head into the waiting room and tell anyone who was waiting, 'We're almost ready.' I didn't want an Academy Award nominee to read for us if we were going to say no. Fred pursued us doggedly. He begged us to let her come in for a meeting, and we kept begging him to leave us alone. But finally we gave in."

Three months before the start of principal photography, Lansing,

Jaffe, Douglas and Close gathered in the small office that Jaffe kept at Paramount, under a turn-of-the-century poster of San Francisco's Sutro Baths, with Lyne videotaping the audition as Close performed her scenes with Douglas. She had changed her look for the meeting: her hair was wild and so were her clothes.

"My hair was long and I didn't know what to do with it," Close explained. "I didn't know whether to put it up or tie it back in a ponytail. I finally said, 'Fuck this,' and I let it go all crazy."

"She just knocked it out of the park," said Douglas. "She already had the Medusa hair. It was a Glenn you'd never seen before."

"She was dangerous, vulnerable, sensual and erotic," said Lansing. "We were all blown away. By the end of the meeting, we knew she had to have the part."

IN FALL 1986, shooting got under way in New York. At first, everything went well on the $11.6 million film: the production hit its marks, and Lyne avoided his tendency to make things look too smoky, with the occasional nudge from Jaffe.

"Stanley's got a good shit detector," said Douglas. "Did he always have to be as tough as he came off? No. But he was concerned about making something the best—both he and Sherry were, and their passion for the project was immense."

The producers, like their director, wanted the film to be as believable as possible, and at times their efforts to ensure realism bordered on the comic, not least in the scene where Archer finds a dead rabbit boiling on her stove. It was a real rabbit—already dead, procured from a butcher.

"We tried to take its innards out to make it real," said Lyne. "But then it didn't have any heft. It was just like a little bit of skin. So we had to boil it with all of its innards, and the stench was beyond belief. It was ghastly, and that probably helped Anne, because the smell was so bad."

Lyne urged Douglas to make his character believably flawed. "I was trying to get myself in shape," said Douglas. "Adrian said, 'No, no, don't worry about it. I like the way you are.' But then I got a little on the chubby side, and one day in the middle of shooting, he came and said, 'Jesus Christ, Mike! You look like bloody Orson Welles!'"

In the sequence where Douglas and Close make love for the first time, getting hot and heavy in Close's kitchen, Lyne loved Douglas's suggestion that he should carry Close draped around him, and get tangled up in his trousers as they fall to his ankles.

"Adrian thought audiences were uncomfortable watching others have sex, and if you didn't give them something to laugh at, they'd laugh at the scene instead," said Lansing. "He was always looking for something to break the tension, so when Michael came up with the idea of carrying Glenn with his pants around his feet, he used it. I thought it was a bad idea. But I was wrong."

The director had flights of imagination that breathed life into what might otherwise have been a genre piece, but he could also be demanding and obstinate. Halfway through filming, he had a heated altercation with Douglas.

"There's a scene where they're arguing as they go down into the subway, and she says, 'I'm pregnant,'" Lyne remembered. "It's this ghastly moment, and he's struck dumb. It's one of very few scenes where I thought of using a Steadicam, and I'm not crazy about the Steadicam. [When that did not work], I got a circular track and laid it around them, and halfway through I realized that was a mistake, too."

Douglas was furious about the delays. He and Lyne started going at each other.

"I said, 'Let's talk about it,' and we go to the trailer," Lyne recalled. "I start yelling, and he comes right back at me. I thought he was going to murder me. He let me have it more than I was giving him. It was absolutely this cathartic shouting match. He was somebody not to mess with. I remember thinking, 'Fuck, that's his dad in there.'"

"Adrian got nuanced performances from every actor, and had a unique visual style," said Lansing. "He made everything so real. He'd rub his hands together, going, 'How can I make it better? How can I make it better?' But that need for perfection could drive a producer crazy. Stanley would threaten him, 'Shoot the damn scene or we're moving on,' and then Adrian would yell at him. The three of us had operatic screaming fights."

At one point when she and Jaffe arrived on set for a simple sequence with Douglas in a hotel room, talking on the phone, they found that the director had added a maid in the background to make the scene more real, and was in the process of elaborately lighting her. It was deep into the night, the crew had been working the whole day, and everyone was exhausted.

"We were on hour thirteen [of that day's work]," said Jaffe, "and he's shooting this woman scrubbing the floor in the bathroom. I said, 'What the fuck? Are you crazy?'"

MONTHS AFTER PRODUCTION wrapped, a test audience saw the movie for the first time. Its title had changed from *Diversion* to *Affairs of the Heart* to *Fatal Attraction*.

"Word around the studio was terrific: 'The two failures have a success,'" said Lansing. "Then we started to test it."

To her astonishment, the movie received a score of 74 out of a maximum 100, nowhere near the brilliant result she had anticipated. "Must have been a peculiar audience. Maybe it was raining that day," Lansing and her colleagues reassured themselves.

The studio arranged for the film to be screened again, and it performed almost identically. Nor did its score improve during any of the test screenings conducted in different cities by the industry's premier research firm, NRG.

"We did about six screenings," said Lansing. "And at every single screening, when Anne Archer says 'If you come near my family again, I'll kill you,' the audience burst into applause. And Frank Mancuso [the studio chief] comes up to me at the popcorn counter and says, 'I think they want Anne Archer to kill Glenn Close.' And I looked at him, speechless, because I thought he was crazy."

From the beginning, the filmmakers had sensed the ending was not quite right. In Dearden's early drafts, Alex frames Dan for her murder, and the police arrest him for killing her. When Jaffe showed those drafts to a screenwriter friend, Nicholas Meyer (*Star Trek II: The Wrath of Khan*), he argued the ending was too harsh.

"I thought, in the words of *The Mikado*, 'Let the punishment fit the crime,'" said Meyer.

Steel had been keen for him to take over from Dearden, who was clearly burned out. When Meyer resisted, the executive had pleaded with him, upping the ante each time. Finally he'd agreed to work on the movie—but only if she would buy the rights to a novel he wanted to adapt. "We'll buy your stupid fucking book," she told him.

It was Meyer's ending that had been filmed, with a redeeming finale in which Gallagher's wife finds a taped message Alex has left, which exonerates her husband. But audiences hated that ending, and after a final screening at the Directors Guild of America, Steel's boss, Ned Tanen, was blunt about Close.

"They want us to terminate the bitch with extreme prejudice," he said.

"Adrian went nuts when he heard that," said Lansing. "He felt that changing the ending was kowtowing to the lowest common denominator, and I agreed. Here was this wonderful film about how all your actions have consequences, and now they wanted to change the whole point. I felt it was morally wrong, and if I agreed to do it, I'd be selling out."

Only Jaffe was open to Tanen's suggestion, but the others resisted him fiercely. Then the executive offered a compromise: he would give the filmmakers $1.5 million to shoot a new ending, no strings attached. "He said, 'Look, shoot it, and if you don't like it, you don't have to use it,'" Lansing recalled. "That was brilliant. How could you say no? I would later use that tactic constantly, whenever I was at an impasse with a filmmaker."

She brought out Dearden once again to rework the ending, and picked him up at the airport. "He sighed and said, 'It's never going to end, is it?'" she remembered.

Everyone knew Close's character had to be killed, but how? Who would do the killing, and under what circumstances? It seemed logical and morally fitting that Douglas should kill her; after all, he was the one responsible for this mess. But somehow that failed to satisfy, and it was only when the filmmakers began to consider his wife, Beth (Archer), that they felt they had their solution. She was the perfect spouse, smart and good-humored, but she had been reactive rather than active for most of the film. To have her, the sole innocent among the lead characters, take this action at the end was nothing if not appropriate.

"We thought of *Diabolique*," said Lansing, referring to the 1955 French thriller in which two women seemingly drown a man in a tub. "Dan draws a bath for Beth, and then goes to the kitchen to make a cup of tea. He doesn't realize Alex has broken into the house. Just as Beth is about to have her bath, she looks in the mirror and sees Alex, but the whistle of the kettle drowns out her scream. It's only at the last minute that Dan hears her, runs upstairs, and drowns Alex in the bathtub. When she pops out of the water, alive, Beth finally shoots her and kills her."

Douglas was on board, but Archer was appalled at the thought of scrapping the scene she liked best, when her husband is carted away by the police. She had been pleased with her performance, a high point in the original shoot, as she reacted to his arrest. Now she was being told the scene would no longer be in the movie. "I burst into tears," she said. "My whole life and career and heart were on my sleeve. I felt like a little kid. Sherry held me in her arms and just comforted me. God love her, she held me tight for as long as I needed."

Close resisted the changes even more vocally than Archer. She felt sympathy for Alex, a woman battling mental illness, and fiercely resisted clichés about another female psycho. And so she categorically refused to do the reshoot.

"She came into Stanley's office, and we couldn't even get through the conversation with her," said Lansing. "Adrian and I were already consumed with 'We're selling out, what have we done?' She looked at us as if we were the most terrible people on earth, and Adrian just said, 'I give up, you're right.'"

Dearden and Douglas stepped in. "I had to pretend it was a great idea," said Dearden. "I had to sit there and tell her what the new ending would be, and tears were running down her cheeks. Glenn said, 'You can take me in a straitjacket, but you can't make me do it.'"

"I had a big talk to her about the theater, and how you take a show out of town and play the show to out-of-town audiences, and then you adjust, based upon what works best for the audience," said Douglas. "The argument was, 'It may not be the best for your character, but it's best for the movie.'"

Close rejected that out of hand, along with all the other arguments. "I remember screaming at Michael, 'How would you feel? How would you feel if they did this to your character?'" she recalled. "He said, 'Babe, I'm a whore.'"

Ultimately, a friend tipped her into saying yes.

"I was desperate," she remembered, "and I called William Hurt, and he said, 'You've done your fight. You've made your point. Now it's your responsibility to buck up and just do it.'" At last Close consented to film the new ending, and agreed to a three-week reshoot, although she never came around to liking the version she filmed.

"We went back to [the Gallaghers' house], and other people had bought it, so we had to reconstruct it just the way it was," said Lansing. "It cost a fortune. Glenn had the worst of it, by far. She was dunked in the bath more than fifty times, and her eyes and nose became infected. But she gave it her all. She was a total professional."

Back in Los Angeles, Lyne assembled a rough cut and then called Lansing into the editing room to show her what he had done. She took her seat at his side and watched the new ending unfold, as Archer enters the steaming bathroom, glances in the mirror and jumps at the sight of Close.

When Archer jumped, "I jumped, too," said Lansing. "I leaped right out of my seat. I'd seen every single frame; I'd been there for every day of the shoot; I knew this inside out, but I was riveted by the whole thing."

FATAL ATTRACTION OPENED on September 18, 1987, and held the number one spot at the box office for eight consecutive weeks, remaining in the top ten for almost six months. The movie earned $156.6 million domestically.

Time put Douglas and Close on its cover and called Fatal "a nightmare parable of sex in the '80s." Still, feminists and many critics loathed it. "It's about men seeing feminists as witches, and, the way the facts are presented here, the woman *is* a witch," wrote the *New Yorker*'s Pauline Kael. "This shrewd film also touches on something deeper than men's fear of feminism: their fear of women."

It had never been Lansing's intention to demonize women. "This was one woman, not all women," she believed. "This was one career woman, not all of them."

Critical attacks failed to quell the movie's momentum, which peaked when it received Oscar nominations for Best Picture, Best Actress (Close), Best Supporting Actress (Archer), Best Adapted Screenplay, Best Director and Best Editor. Douglas alone among the key participants was shut out.

Lansing attended the Oscars as a nominee for the first time. "I went with my friend David Goodman," she recalled. "I felt like a princess. The telecast opened with a montage of the red carpet, and when the announcer said, 'Here's the beautiful Sherry Lansing,' I couldn't believe it. I turned to David and said, 'I don't care what happens. I can go home happy now.'"

Fatal lost the Best Picture race to *The Last Emperor*. Still, she said, "It was one of the greatest nights of my life. We'd bet on ourselves and won."

CHAPTER 10

Lansing's next film would explore a woman's point of view more thoroughly and sympathetically than any she had worked on before.

Reckless Endangerment—which later became *The Accused*—was the story of a rape, and the second project that Ovitz had counseled her and Jaffe to drop when they were struggling. It was inspired by a real-life event that occurred in March 1983 at a bar in New Bedford, Massachusetts, where Cheryl Ann Araujo, a twenty-one-year-old mother of two, was attacked by a gang of men who dragged her across a pool table and sexually assaulted her as others, allegedly, stood by. The ensuing trial became one of the first high-profile cases to get massive television coverage on the nascent CNN, and most media outlets named the victim, which incensed Lansing and many other viewers. In all, six men were charged and four incarcerated.

"I was interested in two things," said Lansing. "One was the guilt of the bystanders. You had a group of guys cheering on a gang rape. Were they as guilty as the rapists? And what would a jury think? I drew parallels to my mother's childhood in Germany. And second, I was worried about the double victimization. When a woman was raped, it was always her fault: 'She must have done something to deserve it.' Effectively, it was as if she'd been victimized twice, first by the rapists and then by whoever blamed her for the rape."

Lansing had been disturbed by her own response to an assault she had witnessed while driving, when she glimpsed a couple arguing on the sidewalk, then saw the man slap the woman and pull her behind a tree. She swiftly turned around, but the couple had vanished. What would she have done had they still been there? Would she have gotten out? And then what? She played the incident over and over in her mind.

It was Paramount's Dawn Steel who had first mentioned the Araujo story to Jaffe and Lansing, and with her blessing they hired former *New York Post* reporter Tom Topor (*Nuts*) to write the script, which focused on the fictional relationship between a district attorney and her blue-collar victim, and their decision to bring charges against the witnesses as well as the rapists.

When Jane Fonda said she wanted to make the film, Lansing was delighted. Now it would be easy to get the picture made. But Fonda insisted on replacing Topor with another writer, *Nashville*'s Joan Tewkesbury, and wanted the story to be told from the point of view of the DA, the character she would play.

"We had a script that nobody wanted to make, and Jane said she wanted a writer to help with her character," said Lansing. "That seemed reasonable, so Tom was replaced without really being given the chance to prove himself. He was angry, really angry, which I understand."

Over the course of a year, Tewkesbury went through multiple drafts, and everything seemed to be moving forward when Fonda called Lansing to say she was dropping out. She had decided to do another picture, 1986's *The Morning After*, instead.

"I was furious," said Lansing. "I was angry and hurt and frustrated. I knew that if Jane pulled out, our whole movie was going to fall apart. So I lashed out. I tried to make her feel bad by telling her she was the one who'd wanted to change the writer. I said, 'You're supposed to have integrity. That's what you're all about.'"

Fonda listened politely but did not relent. "She said, 'I'm sorry you feel that way, but I just don't think the movie is ready,'" recalled Lansing. "She offered to read the next draft, but I told her we were moving on."

Only many years later did she recognize that Fonda was right. "We weren't a 'go' movie," she said. "The script wasn't right yet, and when something else came along with a director she'd approved, Sidney Lumet, it was understandable if she wanted to do it. That was part of my induction into the business. It was part of growing up."

With Fonda out, *Reckless* languished, and the script was rejected by almost every director Lansing approached. In desperation, she and Jaffe mentioned a B-list name to Paramount's Tanen, and he looked at them askance. "Have you actually seen his film?" he asked. Sheepishly, they retracted the suggestion.

The movie went into deep freeze until Jonathan Kaplan approached Lansing out of the blue. The young filmmaker had drawn warm reviews for 1983's *Heart like a Wheel*, and asked to direct.

Lansing was skeptical. Kaplan had only one low-budget credit to his name, and would be jumping from that to a major studio release. But Jaffe supported him. "Stanley said, 'Look, there comes a time when you're either going to make the movie or not,'" she said. "He thought we should just go ahead and meet."

When they got together, she liked the big, bluff and emotional Kaplan at once, despite his blunt assessment of the script.

"I read these drafts and said, 'You guys drove this into the ground,'" he recalled. "Jane basically took control of the draft, did what she wanted to do. I know Joan. I've known her for years. She's a lovely woman and a great writer, but she had to take dictation from Jane, and Jane got exactly what she wanted."

The Tewkesbury-Fonda script had eliminated the best things about the original idea, he argued. "The rape victim became less central, and it was all about the lawyer. It was such a microcosm of what's wrong with the studio development system: they needed a star, and the star had her own point of view, and they ended up boring themselves to death by over-rewriting it. Sherry said, 'I know.'"

Lansing showed him the previous drafts and allowed him to judge what he liked without trying to steer him one way or another.

"Sherry didn't indicate her point of view to me at all, even in the music in her voice," said Kaplan. "She was very fair. She just said, 'Here are the drafts. I'm not going to give you three years' worth of reading to do, just the most significant.' She gave me five scripts to read. I really loved Tom's second draft. I said, 'Why isn't he rewriting?' She said, 'Well, it was really hard to fire him, and he's furious at us and he's furious at everybody.'"

Kaplan urged her to bring Topor back, and Lansing agreed, which meant placing herself in the exquisitely uncomfortable position of returning to the disgruntled writer, cap in hand.

"That was the first time I got to see her in action," said Kaplan. "I was listening to her talk to him on the phone. She just charmed him right back in. First she left a message for him—'I know you're furious at us, and you have every right to be, but we've got Jonathan Kaplan, and he loved, loved, loved your draft. And I gave him your second draft and he loved that even more.' Then he called back, and she was just brilliant. She let him vent—and it was easy, because basically she agreed with everything he said."

Lansing had a somewhat different recollection: "I remember trudging up the stairs to Tom's apartment, a long flight of stairs. And I said, 'I beg you to come back!' And he was suspicious, and he was tough. But he agreed."

Steel was willing to green-light the picture with Kaplan onboard, given that it would only cost around $8 million. But the executive found herself in the minority among a phalanx of Paramount men.

"Dawn didn't have quite enough power to just green-light it," said Kaplan. "And the others [at the studio] would never have made this movie on their own."

The Paramount brass wanted a brand name attached to star, and so Lansing sent the script to Kelly McGillis, who had risen to fame with 1985's *Witness* and solidified her stardom with 1986's *Top Gun*. "Choose any role," she told her. McGillis chose the attorney.

"She said, 'Whoever plays Sarah, the rape victim, is going to win an Academy Award,'" Lansing remembered, "but she wanted to be the lawyer."

As with *Diversion*, the filmmakers preferred a different title. All liked *J'Accuse*, a term drawn from French novelist Emile Zola's open letter in defense of the jailed army officer Alfred Dreyfus, and so the movie became *The Accused*.

Now they needed an actress to play the rape victim. Some candidates

did not seem right; others were unavailable or simply said no. Weeks before filming, the picture's casting director suggested Jodie Foster. Neither
Paramount nor the producers were convinced.

"They thought I was still this child, and sort of a pudgy teenager," said
Foster. "They'd forgotten that years had gone by [since then]. They pretty
specifically said, 'No, we're not interested.' And I just kept bugging everybody." She agreed to do a screen test. "They made a deal. It's called a 'test
deal.' Basically, you agree that you're going to test, and then if you get the
movie, you're only going to be paid [whatever has been arranged]. But I
had to beg to make that happen."

Cloistered with Kaplan, McGillis and the producers, Foster delivered a
powerful audition. And yet doubts remained. Jaffe and Lansing were concerned about the hard edge she had given her character, and asked her to
come back a second time, adding insult to injury. "Jonathan told her to be
sweet and vulnerable," said Lansing, "and Jodie agreed to try, though she
told us it was hopelessly wrong."

That second audition won them over, but not the studio.

"Our biggest problem was the boys' club at Paramount," said Kaplan.
"There were lists [of actresses' names] they submitted, lists that we submitted, and so on. Here's what came from the boys at Paramount: 'We
really don't think she's rape-able enough.'"

That confirmed all the stereotypes *The Accused* was trying to fight. But
Steel was adamant the picture be made, and bulldozed her fellow executives into consenting. "She said, 'I'm making this fucking movie, no matter what,'" said Kaplan.

When McGillis threatened to quit if Foster were not cast, Paramount
backed down, and just before filming was due to start in April 1987, Foster
got the part.

A ROADSIDE BAR in Vancouver was chosen as the location for the rape
sequence, and Kaplan kept his shooting schedule flexible so that Foster
could decide when she was ready to film it. Only twenty-four years old,
she was petrified by the scene.

"I was scared to prepare, so all I did was hang out with my friends, read the script once, and went dancing," she said. "[I was] going out way too late at night, and just painting the town red to escape what I had to do. Which was perfectly in character. I was a kid, and it was hard."

At one point, her mother had to intercede. "Sherry and Stanley called her and [said], 'You really should come up here, because she's a little weird,'" Foster recalled. "I was in the bar, drinking, having a fantastic time with all the actors from 21 Jump Street, who were filming at the same time. My mom got on a plane and came to rescue me. Even though I had worked my whole life, I hadn't really been away from home without my mom for that long. It took a lot of getting used to. I was doing something that was emotionally difficult, and there I was all by myself. It's still hard for me [to shoot away from home], and I've come up with all sorts of interesting rules and structures to figure out how to do that and not be a casualty, how to not be depressed and act out and do weird things."

Early in the shoot, she walked on the set in a slinky T-shirt and short skirt, and said: "Let's rape."

Lansing and Jaffe cleared away extraneous crew members, and Kaplan shot the scene using two cameras, with McGillis present for moral support. The sequence had been planned with great precision, "but it was still brutal on Jodie," said Lansing. "Her arms and legs were black and blue with bruises. She lost her voice from crying out for help." The male cast members took it just as hard. "They were sensitive guys, and they were doing something on film that they couldn't ever fathom doing in real life. They were having nightmares. They couldn't handle the intensity."

Lansing felt enormous stress during the shoot. "I ended up with lock-jaw," she said. "A doctor put me on a liquid-food diet, and I had to do exercises to keep my jaw from locking closed."

AT THE FIRST test screening, some audience members cheered the rapists on. "Then I saw the test numbers," said Lansing. "The movie had scored a 42, one of the worst results in Paramount's history."

"[Marketing executive] Sid Ganis comes up and says, 'Well, I'm afraid your weird little movie just isn't going to be seen,'" said Kaplan. "'Weird little movie!' But the numbers were awful. Sherry was furious—I've never seen her like that, furious but controlled. She turned to the Paramount people and said: 'We're doing this again. We're going to test it with just women. No men allowed.'"

"I said, 'This isn't a true test of the movie,'" Lansing explained. "I told them, 'What happened here is an aberration. These comment cards are asking people if they'd highly recommend this movie to everyone. Would I highly recommend it? Of course not—it's disturbing. But that doesn't mean it isn't powerful.'"

She reminded the Paramount brass: "In this audience, there are women who've been sexually assaulted, and they aren't going to talk about it in front of men. No woman in a focus group is going to say, 'I was raped.'"

The studio agreed to a second screening, which Lansing attended without a single male colleague. The results were far better, and revealing.

"Out of twenty women in the focus group, eighteen had had an experience with rape, either themselves or a sister or a cousin or someone they knew, and a good third of them had experience with gang rape," said Kaplan. "And that's just a random twenty women in Southern California. Sherry was moved. When she came out, she'd been crying. It became something far more than a screening."

That not only reminded Lansing of what was right with the film, but also showed her what was wrong. She realized she and her colleagues had erred in pushing the early scenes with Foster too far. "In trying not to make her seem like a debutante, we'd made her dislikable," she said. "Even women at that screening felt that her dancing was so provocative, maybe she deserved to be raped."

It was clear the original cut of the film had gone in a wrong direction. Kaplan reluctantly acknowledged he needed a fresh set of eyes, and a new editor, Jerry Greenberg, was brought in. Lansing sat at his side as he went through the movie, shot by shot, scene by scene, studying all the material that had not been used, then observed in awe as bit by bit he stitched it back together into a more coherent and powerful narrative. It was the first time she had truly understood how much a film could be built or broken in the cutting room, and the beginning of a lifelong love of the editing process.

Foster, who had been unhappy with aspects of her performance in the previous cut, was thrilled. She had blamed herself for being unable to give Kaplan the variations he wanted in each take during the courtroom scenes.

"I felt terrible about it," she said. "I felt stupid, and 'What's wrong with me?' I was like, 'I'm going to grad school. I'm clearly not a very good actress.' Then the new editor saved my life and saved the movie."

Lansing was delighted with Foster's performance, no matter what the actress thought. "Sometimes she would do one take that was tough and one take that wasn't, one take that was vulnerable and one that was not," she said. "We'd picked the wrong take every time and not allowed the character to build an arc. When I sat down with Jerry, he had all these strips of film and looked at everything. He saw the whole movie in his head and reconstructed a performance that was always there."

Once he had done so, Lansing was left with a new challenge: how to overcome Foster's fears in promoting the movie.

The actress' life had been thrown into upheaval when John Hinckley Jr., a mentally unbalanced man of twenty-five, attempted to assassinate President Reagan in March 1981. Obsessed with Foster ever since he saw her play a child prostitute in *Taxi Driver*, he had stalked her at Yale before turning violent in a bid to get her attention. He was found not guilty by reason of insanity. Seven years had passed, but the firestorm had not entirely abated.

"It was a serious concern," said Kaplan. "Jodie never stayed in the same place for long, even years after *The Accused*. I'd go to dinner with her, and she loved to cook, and it would always be a different place. We had to have a security guy with her in Vancouver all the time. Brandy [Almond, Foster's mother] was very, very specific about what Jodie would and wouldn't do. Sherry negotiated with her, but they had serious security concerns, because there was a whole subculture of Hinckley groupies who had gone from being in love with Jodie to hating her."

In the end, Almond agreed that her daughter would take part in an extensive and highly personalized campaign that would take her to different cities across the country.

"We wanted to go on a road tour, which hadn't been done in years," said Lansing. "So Paramount got us this little plane, and we'd land in a city and spend a day there, then fly to the next."

During their expeditions, Lansing got to know Foster better. She had sensed a growing gulf between them on the shoot, when Foster and McGillis seemed to side against the producers. It was the rebels versus the authorities, and Lansing regretted having been too authoritarian—on one occasion even insisting that McGillis wear a business jacket for a scene, against the actress' wishes.

"I pulled rank," she said. "And that led Jodie to see me as too imposing. I was so concerned with every little detail, I didn't know when to let go, and Jodie was put off either by my obsessiveness or my delivery. I remember Stanley saying to me, 'This is not a sword to fall on.' I went, 'Yes it is,' because I didn't know. Also, Jodie had gone through quite a dance to get the role, and waited forever for us to make a decision. There was a divide, with her, Jonathan and Kelly on one side, and us on the other."

Lansing had yet to master the diplomacy that would become her hallmark. "I didn't know what was important and what wasn't," she said. "Everything was life and death. I hadn't yet learned that you have to pick your battles."

Squeezed together in the little plane as they shuttled from one city to another, the producer and stars began to talk about life away from work, and Lansing was shocked when McGillis revealed she was a rape victim.

"I was sitting next to her on a flight across the country," Lansing remembered. "She said, 'I was raped. And I'm thinking of going public.' Jonathan knew, but he'd never told me. I can only imagine the emotions she must have gone through watching that rape scene when it was filmed."

In a November 1988 *People* magazine cover story titled "Memoir of a Brief Time in Hell," McGillis described how two men had forced open her apartment door, just after she took a shower. She was a young woman studying acting in New York. "One was very tall, the other was short, and they were both physically strong," she wrote. "I'll never forget the way they smelled—like alcohol and old sweat. I felt panic. It was as if time had stopped, and I was desperately trying to assimilate what was happening." She screamed and went for the phone, but one of the men grabbed her and yanked the line out of the wall. "It was clear that one of the intruders had come to rob and the other had come to rape," she continued. "Almost immediately the taller one undid his trousers and crudely demanded oral sex. I refused. He tried to hit me on the head with a beer bottle but caught my shoulder instead. I kept screaming, and they yelled, 'Shut up!' Then they stuck a knife in my face and forced me into the bedroom. The shorter one demanded money and jewelry. I kept thinking, Be rational, you can talk your way out of this. So I kept saying, 'You can have my money and anything in the apartment, just leave when you're done.'"

The revelation of McGillis's ordeal helped propel the film forward, and when it opened on October 14, 1988, it earned $32 million domestically, a substantial sum in relation to its budget.

In February 1989, Foster was nominated for a Best Actress Oscar, her first nomination since *Taxi Driver*. Her joy was tinged with regret that nobody else from the picture was nominated. "It was just me, by myself, running around Mr. Toad's Wild Ride," she said.

In late March, at the 61st Academy Awards, Lansing looked on, delighted, as *Rain Man*'s Tom Cruise and Dustin Hoffman came onstage to present the Best Actress Oscar. After naming the nominees—Glenn Close for *Dangerous Liaisons*, Melanie Griffith for *Working Girl*, Meryl Streep for *A Cry in the Dark*, Sigourney Weaver for *Gorillas in the Mist* and Foster for *The Accused*—they announced that Foster was the winner.

"There are very few things: there's love and work and family," Foster said in her acceptance speech. "And this movie is so special to us because it was all three of those things. And I'd like to thank all of my families . . . And most importantly my mother, Brandy, who taught me that all of my finger paintings were Picassos, and that I didn't have to be afraid. And mostly that cruelty might be very human, and it might be very cultural, but it's not acceptable. Which is what this movie's about."

WITH *FATAL ATTRACTION* and *The Accused*, Lansing and Jaffe were back in the studio's good graces. At a time when other producers were struggling, their contract was renewed for three years. "We received one of the richest back-end deals in town," said Lansing. "As the profits rose on a hit film, our share would escalate exponentially."

She was at her happiest since MGM and perfectly in tune with Jaffe as they moved on to other films, from 1989's *Black Rain* (reuniting them with Michael Douglas on a thriller set in Japan) to 1992's *School Ties* (a passion piece that Jaffe planned to direct, about anti-Semitism in a boarding school). It was *Rain* that tested their mettle the most.

"When we got to Japan, it was far from ready," said Douglas. "I was being a little crabby and bitchy. Sherry was not happy and let me know it. I remember those eyes getting big, and her saying: 'You're being nothing but self-destructive. I don't need this. I don't need your bullshit.'"

There could be moments of levity, despite that. In a bid to distract a local shopkeeper so that the crew could keep filming beyond the tightly restricted hours the authorities allowed, Lansing started chatting up a diminutive but ferocious local, doing her best to charm the woman while the crew lined up a shot—only for the woman to start kicking her in the shins and literally brushing her out of her shop. "I remember this little shopkeeper with a broom, sweeping Sherry out: 'Go, go, go!'" said Douglas. "Sherry was a foot taller than her. She was like, '*What are you doing?*'"

Another time, when Lansing was in a taxi with Jaffe and Douglas, the three became so engaged in their conversation they failed to realize the taxi was heading to Tokyo, three hundred miles away. "We screamed at him, 'Stop! Turn around! We said, *screening room!*'" said Lansing. "But the more we screamed, the less he understood." As they tried harder and harder to make themselves clear, it all seemed so absurd they started to laugh, and dissolved in tears at the back of the cab, puzzling the driver even more. Finally Lansing spotted a phone box and got the driver to pull over—only to discover that the instructions were in Japanese. "We were hysterical," said Jaffe. "The three of us were crying on the floor of the backseat. But at last we remembered how to say the name of our hotel and the driver turned back."

Filming in Japan was near-impossible, hindered by a thicket of arcane rules and endless bureaucracy, all of which Lansing had to navigate. But it became clear here as never before that she was truly her partner's equal, which her *Accused* director Kaplan had believed from the start.

"Sherry and Stanley had this amazing partnership," he said. "They were both interested in the stories and the casting, and Stanley was totally interested in the photography and had a really good eye. He was also a great line producer [in charge of the day-to-day details of a film], while Sherry was interested in taking care of the actors and making sure that everything was working properly. She got the best out of him. That's what she's brilliant at: she recognized what his talents were. She knew how to handle him."

After eight years together, Lansing was confident their relationship would continue for decades, when Jaffe came to her with a bombshell.

"I WAS IN New York in March 1991 when Stanley called and said he needed to see me," Lansing recalled. "He came over and told me he was leaving to become president of Paramount Communications [the renamed Gulf + Western]."

The news hit her hard. Throughout their years together, she had never doubted that Jaffe would tell her the truth. But now she realized that for days, and possibly weeks, he had harbored a secret as he negotiated to become the second-ranking executive in one of America's top media companies.

"We used to talk a dozen times a day," said Lansing. "We'd pour our hearts out, pushing through movies that no one else wanted to make. That was our way of life. And now it was ending. I could barely talk. I felt betrayed. I felt completely out of control. I was afraid I was going to cry. But I didn't want him to see it. I hated the thought that he'd feel sorry for me, so I didn't show what I was really thinking. It was like someone telling me, 'I don't love you anymore.'"

"The day I told her was one of the hardest of my life," said Jaffe. "I wasn't allowed to talk about it before, and probably I should have because

I could trust her, but I didn't. It was tough. I said, 'I have to take it. I just can't let this opportunity go,' which was selfish. It was hard. I did her a disservice."

His departure confirmed Lansing's worst fears: that even the strongest bond was liable to break, the safest relationship crack into pieces. Life was evanescent; everything that seemed most solid could melt into thin air.

"People will go only so far with you, and then they're gone," she reflected. "I'd been with Stanley for years, but in the end he had to do what was right for him."

SHE CONSIDERED FINDING another partner. But nobody held Jaffe's appeal.

"It's a lonely feeling to have nobody to talk to," she said. "I missed Stanley, his mind, his humor, his friendship. I missed having an equal partner. I missed bouncing ideas off him. He made me better, and I hope I made him better, too. But there was nobody to replace him."

Closing the company's New York office, she consolidated her staff in Los Angeles, where she faced the immediate challenge of finding a director for *School Ties*, which was about to go into production, with Jaffe no longer available to direct. In his place she hired a young filmmaker named Robert Mandel, casting Ben Affleck and Matt Damon in two of their earliest roles.

Rather than isolate herself, she plunged deeper into work, both professional and personal. Her nonprofit activities engaged more of her time and helped lift her above her anguish.

"One of the most moving experiences I had was visiting City of Hope, a hospital in Duarte, California, that made free care available to patients with cancer, leukemia and other blood disorders," she said. "Even with all the sick people there, they had an incredible optimism. Outside a doctor's office, there was a sign I never forgot: 'They said smallpox was hopeless. They said tuberculosis was hopeless. They said polio was hopeless. Cancer is only a disease.'"

Earlier, she had joined the board of the American Association for Cancer Research, and later she would serve on the board of the Albert and Mary Lasker Foundation, a group advocating medical research, particularly related to cancer. Along with these activities, she became more involved with Big Sisters of Los Angeles, which paired struggling girls with adult women as their mentors.

Her work with Big Sisters took her into the inner city for the first time since she had left teaching. She discovered a realm apart, just miles from the perimeter of Hollywood and Beverly Hills, where the children seemed to inhabit a different emotional and financial landscape. Crack cocaine had decimated their neighborhoods; poverty and a prison epidemic had made any notion of stability illusory. What she saw shook her all the more as she met the young boys and girls for whom this was everyday life and the teachers who struggled to help them get through it. If her mother's death had been the catalyst in her fight against cancer, so her experiences with Big Sisters galvanized her to fight for improvements in education.

Most of the Big Sisters girls were black or Hispanic, often from single-parent families whose lives had been destroyed by narcotics or physical and sexual abuse. One girl had grown up in foster homes because of her mother's dependence on drugs, and yet somehow had done well enough to win a place in college—even as she shared a room with three other foster kids. Another girl had to look after her sister's baby at the same time as trying to study, while living under one roof with multiple families, mostly illegal immigrants. She dreamed of majoring in engineering at a good university, but how could she ever get accepted, with no time for her schoolwork, no money and no papers?

"These girls often didn't have mothers, or their mothers had serious problems and couldn't look after them," said Lansing. With her friend Sarah Purcell, she set up an endowment, the Future Fund, to provide scholarships allowing hundreds to go to college. Watching the big sisters, "I saw how one person could change a whole life, how if you committed yourself to help, you could touch their lives forever."

———

SHORTLY AFTER HER split with Jaffe, Lansing got a call from their *Fatal Attraction* director, Adrian Lyne, asking her to join him on a new film, *Indecent Proposal*. Once again she was caught in the maelstrom of making a movie.

Proposal had begun as a novel by Jack Engelhard that posed a simple but spellbinding question: would a married woman sleep with a stranger for $1 million? The project had been developed by two young producers, Alex Gartner and Tom Schulman, who had stripped away some of the book's more political elements. Unlike the novel, whose male protagonists were an Arab and a Jew, the screenplay by writer Amy Holden Jones centered on a yuppie couple badly in need of money, who consider a billionaire's offer to have sex with the wife.

"It didn't read as well as *Fatal*, but I remember thinking it was a terrific idea," said Lyne. "The idea, 'Would you fuck somebody for $1 million, and if you wouldn't, would you do it for $5 million?'—the morality, or lack of it, around that question was just marvelous."

Lyne was keen to bring in an experienced producer to join the relative newcomers Gartner and Schulman, and he turned to Lansing.

"Adrian said, 'There's something about this. I'd like you to look at it,'" she remembered. "The script was very dark and twisted, but it had that kernel of a great idea. I knew we were on to something when I was at a dinner with some women and asked what they thought, and they said they'd definitely sleep with a guy for $1 million, as long as he looked right. The men were outraged, and everyone got into a big argument."

Negotiations commenced for Lansing to take over the movie. These were tough, unsentimental talks, and she insisted on being the sole producer, with Gartner and Schulman as executive producers, knowing she ultimately would bear the responsibility. Neither was happy (though Gartner was staggered by the amount Paramount paid him to take a lesser credit), but Lansing knew this was business as usual. "By then I'd grown up," she said.

Lyne wanted to make some script changes and brought in William Goldman, one of the industry's leading screenwriters (*Butch Cassidy and the Sundance Kid*, *All the President's Men*). "I remember meeting him in a large, rather gloomy apartment at the Carlyle Hotel," he said. "He was concerned about his posture, so every doorway had a single word over it, like 'tall' or 'upright.' I thought that would be great in a movie."

Lansing took Goldman at his word when he said he could fix the script in two weeks. "He was the hottest writer in the business," she explained. But when the revised screenplay arrived, the producers' hearts sank.

"Tom, Adrian, Sherry and I sat with Goldman on the speakerphone, marking up the script," said Gartner, "and I went home and literally, with scissors and glue, cut-and-pasted his draft into Amy's. I remember everything spread around my bed, and my wife and toddler watching me cut this script together, and that went to Goldman. He took another pass at it, which I believe was his last."

WARREN BEATTY WAS offered the lead, but as so often in his career, he hesitated. "Warren did his usual dance," said Lansing. "I don't think we ever got an answer."

Lyne, in any case, was keen on a more rough-hewn actor or at least one who would add a genuine sense of danger, and suggested Tommy Lee Jones. But Jones had a reputation for being prickly, and Lansing favored Robert Redford.

Despite everything she had been through on *The Verdict*, she remained eager to work with him, and felt he had both the magnetism and the innate sense of class the role required. Lyne was vehemently opposed, afraid a star of his magnitude would overshadow the young couple and tip the entire balance of the film so that audiences no longer cared about them. His arguments with Lansing became so passionate that he almost left the film—he even quit at one point, but days later, he was back and agreed to meet with Redford.

"We went to his office in Santa Monica," said Lansing, "and Redford walks in and says, 'Hi. It's really nice to meet you, Adrian.' He was warm and charming and gracious. We talked, and he said, 'I'd really like to do this movie. Would you like me to do it?' And Adrian goes, 'Well, uh—yes.' He didn't realize he was giving him the part."

Redford's star power had faded in the six years since his last genuine blockbuster, 1985's *Out of Africa*. Many were dubious about his continuing box office appeal, and Paramount balked at paying him "full freight," the multimillion-dollar fee he might otherwise have commanded. When the actor refused to do the movie for less, the two sides were at an impasse until CAA convinced him to lower his payment in exchange for a larger share of the profits. Redford received $5 million and 15 percent of first-dollar gross—that is, 15 percent of the revenue the studio received from movie theaters.

"Redford worked for a fraction of what he normally made," said Lansing. "He eventually made a huge amount of money"—close to $40 million, sources said.

With their star locked in, Lansing and Lyne set about casting the young couple. One by one, some of the best-known young actresses of the day traipsed through their offices.

"Adrian is a great admirer of beautiful actresses, and he tested every beautiful actress at the time," recalled Gartner. "Oh my goodness! Sophie Marceau, Irene Jacob, Nicole Kidman." Rather than these, however, the director settled on the last actress to audition for him, Demi Moore, fresh off two big hits, 1990's *Ghost* and 1992's *A Few Good Men*.

Then he had to cast her architect husband. The role was problematic: if the man were too wishy-washy, he would run the risk of seeming weak; if he were too firm, he might appear harsh. Lansing argued for Woody Harrelson, but "Adrian wouldn't even see him," she said.

Harrelson was best known for playing Woody Boyd, the not-so-bright barman of NBC's *Cheers*, and Lyne continued to resist until he saw his new film, *White Men Can't Jump*. By then it was too late: Harrelson had committed to another picture, MGM's *Benny and Joon*. It was a much smaller project, but a deal was in place.

Three weeks before *Indecent* was due to start principal photography, Harrelson ditched *Benny* for the Paramount film, and MGM sued the studio for more than $5 million, just about *Benny*'s entire budget. Alan Ladd Jr., the former Fox executive, was now running MGM and knew the long-term consequences he would suffer if he allowed a star to pull out of a deal: it would mean any star could leave any project whenever he or she wanted.

"I said, 'Fine, we'll let you leave, but we'll also sue you,'" Ladd recalled.

Paramount settled for half a million dollars. But Harrelson got to make *Indecent Proposal.*

IN JUNE 1992, the cast and crew assembled in Las Vegas, where they would stay for two months before moving to Los Angeles.

"We all sat around this long table—Adrian, Stanley, Woody, Demi, Redford and myself—and they did the read-through and it was perfect," said Lansing. Any doubts Lyne had had about Redford vanished; his casual, comfortable reading took the director's breath away, as it did Lansing's. "I couldn't take my eyes off him," she said.

Then Redford asked for a meeting.

"We get a call—'Mr. Redford wants to see you'—and we go up to his suite," said Lansing. "I thought he was going to tell us he didn't like something in the script. But he said, 'I want out.'" Lansing couldn't believe what she was hearing. "He said, 'The kids are wonderful, but I'm not. It's their movie.' I said, 'Bob, you're amazing.' And he said, 'That's very kind, but I have to leave.'"

The more Lansing argued, the more he stuck to his position. "We were dumbfounded," she said. "But we couldn't laugh because he was so serious."

Worried that Paramount would shut down the movie if she lost her star, she asked CAA to intervene, and ran through a list of possible replacements. The agency suggested a simple solution: bring in another writer to make script changes that might allay Redford's concerns. "They discussed that with him, and he agreed," said Lansing.

While the search began for a writer, the various parties knuckled down and worked on the script themselves.

"It was a huge moment," said CAA's Bryan Lourd. "Doc [agent David

O'Connor] and I were representing Redford at the time. Sherry, [Paramount executive] Karen Rosenfelt, Doc and I were writing scenes to convince him to do the movie."

CAA understood its client well, and realized that a general malaise was not unusual among stars, especially ones on the brink of tackling an important role. "He was never leaving," said Lourd. "He knew what the movie could be and was committed to getting it right."

He suggested hiring Robert Getchell (*Alice Doesn't Live Here Anymore*), whose empathetic nature made him a perfect fit for the mercurial Redford.

The writer was baffled. "He said, 'The script is wonderful. I don't know what to change,'" recalled Lansing. "I said, 'I agree. So here's what I'm begging you to do: write whatever he wants, but make sure there's nothing you add that we can't cut out in the editing, if we need to.'"

Getchell accepted and flew to Las Vegas, where he ensconced himself in a hotel room and got down to work, adding a snippet of dialogue here, a new sequence there, but nothing so fundamental that it could not be eliminated in postproduction.

Days later, Redford was a man transformed. He thanked Lansing for bringing in the writer and assured her things were going fine.

"I wasn't sure if he lacked confidence or if he just wanted to be certain his character was fully fleshed out," she said. "He'd say things like, 'I don't understand the part,' and then deliver an amazing reading."

She was struck by Redford's acting gift, especially when shooting the scene in which he first meets Moore. "He did it a couple of times, and then said, 'Just a second,' and took out a pen, and started crossing things out of the script until all Getchell's additions were gone," she recalled. "Then he smiled and said, 'You're right. It worked just the way it was.'"

During the sequence where he makes the "indecent proposal" at the heart of the film, "I crouched in the back of the room to watch," she said. "When Redford delivered the line, offering Demi $1 million to spend the night with him, he just threw it away, as if he was asking to borrow a jacket. A bad actor would have paused and delivered it sotto voce. But Redford made it lethal by his casualness."

"What he did, as only a brilliant film actor can do," said Lourd, "was subtly rewrite the script through his performance—not by putting pen to paper but by how he played things. He made you care about this character who was the most horrible guy on the planet. Later, when we got to see the rough cut, Sherry called and said, 'He's now the sympathetic center of the movie.'"

TO EVERYONE'S SURPRISE, Redford was almost always punctual. "I know this will sound crazy: he wasn't difficult at all," said co-producer Michael Tadross. "He said, 'What do you need from me?' and I just told him [where to be and when]. He was only late one day through the whole movie."

On that particular day, the film was shooting in Watts, part of the inner city of Los Angeles. Lyne had insisted on filming there over Lansing's objections because he wanted to use a real-life classroom. This was at the height of gang warfare, and extra security had to be brought in.

"You needed an escort just to get to your trailer," said Lansing, "and then Redford left the set to go off and do something, and nobody could find him."

Tadross was so frustrated by the slowdown, he started pounding his chest in mock-rage. "He said, 'Jesus Christ! What am I doing here?'" Lansing remembered. "There were gang members going by in their souped-up cars. And he thumps his chest, shouting: 'Shoot me! Shoot me!'"

Hours passed, and still Redford did not appear. When word spread finally that he was back in his trailer, safe and unharmed, "Demi was so angry, she marched into his trailer and lectured him," Lansing recalled. "She said, 'You obviously don't like working with me.' He said, 'What do you mean?' She said, 'You're disrespecting me, the crew and the movie.'"

Redford listened, chastened. Five minutes later he reemerged, "and from that day on he arrived early, and he was completely charming," said Lansing. "When we'd break for lunch, I'd shoot him a look and he'd say, 'Don't worry, boss. I'll be back before you know it.'"

———

LANSING WAS SURE she had a hit, but test audiences again disagreed. "Every screening was worse than the last," she said. "The results were a disaster."

She tried to reedit the film with Lyne, but "we couldn't find the movie. Adrian shoots a lot and does a lot of takes and gives many, many possibilities. Then it's a question of: Do you keep this scene or not? Do you move it here or put it there? We couldn't find the arc that would make you root for the couple. Each time we thought we had it, we realized it wasn't right."

The more they worked, the further off they seemed. "We would test it on the Paramount lot," said Gartner, "and sometimes [one part of] the movie would be playing while we were still mixing reels in the cutting room, and we'd run the other reels down to the theater. Then we'd cut all of the next day and test it again the next night."

Women walked out, nauseated by some of the darker moments of the film, which included scenes in which Harrelson fantasizes about Moore having sex with Redford. "They just couldn't handle it," said Gartner.

Little by little, the less palatable elements were removed, while other sequences were restored to make Harrelson more sympathetic. "You had to care for the couple," said Lansing. "That's everything we were trying to do. But the scenes with Redford were so good and so romantic, it took a long time to find the right balance."

While they were editing, word about the film began to spread, eliciting a flood of negative responses. Patricia Ireland, then president of the National Organization for Women, said it demeaned women, even though she had not seen the movie, while Peg Yorkin, chair of the Feminist Majority Foundation, called its premise "disgusting."

"The most astonishing aspect of this picture is that it has made so many people of such varying views so apoplectic," wrote Elizabeth Kaye in the *New York Times*. "Last week, a local Manhattan news show interviewed [sex therapist] Dr. Ruth Westheimer, who categorically stated that the picture cheapens love. . . . One station conducted man-on-the-street interviews with men who stated categorically that the picture demeans them. In the *New York Post*, society columnist William Norwich reported that the English author Barbara Cartland 'has gone ballistic.' 'The whole idea is absolutely disgusting, degrading and vulgar,' Mr. Norwich quoted Ms. Cartland as saying, 'and no woman with any pretensions to being decent would do it.'"

The film's billboard stoked anger even further. It showed Moore lying half naked in a pile of cash, seeming to suggest that a woman was for sale. Anonymous opponents unleashed their rage on Lansing, plastering a picture of her face over Moore's on billboards across Los Angeles.

"It was so personal," said Lansing. "I felt completely humiliated."

When the critics got to see the movie, they savaged it, and its fate looked certain: this was a large-scale flop. Then, curiously, even as the film was being pilloried by liberals and conservatives alike, by art-house reviewers and mainstream pundits, the public's interest grew. The sheer venom the picture provoked made it more intriguing. Audiences wanted to see what the fuss was all about.

When *Indecent* debuted in April 1993, ticket buyers flocked to the theaters and the movie opened to $18 million, a monstrous number for a spring weekend. Redford's career was redeemed. "[That] was a whole reconnect for him in pop culture in a huge way," said his agent, Lourd.

Like *Fatal Attraction*, the movie had penetrated the culture. And like *Fatal*, a controversial theme had given Lansing a massive hit, proving that even without Jaffe, she was among the most capable producers in the business. She was at the height of her powers and she knew it. The uncertainty she had felt in her youth had melted away.

"I was night and day from the woman I'd been before," she said. "I knew how to produce, and I wasn't scared."

CHAPTER 11

With all of Lansing's success, something was missing.

Her brother and sisters were married now, and even Norton, after Margot's death, had found happiness with a new partner in Florida. They were spread across the country, each living full and varied lives, while Lansing was alone.

"I took a hard look at my life and career," she said. "I knew the choices I'd made kept me happy and sane. But I was lonely and I didn't want to stay alone."

In the years since her 1970 divorce from Michael Brownstein, she had never remarried. True, she had had boyfriends, some remaining in her life for years, and yet none had become a life partner. She had spent seven years in an on-and-off relationship with Wayne Rogers, but they were an imperfect pair at best. He saw the world in black and white, she in shades of gray. Her passion for her work added a further strain.

"Studio executives, at that particular time in my life, represented an amorphous sort of group that blended together," said Rogers. "I didn't see anything individually exceptional about any of them."

After Lansing's appointment at Fox, Rogers's irritation with her life-style grew more marked, not least when a reporter arrived at Lansing's house for a lengthy interview and he had to cool his heels, waiting for her to finish. This became a pattern. Once, when they decided to live together,

Lansing felt a wave of panic at the mere sight of his jacket in her closet. He moved out almost as soon as he'd moved in.

"We were like two ships passing in the night," he said. "She was addicted, to a certain extent, to the responsibility of the job, and that was her first priority."

Their relationship sputtered to an end in 1982, though they remained friends.

"Wayne was a very talented actor and a great businessman," said Lansing. "He was intellectually curious and had a tremendous love of life. He was volatile and passionate and unconventional, but he couldn't handle my work. After him, I came to believe I was never going to find anyone, because I couldn't stop working. I thought every man I met was going to take something away from my life rather than add to it. With each man I felt a loss of self, rather than an increase."

THIS WAS LANSING'S state of mind in March 1991 when she was invited to an Academy Awards party at the home of real estate developer Richard Cohen.

It was a small affair by Hollywood standards, with a few dozen people gathered for the most glamorous night of the movie year, all casually enjoying each other's company without having to dress up or ferry themselves to the ceremony.

As Lansing stepped into the den with her friend Martha Luttrell, she noticed a man wearing aviator-style glasses, but did not recognize him. This was unusual because he was one of Hollywood's most famous directors. His name was William Friedkin, and at fifty-five he had already made two classics, 1971's *The French Connection* and 1973's *The Exorcist*. He had won an Oscar for the former while still in his mid-thirties, and was part of the dizzying array of talent that had emerged in the 1970s to alter the landscape of film, along with Francis Coppola, Woody Allen and Martin Scorsese. One of the guests introduced him.

"You can't be William Friedkin," said Lansing. "You're much too young and much too cute."

"And you can't be Sherry Lansing," he replied with a smile. "You're much too cute and much too young."

Their connection was immediate. As they sat down to speak, an easy conversation that roamed across a number of subjects—none of them related to work—Lansing was charmed by Friedkin's wit and his flashes of brilliance.

Her first husband, Michael, had been a good girl's idea of a bad boy, but Friedkin was a bad boy par excellence. He had once raced a car through the streets of New York, shooting a chase scene for *French Connection* at such a speed that he put his life and others' in danger, all for his art. On another occasion, after winning the Directors Guild of America award, he stepped off the stage and saw his onetime employer, Alfred Hitchcock. Remembering how Hitchcock had chastised him for not wearing a tie on the set of *The Alfred Hitchcock Hour,* he snapped his elastic bowtie at him. "How do you like the tie, Hitch?" he quipped.

He had worked with many of the same people as Lansing, and even been in the same places at some of the same times. He had once slipped late into a screening of *The King of Comedy* and asked a friend if he'd missed anything. "Just Sherry Lansing giving her welcome speech," he was told. Another time, he had met with Jaffe in the office right next to hers, but Lansing was too busy to say hello.

Both were Jewish and from Chicago, but their overt similarities ended there. Luck was on Friedkin's side that night, however: he not only won the Oscar pool (*Dances with Wolves* was named Best Picture) but also got Lansing's number.

The following week, while out of town, he called her every day, and their conversations lasted for hours. On their first date, he whisked her to San Francisco, where a car was waiting at the airport to take them to Muir Woods, the Marin County nature preserve he loved.

"We drove to the Rockridge market in Berkeley, ordered some stuff, went up to Muir Woods, and had a picnic," he recalled. "Sherry had a seemingly insatiable curiosity about the things we both liked—many of which, I found out later, she didn't like at all: basketball and classical music. But she was in the moment. Not a lot of people are in the moment."

"I felt I'd known him my whole life," said Lansing. "I could tell him any-thing and he wouldn't judge me. I remember thinking, 'Oh my God, I can present myself fully the way I am.'"

In Muir Woods, they strolled for hours, roaming among the redwoods, staring at the endless blue of the Pacific Ocean, wandering along its path-ways until the last squibs of light faded on the horizon, and still they were there. "We just kept talking and talking," said Lansing. "It was magical."

That night, she called Luttrell.

"I think I'm in love," she said.

SOME OF HER friends were dubious. This was a man with three failed marriages, who even now was in the midst of a divorce.

Herbert Ross, the director whose wife had once scorned Lansing's vi-cuña coat, "launched into a litany of complaints about him at a dinner," she said. Ross was aware they had gone on a date, but did not know more. "He told me how Billy had left all these women brokenhearted and how no woman could ever tame such a beast." Only then did it sink in: Lansing was in love. "Oh my gosh!" said Ross. "I just made him more appealing."

If, in normal circumstances, Lansing worried too much about other people's opinions, she never let them influence her here. "I'd gotten to the point where I didn't give a damn," she said. "I thought, 'This is the man I love, and if you don't like it, I don't care.'"

Many were skeptical, said John Goldwyn, then Paramount's produc-tion chief. "[Agent] Sue Mengers was the only person who said, 'Sherry, you'll never be bored.' She was in love with him. She was absolutely crazy in love with this guy. She had these relationships with men that never went anywhere [including architect Richard Meier and Italian count Giovanni di Volpi], but Billy was tough. She found an excitement with him and she absolutely believed he was a genius."

Three months after they met, the couple decided to marry in Barba-dos. They went alone, without family or friends, and arrived unprepared.

"I wanted a Jewish ceremony," said Lansing, "so when we got there we looked through the phone book and found the number of the only synagogue on the island. But the synagogue was a historic landmark with no congregation, and we were told the rabbi wouldn't be there for six months."

With some trepidation, she agreed to let a local priest officiate, on the condition that the ceremony be nondenominational. When the wedding got under way on the beach, however, the priest could not help himself.

"We are gathered here," he began, "in the name of our lord and savior Jesus Christ—"

"Stop!" yelled Lansing.

"What's wrong?" asked Friedkin.

"Didn't you hear?" she replied. "He said, 'our lord Jesus Christ.' We're Jewish!"

The priest started over, and made the same mistake.

When he did so a third time, Lansing grabbed his Bible, whipped out a pencil and crossed out the word "Jesus."

"I was beside myself," she said. "I wanted our marriage to be real."

MARRIAGE INEVITABLY ALTERED Lansing's life. "Part of me was scared it would ruin our relationship," she said. "But I was happy in a way I'd never been happy before. There weren't enough hours in the day to be together. For the first time since childhood, I'd found unconditional love."

Until now, she had buried herself so deeply in work, it was impossible to think of anything else. Moving forward, she had to create a new life as part of a couple, helped by the fact that Friedkin never seemed to mind if she came home late from a meeting or had to fly out of town for a film. He was a filmmaker, too, and nobody better understood the topsy-turvy nature of the movie business.

Their life could seem glamorous but also startlingly normal. "I went to Lakers games with Billy," said Lansing. "I also went to the symphony, though after the first couple of times I was so bored I started bringing scripts to read on my lap."

She had no illusions that marriage to Friedkin would resemble anything she had known before, or that she could transform him into the sort of Boy Scout her friends might have liked. She made no attempt to change him, nor did he attempt to change her.

"He made me feel adored," she said. "I could gain fifty pounds and he'd still think I was the prettiest woman in the world. I didn't have a face-lift, I didn't do anything—and if I did, he'd have said, 'Oh my God, why would you change the *Mona Lisa?*' He's a complicated man; I'm not going to say he isn't. But he's very romantic, and he's one of the kindest people I've known. He's a genius, and geniuses think differently, and that's the fundamental difference between him and almost everybody else I was with."

Once, when Friedkin was being particularly demanding, a friend shrugged it off. "You married real talent, not a fake," he told Lansing. "You have to deal with all the craziness and the screaming and the yelling, but he's the real thing."

Marrying Friedkin, she inherited a family. He had two sons by different women, and she was determined to make them part of her life. She remembered only too well how abandoned she had felt by the men who came courting her mother, who disappeared from her own life once they vanished from Margot's, and she also recalled her exclusion from the enchanted circle that Margot and Norton had formed. She would never allow that to happen here.

She became a mother to Jack, eight, and Cedric, fourteen, and the younger son began to divide his time between the couple's house and his other home, though Lansing was at pains not to damage the boys' ties to their biological mothers. "The greatest bonus Billy gave me was these two children," she said. "They were guileless, they were kind, they were fun. They were just a joy."

Jack started coming to her office after school, sitting in an alcove where she would help him with his homework before they drove home together. "We'd have dinner as a family, and I'd think, 'This is what my friends have been talking about all these years,'" she said. "I always thought people were bullshitting about what it was like to be truly loved. I thought, 'It can't be that good.' But it is."

There was a downside, of course. During her filmmaking years, Lansing had loved nothing more than going on location, escaping the confines of her office and visiting an exotic locale where she would become part of the film crew family. But now "that lost its allure," she said. When she left Los Angeles to shoot *School Ties*, "most evenings, I'd just go back to my hotel and crawl under the covers and call Billy."

His absence left a gaping hole, deeper than she had imagined. She could not face another prolonged absence. Something had to change. But what?

JAFFE HAD BEEN at Paramount Communications for a year and a half and was just coming to terms with the fact that one of his boldest decisions had backfired: hiring Brandon Tartikoff as chairman of Paramount Pictures.

On paper, the appointment seemed inspired. Tartikoff, the former president of NBC Entertainment, had been among the most brilliant television executives of his era, responsible for launching *The Cosby Show* and lifting NBC to number one in the ratings. But he was a creature of the small screen, not the large, and at Paramount he discovered the chasm that separated the two.

Film, in this pre-franchise age, was all about creating a single piece of entertainment so compelling that audiences would leave their homes to watch it on a Friday or Saturday night. Television was about filling a programming slot. The men and women who worked in each medium existed in separate but parallel universes.

Tartikoff's skills lay in TV, not film, and his pictures reflected that. "He would have these crazy ideas for movies," said Michelle Manning, a senior Paramount production executive. "One was called *Squeeze Boxes*, which was like *Glee* with accordions. He also pitched *Copter Cop*, about a motorcycle cop with a propeller."

His indecisiveness infuriated Jaffe, who had run the studio when he was in his late twenties and knew better than anyone how it should function. Their relationship was not helped when Tartikoff took a leave of absence to promote his autobiography, *The Last Great Ride*, and posed in his swimsuit for a magazine photo shoot.

More than anything, his work was hindered by a tragedy. In January 1991, a few months before he joined the studio, he was involved in a car accident that left his eight-year-old daughter brain-damaged. His attempts to cope with her medical and educational needs, especially when she was moved to New Orleans for better care, placed an almost unbearable strain on him.

"I remember coming to his office one day and he was ashen," said Jaffe. "I thought he was sick. I said, 'Are you OK?' He said: 'My daughter came home for the first time, and her friends came to visit. When she was by herself in the hospital, we thought she was making great strides. Then we saw her against the normal children. It broke my heart.'"

The Jaffe-Tartikoff relationship reached a tipping point at a company retreat in Rancho Mirage, California, where each division of Paramount Communications had to make a presentation. Tartikoff was unprepared.

"Brandon said, 'Oh, we just need some clips from the movies,'" recalled Manning. "We were the splashy part, and the first day was Simon & Schuster's presentation, and all of a sudden there's music and there's factoids on the screen. Then after that was the Paramount Parks guy. He just was so funny, talking about rides and people throwing up, and I'm like, 'We are fucked. We are so fucked.'"

Jaffe and his boss, Martin Davis, conferred. "I said, 'This can't go on. This is crazy,'" noted Jaffe. "I said to Brandon, 'I think we should meet up.' He came in the next morning. I said, 'Look, we're going to have to make some changes. I'm going to get more involved until we get this ship righted.' Brandon said, 'I just think I should leave.'"

Within days, he was out and Jaffe turned to Lansing. Would she become chairman of Paramount Pictures?

"I'd had two other offers, to run a studio and a mini-major [a company with the money to make movies and distribute them]," she said, "but I'd never made it past the appetizer before saying no. Now things were different. The key issue was quality of life. I wanted to enjoy my marriage. I wanted to be back home for dinner. With this job, I'd be based in L.A., I'd be more in control and I wouldn't have to travel as much."

For days she wavered, reluctant to go back to corporate life even as she felt this was the best solution. Friedkin encouraged her to do whatever she thought best.

"I remember the two of us meeting with [Jaffe]," he said. "He told her, 'Make sure Billy is OK with this.' I said, 'Don't even take me into account.' I said to Sherry, 'If you want to do this, you should. If you don't want to do it, you shouldn't.'"

In weighing her decision, Lansing remembered a friend's advice: at Harvard Business School he had learned that a person should reconstitute herself professionally every ten years.

"In the end, I applied the same question I did when I thought of getting married: would I regret it if I didn't?" said Lansing. "So I accepted, on certain conditions: marketing and distribution would have to report to me, and I would have to have green-light authority, though I'd always consult with Stanley."

Jaffe said yes to both demands, and on November 5, 1992, less than a week after Tartikoff's resignation, the trade press and major newspapers broke the news that Lansing had been named chairman and CEO of the Paramount Pictures motion picture group.

Once again, she was the highest-ranking woman in film.

CHAPTER 12

Twelve years had passed since Lansing was named president of Fox, and the landscape for women had altered—if not quite irrevocably, at least for the better. She was still a pioneer in the eyes of other women, but not quite the leader of a revolution.

Women were still nowhere near equal to men in the uppermost sectors of Hollywood, nor were they doing any better in America's largest companies: only 19 of the 4,012 highest-paid executives were women, according to a 1990 survey in *Fortune* magazine. But they were rapidly ascending the ranks.

"A decade ago even women's staunchest male advocates said time had to pass; women lacked the seasoning and seniority to run the show," noted *Fortune*. "Today that explanation rings increasingly hollow. Women have gained access to virtually every line of work and are bulging in the pipeline. The U.S. Department of Labor says they make up 40% of a loosely defined category of managers and administrators that covers everyone from President [George H. W.] Bush to the person running the local Dairy Queen."

In the entertainment industry, several women held senior positions and were ready to progress further. A 1991 study commissioned by the nonprofit group Women in Film showed that women held 30 percent of middle-management posts in the top twenty film and TV companies, holding 378 jobs in all. Within a few years, they would become familiar presences in the corner offices of networks and studios alike.

Indications that a tectonic shift was under way were all around. After more than a decade in which Lansing and Steel had stood in splendid isolation at the epicenter of power, others were starting to join them. Lucy Fisher, a few years Lansing's junior, was an executive vice president of production at Warner Bros. and would soon become vice chairman of Columbia-TriStar Pictures, a division of Sony. Amy Pascal was executive vice president of production at Columbia, already on her path to being chairman of the studio. And Stacey Snider was president of production at TriStar and later would be named chairman of Universal Pictures and also 20th Century Fox. Only an increasingly frail and contrarian rear guard still considered these women upstarts or dared to treat them with the kind of condescension that was routine in Lansing's formative years. As far as the majority of industry members were concerned, women were here to stay.

"It didn't feel that things were utterly impossible, but at the same time there were very, very few role models," said Snider. "I didn't know how hard it had been for other women, because I came of age when women had pushed out the boundaries."

That, at least, was in the executive field. It was another story in different sectors of the entertainment world, and Lansing was endlessly baffled that the strides made by women executives were not matched by the writers, directors, cameramen, editors and other technicians who toiled on the shop floor. Why had women grasped the gold ring in one arena but not all? Was it that motherhood interrupted their careers? Or was it that Hollywood, to all appearances the most liberal of enclaves, was in fact deeply averse to change?

The promise that rippled through Hollywood in the early 1990s proved fleeting. A decade later, the surge had plateaued, and a 2016 report by USC's Annenberg School for Communication and Journalism noted that only 15.2 percent of directors were women, along with 28.9 percent of writers and 22.6 percent of the creators of television series. In film (as opposed to television) only 3.4 percent of movies were directed by women. Over the course of a quarter century, things had hardly improved at all.

Lansing rarely paused to reflect on such matters.

"I certainly experienced prejudice in my life," she said. "But by the time I got to Paramount, things really had changed. I didn't experience any sexism there. How could I say I did? I was getting fair pay, and I was running the place, and whenever we came to hire a writer or producer or executive or director, we never thought about whether it should be a man or a woman. We hired the best person for the job, man or woman, pink or green."

WITH LANSING IN place, a new sense of urgency coursed through the studio.

From day one, she was on the phone, in meetings, reading scripts, studying budgets, cutting trailers, attending screenings. Her decisiveness contrasted with Tartikoff's lack of it.

She had developed a style of her own, with a gracious manner that did little to hide the firmness. She knew that each person and situation had to be handled differently. "Some people respond to cajoling, others need emotion and still others need strength," she said.

She drew deeply on her instincts as an actress. The same intuition that had propelled her to be curious about her characters made her wish to understand the men and women she worked with, knowing that few people were as complicated as artists. At the same time, some inner force kept pushing her to make things better.

"I had a need to make everything as good as it could be," she said. "It was something I was born with, a desire, a compulsion."

In luring her to the studio, Jaffe had promised the work would be easy. This would be a year of sequels, he said, a time when Paramount could cruise to victory simply by winding up the mechanical toys in its box and letting them chug to the finish line. Then Lansing met Tartikoff to discuss the transition, and he opened a binder revealing the status of the studio's projects.

"It wasn't that Brandon had left bad stuff," she said. "He'd hardly left anything."

She summoned the senior production team to a meeting. These were the men and women charged with shepherding pictures from inception to completion, from the faintest wisp of an idea through to the finished, multimillion-dollar product. They were a motley crew, mostly in their twenties and thirties.

There was Goldwyn, the president of production, a tall and lean scion of Hollywood whose ferocious ambition was fueled by his need to escape the shadow of his legendary family. There was Karen Rosenfelt, the daughter of a former MGM chairman, whose rumpled presence and squeaky voice belied her intellect. There was the solid, down-to-earth Don Granger. And there was Manning, a film buff and USC film school graduate who had worked for Coppola and Tanen and directed a film of her own, 1986's *Blue City*. She was the only one who did not know Lansing. "I'd never met her," she said. "I was a worker bee doing my job."

Lansing offered words of support. "I said none of them were going to lose their jobs," she recalled. "I wanted to assess everyone's strengths and weaknesses. I thought they were good and believed they could be better."

IT WAS CRUCIAL to get at least one franchise film out of the gate this first year, but Lansing hit a wall.

Mike Myers's debut feature, *Wayne's World*, had come as a bolt from the blue, an unexpected hit that earned $183 million around the world when it was released in early 1992, far more than Paramount had expected from a low-budget riff on the character he had created for *Saturday Night Live*, a metal head with a cable-access show.

On-screen, Myers was an endearing personality, but offscreen he was more nettlesome. He trusted only his wife and alienated some of his strongest supporters, including his agents, who would bemoan his unerring ability to call them at the worst possible time, usually minutes before they were due to leave the office. He had rubbed his fellow *SNL* cast members the wrong way by creating a backstage character named Fucky, who would moon them and dry-hump some of the women. He was insecure, introverted and often insensitive, as phobic about physical contact as he was about the emotional kind. Fans loved him, Paramount did not.

Lansing was willing to overlook his flaws until a legal affairs executive told her about an act of carelessness in the creation of *Wayne's World 2*.

"He had based his script on a classic English movie from 1949, *Passport to Pimlico*," she said, referring to the Ealing comedy in which a group of British citizens declare their own tiny country. "One of our lawyers discovered weeks before the movie was scheduled to go into production that nobody had ever bought the rights."

"Mike had always wanted to do *Passport to Pimlico* as the basis of *Wayne's World*," said Lorne Michaels, the *SNL* executive producer who also produced *Wayne* and its sequel. "We toyed with that in the first go-around. So he went and wrote it. I think he believed the studio understood that, and I think he even believed they had bought the rights to the other movie so that he was free to use it."

It would take months to acquire those rights, assuming Paramount was able to buy them at all, and the discovery threatened to topple the project. If the film had been shot, the *Pimlico* rights holders could easily have gotten an injunction to stop its release. And yet the studio was moving full steam ahead, with promotional materials in place, a release date, and a massive campaign under way.

Myers blamed Michaels, who was also the movie's producer, for failing to obtain the *Pimlico* rights; others pointed a finger at Myers himself.

"Whoever was at fault," said Lansing, "it was clear we had a problem. There was only one person who could solve it, and that was him."

Calling an immediate halt to work on the film, she summoned Myers to her office, along with his managers and Goldwyn.

"Going into that meeting was like the Bataan Death March," said one participant. "It started fine, and then she went crazy. She said, 'How dare you? How dare you put us in this position?' She turned to Mike and said, 'We'll sue you. We'll take your fucking house. You won't even own a fucking home.'"

"Mike came in wearing a T-shirt and tennis shoes and sat on a couch, looking forlorn," said one of the others present. "He said: 'This is the movie I want to make. If I can't do this script, I'm not doing the film.' Then she let him have it. She said, 'Let me tell you something. As we're sitting here, there's a team of lawyers assembled in Stanley Jaffe's office that has nothing better to do than figure out how to sue you for everything you're worth.'"

"She made up this fabulous story about all of the lawyers sitting with Stanley Jaffe," said Goldwyn. "She said, 'As I'm sitting here with you, there's a team figuring out how they can take every single thing away from you.' The guy literally went into a fetal position. Then she got Lorne on the phone and said, 'I want that script even if you have to write it yourself.' He said, 'Sherry, I'm on your side. I get it. You're absolutely right.'"

Lansing turned to Myers. "He muttered, but nothing came out," said one source. "She said, 'If I were you, Mike, I'd go to Lorne's office right now, and stay there until you come up with a new script. We'll slide food under the door.'"

Myers did as he was told, and Lansing got her film shot and edited in time for a December 1993 opening. It did well enough to cover its cost, but was far from the blockbuster she needed.

NOR DID THINGS fare better with another promising sequel, *Beverly Hills Cop III*. The first in the series had taken in a gigantic $235 million domestically, solidifying Eddie Murphy as a superstar. The sequel had also done well, but now the third iteration, which placed Murphy's character, Axel Foley, in a theme park, was in trouble.

Jaffe had refused to give the series' original producers, Don Simpson and Jerry Bruckheimer, final cut, and so they left the project. So did the next producer, Joel Silver, an extravagant bear of a man who specialized in action films such as *Lethal Weapon*, who walked away when Jaffe insisted *Cop III* be made for under $55 million. The picture had a problematic script and a reluctant star, and was rudderless when Lansing took charge. Then Murphy said he did not plan to play it as a comedy.

"At the eleventh hour, a memo comes in: 'Eddie doesn't want to be funny,'" said Steven E. de Souza, one of the writers. "Yes, believe that or not. He was looking at some other actors getting big, dramatic roles, like Denzel Washington, and suddenly he doesn't want to be funny. [He said] 'Take all the jokes out.'"

Lansing had an action movie with no action, a comedy with no comedy. She knew she needed the right producer to salvage this wreck.

In her first week as chairman, she asked Robert Rehme and Mace Neufeld to have lunch with her in the studio commissary. They were strong producers, whose hits included *The Hunt for Red October* and *Patriot Games*, but they were reluctant to take on another picture, as they were about to start a new Tom Clancy adaptation, *Clear and Present Danger*. Lansing insisted. She promised them latitude and authority, their pick of other films, and above all her gratitude.

"Sherry's the greatest diplomat in the world," said Rehme. "It was hard to say no."

The partners agreed that Rehme would concentrate on *Danger*, while Neufeld focused on *Cop*.

"It wasn't particularly the kind of script I liked," said Neufeld, "but there was very little we could do about changing it at that point. All we had to do was reduce the budget."

Lansing's hopes sagged when Murphy's *The Distinguished Gentleman* opened in December and sank like a stone, giving the comedian a fourth consecutive flop, following *Harlem Nights*, *Another 48 Hrs.* and *Boomerang*. Convinced that neither the budget nor the screenplay was in good shape, she halted production a month before shooting. This was the second picture she had shut down in less than two months.

"The script wasn't working," she said, "and they all realized it. There weren't any fights. This was about saying, 'We need more time.'"

The movie resumed several weeks later, after four separate writers were hired simultaneously to fix the screenplay. It failed to restore Murphy's box office sheen or the studio's reputation.

———

THESE WERE BOLD and even brazen moves, not just because they involved putting pictures on ice after millions of dollars had been spent, but also because Paramount's gaping distribution maw needed to be fed.

Hundreds of staff were tucked in offices around the country, and even more around the world, all forced to put their professional lives on hold until these films could be completed, when they would embark on the long, slow process of overseeing their release. Lansing knew they would be anxious and that there would be pressure from below as well as above for her to green-light a slate of movies in no time at all. But she stood firm in the belief that it was better to proceed with caution than rush something forward that inevitably would fail.

Reports spread that the studio had so little in the works it might as well shut down for a year. Phone calls came pouring in, as insiders demanded to know what was happening. And still she bided her time.

"We were dealing with everything from a lack of development to budgets that were out of control," she said, "and in a situation like that, all you can do is keep calm."

A THIRD STUMBLING feature was in the works. *Sliver*, a psychosexual thriller based on Ira Levin's 1991 novel, had been brought to Paramount by Robert Evans, a flamboyant former production chief who had resuscitated the studio in the 1970s with films such as *The Godfather* and *Chinatown* before descending into a haze of drugs and accusations of drug peddling. After leaving his post in 1974, he had been convicted of cocaine trafficking and was in such a bad state that he had contemplated suicide, until Jaffe revived his career by bringing him back to Paramount as a producer.

"I'd met Bob when I auditioned for *Goodbye, Columbus*," said Lansing. "He was a legend. I remember seeing pictures of him and his then wife, Ali MacGraw, and they were the most beautiful couple you could imagine."

Now, however, Evans was a shadow of his former self, as charismatic as ever but no longer the gimlet-eyed filmmaker he had once been.

"He'd gone through horrible things, but there wasn't a mean bone in his body," said Lansing. "I expected someone who was bitter, someone who was manipulative, someone who was tough; instead I met a very kind man. All he wanted was to have a hit movie. He was still hopeful, and he still loved films."

Sliver showed none of the taste he had brought to his more celebrated work. Rather, this was a sensationalist story about a beautiful young woman and the Peeping Tom who stalks her, who may or may not be a murderer.

By the time Lansing got involved, the film was sinking fast. Its stars, Sharon Stone and Billy Baldwin, loathed each other, and one would refuse to act in a scene when the other was shooting a close-up. Stone, reveling in her newfound stardom following 1992's *Basic Instinct*, despised Evans as well as Baldwin. Believing the producer had kept one of her girlfriends locked up in his house, she had him banned from the set.

"Bob would say things like, 'Why wouldn't you just fuck [Baldwin]?'" she recalled. "'Why don't you just fuck the kid? Back when I was doing that bullfighting movie with Ava Gardner [1957's *The Sun Also Rises*], I tried to seduce her. That's how I came in the business. I would fuck people.' Sherry would look at me and put her arm around me and walk me away from it. She'd say, 'Sharon, just come to work and do your job.' She was never invested in continuing to dramatize [a situation]."

Three weeks into Lansing's tenure, things almost turned deadly when a helicopter carrying a cameraman vanished inside a Hawaiian volcano, where he was shooting backdrops for the movie's conclusion. "As an ultimate dare, the [protagonists] fly into the lava," said director Phillip Noyce, noting that test audiences later rejected that ending "because it was so nihilistic."

The director was in Los Angeles when he got a call from the production office telling him, "We've lost the bird," he remembered. "That was the beginning of a forty-eight-hour nightmare. There'd been a malfunction and the pilot had to crash-land the helicopter inside the volcano. The pilot stayed with the helicopter, which was sheared in half. The cloud and sulfur cover closed in, and the cameraman and camera operator decided to try and climb out, but they became enveloped in the vapor and couldn't see. It was a hellish situation."

Lansing waited on tenterhooks to see if every producer and executive's nightmare would come true: the loss of human life. "Sherry was very much in support of us sitting down in the morning, where we wanted, to have prayer and meditation circles for them," said Stone, "because we wanted to send them all our thoughts and prayers."

It took two days before the men were rescued, when a helicopter trawled a net inside the volcano, picking them up and carrying them to safety. Lansing's relief was palpable, but after that filming proceeded at a glacial pace thanks to the time it took to light Stone and a soundstage that creaked during every shot, the result of being built over a swimming pool. Noyce, who had been battling a six-pack-a-day smoking habit, was so exhausted from all the difficulties, he almost collapsed and needed vitamin shots just to drag himself off the floor.

When the shoot was over, he and Evans clashed during the editing, and Lansing was forced to intercede. In usual circumstances, given her background, she would have sided with the producer; but Noyce was reliable, his judgment sound, and Evans was no longer the life force he had been at his peak. She conducted shuttle diplomacy between the two men, while making sure Noyce had the freedom to work.

"Bob at one point asked for an editing room and wanted to take over the cut," said Jaffe. "We said, 'We'll give you an editing room for four weeks.'" Evans spent that entire time cutting two scenes. "We said, 'We've got to see the film.' We [saw the scenes and] they were terrible, terrible."

Meanwhile, the production was thrown into turmoil by the news that Stone was having an affair with *Sliver*'s co-producer, Bill MacDonald. If this had been just one illicit relationship more or less, it would have been manageable, but Stone, Hollywood's resident femme fatale, was caught up in a game of dominoes with some of the movie's other key players. When MacDonald left his wife for Stone, writer Joe Eszterhas left his own wife for MacDonald's and the tabloids had a field day.

"My engagement with Bill MacDonald was very, very brief," said Stone. "Then the team of geniuses came over to my house—Joe Eszterhas and [his agent] Guy McElwaine and others—to tell me what they thought I should do. My thoughts were that I should get very far and very quickly away from all of them. After *Basic Instinct*, the thrill of that success and the greed of that success were really driving people. I wasn't as invested in all of their shenanigans as they were. But I was getting a ton of pressure from everyone. It was very, very hard."

"I felt I was in a David Lynch film," said Lansing. "I'd go into my office like this studious little girl, with my book bag and my scripts. No one would tell me anything. I used to get angry and say, 'How come I'm the last to know?' They'd say, 'Well, you never ask. You come and go, boom-boom, like a machine.' I was so consumed with my checklist of stuff that I'd be exhausted by the time I got home. If someone had stopped and said, 'Do you want to hear some dish?' I probably would have said, 'Let me finish what I'm doing first.' I only found out about the affair late, when Bob told me."

One crisis seemed to follow another, leaving Lansing with no room to breathe, let alone do things the way she wanted. "That's what it's like when you start a job like this," she said. "You're so overwhelmed, you hardly leave your office. There are no movies in place, no marketing plans, no deals, nothing. You just try to keep your head above water."

The first screening of *Sliver* was a disaster; the audience was confused by the murders and turned off by the sex. Lansing ordered the ending to be reshot—replacing the volcano scene with one inside Baldwin's den, where Stone shoots out each TV screen in his high-tech voyeur's hub and tells him to "get a life"—only to find the sets had been scrapped and had to be rebuilt from scratch. Knowing this would add millions to the budget, she nonetheless gave the go-ahead, believing it was her only chance to save the movie.

She sat in the editing room with Noyce, working to fix the film even as the Motion Picture Association of America screened a rough cut and came back insisting on dozens of changes if Paramount wanted to avoid an NC-17 rating. When Lansing called the principal players into her office to discuss alterations, Evans exploded.

"Fuck 'em!" he said, hammering his fist on the table.

He refused to listen, and in a fit of anger stormed out of Lansing's office and strode away across the lot. Suddenly he collapsed with what looked like a heart attack. A studio nurse was called and found his blood pressure registered 215/110. The producer was rushed to the hospital, where he was diagnosed with a case of extreme anxiety.

The filmmakers moved forward with the changes the MPAA wanted, along with the revised ending. "We shot the new ending about a week and a half before the movie came out," said Noyce. "We started making prints of the film on a Tuesday, and they had to be in all the cinemas on the Friday."

Throughout, Lansing clung to the belief that the picture was salvageable. Her experience in editing rooms had convinced her that a movie's problems could almost always be repaired, regardless of their scope. But critics savaged the film and it did dismally at the domestic box office, though it performed strongly abroad, an early indication of the burgeoning international market that would transform the entertainment business.

Despite that disappointment, Lansing stuck to her core belief. "You can never give up," she said. "You have to keep working to make it the best it can be."

THE FIRST SIGN of a turnaround did not come until June 1993, when Paramount had a smash hit with Tom Cruise's *The Firm*, a big-budget legal thriller adapted from John Grisham's novel, though that was largely set in motion before Lansing joined the studio.

Whatever credit she might have received was undermined by a *New York Times* article that slammed her for lavishing gifts on *The Firm*'s filmmakers just when the country was going through a prolonged recession that would cost America 1.6 million jobs. Ironically, Lansing had attempted to emulate the strategy of another studio, Warner Bros., which was famous for bestowing perks on its stars. Anxious to retain their loyalty when her regime was brand-new, she had been too generous, without considering the implications.

"The studio bought new $100,000 Mercedes-Benz 500 SL convertible two-seaters for the film makers and star," wrote the *Times*, which quoted Lansing as saying, "We just wanted to say: 'Hey, thank you. You've worked

tremendously hard. You're special to us. You've gone that extra distance.'"
Those who went the extra distance "were Tom Cruise, the star of the film,
who also received about $12 million and will make millions more from
his share of the gross receipts; Sydney Pollack, the director, who hauled
in about $5.5 million and will also make a few million more from the
grosses, and Scott Rudin, a producer, one of the most prolific and successful in town." Even by the town's "wacky standards," the article concluded,
"the cars bought by Paramount left many executives and agents in Hollywood amazed."

It was the last time Lansing would copy others. From this point on, she
said, "I had to do things my way."

JUST AS LANSING was beginning to feel settled in, on the morning of September 12, 1993, Jaffe called with important news.

"He said our board of directors had voted to merge with Viacom," she
recalled. "Viacom's chairman, Sumner Redstone, and Paramount's chairman, Martin Davis, would head the new entity, and Stanley would be their
first lieutenant, sharing the job with Viacom's president, Frank Biondi Jr."

She listened skeptically. She had been around money men long enough
to know it made little sense that Redstone would allow his right-hand
man, Biondi, to share the job with Jaffe. This was not a merger but a take-
over.

"It sounds like we're being bought," she said.

Paramount's would-be purchaser, Redstone, then seventy, was a shrewd,
driven businessman whose Brooks Brothers suits and Boston accent might
easily have led others to underestimate his skill. A man whose temper
matched his flaming red hair, he had inherited his father's theater business
and built it into an empire, but was most famous for having survived a
1979 Boston hotel fire by dangling from a windowsill until his fingers were
burned raw; he had then spent months in a hospital, enduring agonizing
skin grafts, until he emerged even more ruthless and ambitious than before. He was willful and capricious, volatile and egotistical, and singularly
determined to win.

"All the way back, when Sumner just had a few drive-ins and the multi-plexes were getting started, everybody in the [other] studios gave him the back of their hand," said Biondi. "But [Paramount executives] Bob Evans and Barry Diller didn't. They'd speak to him personally. They'd take him out to dinner. So Sumner had a warm spot in his heart for Paramount. This is like the Yankee bat boy in the 1930s who grows up and becomes wealthy and has the opportunity to buy the team."

Paramount's Davis had none of Redstone's vision and only a fraction of his zeal. He had spent too many years toiling at the feet of his late boss, Charles Bluhdorn, to have enough energy left for his own dreams. Instead of thinking big, he had started to manage small, nitpicking at his employ-ees in a way that inspired loathing rather than loyalty.

At first he rebuffed Redstone, and early talks to merge their companies fell through. But in spring 1993 he heard that other raiders were turning their sights on Paramount, and decided to go with the devil he knew.

Redstone had thought the deal was never going to happen, and had already begun talks to buy NBC instead. He was sitting in his office, wait-ing to hear from Biondi, who was returning from a meeting about buying that network, when his phone rang, and it was Davis.

"We were coming back from [the NBC talks], really excited, thinking, 'God, we potentially have the steal of the year,'" said Biondi, when "Red-stone called and said, 'Get back here as fast as you can!' [He said] 'Marty Davis called me, and the deal is back on.'"

The two parties entered into secret talks. Back and forth they went for weeks, until in early September they closed a deal. Redstone's company, Viacom, agreed to pay $8.28 billion to buy Paramount Communications, putting Redstone at the top of one of the biggest media companies on earth. He was about to join the ranks of the true moguls, alongside News Corp.'s Rupert Murdoch and TCI's John Malone, the place he had dreamed of being for years.

It was "an act of destiny," he declared.

———

BUT NOT IF Barry Diller could help it. Nine years had passed since a clash with Davis had led to his exit from Paramount, and his luster only gleamed brighter.

He had stunned Hollywood by leaving Fox and betting heavily on a shopping network, QVC. Anyone who thought that would keep him happy, however, was wrong; insiders guessed he was biding his time, waiting to assert his place at the top of the Hollywood pyramid.

Lansing knew he was circling Paramount, and knew it would be wrong to underestimate him. She remembered his brilliance. Each time she had asked for more money for a film, he had asked incisive questions about the budget that no one else would have thought of. But his need for control was scary.

"I went into a meeting once when he was still running Paramount," she recalled. "As I was waiting for him, I noticed one of his assistants had pulled a cigarette halfway out of the pack. It was on the edge of the table, ready for him. Everything was so controlled."

Davis, sniffing the danger "Killer Diller" posed, decided to confront him when Diller dropped by his office one day. Was it true, he asked, that Diller was going after Paramount? Diller tried to dodge the question, but Davis was convinced the answer was yes.

A week after Viacom went public, Diller announced he would top Redstone's bid by more than $1 billion, offering $9.5 billion, money he would have to cobble together through a series of loans and partnerships. In doing so, he unleashed a bidding war that would have Hollywood and Wall Street watching amazed for months.

Lansing observed from the sidelines as the bidders played financial ping-pong with her studio and her life. Each week, one would raise his bid, only for the other to go higher.

Financially, this could not have been better for her. "I'd negotiated for the most possible stock in lieu of a large salary, thinking this might happen," she said, "but I never dreamed the numbers would go so high."

Professionally, her life was in upheaval, and so were the lives of her staffers, many of whom were frightened about what this would mean for their careers. They were inundated by calls from friends and sometimes enemies, all whispering the latest gossip.

"You'd be on the phone with an agent and hear him say, 'I heard it's Diller,'" said Manning. "Then someone would say, 'No, it's Viacom.' You'd find the vultures that are in Hollywood. Sherry said, 'Look, one of these guys, or maybe somebody else we've never even heard of, is going to buy us. The best thing we can all do is put our nose down, stop engaging in rumors, and when people want to stir this up, just say, "I'm calling to cast my movie." Let's do our job and everybody will be fine.'"

"I told them, 'Other people's lives are at stake, as well as ours,'" said Lansing. "I said, 'The filmmakers didn't ask for this war. And what will happen is, you'll get distracted and the movies will suffer, and that's the only legacy you have.'"

As Diller gained an edge, both sides did everything they could to line up allies, aware they would need extra funds to close a deal. The price rose so high—above $100 per share—that some of Redstone's advisers begged him to back off, arguing that the stratospheric numbers made no sense. But he was as immovable as the Paramount mountain.

"Sumner said, basically, 'I'm doing it,' pretty much the way he does business, and 'If you don't like it, you can leave,'" Biondi recalled. "It got to the low $108s or $109s [per share], and we were literally out of money because the price had gone up so much."

Diller raised Redstone once again. He was on the brink of winning.

Then Redstone made one of the deftest boardroom maneuvers any of his colleagues had seen, persuading Blockbuster's Wayne Huizenga to merge their two companies, thereby adding enough value that Viacom could raise its tender one last time. He made his final offer—just under $10 billion.

"Diller said, 'I'm done,'" noted Biondi.

If Diller had gone up even the tiniest amount, just $1 per share, Redstone would have been forced to pull out, as he had no more money. But he had won, and Diller had no choice but to withdraw.

"Our current position demands brevity," he said in a February 1994 statement. "They won. We lost. Next."

THE DEAL HAD brought Lansing millions, but it also cast a shadow over her future, and her staff laid grim bets on how long she would survive.

"She was very vulnerable," said Goldwyn. "We were all vulnerable. But Sherry was very matter-of-fact about it. She said, 'I could get a call saying I'm fired. It's not my company, it's theirs. I'm an employee. If they don't want to keep me, they don't want to keep me.'"

Martin Davis was edged aside, and Jaffe was pushed out soon after, in the beginning of what seemed like a mass exodus of Paramount's top players.

"There was a house-of-cards theory," said Rosenfelt, the production executive. "Would Sherry follow Stanley? And would she want to stay without him?"

Days after the deal closed, Redstone flew to Los Angeles to address the troops. Gathering them in one of the studio's theaters, he spoke about his business philosophy.

"He said, 'I'm going to prove that synergy works,'" recalled Goldwyn. Mentioning the different Paramount and Viacom divisions, "he said, 'I want to see MTV and Paramount working together. I want to see Nickelodeon and Paramount working together. We're the Viacom family.'"

That night, Redstone invited Lansing to a private dinner at the Ivy, the fashionable West Hollywood restaurant where insiders went to see and be seen. It was hardly the best place for a private meeting, but perhaps that was what Redstone wanted. He was flaunting his new role as a Hollywood boss. Here, Lansing knew, all of Hollywood would be watching, her body language dissected by the seemingly casual crowd whose impressions would soon cascade through the industry.

Arriving early, as always, she navigated her way through the tables, meeting and greeting the dozens of men and women for whom the Ivy functioned as a second office, until she found herself sitting with Redstone and his colleagues. She was the sole woman among this tight-knit group of men, all dark-suited strangers.

There was the pale and beady-eyed Redstone, his red hair glowing demonically in the candlelight; Biondi, the most laid-back of his adjutants; and two top Viacom executives, Philippe Dauman and Tom Dooley, corporate insiders to the core. Lansing barely knew them, though she had met Redstone recently when both were honored by the American Academy of Achievement, a Washington, DC–based nonprofit.

Still, she knew what she wanted to say.

Weeks earlier, she had attended a company-wide retreat at the San Ysidro Ranch, near Santa Barbara, California, where she gave an elaborate presentation about her filmmaking philosophy. Now she explained this to Redstone and his team.

"I told them about the four points we were following," she said. "First, we were a producer-based company. We truly believed that producers mattered and should be treated with respect, as they brought in the best material. That's why one of the first things I did when I joined Paramount was ask John Goldwyn to create a list of the most talented producers and see who could be wooed."

Second, she said, "scripts mattered above all else. You had to spend time to get the material right before you green-lit a movie, regardless of who was in it, and if the screenplay wasn't working, I didn't believe we should move forward. That was the opposite thinking to some studios that believed stars were the key."

Third, she said, "I felt there was an opening for the sort of midbudget movie that studios increasingly were veering away from, the kind of character-driven dramas that could be made for a reasonable price and would still find an audience"—pictures that were fast becoming anachronisms in a Hollywood that believed bigger was always better.

And fourth, most radically, Lansing said she was beginning to explore a relatively new financial strategy of sharing the cost of individual films with other studios—a break in Hollywood's tradition of pitting one studio against another.

"Because the cost of movies was getting so high, thanks in part to the spiraling expense of marketing," she said, "we believed we could partner with others and share some of the risk. That meant we'd divide the profits, but we'd also protect our downside."

On a personal level, she added that she was used to maintaining close contact with New York, that she enjoyed having a partner and hoped to find one in Redstone.

All this he listened to carefully, nodding but never revealing his cards. Lansing felt his response was positive, but she also knew he was far too wily to tell her everything he was thinking.

Nothing interested him as much as the films themselves. As they spoke, Lansing was pleased to learn how much he knew about them. She did not know that Redstone was a master of due diligence and would routinely call industry insiders—even people he had never met—just to pick their brains on Hollywood.

One film intrigued him more than any other, far from the most high-profile of Paramount's projects. Over and over, he kept asking about the movie, the talent and the marketing plan, and the more they spoke, the more Lansing realized her future was riding on its success.

Its name was *Forrest Gump*.

CHAPTER 13

One night early in her tenure at Paramount, Lansing lay in bed reading, transfixed. When Friedkin asked what was so special, she answered, "The most beautiful script I've ever read."

This most beautiful script was hardly obvious commercial fare. It lacked a conventional protagonist and antagonist; its structure was rambling and even episodic; and it featured touches of magical realism that seemed to belong to a different realm than the quasi-historical world in which it was set, including a trip into space with an orangutan, and animated characters that accompanied the hero on his journey like so many disembodied souls. But Lansing was enthralled.

"I remember how it progressed through time, and finding that fascinating," she said. "And I remember how moving the love story was. This was my generation's story, going back through our history, and we were looking at it through one very unusual man's eyes."

Forrest Gump was the brainchild of Winston Groom, a southern novelist who divided his time between New York and Point Clear, Alabama, where he had grown up. His 1986 novel told the story of a decent but simple-minded fellow with peculiar abilities, and followed him through a series of adventures that took him from Washington to Vietnam, from a fishing boat to the moon.

In the hands of screenwriter Eric Roth, the book's more whimsical elements had been expunged, and the script Lansing read was richer and altogether more ambitious than the novel: a voyage through the second half of the twentieth century that was wry, witty and deeply emotional, if also sentimental.

"The book had its charms, but it was a little more farcical than my taste," said Roth. "[Forrest] weighed 240 pounds and went to the moon with a monkey, and there were all sorts of things like that."

The screenplay he hewed was an exploration of what it meant to be American in a country that had endured a major war (Vietnam), a presidential assassination (Kennedy), a battle for civil rights (Lyndon B. Johnson and Martin Luther King Jr. both appeared in this draft) and the onslaught of AIDS.

Lansing was haunted by many of these things. She had been shattered by Kennedy's death, and indeed had stayed home for days trying to process the assassination. She had seen racism up close in Chicago, some of it directed toward herself as a Jew, some of it toward the black friends she had made at the Lab School. And she had lost friends to AIDS in an industry more afflicted by the disease than any other. "That was the epidemic of our time," she said. "It gave this film a contemporary quality that made its historical parts undeniably relevant."

Forrest had been developed by Warners, but the studio had lost faith in the material after being unable to get it off the ground, and felt it bore too much of a resemblance to 1988's *Rain Man*. Eager to get hold of a Paramount action screenplay, *Executive Action*, Warners made a rare deal: it offered $400,000 and agreed to trade the two scripts.

One of Lansing's top priorities became finding a director to join the movie's producer (Wendy Finerman) and its star (Tom Hanks), both already in place when she started her job. Barry Sonnenfeld seemed perfect to direct. A former cinematographer, he had had a big hit as a director with Paramount's *The Addams Family*. He loved the script, but there was a snag: he wanted to direct the *Addams* sequel, and the movies were on a scheduling collision course. When *The Addams Family*'s producer, Scott Rudin, pressed him to shoot that picture first, "he had to make a Sophie's choice," said Lansing. "He didn't want to turn over those characters to someone else, and his fee for the sequel was three times what he would have been paid for *Forrest*."

Sonnenfeld reluctantly stepped aside, and Lansing looked for a replacement.

"The script went around to any number of directors," said Hanks. "Some weighed in and said, 'Here's what I would do,' or 'If I'm going to get involved, this has to be the nature of it.' But all of that interest never graduated to anybody saying, 'I'm doing this. I want to make this movie.'"

Then Finerman, who had bought the rights to the story when nobody else thought it could work, took it to her friend Penny Marshall, an actress turned director who had worked with Hanks on 1992's *A League of Their Own*. Marshall said she was interested.

Privately, several studio executives had doubts. They warned Lansing that Marshall was too disorganized for a picture of this scale and had no experience with special effects, which would have to be handled with extraordinary care, in ways that had never been done before. In any case, Marshall herself seemed unsure. While she dawdled, Robert Zemeckis pounced.

After a slow start as a writer-director, both helped and hurt by being one of the two writers on a rare Spielberg failure, 1979's *1941*, Zemeckis's career had moved into high gear with a series of mighty hits, including 1985's *Back to the Future* and 1988's semi-animated *Who Framed Roger Rabbit*.

"I remember reading the script on an airplane," he said. "It's so rare that I read a screenplay and just keep turning the pages, wanting to find out how it's going to resolve. I saw that there were flaws: Forrest would imagine these little characters—Curious George would come alive from his books—and there were cartoon creatures, like angels popping up on his shoulder. There was an element of animation, and I said, 'All this has got to go.' The screenplay needed work, but the bones of a really magnificent movie were there."

Lansing had come close to working with Zemeckis on Fox's *Romancing the Stone* and was eager to sign him now.

"He was exceptional," she said, "because he could handle the technical aspects at a level beyond almost anyone else and was also masterful with the actors. He was someone who always completely believed in what he was doing and wanted to push himself into untested territory."

It was still unclear whether Sonnenfeld had fully relinquished the film, and Marshall had never given a firm yes or no. Now Lansing pushed Sonnenfeld to commit to *Addams* while nudging Ovitz to ease his client Marshall aside, and then arranged for Zemeckis to meet Hanks in a Century City hotel.

"I had just done [1993's] *Philadelphia*, and I weighed about 115 pounds," said the actor. "I was a guy coming in who had just been through a pretty extreme physical and emotional movie experience. But two and a half hours went by in the blink of an eye because we were feeding off each other's ideas. Bob begins a conversation as soon as you start working on a film, so that on the day when you're shooting, and it's 120 degrees and the trucks are all rented and there's helicopters in the sky and you're in Monument Valley and you only have eight hours, you cannot be confused as to why you are there."

At the end of their meeting, Zemeckis called his agent, CAA's Jack Rapke, and put him on speakerphone. "He said, 'Jack, I'm here with Tom Hanks, and we're going to do this,'" recalled Hanks. "What that means is, you are now officially making the film."

With Zemeckis and Hanks committed, Lansing gave the green light.

Gary Sinise was chosen to play Forrest's war colleague, Lieutenant Dan Taylor; Sally Field was cast as his mother (despite being only ten years older than Hanks); and Mykelti Williamson was hired as the shrimp-loving Private Benjamin Buford "Bubba" Blue. That left only the all-important role of Jenny Curran, the woman Forrest loves at a distance, who provides the emotional through-line for the film.

When Jodie Foster turned down the role, Lansing agreed to screen-test a very pregnant Robin Wright, who had come to fame with 1987's *The Princess Bride* but had never become a full-fledged star in her own right. Zemeckis shot her entirely from the waist up so that her stomach would not show, and she won the part.

After working on the screenplay with Roth and assembling his cast, the director set up shop in Beaufort, South Carolina, where he expected to start shooting within weeks. Then everything came close to collapse.

"The budget had come in at $40 million," said Lansing, "and that was the amount we expected to pay. This was before the Viacom takeover, and I was careful to have Stanley and Marty Davis sign off on it because that was a high number at the time and we had no financial partner. But the costs started multiplying. Bob's producer, Steve Starkey, broke it down and said it was going to come in at $50 million."

Her hesitation turned to genuine concern when the special-effects house Industrial Light & Magic told her that whatever money had been allocated for effects—critical to this story, where Hanks would material-ize in real-life footage of Kennedy and John Lennon—was only half what was needed, if that. It was the dawn of computerized effects, and Lansing was expecting a movie that would use them with more originality and realism than ever before. But it was impossible to accurately gauge what they would cost.

"I'd gotten board approval based on the $40 million budget, and then this different number came in," she recalled. "I said, 'I can't go back. It's too much.'"

She was still new at Paramount, without a track record, and she faced a dilemma: should she support a director who was known for spending liberally, or place a lid on the budget, alienating him but satisfying her bosses?

Goldwyn had given her a warning. He had been driving across the lot in a golf cart with producer Frank Marshall, just after Marshall had worked with Zemeckis on *Roger Rabbit*. "He said, 'Let me tell you some-thing: it's going to cost way more than you want, but you're going to get a great movie,'" Goldwyn recalled. "I said, 'What do you mean by way more?' He goes, 'I'm just telling you, open the checkbook. But it will be worth it.'"

Lansing clung to the belief she was still a producer at heart. But she also craved Jaffe's approval and knew he was seething over *Gump*'s escalating expenses; what she did not know was that his irritation was fueled by the pressure from the secret Viacom talks. She decided the budget must come down.

"I wanted to scream, 'I'm not a suit! I'm a producer!'" she said. "But I couldn't."

With Zemeckis already in South Carolina, where preproduction on the movie was under way, she called his agent, Rapke, to tell him the budget would have to be slashed by as much as $10 million.

Rapke was sitting calmly in his Century City office, enjoying the week after putting the final touches to his client's *Gump* deal, when his assistant told him Lansing was on the phone.

"It was a pretty nice day, and then there's all these dark clouds," he said. "No one can deliver bad news better than Sherry. The call went, 'Hi, honey. How are you? Everything's going to be great, but you know, the budget is too high and we're going to have to make some cuts. And if we can't get them resolved, we're not going to make the movie.'"

The agent tried to process what she was saying. A whole production was gearing up to shoot across the country, and it was too late to pull the plug without paying millions of dollars in prior commitments. And yet the studio was telling him it might all be over.

"But you're three weeks away from photography," he said.

"I know," Lansing replied. "But that's what we've got to do.'"

The dark clouds were looming closer. Rapke considered calling Zemeckis's lawyer and getting him to intervene; then he thought of hashing it out with his CAA colleagues before taking any drastic measures. Only after weighing all that did he decide to call Zemeckis directly at the production office.

"I said, 'I've got to get ahold of Bob, it's urgent,'" he recalled. "He gets on the phone, and I report the conversation, and he's devastated. He said, 'What do I have to do for people to believe in me?' and 'Why am I even in the business?' He was really rocked. I'm sure this wasn't the only movie they did this on. It was, 'Get the filmmakers invested. Get them really creatively and emotionally invested. Get them hooked. And then, at the proper time, renegotiate the deal.'"

He was experienced enough to know there must be pressure coming from a higher level, and so he did not entirely blame Lansing. "This wasn't a decision made unilaterally by Sherry—there's an institution there," he said. "But I honestly thought it was their standard operating procedure."

In South Carolina, the more Zemeckis thought about it, the angrier he became.

"We were forty-eight hours from turning on the camera," he said. (Others remembered it being three weeks before the shoot.) "And we got these calls, saying: 'Figure out a way to slash $5 million or $10 million out of the budget or we're shutting the show down.' Was I angry? Excuse me? About being told to take millions out of the movie before we started shooting? Absolutely. It's horrible to do that. Looking back, I don't know if I would have made the movie solely for the back end. I probably would have passed. But now I was so in love, I had no choice."

Rapke reminded him that he hadn't entered the film business for money alone, though privately he was just as upset as his client. He knew Zemeckis well enough to know it would be a terrible mistake for him to pull out of a project for which he felt so much passion.

"I said, 'There's only one reason to continue, and that's because this can be great,'" he said. "'You've always been about the material and never about the economics.'" Zemeckis reluctantly agreed, and continued to prepare the film.

Meanwhile, Rapke searched for other solutions. He asked Lansing if he could take the movie away from Paramount and give it to another studio. She refused.

"It was inconceivable to me," she said. "This was one of my favorite scripts, and I was willing to take the wrath and the anger to keep it. That's when the fighting started. I wasn't going to give away a great script because they couldn't make the movie for a reasonable price."

Rapke huddled with his CAA partners, looking for other options. He tried to find additional outside financing, but nobody bit. And as he battled over the money, the tension between the filmmakers and the studio grew thick enough to cut.

"There was a donnybrook going on," said Hanks. "There was blood in the water. Bob had fought those kinds of battles before on the *Back to the Future* films. For Bob, it's a very long express train that needs to run [in one piece], and you just can't go and say, 'Well, take out that car and knock off that caboose.' There was a substantial budget battle that went on, and true fisticuffs with the studio."

Time was running out. Three weeks had fast become two, and two weeks soon became one. After days of talks, both sides finally decided to compromise. CAA agreed that the director and star would each take 50 percent of their up-front fees—Hanks was getting $6 million and Zemeckis $5 million—in exchange for a larger share of the profits and an agreement that the studio would reimburse the money they had given up once the picture was in the black. At the same time, Lansing persuaded Jaffe to meet the talent halfway, slashing only $5 million from the budget instead of the full $10 million.

"I went to Stanley to get his approval for an extra $5 million," she said. "He wasn't happy, but he agreed. I was concerned the budget was running out of control, but I never wanted to hurt the movie."

The revised deal would make Hanks and Zemeckis millions when *Forrest* became a blockbuster. But Lansing never regretted it: it was fair that the players should benefit in success, just as she and Redford had done on *Indecent Proposal*.

"I'd deferred everything to make *Indecent Proposal*, and Redford deferred a lot, too," she said. "If you're making millions and you don't defer, why should I think you believe in this movie? We all shared in success. That was a high-class problem."

She signed off on a final budget of just under $46 million—halfway between the $40 million she had planned to spend and the $50 million Zemeckis's team wanted.

Even then, the difficulties continued. With no money to film a sequence in which Forrest takes off on a marathon run across the country, requiring a multi-location shoot, Zemeckis called Hanks to discuss it.

"I was alone," said Hanks. "The family wasn't with me there, so we were just making a little food. I said, 'How are you doing, Bob?' He said, 'Well, not very good, Tom.' He said, 'Look, I cannot make a movie called *Forrest*

Gump without the guy who's playing Forrest Gump as my soul mate on the film. I will listen to everything you have to say. We will work in total, absolute concert, and when the film is done you can sit over my shoulder and I will show you every frame of footage.' He was essentially saying, 'We are going to make this film together or we're not going to make this film at all.' [Then] he said, 'It's come down to this. The run has been budgeted at $1.6 million. I think we should split that.' I said, 'OK.' It was that simple, and my agent thought I was insane."

During the shoot, the two men and producer Starkey effectively ran a shadow operation alongside the main shoot, vanishing each weekend to various parts of the country with a tiny crew in order to film the bits and pieces that would be stitched together into a bigger sequence.

"We shot on Sundays with a splinter unit," said Zemeckis. "We got on a plane and flew to all these different states to shoot different sections of Tom running."

"We worked twenty-seven straight days in a row," added Hanks. "We'd have a regular workweek, and then late Saturday or Sunday morning I would go get in a helicopter that flew me to the airport and would fly on a plane to either North Carolina or New Hampshire, then be back at work on Monday morning. It was brutal."

Zemeckis's exasperation grew as he raced to complete his movie, and his relations with the studio went from frosty to icy. Concerned, Lansing sent Manning, her production executive, to keep an eye on the show, but Zemeckis could not stand the thought of seeing a studio representative, even one he deemed an ally. Shortly after her arrival in Beaufort, he tracked her down in a local restaurant and berated her as crew members watched through the window.

"Bob finds me there and drags me out," said Manning. "He's screaming at me, 'Don't fuck with my movie!'"

She begged to be allowed to go home. "But Sherry said, 'You have to stay,'" Manning recalled, noting that even when she was allowed to head home, she had to go into quasi-hiding, terrified that Jaffe would find out she was no longer in South Carolina.

Jaffe also clashed with Zemeckis when the director asked for a few hundred thousand dollars more to film the climax of the running sequence in Monument Valley.

"Everybody at the studio was pissed off," Zemeckis explained. "Stanley Jaffe said, 'Shoot in Griffith Park. It doesn't matter.' He was screaming at me, saying, 'You don't realize how much stress you've put on us from New York,' where corporate headquarters was. I said, 'I think I do,' and he said, 'I don't think so.'"

In fact, the stress was enormous, as Jaffe was being buffeted between Redstone and Diller, uncertain of his future or the studio's. Finally, he agreed to pay for the shoot, but "Tom and I had to put up an insurance bond ourselves," said Zemeckis.

"It was very, very tense," said Goldwyn. "Zemeckis hated us. He hated everybody. But he really hated me and hated Sherry."

Even when the movie was edited and about to be screened for a test audience, Lansing and Zemeckis butted heads, this time almost comically.

"Bob was adamant the audience shouldn't fill out preview cards," said Lansing. "And I was adamant that they should. When the lights came up and the research guys fanned out to distribute the cards, Bob raced down the aisle after them. And I raced down the aisle to stop him. We collided in the middle of the theater. I kept saying, 'Keep the cards! Keep the cards!' And Bob was yelling, 'I'm not having cards!'"

The situation was so absurd that the audience started laughing. Then one man rose to his feet.

"He shouted: 'I don't know what your problem is,'" said Goldwyn. "'I've just seen God and his name is Forrest Gump.'"

THE FILM WAS a sensation when it opened on July 6, 1994. Gump-isms became part of the parlance of the day, and "Life is like a box of chocolates" entered the vernacular.

"Forrest Gump is one of those movies, like The Graduate or Rocky, that taps into a deeper public mood than anyone imagined, its creators no doubt included," critic Frank Rich observed in the New York Times. He attributed this to "the audience's identification with the title character—a man so blank we can project our own dreams onto him—that turns a clever, manipulative entertainment into something more."

The picture became one of the highest-grossing movies in history, earning $330 million domestically and another $347.7 million abroad. It won six Oscars, including for Best Picture, Best Director, Best Adaptation and Best Actor.

Redstone was pleased. Its success had vindicated his judgment. He knew that Lansing had not flinched in her belief in the material, and whatever doubts about her he might have had were dispelled.

But a bitter taste remained from the battles, and when the filmmakers held a party just before the Academy Awards, they did not invite any of the Paramount executives. Later, when they arrived at Lansing's own pre-Oscars party, they were worse for wear.

"They were all so hungover that Bob, Tom, all of them, were throwing up," said Manning. "Somehow Sherry found out. She goes, 'Michelle, did you know they were having a party?' I go, 'Yeah, but I didn't get to go.'"

"It was rough," said Zemeckis. "Sherry had these people above her, telling her, 'This is never going to work.' She was put in that horrible place executives are in, where she's got to serve her masters and make sure the movie doesn't get destroyed. But I do believe her heart was always in [it]."

"I felt terrible," said Lansing. "I feel terrible to this day that someone I admired and respected, who made one of the greatest films in the world, should resent me. But there's a natural tension between a studio and a filmmaker: if you're a filmmaker, you push for as much money as you can possibly get, and if you're an executive, you try to manage it as responsibly as you can. In hindsight, I wish I'd had more time to go to the set and explain it. But I couldn't, and it was painful, because I loved the dailies, I loved what I was seeing. I loved that movie from the first time I read the script to the very last screening."

CHAPTER 14

After *Gump* opened, Viacom's president, Biondi, flew to Los Angeles to address the studio's employees. "When we got here, everybody was asking if we were going to keep Sherry," he said. "Now the question is, will she agree to stay?"

The picture not only solidified Lansing's position but also marked the beginning of an extraordinary run of success, among the most impressive any executive had known. Thanks to *Gump* and the films that followed, Lansing was able to relax in her job, confident she had Redstone's unwavering support.

The same was not true for Biondi, who was fired in 1996. After years of working side by side with Redstone, his relationship with his boss had cooled, perhaps because he did not play Redstone's game, refusing to arrive at his office first thing in the morning, and rarely wining and dining him as much as Redstone might have liked. One morning the Viacom chairman called Biondi into his office and handed him a press release announcing his resignation.

It was a chilling warning for others that Redstone could turn against his most intimate associates. He also severed his relationship with his son, Brent, and for years was alienated from his daughter, Shari. Once, flying on his corporate jet, he unleashed such venom at his then-wife that she got up and moved away, only for him to unleash even more when she returned.

"Boy, he could blister people," said Biondi. "He wasn't a guy who saw his own flaws easily."

Lansing was aware of this but chose to ignore it. While others trembled before Redstone, she barely noticed his rages; she did not so much defuse his anger—like that of some of her other colleagues—as fail to let it land on her. Just as she had dealt with sexism early in her career by turning a blind eye to it, so she deflected their fury by failing to truly notice it.

"I never minded shouting," she said. "For me, it was just a style. It didn't mean anything at all."

Instead, she stressed Redstone's loyalty, which became clear during the making of one of Paramount's more troubled pictures, *Congo*, the studio's big summer release of 1995.

Lansing had always been high on the movie, adapted from a Michael Crichton novel about the search for diamonds in Zaire, and had bragged about it during a Viacom board meeting. She had even hired an actor to play an ape and interrupt the meeting, causing the board members to scatter in fear before they realized the ape was a fake. Now, months before the picture was due to open, she was confident enough in its prospects to leave the first test screening in Goldwyn's hands while she flew to New York for a Wall Street presentation.

"The plan was for John to fax me the results after the screening," she said. "I'd have them before the presentation took place the next day."

That night she woke from a deep sleep and got up to see if the fax had been slipped under her door. But there was no sign of it, and when she called Goldwyn, he did not answer his phone. Assuming it would arrive in the morning, she went back to bed. When she got up, nothing had arrived.

"I called John at home, and this time he picked up," she remembered. "I said, 'Where are the numbers?'"

"I didn't want to wake you," he replied. "It was one of the worst screenings we've ever had. It was so bad I decided not to do the cards, because half the audience was laughing and the other half walked out."

Lansing was shaken. "We had a disaster on our hands," she said. "We were in a highly competitive business, and if news leaked that *Congo* was bad, another studio would quickly shift one of its films to our June ninth release date. Those dates were hard to find, and getting the right one, when no other big movie was going to open, was crucial for a summer hit."

Leaving her hotel, she headed to the auditorium where the presentation was about to take place and tracked down Redstone.

"He said, 'Just tell me what's wrong. I can handle it,'" she recalled. "I told him the unvarnished truth. He wasn't angry; he was stoic. He was completely supportive. He reassured me, 'It's a best-selling book. You got Frank Marshall and Kathy [Kathleen] Kennedy [two major producers] to produce. You did nothing wrong.'"

Back in Los Angeles, she gave detailed notes to Marshall, who had also directed the film. While he believed the test results were skewed by the absence of effects shots, he accepted her argument that the movie should lean toward the scary rather than the lighthearted. "I'd wanted it to be more fun; she wanted it to be more of a thriller," he said. "We reedited it with that in mind. And the test scores came up."

Lansing knew the picture was no classic, but her belief in its prospects rose when her son, Jack, and one of his friends saw it and expressed their enthusiasm. "Before that, we'd always thought the movie would only appeal to adults," she said, "but afterward, we targeted a huge part of our ad buys to teenagers, too."

A critical drubbing did not sink the film at the box office: it opened to $24.6 million—"a huge number in those days," said Lansing—and earned $152 million worldwide, less than she might have hoped for, but enough to make it profitable.

Redstone called the day the film opened. "I knew you could do it," he said. "In situations like this, it's easy to lose faith in yourself, and that's something I never want you to do."

"SHERRY UNDERSTOOD HOW to deal with complicated men—angry, volatile, neurotic, insecure, dangerous men," said Goldwyn.

Few were as demanding as Lansing's partner, Jonathan Dolgen, who was named chairman of the Viacom Entertainment Group right after

Redstone bought the studio. Unknown to her, Redstone and his team had approached Dolgen while closing the deal for Paramount, and talks were already under way when they were dining her at the Ivy.

A man of considerable financial acumen, Dolgen had built a reputation for imaginative deals and unrivaled attention to detail while at Columbia and Fox. But with his glowering eyes and booming baritone, he unnerved his colleagues at Paramount.

"He could be ferocious," said Goldwyn. "He was always screaming. He used to smoke Winston menthols. He'd start smoking his cigarettes and his eyes would light up and the smoke would come out of his mouth and nose and eyes. These accountants would follow him into his office, and they had all these huge binders. They'd have spent months preparing the numbers, and Jon would point and go, 'Is this right, this number here? That number doesn't look right to me.' The head accountant would go, 'Oh, we're actually off by ten grand.' Meeting over. 'Go back, do all the binders.' Then everybody would file out. 'Fucking morons. They can't even get a fucking number. Do I look like a math teacher?' It was just really, really intense."

Lansing formed a bond with Dolgen regardless, and their affinity was sealed on his first day at Paramount when he declined her offer to take her large office, insisting she keep it while he moved into a smaller space.

It was Dolgen who took charge of the television wing of the studio, in which Lansing had no interest; it was he who carved out brilliant business deals that allowed her the freedom to make her films; and it was he whom she credited as the real architect of the studio's co-financing strategy, which she had initiated before his appointment.

That strategy protected Paramount in the event of failure, though it also limited its upside in success. As budgets spiraled ever higher, thanks to increased star salaries and the huge amounts needed to pay for television advertising, it became essential to survival, minimizing the damage that could be inflicted by a single gargantuan flop, though Paramount would later be criticized for being too cautious.

"We had to be fiscally responsible, and that often meant bringing in partners, because we knew we weren't going to be right all the time," said

Lansing. "But we were vilified for not taking the whole burden. People would say, 'Are they crazy? What are they doing?' even though costs were spinning out of control. And then other studios started to do the same thing, and sharing the risk became business as normal."

Within months of Dolgen's arrival, the two executives became so close they started vacationing together, which baffled their staff no end.

"I trusted Jon with my life," said Lansing. "If you have a partner like that—and I was blessed to have two, along with Stanley—you're not afraid to take chances. I can't speak highly enough of what that does—in a corporate relationship, in a marriage, in anything. I know they were both demanding and had a way of raising their voices, but under that was real kindness, decency and loyalty. With Jon at my side, I felt free to take risks, and without taking risks you can never make a great picture."

LANSING WAS PREPARED to risk a great deal on one of her first great bets, *Braveheart.*

The story of an obscure, real-life thirteenth-century warrior who had led a Scottish rebellion against England, the film seemed to have everything going against it: it was a period piece whose hero spends most of his life in a kilt; a sprawling epic with a largely male cast, most of them speaking in an incomprehensible accent; and a tragedy that ended with the death of its hero, who's disemboweled at the hands of the English. Throw in the fact that its director wanted to shoot the picture in Gaelic, and no executive in her right mind would have gone near it.

And yet Lansing was passionate about the project. Unlike many of her peers, she had not succumbed to the growing ardor for superheroes and cartoon characters, for the effects-driven "event" films that would become a studio staple by the end of the decade. Rather, she sought stories that touched her in a deep and often personal way.

"I don't usually like classic period pieces," she said. "It's a flaw, but they seem arch to me, and I can't relate to the way people move and talk in them. But there was something about this story, and the courage of a man sacrificing his life for a cause, that moved me. Stories like that always did, because they were about the highest kind of morality and giving it all up for something bigger than yourself."

The picture was the brainchild of a little-known writer named Randall Wallace, who had first heard of the man who shared his family name, William Wallace, during a visit to Scotland.

"I knew nothing of my genealogy," he said, "so I went to Edinburgh Castle, and I'm standing in the entrance and there's a statue of a man named Wallace. I said to the Black Watch guard who was there in his kilt, 'Who's he?' And the guard says, 'He's our greatest hero.'"

The writer tucked William Wallace away in the back of his mind. But after losing his day job working on television action-adventures—and then selling a script for $900,000—he had the luxury to return to his dream project. After MGM commissioned a screenplay, Alan Ladd Jr. (then serving as the studio's chairman) took it to Mel Gibson, who loved it and yet was reluctant to commit.

"I decided to pass," said Gibson. "There was a lot of stuff coming at me in those days, and it was a judicious process of just wending your way through the multitudes of scripts. I was in my late thirties, in that Bradley Cooper–Leo DiCaprio stage, right in the prime."

The film was relegated to the back burner, where it remained until Ladd left MGM after conflicting with the studio's owner, Giancarlo Parretti, later to become an international fugitive. When Lansing asked him to come to Paramount as a producer, he agreed. His exit deal allowed him to take two screenplays, and *Braveheart* was one of them.

By the mid-1990s, a year and a half had passed since Gibson first heard about the movie, and he had been unable to stop thinking about it.

After finishing 1994's *Maverick*, he recalled, "somebody asked me, 'What do you want to do next?' I said, 'You know, there's this script I can't get out of my head. I've been constructing shot lists. I know how it's supposed to look.' So I told the story. And it was amazing—I'd maybe read it twice, but I remembered a fair bit. He said, 'Let's drag that one out of the cobwebs.'"

Gibson got back in touch with Ladd, and Ladd arranged for him to meet Lansing over breakfast at Los Angeles' Four Seasons Hotel, where they were joined by the actor's business partner, Bruce Davey. It was yet another lopsided meeting of one woman and three men, but Lansing was not intimidated.

"Mel lit a cigarette," she said. "He was nervous and seemed uncomfortable, and didn't look me in the eye. He had a lot of nervous energy. He was jittery."

Off camera, Gibson was one of the most high-strung actors she had met, but she warmed to him, and he to her, when he learned she was married to one of his directing heroes, Friedkin. As their conversation progressed, Lansing was relieved to find him deeper and more sensitive than she had expected.

"He was intelligent, he was direct, and I liked him," she said.

She had hoped Gibson would agree to star, but on this he was adamant: if he did the film at all, it would be as a director, not an actor. Reluctant to take both roles on his second feature as a director—vastly bigger in scope than his previous endeavor, 1993's *The Man Without a Face*—he suggested that Brad Pitt play Wallace.

"I thought, directing this thing is going to be a big, epic deal and I have to get somebody else to be in it," he said. "Everybody was going, 'Be in it, you idiot.' I thought I was a little old at that time to be William Wallace, because he was like twenty-eight when he bit the dust, though no one knew [for sure]."

Months went by, however, without Pitt or any other star signing on, and the project appeared to be stuck when Ladd called Gibson again. Somewhere he had read that Wallace was thirty-eight, the same age as the actor.

"I said, 'The fates are saying you've got to play the part,'" said Ladd.

Gibson agreed. Now he and Paramount had to come to terms on the picture's cost. A preliminary budget came in between $65 million and $70 million, which was way too steep for Paramount to take on alone, and Lansing insisted on finding a partner.

"Sherry wanted to pay $20 million or $30 million all in," noted Ladd. "I went down to her office and said, 'Sherry, the battle scenes alone are going to cost that.' But she said, 'That's all I'll put up.'"

Warners said it would join in, on the condition that Gibson make another *Lethal Weapon* for the studio, but he demurred. Then 20th Century Fox said it would take foreign rights and would provide two-thirds of the budget, leaving Paramount with one-third of the total outlay and the right to handle the domestic release. Still, the budget was frighteningly high.

Gibson came to the studio to negotiate a deal and met with Bill Bernstein, its head of business affairs. Perhaps the actor-director had expected the talks would be simple; if so, he was disappointed. Bernstein told him Paramount would pay no more than $15 million, and would take a distribution fee of 25 percent—that is, Paramount would get 25 percent of the money received from movie theaters.

Gibson was furious. In a fit of anger, he picked up an ashtray and hurled it across the room.

"He felt he wasn't being respected, and he felt he was bringing something of considerable value," said agent Jeff Berg, who was present at the meeting. "So he grabbed a large glass ashtray and threw it through the wall. He threw the ashtray through the wall! We were stunned."

Years later, Gibson was penitent. He even called Bernstein to apologize, though Bernstein discreetly pretended not to remember a thing.

"We were right up to the moment of [shooting], and I'd turned a whole bunch of other jobs down," said Gibson. "I was loud. I was like, 'What the fuck do you people mean? I turned down three jobs—blah, blah, blah.' I was kind of upset, probably a little over the top. It was all posturing bullshit."

A week later, Gibson and Davey accepted a slightly revised offer, with Paramount agreeing to put up a third of the $54 million budget and take a lower distribution fee. The movie was a go.

PRODUCTION GOT UNDER way in Scotland, where atrocious weather forced the filmmakers to call off the shoot, and the entire project—cast, crew, sets and all—had to relocate to Ireland.

The problems were compounded by the banks that were handling the finances but were so slow to pay up that Gibson and Ladd had to spend millions of dollars of their own money to keep the production rolling.

"I got on a plane from Prague, where we were also shooting *Immortal Beloved*, and went to see Mel," said Davey. "We were shooting on Ben Nevis mountain at the time, and during an opportune break I went up to him and said, 'Listen, we're in all sorts of trouble here. You and I are financing this and we are out of dough, mate.' I drafted an email to Redstone and Murdoch and all those guys and I just told them, 'I'm shutting down production.'" The money came through.

Halfway through the shoot, Lansing flew to Dublin, where she spent two days with Gibson and watched him film some of the picture's biggest battle sequences.

She looked on in wonder as epic scenes unfolded before her, with some seventeen hundred Irish soldiers filling in as extras, all supplied free by the Irish government. She stood at Gibson's side as he rode a two-hundred-pound metal horse, built over a steel skeleton, for his close-ups. And she stared fascinated as hundreds of archers fired ten thousand arrows, creating a moment reminiscent of Kurosawa's *Throne of Blood*.

She knew the stress Gibson was facing as actor, director and producer, a challenge rarely taken on by any major star, and admired his self-discipline.

At the end of Lansing's first day on the set, "I walked over to Mel's editing room and he showed me twenty minutes that he'd cut together," she said. "It was pouring rain, and I was wading through the water in these galoshes, wet and cold, but all I could think about was the film. I said, 'Do you understand how great this is?' And he just sat there, looking at me blankly, as if he really didn't know."

Gibson was too exhausted to think. He had spent months dealing with the financing, weeks wrestling with the inclement weather, and now days on end orchestrating vast battles, acting in almost every scene as well as directing, without rest.

"It took everything I had," he said. "These were eighteen-hour days, sometimes seven days a week. You'd sit in a dark hotel room and just drool. Honest to God, that's what it was like. I didn't want to talk. It was, 'Leave the lights off. Just send me up some toast.' It was five months, nonstop. By the end, I could hardly put a sentence together, I was so depleted. That's when I first noticed gray hairs. [On days off] I stayed in the hotel and didn't get out of bed. It was only my second outing as a director, so I was pretty scared. I don't think I'll ever do anything like that again. It just leaves you bankrupt. You age. At the end of it, I was exhausted. I couldn't even talk to anyone for a month."

"That was one of the toughest shoots I'd ever seen," said Lansing. "The logistics were overwhelming. I felt for him. But I knew it was going to be worth all the effort in the end."

WEEKS AFTER THE film wrapped, she got to see a first cut. "Something didn't work," she said. "The film was too long, and the emotion wasn't fully there."

"Some of the stuff was way over the top," Gibson acknowledged. "There were people's intestines falling out, and their eyes were being gouged."

Lansing had learned just how much could change in postproduction, and so she wasn't too worried. She gave the filmmakers detailed notes, reminding them of her enthusiasm and her belief in them. Even though Gibson knew "she didn't want an X rating," he never felt pressured to remove an excessive amount of violence or trim the movie more than he might like. Instead, he came to admire her shrewd observations.

"Sherry is probably the smartest executive I've seen in a screening room," said Davey. "Her notes are precise, and she has a great gut feel for what works and what doesn't. Any notes she gives, ninety-nine times out of a hundred, are spot-on. But she was concerned."

Lansing suggested a test screening, and together the filmmakers traveled to Sacramento to see how the movie played before an audience. Gibson's method of attending such screenings was to go incognito.

"He had this latex mask made, and nobody could recognize him," said Lansing. "It was done by a makeup artist, and he put it over his head so no one ever knew it was him. He came up to me once and said, 'Hi, Sherry.

You don't know who this is, do you?' Then I recognized him, but only from his voice."

Both were nervous about the audience's reaction, and the result was worse than they had feared. People were running out of the theater, some throwing up.

"It was extreme," said Wallace, the writer. "Seventeen people walked out before the screening ended."

When the group left to take the studio plane back to Burbank, they were despondent. Gibson was in turmoil, and Lansing privately was extremely anxious. When the plane landed and the group disbanded, Gibson came over to Wallace.

"It's two in the morning and I'm at the hangar in Van Nuys airport, and Mel says, 'Let's get something to eat,'" he recalled. "We drive to Jerry's Deli on Ventura Boulevard, and we're sitting there together, and Mel says, 'I've lost my perspective.'"

THE NEXT DAY, Lansing wandered over to the filmmakers' tiny cutting room and huddled with Gibson and his editor, Steven Rosenblum. Gibson knew the movie was too long, but he was at a loss how to tighten it.

"Steve and I had the film down to three hours and fifteen minutes," he said. "We were just about hanging ourselves trying to figure it out. Honestly, we were looking at it, going, 'We don't know how to make this shorter and quicker and better.' And Sherry gave us a note. She said, 'I think you're letting the audience get too far ahead of you and you're spoon-feeding them where you don't need to.' Steve and I were cranky, like, 'Easy to backseat-drive' and all that. Twenty-four hours later, we were both trying to call each other at the same time, and saying, 'She's absolutely right.' We sat down and we said, 'Fuck! Yeah, she's right.'"

That note, said Gibson, "made us look at stuff differently. We were able to cut three hours and fifteen minutes to two hours and forty-eight minutes [not including titles]. We streamlined it and made it a much better film."

A second screening went like magic. There were no more walkouts and no throwing up; and even though Bill Mechanic, the Fox executive who had co-financed the picture, tried to persuade the filmmakers to trim a few more minutes, Lansing stood firm.

"Mel cut it back more and had an even shorter version," she noted. "I saw it and said, 'Put the five minutes back. It was better longer.'"

Braveheart opened May 24, 1995, to a $9.9 million weekend. By the end of its run, it had earned $76 million domestically and an impressive $210 million worldwide. At the 68th Academy Awards, it led the field with ten nominations and became Paramount's second consecutive Best Picture Oscar winner, taking home five statuettes in all, including two for Gibson as producer and director.

Lansing remained loyal to him over the years, through all his ups and downs, and refused to join his assailants when his rash words and drunken outbursts helped ruin his career.

She remembered how generous he had been after their tough negotiation. "I called him afterward," she said. "I told him, 'I know we've been through a lot, but I really love this movie. I'm sure you have a dartboard with my picture on it that you're throwing darts at every day.' He couldn't have been more gracious. He said, 'No. You were doing your job. I was doing mine.'"

She added: "He has his demons, and when he drinks he becomes another person. But he's not anti-Semitic and he's not homophobic, or any of those things that people believe. He's honest, shy, funny and real."

CHAPTER 15

By the time of *Braveheart*, Lansing had settled into a comfortable routine.

"I'd set my alarm for six-thirty a.m.," she said, "then I'd grab my bag of scripts and climb on the treadmill. The workout was crucial—if I didn't exercise, I'd lose my sense of perspective. But the phone would start ringing before I'd walked a mile."

After skimming through two or more screenplays, she would shower and dress, glance at the news in the *Los Angeles Times* and then leave home for the lot. Frequently, she would stop off for an eight-thirty breakfast meeting. "Hollywood has a thing about talking over meals," she said, "and whenever I was chasing a director I'd insist on getting together for breakfast or lunch."

While she was at breakfast, one of her two assistants would arrive at the office and the calls would pour in. "She'd roll them like an air traffic controller," said Lansing. "One would come after another. They never seemed to stop." Important or unimportant, each caller would hear back by the end of the day.

She chose not to socialize outside work with the actors and directors whom other executives craved to know well. She wanted to keep a professional distance. "It was hard enough to say no in the best of circumstances," she explained, "but it would have been impossible if they'd become my intimate friends. That would have impaired my judgment."

She was now an established public figure, courted for charitable work, targeted for social events and wooed for political endorsements. A longtime Democrat, she was invited to spend a night in the Lincoln Bedroom during the early years of the Bill Clinton administration.

"I came in through a guest entrance, and someone was waiting to give me a tour of the White House," she recalled. "Then they took me upstairs and asked if I was comfortable, and showed me around the private quarters. In the Lincoln Bedroom, I was overwhelmed. There was an ornate Victorian bed, and a few pieces of mahogany furniture, and a copy of the Gettysburg Address on a stand. The odd thing is, by the time I said good night to the staff, the Clintons hadn't arrived. I was alone in their residence, and they were nowhere to be seen."

She took out a script and got into bed. After a while, the Clintons still had not appeared, and so she got up, snuck out of the room, crossed the hall and peeked into the Queens' Bedroom.

"I didn't want to look like I was prying," she said. "Maybe they'd be there and say, 'What are you doing?' I'd met the Clintons, but we weren't close friends. I was nervous. But I wanted to see what was going on. And after that, I had nothing to do. It wasn't late, and nobody was there, and it was strangely silent. So I got back into bed and carried on reading my script."

An hour later, there was a knock at her door. It was the president and the First Lady. They opened the door to find Lansing in a robe, somewhat to her embarrassment.

"The president said, 'Welcome to the White House. Are you comfortable?'" she recalled. She fumbled for words. "The next morning, I had breakfast with Hillary on my own, and we talked and talked, not about politics, just life. She was so open and accessible. It was a wonderful conversation."

Lansing was invited back to the White House sometime later in the Clinton administration, and was sitting next to the president at a formal dinner when he leaned over and asked, "Do you know Kinky Friedman and the Texas Jewboys?"

"I thought, 'Oh my God, the president of the United States is telling an anti-Semitic joke,'" she said. "I wanted to hide under the table."

Instead, he told her about the country singer and satirist of that name, and his band, the Texas Jewboys, and mentioned that one of Friedman's books (he was also a mystery novelist) would make a great movie. After dinner, he introduced her to the musician, another of the evening's guests.

"I felt really stupid," she said.

She never bought the book.

SUCH EVENTS WERE pleasant diversions from her frantic schedule, but they also took her away from her family. Life with a husband and children was a stark contrast to the life she had known before. Her schedule was no longer just hers to control, her priorities quite different from the way they had been when she was single.

"I used to go to Jack's baseball games, and we'd have all his friends over for the weekends," she recalled. "We'd have five or six kids come over and they'd all sleep in his room in sleeping bags. We had an attic with a pool table and a big television set and couches, and they could run around and do whatever they wanted there. At the end of the weekend, you'd find pizza on the ceiling—literally. I never knew how it got there, but that was the kids' room. They were fun. Spending time with Jack and Cedric was pure joy for me."

Having a family gave ballast to Lansing's work life and served as a relief valve in an environment that could too easily become toxic. "The hardest thing about that job is not losing yourself in it," she said. "You're not finding a cure for cancer, and yet you think you are, in a funny way, because it becomes all-consuming. But it can't be when you have kids."

She resented accusations that her husband benefited from her position; this was, she pointed out, an Oscar-winning director. She was particularly disturbed when the *Los Angeles Times* blasted her for hiring him on the 1995 thriller *Jade* in a story headlined "Selection of Paramount Chief's Husband as Director Raises Eyebrows, Even in an Industry Known for Nepotism."

She had bought the project, based on a Joe Eszterhas story about a San Francisco executive and a prostitute linked by a murder, within days of taking over at Paramount. She insisted she had recused herself from the decision to hire Friedkin, though others were skeptical. "I was upset because it wasn't true," she said.

Jaffe said he and Lansing discussed the matter early in her tenure. "Billy was going to direct [the 1994 sports drama] *Blue Chips*," Jaffe noted. "She came to me and said, 'Look, this is really awful. I can't really oversee this. I want you to.' I said, 'Sherry, I'm running the company and I don't live in California.' She said, 'Please.' So I did. I was involved in the discussions with Billy."

It was perhaps naive of Lansing to think anyone who worked with her would forget Friedkin was married to their boss. In a rare misstep, she had failed to consider public perception and neglected to put in place measures that would insulate her from charges of favoritism. After *Jade*, that changed. Five years would pass before Friedkin made another film for Paramount, 2000's *Rules of Engagement*.

"I knew from then on we had to avoid even the appearance of favoritism," said Lansing.

When *Jade* failed critically and commercially, Friedkin blamed himself for hurting his wife, and she in turn blamed herself for allowing this to happen.

"Sherry was the head of the studio and I had directed this picture," said Friedkin. "I remember feeling really depressed, because I thought the film was good and other people didn't. I felt, more than anything, that I had let her down."

"He felt like a failure and I felt responsible," said Lansing. "He went off to do a remake of *12 Angry Men*, which I thought was a terrible idea. I said, 'I'm telling you, why would you set yourself up by remaking a classic?' I was wrong." The Showtime movie was nominated for six Emmy Awards. "That's when I realized I couldn't have anything to do with his creative life. He had to follow his own instincts or I'd lead him astray."

Their marriage succeeded, in part, because they kept their work lives separate. "How do you handle that?" Lansing asked. "The answer is, you have a life that's not just based on your work. I fell in love with an extraordinary director, but that was only one of the things that make him special.

I fell in love, first, because I was attracted to him, and then I fell in love with his mind and his humor and his kindness. And I fell in love with the way he loved me. He didn't want to change anything about me. That's the greatest gift anyone can give you."

Whatever she had achieved before, she believed, "I'd never have been that successful without him. I knew that if I was fired or had the biggest humiliation in my career, he wouldn't care. It wasn't going to change our marriage one bit. Our house became an island of security, where we were thrilled by each other's successes and suffered each other's disappointments viscerally and painfully. When I cried, or didn't want to get out of bed because a movie hadn't worked, he'd say, 'It was great.' He was my biggest fan and cheerleader. And I was his biggest fan and cheerleader. To this day, I feel his pain as if it were my own, and he feels my pain as if it were his, too."

They did not always see things the same way, but that didn't matter, said Friedkin.

"Sherry and I could not be more different in so many ways," he observed. "We have major differences about people and politics and even movies. We disagree, but it's not important to me to resolve those disagreements. We love each other. I not only love her, I respect her tremendously and I admire her."

IN 1996, LANSING took her biggest bet yet on a hugely expensive period piece about the greatest shipping disaster in history.

The industry was abuzz with rumors about *Titanic*, the first film director James Cameron had made since 1994's *True Lies*. Everybody knew how expensive it was going to be (though its eventual cost would surpass the most extreme projections), but the picture had been shrouded in mystery, its script unavailable to any of the Paramount executives until Goldwyn's wife, actress Colleen Camp, auditioned for a role, and then a Fox executive gave her husband a copy of the screenplay.

Goldwyn had been to a recent exhibition about the real-life ship, which foundered in the North Atlantic in 1912 after colliding with an iceberg, at the National Maritime Museum in London. He had even chatted about it with Cameron at a party celebrating—in true Hollywood style—the fifth anniversary of actor Tom Arnold's sobriety. When he read the script, he was convinced Paramount should get involved.

Lansing, too, was fascinated by what she read. She was thrilled by the way Cameron had used a real-life tragedy to propel a fictional story about class and romance, a *Romeo and Juliet*–tale set against an epic backdrop, as modern in its style and themes as it was historic in its setting. The movie may have been largely set in 1912, but it was utterly contemporary in its feel.

"It was a great love story, with an underlying message about female empowerment," she said. "Rose [Kate Winslet] was strong and feisty from the beginning—she's an independent woman who breaks with her class to be with the man she loves [Leonardo DiCaprio] and even lets him paint her nude. One of my favorite moments was when you see Rose at the end and realize she's had this huge life and has become a force in her own right. People underestimated the strength of those characters and how unconventional they were."

She was eager to make the film, but there was no obvious way to get involved. She knew Cameron was locked into a deal with Fox, and nothing led her to believe he was thinking of switching studios. Then word began to spread about the picture's cost. Stories rumbled through Hollywood that the price was too steep, that Fox executives were sweating bullets. Soon Lansing learned that the studio was in talks to co-finance the movie with Universal.

Universal was an obvious partner, having joined Fox to release *True Lies*. But Lansing knew it was contending with a slew of troubles, including the fallout from Kevin Costner's 1995 drama *Waterworld*, an ocean-based action film that became a byword for profligacy.

Waterworld had started out with a budget of $100 million, which had gone up and up until the movie came in at an astronomical $175 million. Costner had almost died along the way when he got caught in a squall; even then, he was shooting six days a week, and the stress showed in his performance. Wags dubbed the movie *Fishtar* and *Kevin's Gate*, playing off two other celebrated disasters, 1987's *Ishtar* and 1980's *Heaven's Gate*. The idea of backing another sea-based epic was inconceivable to Universal's top executives.

"[Universal's] Casey Silver couldn't run away fast enough," said Fox's Bill Mechanic. "Everybody thought the movie was nuts."

When Lansing heard Universal was wavering, she pounced. "I said, 'We have to win this. We have to get in there before anyone else,'" she recalled. Calling her executives together, she launched a coordinated assault and arranged for them to bombard Fox with calls, reminding its production staff about the great experiences the two studios had shared on *Braveheart*.

Mechanic did not see things quite the same way. A down-to-earth former distribution executive, he was still angry with Paramount for failing to do the paperwork that would have allowed Fox to share the Best Picture Oscar, and believed the neglect had been deliberate.

"They were all calling, saying, 'We had such a good thing on *Braveheart*,'" he noted. "And I'm like, 'Well, there were some issues.'"

Mechanic would have liked to finance *Titanic* on his own. He believed in it, was invested in it and clung to his conviction that it would be a hit, no matter what others might say. But there were pressures. As Fox's second-ranking executive, he reported to Peter Chernin, the head of the studio, and Chernin reported to Rupert Murdoch, the head of News Corp. The higher up the ladder the decision-making went, the more anxious everyone seemed. There were bosses to please, shareholders to keep happy, and all these executives were wise to the ways of Hollywood, knew only too well how easily their careers could be toppled by a single ill-advised decision. Mechanic increasingly seemed like a voice crying in the wilderness.

Chernin had loftier goals. He was soon to be promoted, and the last thing he wanted was a stain on his record as studio chief. He was desperate to do a deal.

"I told Peter that finding a partner was his problem, I had a movie to make," said Cameron, "so I just proceeded hell-bent toward production, and Fox continued to fund the film while they scrambled to find a partner."

Unable to get an answer from Universal, Chernin insisted that Mechanic consider Paramount's offer before it was too late. Fox told Paramount it would have five days to close the deal, and if it could not be completed within that timeframe, Fox would be free to look elsewhere.

Lansing sent Bernstein, her chief of business affairs, to negotiate, and for much of the following week he went back and forth over the intricacies of the arrangement. At the end of five straight days of talks—at precisely 2:00 a.m., technically two hours past Fox's deadline—he concluded his work.

The two sides agreed to split the film's $109 million budget right down the middle, with Paramount releasing the film in North America and Fox handling the rest of the world. All the revenue would be shared equally between them.

"The contracts were faxed back and forth and hastily signed," said Lansing. "The deal was done."

THEN TROUBLE BEGAN. When Lansing was given a detailed budget and pored over it with Bernstein and her head of physical production, Fred Gallo, she saw one red flag after another.

"I hadn't produced such an elaborate movie, but I knew it was light by millions of dollars," she said. "Fox had only allowed around $25 million or $30 million for special effects, most of which would be spent during the shoot, which meant there'd only be a few million dollars left for the computerized work. And it was going to take a lot more than that."

She had gone through this with *Forrest Gump* and knew how easily that number could balloon. Concerned, she sent Gallo to Baja, Mexico, where Cameron had built a gigantic water tank and multilevel sets on a twenty-four-acre piece of land and was well into making his picture. He had already shot part of the movie in Nova Scotia, Canada, and was preparing to film the ship itself, when Gallo arrived.

He found an operation bigger than anything he had ever seen. Some ten thousand tons of dynamite had been used to blow a hole large enough to build the tank, and fifteen hundred construction workers were hammering away at the vessel itself, which was almost as large as the original ship. But even this brief visit revealed all sorts of things that could go wrong.

"Cameron wanted real wallpaper and things like that," said Gallo. "I said, 'Why don't you build the sets and have them paint on the wallpaper? No one will ever know in a million years.' He wanted a special submarine, and there was only one in the world. It was Russian and he had to have it. They bring it in, and on the first day they have it they have power problems and can't shoot."

When he reported back to Lansing, she grew more concerned.

"In the climactic sequence, the ballroom was going to be completely flooded, which meant there'd be no way to do any reshoots unless they rebuilt the whole thing," she said, "and that would cost millions of dollars. But there was no provision for any reshoots in the budget, and that was just one of the problems. Tilting the ship was also complicated, and likely to be very costly. But precisely how costly, nobody could say."

Anxiety turned to anger as the Paramount team suspected it had been deceived. Why had Fox not told them about this? Why had they shown Paramount a budget with such gaping holes? Dolgen called Chernin. The two were friends and former colleagues, having worked together at Fox before Dolgen came to Paramount, but that did not mitigate his rage.

"He said, 'Your budget's running way over! You knew this! We're going to sue you for fraud!'" recalled Mechanic.

Dolgen said Paramount would only stick to the deal if Fox guaranteed that the budget had been "properly vetted and validated." This was legalese for accepting full responsibility, effectively meaning Fox would have to pay for any cost overruns.

Chernin refused. But he was under immense pressure, having been named president of News Corp. in October 1996, and the last thing he needed was a runaway picture whose entire expense rested on his shoulders. So he offered new terms.

Instead of a straight fifty-fifty split, he allowed Paramount to "cap" its investment: it would pay a set amount for half the film, and Fox would cover the rest, including overages. "We'd never have to pay a dime more," Lansing explained, "no matter how over budget the movie went."

In exchange, Chernin asked Paramount to up its investment. Assuming the picture would never cost more than $130 million, Paramount agreed to pay half of that far-out number, or $65 million.

That deal has gone down as one of the most remarkable in motion picture history, and an embarrassment for Fox, given that *Titanic's* budget would soar to $210 million, less than one-third of it paid for by Paramount. (Fox later benefited from having a slightly larger share of the profits.) It was a triumph for the Lansing-Dolgen regime. As it was, neither party ever imagined how much the movie would eventually take in.

"Jon must have run ten different scenarios to show how much we could make or lose," said Lansing. "We did them until we were blue in the face, but nobody had ever heard of a movie making $2 billion."

As THE MEXICO shoot commenced, Lansing was able to relax, confident in the knowledge that she was off the hook for whatever went wrong.

But as weekly cost reports came in, indicating that the budget was careening out of control, the Fox leadership was in a frenzy. Mechanic and Chernin were furious at the thought that Paramount had gotten away scot-free, while their own relationship was deteriorating as Mechanic felt he was being blamed and Chernin had moved out of the line of fire.

"This proved later to be an enormous source of animosity between the studios," said Cameron.

Nor did the tension ease when Redstone bragged about the deal. "Sumner does a big thing in the press about 'my genius Jon Dolgen, my genius Sherry Lansing,' and 'Fox is going to eat it,'" said Goldwyn, "because he was competitive with Murdoch. Peter felt diminished. He was being played as a financial wimp. He was very unhappy."

Chernin and the other executives feared *Titanic* would become a disaster along the lines of Fox's own *Cleopatra* or the more recent *Heaven's*

Gate, a western directed by Oscar winner Michael Cimino that had almost bankrupted United Artists in the early 1980s.

"Everyone thought they were going to lose money, and all efforts were simply to make sure the hemorrhage was not fatal," said Cameron. "Nobody was playing for the upside, myself included."

Not even Lansing was sure she had a hit until she traveled to Mexico early in the shoot and watched Cameron and DiCaprio in action. Initially she had feared the actor might be too young, remembering him from such movies as 1993's *What's Eating Gilbert Grape* and 1996's *Romeo + Juliet*. She realized she was wrong.

"They were doing a sequence in the tank, and Leo was soaking wet and gorgeous," she said. "He was really into the role, and that was all that mattered to him. I don't think he ever cared about being a sex symbol or a movie star, though this picture made him one. He cared about the quality of the work, which was stunning."

Cameron, whose fights with Fox (along with his crew) became epic, greeted her with unexpected enthusiasm before leading her on a tour of his massive set. She remained one of the few executives toward whom he harbored warm feelings.

"He said, 'Oh, I'm so glad you're here,'" recalled Lansing. "He'd been asking me to come down and wanted to show me what he was doing. I walked through the ship, and I was taken back in time. They'd recreated everything, and the specificity of the details, right down to the period dishes, blew my mind. He was really excited, showing me: 'Look at these plates. These are exactly like the plates on the real *Titanic*.' He was so dedicated to what he was doing that nothing else existed."

Even as she and Mechanic were thrilled with the dailies (Cameron was sending batches of footage back to Los Angeles at the end of each week), the pressure was growing—especially on Mechanic.

"Peter was hiding his head in the sand," he said. "We were losing three out of every five days. We had no estimate of cost to date; we had no estimate of when it would finish or what it would cost to finish at all."

Production delays grew even worse as the building of the ship took far longer than anticipated. Then, during the shoot, Winslet chipped a bone in her elbow and fought with Cameron, while three stuntmen suffered broken bones. The film's director of photography was replaced; several cast members got the flu; and almost everyone cowered at the sight of Cameron, terrified of his temper.

Mechanic was so concerned that he drove down to Baja, armed with a list of proposed cuts. There he confronted Cameron in the middle of the night.

"Jim exploded," he said. "It was three or four o'clock in the morning, and if he'd had a gun in his trailer he would have shot me. The gist of it was, 'If you're so fucking smart, you direct the picture.' And he walked off. He stormed out of his trailer, pulled his chauffeur out of the car, and sped off. He was screaming. I said, 'Shut down the shoot until he calls me,' and got in my car and drove back to L.A."

"It was one of those meetings at night, in the middle of a 150-day shoot, where people just didn't see eye to eye," said producer Jon Landau.

Cameron and Mechanic reached a tentative peace and filming resumed. The director even offered to give up his profit participation—meaning that he would receive nothing in the event of success—which both Fox and Paramount accepted. (His profits would later be restored.)

All this Mechanic discussed with Lansing over the phone. She empathized with the troubles he was facing, while feeling a huge sense of relief.

"It was terrible," she said. "The picture was going over and over. Everybody had written it off: 'It's going to be the biggest disaster ever.' Everyone was saying, 'Bill's going to be fired.' He kept believing in the film when a lot of other people at that studio didn't. I knew how hard it was to shoot on water, where all sorts of things can run out of control, but I'd never imagined the film could go so far over budget."

As word leaked about the nightmare shoot, some of the cast and crew turned against their director. Winslet said at times she was "genuinely frightened of him," while others called him a tyrant. Several crew members were fired or quit, and many called him "Mij" (Jim in reverse) when he revealed the dark side of his personality.

The press turned savage. *Newsweek* headlined a story "A Sinking Sensation," while *Time* wrote "Glub, Glub, Glub . . . Can James Cameron's Extravagant *Titanic* Avoid Disaster?" The trade paper *Daily Variety* started to run regular, biting columns under the rubric "*Titanic* Watch."

But Lansing supported Cameron throughout.

"She was very excited that the raw footage captured the sweep and emotion promised by the script," said the director. "I had only ever done sci-fi, horror and action previously, so this must have been a relief. However, the costs were spiraling out of control, so I remember the praise from all parties becoming more sparing as time went on."

MONEY CONTINUED TO hemorrhage in postproduction, and relations between the two studios, already cool, became frigid. When Chernin asked Dolgen to kick in some more cash, and Dolgen refused, the two friends split irreparably.

"Chernin said, 'Jon, I need relief,'" recalled Goldwyn. "And Jon said, 'I'm not giving you relief.' Chernin said, 'Jon, if you just give me some relief, we could renegotiate the profit participation, but man, I'm really exposed.' Jon said, 'No!' It ended their friendship."

"We were carrying the movie on our books as a $55 million loss," Chernin explained. "I went to Paramount and said, 'Jon, you can't make what you're making while I'm still underwater. You can't do that to me. I'm going to get fired for this and you're going to make money standing on my neck. And that's just wrong.' He turned me down. I was very, very angry."

While Paramount and Fox were at loggerheads, Cameron was at war with both. At the former, his wrath fell on Robert Friedman, a longtime Warner Bros. executive whom Lansing had hired as her vice chairman, with a particular emphasis on marketing and distribution.

Cameron despised Friedman's plans for selling the picture, and loathed a trailer he had created, which stressed the film's action sequences, as if the movie were merely a continuation of Cameron's previous work rather than a great leap forward, as the director saw it. When he cut his own trailer, Friedman hated it.

"We got a call from Robbie Friedman saying—and I quote—'I just saw your trailer and threw up on my shoes,'" said Cameron. "Sherry always loved the film, but the business heads at Paramount acted like they'd been diagnosed with terminal cancer. It was a highly contentious time and close to open warfare between the studios."

That warfare continued over matters large and small, including everything from the design of the poster to the date when the movie should open. As it became clear that Cameron would not be able to make the planned release—the July 4 weekend of 1997—the parties fought even more furiously. Late July was considered but deemed too early; then Thanksgiving was mentioned, but Fox disliked that idea.

When Lansing called Chernin to discuss the movie's opening, "Peter was very upset with me," she remembered. "He said, 'My dear, you don't have the kind of money that we have in it, and we'll determine when it's going to be released.' I said, 'Good luck to you.'"

Both sides had other movies that complicated the *Titanic* release, and for neither one was it as simple as choosing the date that was best for *Titanic*. Fox had two big pictures coming up at Thanksgiving, which made it the worst possible time to open Cameron's picture, while Paramount was trying to keep Harrison Ford happy, knowing it would need him for its ongoing Tom Clancy action franchise, as well as a return to Indiana Jones.

"Harrison Ford angrily warned studio executives that if 'Titanic' opened in late July, he would sever his relations with the studio that made some of his biggest hits, including 'Raiders of the Lost Ark' and 'Patriot Games,'" reported the *New York Times*. "Mr. Ford was disturbed because his new film, 'Air Force One,' is set to be released by Sony on July 25."

The conflict over *Titanic*'s release spilled into the open at the Cannes film festival. "Tensions between the two studios over the film grew so intense . . . that Mr. Friedman and Mr. Mechanic came very close to a fistfight," noted the *Times*. "Fox, eager to start earning income on the film, sought an August release [while] Paramount said August was too late to lure the summer audience and suggested Thanksgiving."

Cameron wanted to go even later. "I argued strongly for Christmas," he said, "because only by having an open playing field, with little competition, could a three-plus-hour movie run long enough to make its money back."

He called Chernin to make his case. "I remember my hands shaking as I placed that call. I made my pitch, and Peter, to his credit, took the news soberly that we couldn't make a summer date and still maintain quality, and he listened to my arguments. He said he needed twenty-four hours to think about it. He called the next day and said we were going with my plan. I'm sure by now it's remembered as their idea."

Throughout "this ugly period," said Cameron, "Sherry remained staunchly supportive of the movie."

At no point was she more so than when she saw parts of it pieced together at Cameron's Malibu home—the first time she had seen anything other than the raw footage—months after the shoot was over. The director was cutting the film in his compound and invited her to see it on an Avid editing machine.

"Jim said, 'Come out, and I'll show you a few scenes cut together, just a couple of scenes,'" Lansing recalled. "It was a Sunday, and I'd made plans to have dinner with my husband later on. John Goldwyn and I drove out to Jim's home early in the afternoon, and we had a little lunch, and then Jim made the room dark and showed us the first scene, and I was speechless."

Cameron asked if she would like to see some more. "Of course," she replied. "And he showed me another scene, completely different, and that was incredible. Then he said, 'Another scene?' And I said, 'Yes!' Each time he showed a scene, I was in awe. He just kept showing us more and more, reacting to our excitement. Even with a temp [temporary] score, it was fantastic. I lost all track of time."

After an hour had passed—or what she believed was an hour—she said she should call Friedkin to say she would be late for dinner. "I told Jim I was meeting Billy at six," she said. "And Jim said: 'What are you talking about? It's already eight p.m.'"

"She had a very emotional reaction," Cameron remembered. "She said she thought it was a great love story, on the order of *Gone with the Wind*, and it really held her throughout. She had a few comments, all of which were positive and insightful. I don't recall her being overly concerned about length, although there was an overall sense from everyone involved, myself as well, that it needed to be shorter. But to her, the important thing was that the chemistry between Jack and Rose [DiCaprio and Winslet] worked, and the drama paid off at the end."

The screening "was a big turning point for me," he added, "because we were in a very bleak place emotionally, trying to finish the movie. Everyone was against us, and we knew we would always carry this huge albatross of going almost twice [over] the proposed budget for the rest of our careers—if there even was going to be a career after that. And all of a sudden we had a studio head saying that somehow, at some level, it had all been worth it. Mind you, nobody thought we were *ever* going to break even. And I pretty much assumed at that time that I'd never work again."

Lansing only had one reservation: when the score was completed, she argued against the song "My Heart Will Go On."

"The movie ended so beautifully, and now we had Celine Dion," she noted. "I said, 'Jim, isn't this a little corny? Do we really need it?' He said, 'Oh my God, Sherry! The song is fantastic.'"

TITANIC PREMIERED NOVEMBER 1, 1997, at the Tokyo International Film Festival and opened domestically December 14 on 2,674 screens.

Contrary to industry expectations, it came in number one at the box office, earning $28.6 million its first weekend and beating the anticipated leader, the latest James Bond thriller, *Tomorrow Never Dies*. More surprising still was its second weekend, which outpaced the previous one, taking in $35 million on its way to a worldwide total of $2.19 billion. That made it the most successful movie ever, a record broken only by Cameron's *Avatar* in 2009.

"The picture went 'clean' [into the black] on theatrical alone," said Bernstein, the business affairs executive. Most movies have to wait for cash to flow in from cable television, home entertainment and ancillary markets before they turn a profit. "I never saw that happen before. DiCaprio wanted more money, and I think we gave him a $5 million bonus."

Lansing bought Landau a home aquarium and Cameron an African safari—gifts that not even the most cynical observers could question, given the enormous profits Paramount reaped from *Titanic*. "Jim gave up his salary and profits when there were all those budget problems, and we restored them," said Lansing. "He made a fortune and deserved it."

Titanic was nominated for a record-tying fourteen Oscars and won eleven, including three for Cameron. The day after the Oscars, Lansing ordered a photo of the moment when he and Landau learned their movie had been named Best Picture.

"She sent over the photo in a silver frame," said Landau. "It's a moment I'll have forever."

CHAPTER 16

With *Titanic*, Lansing was at the peak of her game.

"I was in a producer's candy store," she said. "I relished every moment I got to read a great script, or one that had the potential to be great. Each time I said yes, I was furthering a filmmaker's dream, and becoming part of that dream myself. I loved everything about being at Paramount, except for the rare times when the problems became so contentious they made me nauseous. But they had to rise to a pretty high level for that."

Her executives adapted to her hands-on management style, which involved rapid-fire calls, multiple meetings and an immersive involvement in every project, from the first draft of a script to every aspect of a film's marketing and release. If some studio chiefs were absentee landlords, this one believed in examining each building as carefully as her mother had done.

"She was tough when she needed to be tough, and played ball when she needed to play ball to make things happen," said CAA's Bryan Lourd.

Staffers got used to being inundated with calls, even first thing on Saturdays when Lansing would ask about their "weekend read," the stack of screenplays they regularly took home, which was usually the subject of a Monday-morning conversation at other studios.

"She would do her reading on a Friday night or Saturday morning, expecting you had done it, too," said Rosenfelt. After meetings during the week, "she'd say, 'Call so-and-so,' but by the time you got back to your office, she'd already have called them. You'd hear from her all through the day. She couldn't let go."

Lansing would buzz each executive directly from her office, bypassing their assistants. "I called it the 'bat line,'" said Manning. "If she was in her office and had a question, she could press 'Michelle' and the phone on my desk would ring. It didn't matter who else was on the phone with me when she called; I had to grab it. I was like, 'Oh my God! The bat phone's ringing! I gotta go.'"

As demanding as Lansing was professionally, she was personally caring. "If there was anything to do with an illness, anything medical, she was great, making sure you got the best doctors," said Manning. "But there's the leadership of somebody who's your friend, your mentor, the shoulder to cry on. And then there's the general. She was the general."

This general instituted a weekly meeting with Goldwyn and his production team, who would gather privately just to prepare. Similar regular meetings took place with all the senior staff, as well as those involved with marketing and distribution, and her business affairs team. She was also in constant contact with Dolgen, who would speak to Redstone multiple times each day.

"Sherry was a really hard worker," said Scott Rudin. "There was no muscle in her body that was not working 100 percent, all the time. She liked elbowing her way into things, but she had massive available charm, so you didn't feel like it was elbowing. And if she believed in you, you knew it. She had the ability to make you feel the wind at your back. If you were emotionally endorsed by her, it meant an enormous amount."

When Jordan Kerner, a producer, suggested she add weekly get-togethers with her key producers on top of the other meetings, she did so, "letting us decide the agenda and the things we needed to do to cut through all the red tape," he said.

Having dealt with several studios, Kerner was struck by Lansing's decisiveness, in contrast to others' bureaucracy-laden process, more and more evident as Hollywood moved deeper into the 1990s, when flotillas of senior executives had to sign off on any major decision, "green-light committees" were instituted to determine which movies should be made, and studios developed computer algorithms to help estimate a picture's success. Lansing believed in none of this; like the old-fashioned moguls, she went on her instinct alone.

During Kerner's first sit-down with her, she gave an immediate yes to six of the seven ideas he pitched her. Later, when he was developing a screen version of the children's novel *Charlotte's Web*, he said, "Her notes were specific about wanting to stay true to [author] E. B. White's intentions. I went to Cornell University, where he had all his handwritten notes, and spent a week and a half researching, and she was really happy about that."

Bringing the Paramount-based producers together engendered a loyalty, both to herself and the group, that lasted for years, and a handful of them would have regular reunions well after Lansing had left, dubbing themselves "the green-light club." "Rather than be competitive," said Kerner, "we became close."

Producers were of vital importance to her, and Paramount became a creative hive of men and women who would ferret out material and send it her way, and then push pictures through the studio pipeline. They included Mace Neufeld and Robert Rehme (who worked on the Clancy movies, along with *Beverly Hills Cop III*), Kathleen Kennedy and Frank Marshall (the husband-and-wife team who made *Congo* and were longtime associates of Spielberg) and Rudin (*The Addams Family*, *The Truman Show*). These were among the most able producers in Hollywood, each there to feed Paramount some of the fifteen to twenty movies it needed to release per year.

Many of these producers considered Lansing a friend ("Everyone was an 'FOS,' a friend of Sherry's," said Manning), though she spent her real social life outside the business. She would have weekly lunches with her girlfriends, just to remind herself of the world outside work. "It was an attempt to keep a balanced life," she said.

Even her best films would be taxing. Conflict was rarely absent from any project.

Hiring Demi Moore (right) for *Indecent Proposal* was easy. But signing her costar, Woody Harrelson, led to a $5 million lawsuit.

With husband William Friedkin.

Celebrities from Diane Keaton to Sidney Poitier came out when Lansing received her star on the Walk of Fame.

As Paramount chairman, Lansing became Hollywood's most powerful woman for the second time in her career.

Lansing only became friends with Jodie Foster (right) after they wrapped *The Accused*.

Even after Mel Gibson hurled an ashtray through a wall during the *Braveheart* negotiations, he and Lansing remained close.

"Everyone thought they were going to lose money," said James Cameron, seen with Lansing on the set of *Titanic*. "Nobody was playing for the upside."

Jonathan Dolgen, Sumner Redstone and Harrison Ford (left to right) with Lansing at the premiere of 2002's *K-19: The Widowmaker*.

Actor Jon Voight cautioned Lansing against hiring his daughter, Angelina Jolie (left), for *Lara Croft: Tomb Raider*, warning that she was extremely fragile.

Lansing was trapped between two warring giants, Harvey Weinstein (left) and Scott Rudin (right), on *The Hours*.

Delivering the commencement address to the UCLA School of Theater, Film and TV graduates in 2004.

Lansing with some of the girls from Big Brothers Big Sisters, whom she championed through the Women in Entertainment Mentorship Program.

Katie Couric, Sue Schwartz (front row); Kathleen Lobb, Lansing, Ellen Ziffren, Lisa Paulsen, Rusty Robertson and Pam Williams at the 2014 Stand Up to Cancer telecast.

With President Jimmy Carter and First Lady Rosalynn Carter.

Presenting Meryl Streep with the *Hollywood Reporter's*
Sherry Lansing Leadership Award.

With sons Jack
and Cedric.

Lansing adored
Tom Cruise, though
both could be
like "immovable
mountains," according
to one executive.

The paparazzi turned out in force when Lansing received her star on Hollywood's Walk of Fame.

Receiving the Jean Hersholt Humanitarian Award, an honorary Oscar, in 2007.

She tussled with one of the most promising young directors in America, Alexander Payne, on his second feature, *Election*, about a teacher's efforts to prevent a nakedly ambitious girl from being elected student president. When she asked him to revise the ending, he complied. But when she wanted further revisions, he resisted. What had been a sweet experience for both suddenly turned sour.

"To my dismay, she now said she wanted changes to even this new ending," said Payne. "When I insisted that she had already approved these pages, and we had scouted and prepared the shoot, the meeting grew very tense. She became angry and accused me of suggesting she was lying. I said no, I was just going by what we'd all agreed upon previously, and I couldn't permit any more changes to what I thought would be a successful outcome for the film."

Lansing leveled a finger at him. "She went, 'Listen, do you know who's sat on that couch?'" Goldwyn recalled. "'Bob Zemeckis has sat on that couch. Sydney Pollack has sat on that couch. Peter Weir has sat on that couch. Every one of them is a final-cut director and you aren't. And let me tell you, they're my partners. They understand how to be a partner with a company that has spent money making a movie, and you had better learn how to be a partner if you want to stay in the business.' It was just incredible. Alexander looked at her—and there's something about having a woman of that stature yell at you. It's intimidating. She was Sherry Lansing and she had that giant job and was coming at him."

Later, despite their clash, Payne credited her with financing "a new ending that was not more sentimental, but rather more cynical than the original" and for "being good enough to offer a half million dollars or so for us to shoot a new ending."

Lansing's irritation welled up when Edward Norton repeatedly refused to take the roles Paramount offered him, despite being under contract to the studio.

After being cast in 1996's *Primal Fear*, Norton had committed to make two more movies for the studio, though which ones were never specified. According to the terms of the deal, he would receive $75,000 for one and $125,000 for the next—a lot of money at the time the near-unknown signed the deal, but nothing compared to the $10 million he would soon be getting elsewhere.

When Fox cast him in 1997's *Fight Club,* Paramount sent a cautionary letter reminding that studio he was under contract to make a movie for Paramount and warning that it would sue. Fox refused to move forward until the situation was resolved. In the negotiations that followed between Paramount and Norton, Lansing offered a compromise: she would allow the actor to make one movie for Paramount instead of two, and she would pay him $1 million—but he had to make a film.

Still he wavered, and over the following five years he turned down everything Paramount showed him. When he finally said no to *The Italian Job,* it was one time too many. Lansing called Mark Wahlberg, who was set to co-star, and asked him to intervene. For Wahlberg, it was an extremely important film, given that he was coming off two flops.

"Did he have a deal?" he asked.

"Yes," said Lansing.

"And no one held a gun to his head?"

"That's right," she replied.

"Then he should do it," said Wahlberg.

Norton continued to resist. "It wasn't a film I had much interest in," he said, "and I was going to do a play for my theater company at the same time, so I asked [Lansing] to not force me to do the film, but she insisted. I tried to be politely firm that I really couldn't bail out on the commitment to the play, which had a lot of our company's economics on the line."

Lansing maintained her ground, though she later gave a generous gift to Norton's theater company to make up for any losses.

"Sherry said, 'We're going to force his hand,'" recalled Wahlberg. "At first I didn't think that was a good idea, because unless somebody is really passionate about something, they may not do their best work."

Lansing had no doubt that Norton would deliver a stellar performance, as gifted as he was. When he persisted in saying no, she hired a litigator and the actor hired another.

"I was informed, again, that Paramount would sue me," said Norton, "and this time was told specifically that they'd sue me for $20 million."

Faced with the real possibility of a lawsuit, he gave in, only to arrive on set with an assistant ready to videotape his every move, almost daring the studio to find him out of line.

"It was surreal," recalled Donald De Line, the picture's producer. "I said, 'What's going on?' He said, 'I'm going to protect myself and have it documented that I'm doing what I'm told.' He was clearly shaken up. But Sherry was like steel. She wouldn't back down."

HER PRODUCERS WERE not always any easier than her stars. Rudin, in particular, could be a handful.

A rumpled and bearded former wunderkind, he was obsessive in his perfectionism, which Lansing found out on her first day at the studio when he left four phone messages for her before she could return a single one. Despite that—or perhaps because of it—for years they were ideally matched.

In their early days, reveling in each other's company, they perfected a one-two punch to lock in talent and projects that resulted in such hits as *The Addams Family*, *Clueless*, *Zoolander* and *School of Rock*.

"Scott was exceptional at finding material and remarkable at developing it," said Lansing. "He was one of the most gifted producers I knew."

Who else could have turned an accidental slip in an Oscar speech (Tom Hanks's revelation that his high school acting coach was gay) into an acclaimed comedy (*In & Out*)? Who else could have shifted so easily from the cerebral (*The Reader*) to the scatological (*South Park: Bigger, Longer & Uncut*)?

At his best, Rudin would use charm to bend others to his will; at his worst, he would promise to kill them. His tantrums were legendary. Once he left a voicemail threatening to burn down the house of Paramount's Robert Friedman. Another time, furious at a Lansing staffer for the way she had handled a premiere, he wrote her: "Be aware that the only thing separating my hands from your neck is the fact that there are 3,000 miles between us. Be aware that in 15 years of producing movies and running companies, I have never been treated so disrespectfully, rudely, insolently or been dismissed . . . by any low-level flunky as I have by you this afternoon."

Rudin's rage was fueled by the same passion as his talent, which Lansing admired enormously, even though he could drive her to distraction—not least during the making of 1998's *The Truman Show.*

Paramount had paid $1.5 million for Andrew Niccol's satirical script about a man who is trapped inside the bubble of a TV series, not realizing his whole life is being watched on television. Lansing liked the script so much that she agreed to wait a whole year for Jim Carrey to star, despite reservations. "Carrey brought little insurance," she said, "because this wasn't a mainstream comedy."

Shooting began in Florida in 1997, and days into filming, Rudin called Manning, the studio's point person.

"I got a call very early in the morning, saying, 'Mich, we've got to get rid of Dennis Hopper,'" said Manning. "I go, 'Well, I'm going to go see dailies today.' He said, 'No, you can't see them. They're too embarrassing. We need to protect him.'"

Manning watched the dailies, regardless, and realized Hopper, cast as the godlike television guru who oversees the *Truman* show, could not remember his lines, probably following years of drug and alcohol abuse. He had to be replaced, but by whom? Peter Weir, the director, suggested himself.

"Crazy idea," said Rudin. "I said, 'I am not doing this movie. Let's just shut it down and go home.' He kept going to Sherry. But she was very smart. She said: 'All right, shut this movie down for a year if you have to. When you both agree, go finish it.'"

Weir backed off, but the casting issue remained unresolved until both he and Rudin united behind Alan Arkin. Lansing demurred, saying she wanted a bigger star (she eventually opted for Ed Harris), and the producer went on the warpath.

"He was blowing up my phone," said Manning. "He had every one of his assistants calling, saying, 'Martin Scorsese on line one about Alan Arkin,' 'Sydney Pollack on line two.' He was desperate."

When Lansing stood firm, a letter came to Manning, purportedly from Arkin.

"I write to you because a grave injustice has been committed," it began, "and as we both know, you are the perpetrator. You have denied me personally and artistically, and I am mortified and disgusted. For reasons unknown to myself and others, you have marked me as your enemy, or more appropriately your prey. For the moment my suffering has satiated your appetite for destruction. How could you? How dare you direct such an atrocity at me? Are my years, my blood, my flesh, my sacrifice a fair trade for the work of your evil hands? Is all that I have done so unremarkable in your eyes? Are you so corrupted, your mind so polluted, that my work is beyond you? It is painfully clear that your cantankerous hand and wicked deeds [extend] far and wide but I know even you cannot poison every cup. Despite your efforts to sabotage my work, [it] will survive and vengeance will be mine."

"It was Scott's writing," said Manning, "but written with his left hand instead of his right hand."

Both Rudin and Arkin denied writing the letter.

DEALING WITH THE egos and excesses of producers and stars was only one element of Lansing's working life as she oversaw a city-state with dozens of soundstages, hundreds of offices and thousands of employees.

"People don't understand what a studio is like," she said. "There's a clinic, doctor's office, shops, a commissary. You can get your shoes shined. You can get your hair done. You're managing a city. And I wanted to instill a good culture in that city, a really warm culture. So we had a Christmas tree, we had a volunteer day, we went to a school and gave them computers, we had the AIDS walk, and we redesigned the studio, adding areas for sitting and a whole new walkway. We also did everything to minimize studio politics: anyone could call me or come by my office, no matter who they reported to."

She did her best not to be too removed from her employees or the outside world. On Saturdays, she and Friedkin would buy tickets to the pictures just like regular moviegoers, many of whom would have been stunned to know who was in line with them. Whenever possible, she wanted to see the latest releases at a local theater, avoiding the hermetic bubble of industry screenings. Then on Sundays, almost religiously, she would go to the studio and run parts of the films she had missed, searching for an actor here, an editor there. Few other studio chiefs conducted their business like this.

She wanted her audience to be as swept up by their emotions as she was. "I wanted to make films about people that you cared for," she said. "They could be twisted, they could be dark, but if they evoked an emotional response, the films were worth making. Sometimes a script would take years of work, but it was only after it was right and a producer was in place that we'd search for a director and cast."

Having erred in failing to visit the set of *Forrest Gump*, Lansing did a course correction and made sure to spend time on location with her other pictures, partly to support the filmmakers and partly to escape the claustrophobia of her office. She loved nothing more than sitting in an editing room, weighing in on a movie's progress.

"I was completely invested in these movies," she said. "I read every script, gave notes on each draft, saw all the dailies. I went to every test screening, joined in the marketing meetings. When a picture didn't work, I knew how that felt. I remembered when *Fatal Attraction* was going through hell. I knew how much it hurt when *The Accused* had to be reedited. Whenever there was bad news, I'd say to the filmmakers, 'I'm really sorry. I know this is tough.' And I always tried to share the blame, because ultimately I was the one who'd green-lit their movie. I bled with each picture that failed and I bled with it on the way to success."

WHILE OTHER STUDIO chiefs allowed their subordinates to oversee each project's development, Lansing waded waist deep into all of them, just as she attended every test screening. She believed executives' failure to do so added to the widening gulf between studios and filmmakers.

She orchestrated these test screenings in her own special way, trying to ensure that her position would not influence those around her.

"Sherry had a specific method for how she would handle the post-screening conversation," said Don Granger, one of her production executives. "We'd leave the studio theater—the producers and director and executives—and walk a very short distance to her office. Nobody was allowed to speak. You couldn't huddle aside and rehearse what you were going to say. We'd go in the back door and sit down on couches and Sherry would sit in her chair, and we'd start talking about how we thought the movie played. And at some point [market researcher] Joe Farrell would come in with a sheet of paper that had the test scores on it. And Sherry would take the paper and not allow anybody to look at it—including herself—and put it facedown on the coffee table. You'd be sitting there with that piece of paper holding your fate in its hands for maybe an hour. She'd say, 'This is useful, but that's all it is. We don't have to go with everything it says.' And at the end Sherry would give her opinion, and it was only then we'd see the score."

Lansing wanted to be able to express her opinion uninfluenced by the test results, and she wanted her staff to do the same, though that might have been wishful thinking. Granger recalled feeling a cold sweat as he and the others in the room discussed the merits of 1996's *Star Trek: First Contact*.

"It seemed clear the movie had tested well," he said, "but you never know. So we start to talk and Sherry says, 'The scores don't matter. They shouldn't sway any of our reactions. They're only a tool.' The junior person in the room starts talking—that's me—and you knew you were dead if you said, 'The movie's great, don't change a thing' and the scores were terrible. So I mentioned a few things that [director] Jonathan Frakes and [producer] Rick Berman had left out of the movie, and Goldwyn picked up on them, and there was a lull. Then Sherry says, 'Well, I thought the movie was just great.' And she turns over the piece of paper and the movie scored an 84. The highest score in Paramount history was an 88, which

Forrest Gump got. And she says, 'See! Don't change a thing!'" Granger laughed. "We all looked at her like, 'Uh, what about that 'scores don't matter . . .'?"

THE *STAR TREK* franchise, which had been launched as a film series with 1979's *Star Trek: The Motion Picture*, was of prime importance for Lansing, though at first she was flummoxed by its terminology. "What's 'Beam me up, Scotty' mean?" she asked Berman, much to his amusement. "What's the bridge? What's warp drive?"

Aware that she was an outsider to the *Star Trek* ecosystem, Lansing gave the producer more room to maneuver than she might otherwise have done.

"He was the keeper of the flame, and I knew I had a steep learning curve," she said, noting that Berman had taken over the brand created by Gene Roddenberry and ran the *Star Trek* TV spin-offs as well as the movies. "I was nervous, because when you're given an important franchise like *Star Trek*, it's a huge responsibility, and in this case it's one where I had no history with the material. I was terrified I might damage it."

She was eager to hire Leonard Nimoy as the director of 1994's *Star Trek: Generations*, the first of the film series released on her watch, but he declined.

"When I brought it to Leonard, his attitude was, 'There's a great deal of rewriting needed on the script,'" said Berman. "And our attitude was, 'Well, we really don't have time for that.'" Berman was used to the television world, where directors were guns for hire, not auteurs—as opposed to film, where they were the be-all and end-all behind every decision. "It was my naïveté. Leonard probably had every right to do that. But we ended up parting ways."

Lansing was disappointed, and so was Berman when she passed on the chance to sign Marlon Brando as the villain.

"I got a call one day that Brando was interested," he remembered. "I went to Sherry and said, 'Marlon Brando wants to play Soran.' But he wanted a huge amount of money. It was numerous millions of dollars, much more than she had any interest in paying. This was also at a point when he was quite overweight, and it was an action-hero type of role. My feeling was, 'We're talking about Marlon Brando here!' But Sherry had remarkable experience in the motion picture business and said: 'Brando's presence is not going to justify the expenditure.'"

When the movie opened in November 1994, the producer got flak from die-hard fans, who learned that their beloved Captain Kirk (William Shatner) was dead.

"There was a lot of controversy," he noted. "Yes, we did kill him—but we'd brought him back to life prior to doing that, because it was a hundred years [since the original *Star Trek* adventures] and he would have been two hundred years old if he hadn't been stuck in this nexus for a century. We thought he died a noble death saving the lives of millions or perhaps billions of people. Sherry did not have the slightest problem with that."

On the next *Star Trek* picture, *First Contact*, when Brent Spiner's agents started playing hardball during negotiations, Lansing told Berman to cut him loose. The actor played the android Data and was a pillar of the modern-day franchise, second only to Patrick Stewart as Captain Jean-Luc Picard. Berman was afraid she really meant it, while Lansing said she wanted to call the agents' bluff. The strategy worked. They capitulated, as she had expected, and Spiner returned to the role.

"Brent and I are close," said Berman, "and he knew he was not going to win this battle."

SUCH BATTLES WERE par for the course on almost any major film, except Lansing's first collaboration with Steven Spielberg.

She was driving home one evening, fully anticipating a quiet night with her husband and sons, when CAA agent Richard Lovett called her in her car. The line crackled as she passed through the hills, and his words floated in and out of hearing.

"Sherry," he said, "how would you feel about Tom Hanks and Steven Spielberg doing *Saving Private Ryan?*"

Paramount had been developing the screenplay for *Ryan* for a while; it was one of three World War II movies the studio had in the works, and earlier that week Rob Cohen (*The Fast and the Furious*) had committed to direct. Now Lovett was telling her that Spielberg wanted to do it. Was this a prank, some kind of elaborate hoax? Nobody had ever called out of the blue to offer her the biggest director in Hollywood and one of its biggest stars. The contrast between Lovett's monotone voice and the news he was imparting made the whole thing seemed surreal.

"There was no drama, no typical agent build-up," said Lansing. "He might as well have been asking if I wanted cream in my coffee. I said, 'I'd feel just fine.'"

"DreamWorks would have to be your partner," the agent resumed, referring to Spielberg's production and financing company, "and you'd have to split the budget and the rights. Is that OK?"

"Of course," said Lansing.

"Then they want to do the picture," said Lovett.

And with that he hung up, leaving her too stunned to know what to do next.

"I told myself it was ludicrous," she said. "Nothing like this had ever happened, because anytime I got to that point it was after months of chasing the talent or begging them to do it. I thought, 'What's he been smoking?'"

That night she called the film's producer, Mark Gordon, who assured her it was true. And then Dolgen called to say that he, too, had spoken to Lovett.

"Jon was ecstatic," she said. "He told me [DreamWorks partner] David Geffen had just called about working out the rights split. He wanted to flip a coin to see who would get the domestic release and who would get foreign." That seemed no stranger a solution to the problem than anything else in this weird experience.

"We agreed that Sumner and Steven would represent their respective companies," she said. "The winner would take *Ryan* domestically and the loser would take it internationally, with all the costs and revenues divided equally."

Spielberg and Redstone met for the coin toss.

Spielberg won.

SAVING PRIVATE RYAN was the unlikely brainchild of Robert Rodat, a Harvard Business School and USC film school graduate best known for romantic comedies and for the 1996 family drama *Fly Away Home*. But the writer was also a history buff, and had begun to think about World War II when an avalanche of books and articles appeared in June 1994, in anticipation of the fiftieth anniversary of D-Day.

Rodat had been mesmerized by a memorial to the war dead in the small New Hampshire town where he and his wife had spent their summer.

"There were multiple last names that were the same, with the same year of death," he said. "One family had lost five sons in the Civil War, and another had lost three in the American Revolution. All the guys from a town would enlist, and they would keep those guys together because it was good for unit cohesion. Unfortunately, that meant the entire town's young men could be wiped out in a moment."

He knew of the five Sullivan brothers from Waterloo, Iowa, all killed in action following the sinking of the USS *Juneau* in 1942. He began to wonder, would it be possible to tell a story centered on a small group of soldiers out to find the sole surviving sibling before he is killed?

Rodat took his idea to Gordon, the producer of *Speed*, and they went out to present it. "We pitched the story to pretty much every studio in town, and nobody wanted it," said Gordon. "The only place that was even a little interested was Paramount."

There was a hitch. The studio had two other war movies chugging along at various stages of development: a Randall Wallace screenplay, *With Wings of Eagles*, designed to star Arnold Schwarzenegger as a Nazi officer who saves escaping prisoners of war; and *Combat!*, based on the 1960s television series about a U.S. platoon fighting in France, which had attracted the attention of Bruce Willis. Both stars were nibbling at the edges, but neither had bitten, and Lansing knew that only one of these pictures would get a green light, very likely the one whose star committed first.

"They all had things about them that I liked," she said. "But we weren't going to make all three. We were going to make the one that came together the best."

She offered to help each project in any way she could, and when Gordon got Cohen interested, true to her word, she arranged a meeting with him, designed to lock him in. Over breakfast, she discovered the director was more passionate than she had realized: his father had served in the war, and he wanted to make a movie that would honor him. He pushed her to make *Ryan*, arguing that it was far better than either of its rivals. "You can't seriously make a script with an SS officer and just pretend he didn't go around murdering Jews," he said, demolishing the Schwarzenegger film. "This one's going to be a masterpiece."

Thrilled about their meeting, Lansing called Gordon right afterward, expecting he would be overjoyed. She was taken aback to get only a lukewarm response. Wasn't it Gordon who had asked her to meet Cohen? Wasn't he the one pushing to get this made?

"I didn't understand," she said. "Finding a director was a key part of getting the movie off the ground, and that was Mark's dream."

She did not know that a bigger fish was circling. During a visit to CAA, on his annual pilgrimage to what was then the mecca of Hollywood, Spielberg had heard about *Ryan* from a young agent, Carin Sage, who blurted out her belief in this obscure piece of material even though she did not represent it.

"The screenplay first came to me through my agents," Spielberg recalled. "It had been sent to me on offer to direct, and I took to the story immediately. I phoned Tom Hanks, having seen him on every page playing [the leader of the searchers] Captain Miller, only to discover that CAA had sent [him] the script at the same time. We decided on the phone that afternoon to do the movie together."

Hanks's office was next to Gordon's on the Fox lot, and the actor had turned down the script when he first read it, fearing the material was too familiar and too jingoistic. But Spielberg was proposing a hyperrealistic account of war.

"Steven said, 'Look, with the technology that now exists, we have an opportunity to go back and literally recreate World War II,'" Hanks noted. "I said, 'Steven, please tell me you'd like me to be in this movie, so I can say yes.'"

When the star and director told Gordon they were on board, he was sworn to secrecy by CAA, anxious that its clients' plans would leak and result in a wave of publicity before the deals were done, possibly scuttling the whole endeavor. Hence Gordon said nothing when Lansing called after meeting Cohen, who would soon learn he had lost the job.

Now the coin had been tossed and the deal had been done. The budget was set at $69 million and the picture was a go.

LANSING SHUTTLED BETWEEN Paramount and Spielberg's compound on the Universal lot, a low-level adobe office complex built just for him and decorated with classic movie posters and casual Santa Fe–style furniture. It was the first time she had had any significant dealings with him.

"He made me feel instantly comfortable," she said. "Everybody there was dressed in baseball caps and jeans, and there was free food for everyone. He made you think you were talking to an equal, and you'd forget you were sitting with someone of his brilliance. He was relaxed and interested and open to any suggestion, and curious about everything you thought: 'Did you like the script? What are you thinking? What would you like to change?'"

Despite how laid-back Spielberg appeared, she realized he was more complex and also more vulnerable than many realized, and it was that part of him she responded to most. The two developed a warm rapport.

"[She] was a great team leader and inspired us all to do our best work," he said.

At the same time, Rodat polished the screenplay with Spielberg, and was even invited to the director's Pacific Palisades home for a script meeting, along with Gordon, Hanks and DreamWorks executive Walter Parkes.

"I got there early," said Rodat. "I was wandering around like, 'Where the heck am I?' There's a bunch of offices. There's an editing bay and this gigantic office at one end of it. I go into this room and I hear this harsh voice that says, 'Can I help you?' I panicked. It was a parrot."

Sitting down, he and the others stared at a blank TV screen, waiting for Spielberg—who was away on vacation—to be teleconferenced in. "First we see the screen," said Rodat, "and it almost looks like there's an iris in a silent film. This circle of light comes in, and then [the camera] pulls out. We realized Spielberg had taken the camera that was on a little umbilical cord, and put it in his mouth as a gag."

When the laughter died down, they discussed the script.

"He wanted to break it apart," said Rodat. "We considered all sorts of crazy stuff, like having Ryan be wounded and heavily bandaged." He told Spielberg he clung to a secret wish: that Captain Miller should die toward the end of the movie. "He said, 'Absolutely. There's no question about it.'"

In June 1997, Hanks and other key cast members arrived in England, where they were put through a fierce boot camp led by military adviser Dale Dye.

"It was five days," said Hanks. "It rained, we were wet, we were very cold. I was worried that we were all going to get sick, and Dale was relatively merciless." When the actors rebelled, Hanks had to convince them to carry on. "There was a point where the guys said: 'We've had enough of this. We're actors.' But the rebellion fell apart and we all ended up staying."

This was the beginning of a grueling experience that saw them wade through water, slosh through mud, heave bulky backpacks, and live in a state of high alert that lasted from the beginning of the shoot to the end.

"That was an incredibly physical film to make," said Hanks, "and it played tricks with the mind because so much of it was a very, very tactile experience. It was loud, it was wet, it was uncomfortable, it was hard—

literally—on the knees and on the shoulders. Eddie [Edward] Burns got a horrible third-degree burn on his hand because the weapon he was firing was incredibly hot. His hand swelled up and blistered like a baseball bat, but we had to keep going."

There was only one break, after the August 31 death of Princess Diana. When her funeral took place, "the country shut down," said Hanks. He and Spielberg traveled to London for the funeral, which they attended with Tom Cruise and Nicole Kidman, both there for Stanley Kubrick's *Eyes Wide Shut*. "We showed up with a few thousand other people, and there were people on the roofs of every building, and every open space had somebody standing in it. We were in front of Westminster Abbey, and all you heard was the footfalls of the people in line. There was no other sound."

Despite the difficulties his actors faced, Spielberg was in his element, and when Lansing arrived in England she found him more relaxed than any filmmaker she had ever seen.

"I was struck by how calm the set was," she said. "There was no tension and no yelling. The crew moved about, doing their jobs efficiently. They broke on time for a civilized lunch, and the cast ate with them. Steven would eat and then go into a facility to finish editing *Amistad*. There were no frantic, last-minute script conferences or haggling over the afternoon schedule. His confidence filtered through the ranks. I said, 'Steven, I've never seen such a relaxed set.' He said, 'Well, that's how you do your best work. You have to be loose.'"

MONTHS LATER, HE showed Lansing the finished film in Paramount's main theater. She and a handful of other executives settled in to watch the first cut, before anyone other than Spielberg's closest associates had seen it. Unlike Lansing, the director despised test screenings and preferred to show his film to a few select friends, such as Robert Zemeckis and George Lucas.

No matter how many drafts of the script Lansing had read, and regardless of how impressed she had been on the set, she was stunned by what she saw, and amazed that the director could have made a film this visceral, this groundbreaking. In the first drafts of the screenplay, the Normandy invasion had been a brief flash, witnessed rather than lived; here it was long and real and almost too much to bear.

"That sequence when they land on the beaches of Normandy, I'd never seen anything like it," she said. "The camera moved in and out of real horror; the cutting was so fast you felt you were trying to catch up with the chaos all around you. This was one of the strongest of antiwar movies, but also one that showed the greatest respect for the soldiers. I couldn't even breathe, it was so intense. I knew how great it was the moment I saw it, and so did everyone else in that theater."

"I'll never forget it," said Terry Press, DreamWorks' head of marketing. "People couldn't speak afterward. Nobody was saying anything, because nobody could speak a word."

Lansing only had one concern: that the movie's violence could lead to an NC-17 rating. The very notion that a Spielberg picture might warrant this showed how far the director had come from his early days.

"I discussed the rating at length with Sherry," said Spielberg, "and she advised that I should preemptively sit with the ratings board to place into context what my intentions were in showing such a vast quantity of violence to depict what it was like for these young men landing on Omaha Beach. They very kindly allowed me to present my reasons for depicting *Saving Private Ryan* in this way before they viewed the film for the first time. I was never concerned about making the D-Day invasion too violent. I was concerned that the audience for such a graphic depiction of combat would not go out to the movies to give us a chance. I am very happy I was wrong about that."

The MPAA gave *Ryan* an R rating, and the picture was a hit when it opened on July 24, 1998. Despite its near-three-hour length, it made $30.6 million over its first weekend and brought in a total of $482 million worldwide, an astonishing number for a war film this intense.

"Here Spielberg, the creator of *Schindler's List*, the film that more than any other justifies the justness of World War II, asks us to examine the war's morality in a different light," wrote *Time* magazine's Richard

Schickel. "What we may hope is that *Saving Private Ryan* will be perceived for what it is—a war film that, entirely aware of its genre's conventions, transcends them as it transcends the simplistic moralities that inform its predecessors, to take the high, morally haunting ground."

Other critics concurred, and audiences raved about the movie. It seemed destined to scoop the top prizes at the upcoming Oscars.

As the Academy Awards approached, and as the industry entered the months-long period known as awards season, Lansing felt sure that this picture had the substance, the brilliance and the imagination to go all the way. It had beautiful performances and masterful cinematography. How could it lose?

But in the run-up to the March 1999 event, something unexpected happened. Another picture, *Shakespeare in Love*, began to gain traction. It was funny and charming and joyful, but it was also relatively lightweight and lacked the cinematic originality of *Ryan*. Rumors of ugly tactics surfaced. There was talk that Harvey Weinstein, the swaggering chairman of Miramax Films—and one of *Shakespeare*'s producers—was working behind the scenes to undermine his rival. Nobody could prove anything, or fathom his honed and tested methods for winning, but Paramount and DreamWorks insiders began to worry.

"Somebody told me that Harvey had hired all these people to go around saying our movie was all in the first fifteen minutes, and beyond that it was mundane," said DreamWorks' Press. "The idea that you could hire people to go bad-mouth somebody else's movie—to me, that was a completely foreign concept. So I went to Steven and said, 'This is the world of Harvey Weinstein, and this is what he's saying about the movie.' And he said, 'I will not get in the mud with him. I will not lower myself.' I said, 'Are you sure? Because this is like a war now.'"

On Oscar night—March 21, 1999—everything looked good. The key players arrived and took their places, all positioned in the first few rows of the Dorothy Chandler Pavilion in downtown Los Angeles, where they could be observed by a dozen or more cameras, each zooming in for a close-up whenever it was needed. The usual meet-and-greets and perfunctory congratulations were dispensed with. And then the host, Whoopi

Goldberg—Spielberg's discovery in 1985's *The Color Purple*—emerged to introduce the show, and the initial batch of awards was handed out.

Hours later, when Spielberg won for Best Director, optimism surged through the *Ryan* team. Gordon, the producer, was so confident that he began to button up his tuxedo jacket, ready to walk onstage and pick up his Best Picture Oscar. When Harrison Ford came out to present the final award, it seemed like a good-luck omen. And then he opened the envelope and announced the winner: *Shakespeare in Love.*

Lansing turned to the others in disbelief. As five producers walked onstage to collect their Oscars for *Shakespeare*—four of them jostling for space around Weinstein, who seemed to suck the air from everyone else—it became clear that Spielberg had made a film about one kind of victory, only to have another snatched from his grasp.

"I remember feeling flushed, like I had had some kind of chemical reaction," recalled Press. "I said to my husband, 'I need to get out of here.' I should never have listened to Steven. It was very noble not to get in the mud, but we lost."

Spielberg was relatively stoic, said Press—he had won the directing Oscar, after all. But a sense of gloom settled on the others.

"It was so crushing," said Lansing. "You could feel how shattered everyone was. I felt guilty, as if I'd let everyone down. Whenever I failed, that's how I felt. I'd ask myself, 'What did I do wrong?' But there was nothing that hadn't been done right. It was hard for me and for all of us, but it didn't change how great that picture was."

CHAPTER 17

While Lansing formed a close relationship with Spielberg, she formed an even closer one with Tom Cruise.

She had first met the actor at Fox when she oversaw *Taps*, the 1981 military drama in which he starred with Sean Penn, Timothy Hutton and George C. Scott. Back then, he was an eager if somewhat naive nineteen-year-old with a strong work ethic and an even stronger sense of loyalty, who was grateful to Lansing for being gracious to his mother.

"He was cast in a smaller role, then given a much bigger one in a film with an amazing cast, because you could see right away that he had a giant talent," she said. "He was always extremely focused and exceptionally polite."

Lansing had not worked with him since, and production was already under way on *The Firm* when she took up her post as Paramount's chairman in 1992. But the Cruise she had met at Fox had not changed. "He was just as focused and just as polite," she said.

The actor was in the middle of creating a production company with his former agent, Paula Wagner—CW Productions—and had just closed a deal to be based at Paramount when Lansing was named studio chairman. As she moved out of her production offices and into the executive suites, Cruise and Wagner took over her old space in the Lucille Ball Building.

"The goal was to make a couple of movies a year, preferably for Tom to star in," said Wagner. "But we also wanted to do other films."

Lansing approved, and was in the thick of finding producers whom she could count on when Cruise and Wagner started their new company. "I knew Tom was hardworking and would take this seriously, because that's who he is," she said. "I'd also seen a good success rate with actors who became producers and directors. They have an innate sense of truth and know when material works."

After developing several projects, Cruise locked into the idea of making *Mission: Impossible*, based on the CBS series that ran from 1968 to 1973 about a group of secret CIA operatives tasked with mind-bending challenges that they would solve using the latest gadgetry and appearance-altering masks. Paramount had been trying for years to adapt the series, a favorite with Cruise's generation, but its surface appeal—an action-heavy spy thriller—hid numerous problems. It was an ensemble piece rather than a star vehicle, and it was rooted in the Cold War, when the world had moved away from that conflict following the fall of the Berlin Wall. Still, this was the picture Cruise wanted to make.

"I kept thinking, why does a star of his stature want to do this ensemble piece?" said Lansing. "I knew each character in the series had the potential to be distinct, but it was strange that he wanted to make a new version of an old TV show, and a showcase for half a dozen characters."

Lansing waited as the partners commenced the arduous task of developing a screenplay worthy of their producing debut. A draft by *American Graffiti*'s married screenwriters Willard Huyck and Gloria Katz, while prescient in putting an ecological crisis at the heart of the story, was rejected as not thrilling enough, and over the next three years a host of leading writers came and went, adding millions of dollars in development fees, but never resulting in a finished screenplay.

"The mandate from Sherry and John Goldwyn was: make *Mission*," said Wagner. "Then you start asking all the questions: Is Tom going to play Jim Phelps [the leader of the missions, originally played by Peter Graves]? Are you going to keep the same characters? Are you going to change it? How?"

Early in the process, *The Firm*'s director, Sydney Pollack, came in to oversee the process, only to drop out. "He wanted it to be a spy film, like something by John le Carré," said Wagner. "He was really helpful in defining the tone, but he didn't feel it was his cup of tea, with all the action." When he left, "we started talking about, 'Who can we bring on?' Mike Ovitz had just signed Brian De Palma, who had done *Bonfire of the Vanities*, then *Raising Cain* and *Carlito's Way*, which didn't work. But Tom was game."

After three failures in a row, De Palma was in "movie jail," the place stars and directors went when they had suffered a colossal bomb or two and nobody in the industry wanted to take a risk on them. Wagner felt the studio was nervous about hiring him, but Lansing was impressed that Cruise chose this director, rather than a more fashionable one.

Her relationship with De Palma had been strained on *Fatal Attraction*— "Brian's defection wounded her," said Goldwyn—but had grown warmer after he acknowledged how good Michael Douglas was. This was the man who had made such visually arresting films as 1976's *Carrie* and 1987's *The Untouchables*, and Lansing had never forgotten Melnick's counsel to judge an artist on his best work, not his last.

"Right away, Tom started talking about scenes in *The Untouchables*, and everything else De Palma had made," she recalled. "He wasn't going with the flavor of the month."

De Palma brought in writer Jay Cocks (*Gangs of New York*), and together they started to explore ideas for the film.

"When Brian called asking for help, I called the Huycks, old pals, to check in that everything was copacetic with them," said Cocks. "This was the first they'd heard they were being succeeded. Awkward all around. But the fact we were friends and—I hope—professionals made the transition easier."

Cocks worked on the movie for only a week, but that week was productive. Ideas came bubbling forth, influenced by his wide-ranging knowledge of film, which was more than matched by De Palma's own.

"Jay is a phenomenal film historian," said Wagner. "He came onboard and we started doing all this research. We looked at every single film that had twists and turns in it that you didn't see coming."

In particular, they studied Hitchcock, a tremendous influence on De Palma, and looked at all the old *Mission: Impossible* episodes, as well as at everything that had inspired its creator, Bruce Geller. They explored the lives of some real-life spies, including CIA mole Aldrich Ames, an agent for the Soviet Union until his arrest in 1994.

Before locking into a story, the production team agreed it must be rich in complications, packed with unexpected revelations. "Brian wanted it to be done with sleight of hand," said Wagner. "He loved twists and turns."

In these first conversations, the filmmakers decided on one of the movie's biggest revelations: that Phelps, the leader of the missions in the television series, where he was the embodiment of authority and integrity, would not be who he seemed.

"I suggested making [him] the major villain," said Cocks, "an idea Brian loved, and which, to our glee, discombobulated, upset and incensed *Mission: Impossible* traditionalists the world over. And we came up with and refined the idea of the long sequence in the Chunnel [the rail tunnel under the English Channel, linking England and France]. I don't recall ever writing anything beyond scrawling a lot of notes on a yellow pad. But it gave some shape and thrust to the finished film."

When Cocks left the project for other commitments, new writers stepped in, including Steven Zaillian (*Schindler's List*), Robert Towne (*Chinatown*) and David Koepp (*Jurassic Park*).

Koepp recalled how De Palma created the film's most memorable sequence, when Cruise breaks into a super-secret CIA vault in eerie silence. The gleaming vault had echoes of *2001: A Space Odyssey* and *Star Wars*. It was very much a technocrat's vision of the future rather than a reflection of the prosaic present.

"We'd done a bunch of research into how the CIA actually protects its corridors and its physical property, and it was all very boring," said Koepp. "You know there are video cameras; there's a guy in a room. It was rather familiar. After wrestling this research into the ground, Brian and I said, 'Screw all that. Let's make everything up.' I loved the Michael Jackson video where the floor lights up [for *Billie Jean*]. So I said, 'Why don't we do that?'"

Two years had passed since Lansing agreed to back the movie; she was still without a working screenplay, and had to stand by as other studios bombarded Cruise with offers. "I understood the process and I understood how long it takes to get something great," she said. "I had faith in them." Still, she had a company to run.

"She said, 'OK, kids, here are your rules. Here are the players. Here's what we're going to do. We have to have this movie,'" Wagner recalled. "She said, 'We have to have it and we have to have it soon. Whatever you need to get there, we're going to support you, but you better damn well get a great script and a script that's action and that's going to be a big hit.'"

Finally Lansing received a draft during a business trip to Chicago. Locking herself in her hotel room and refusing to answer the phone, she tore open the package and whipped through the pages.

The first part of the script seemed predictable. "It started with an action sequence, but it was still very much an ensemble piece," she said. "And suddenly everybody's killed and Tom's character [the newly created Ethan Hunt] has to take control of the mission. From that point on, you couldn't stop reading. Even with the thousands of scripts I'd read, I hadn't seen that coming."

CASTING WAS AN immediate priority, and it was influenced by the growing globalization of the business and Lansing's own willingness to consider unorthodox actors.

"The role of the spymaster was written for a man," she said, "but we gave it to a woman and brought in Vanessa Redgrave. We also very consciously gave the movie an international feel: we had two French stars, Emmanuelle Béart and Jean Reno, and decided to make this the first major American production to have a substantial shoot in Prague."

Adding stars and major new sequences inevitably raised the budget. When the picture seemed to be heading out of control, Cruise offered to defer his salary.

"Tom and I were partners," said Lansing, "and he was one of the few producers and stars who truly understood and sympathized with the problems of the studio. He said, 'I'm going to defer $20 million,' which allowed him to make the movie he wanted without having to make other cuts."

Cruise, in fact, had been given some stern counsel by one of his closest advisers. Knowing the cost might lead the studio to pull the plug, one told him: "You have to give up your salary. Take it on the back end. But you can't have your first film as a producer go down in flames."

In the race to get the screenplay completed before shooting began, Towne and Koepp moved to London, where preproduction was under way, living in separate hotels while rewriting different sections of the story. This was precisely the kind of situation that made Lansing anxious: the script was not locked, money was gushing out, and everyone making key decisions was six thousand miles away.

Wagner, a newcomer to the production realm, had to serve as a middle-man between the production and the studio. "I was a first-time producer, forced to jump into the deep end," she said. "I remember crawling around, listening under Robert Towne's door to make sure he was typing at night. Then Sherry would call at six o'clock: 'Where's that shooting script? We have to have it.'"

Lansing sent Don Granger, her production executive, to the set. After some initial missteps (the film's line producer, the man in charge of the day-to-day aspects of the shoot, had to be replaced), he told her to rest easy: Cruise was doing good work.

At one point, a crew member noted, the actor simulated clinging to the top of a bullet train—a sequence that had to be shot in a studio with CGI—and insisted on using a fan the size of an airplane propeller to create a wind violent enough that people would believe he was hurtling forward as a helicopter explodes overhead. "Tom's big thing was, there wasn't enough wind," said the crew member. "He said, 'Well, suppos-edly these trains go at 120 m.p.h.' I was like, 'If you get a piece of dust in your eye at that speed it could blind you.' He said, 'I want the wind blowing in my face and I want my jaws to be blowing.' That's Tom. He's a guy's guy."

Cruise was as committed to producing as acting, even when it came to such small matters as negotiating how much it would cost to shoot on a bridge in Prague.

"I thought it was $10,000 for this location," Wagner explained. "Then we get a call from the production manager. He said, 'No, no, no. Add a zero. It's $100,000.' We were $90,000 in the hole, and we knew the studio wasn't going to give us that for a bridge. So the first person we go to is the lord mayor of Prague. He can't help us. Finally, we find our way to Václav Havel, the president. Tom's doing double duty now: he's an actor and he's a producer and he has to help. Havel's thrilled to be meeting Tom, and he's an extraordinary man, and he talks about his plays. He says, 'I have sympathy and care for the artist. I am an artist.' Then he says, 'But I have no power.'"

WHEN THE PICTURE wrapped, Lansing was delighted with what she saw. Cruise had been right to pick this as his first production and to go with De Palma, whose work was at its most visual and visceral.

The two had gotten on well during the shoot, so she was puzzled when she heard of strains now, right at the end of postproduction. Differences between them had emerged while the film was being cut. Perhaps De Palma, whose roots were in independent film and whose friends were such iconoclasts as Martin Scorsese, had not anticipated Cruise's desire for control; perhaps he was simply exhausted from one of the most challenging productions in his experience.

"Brian saw the enormity of Tom's star power and the control that he had," said Cruise's agent at the time, Rick Nicita. "He wasn't used to it and took advantage of his tendency not to talk to anyone and slipped out the side door and never came back."

"He got a lot of interference, an enormous amount of input from the star," said one insider. "It was exhausting. At the end, he really felt like, 'There, fuck it. It's done.' And he threw his luggage in his car and drove across the country."

Lansing could not reach him, no matter how hard she tried, and when the movie premiered in May 1996, De Palma did not attend. "I called him," she said, "but he never called back."

MISSION'S SUCCESS, WITH earnings of $458 million at the worldwide box office, made it imperative for Paramount to develop a sequel.

"The big idea behind the *Mission: Impossible* franchise was that each movie would be different in its approach, and shot in a different style," said Lansing. "The first picture was a thriller with an intricately woven story line. We wanted the next one to be more action-oriented."

After talking to a number of directors, she and the producers settled on John Woo, who had helped define the Hong Kong action genre with such kinetic works as 1989's *The Killer* and 1992's *Hard Boiled* before coming to Hollywood, where he had had a big success for Paramount with 1997's *Face/Off*, starring John Travolta and Nicolas Cage.

Work on the screenplay moved fast, and when Cruise felt it was in place he told Lansing he was ready to shoot. But she was less sure; she argued that more work was needed on the script. That would delay the start of production, and the delay would cost money. Cruise said the studio should provide the extra amount; Lansing said no. They met in her office to hash out their differences.

"It was like these two immovable mountains," said an executive who was present. "Tom said [if Lansing would not go higher], 'I'll make it in a year's time,' the last thing a studio chief wants to hear. Sherry said, 'OK.' Then they stood up, meeting over. Tom starts walking to the door, and Goldwyn and the others are staring at each other, like, 'Who's going to give in first?' Finally Tom looks at her and says: 'I can push two weeks. But you pay for it.' And she looks at him and says: 'Three weeks. And I'll pay for half.' And it was done. Done in a moment. She wouldn't cave. Nor would he. Both got what they wanted."

Later, Cruise was scouting locations in Sydney, Australia, when Lansing called to ask for further cuts and changes. Cruise and his partners resisted. When they got off the phone, the walls began to tremble. Woo, who was there with Wagner and Cruise, was convinced a giant earthquake had hit. "We thought we were cursed," he joked.

"We start hearing these things," said Wagner. "We hear this 'boom, boom, boom!' We all hit the floor, thinking we were being attacked. The building was shaking. It was the biggest hailstorm ever in Sydney—there was more than $1 billion of damage. I said, 'Sherry's really mad.' We were laughing. Tom and John were like, 'Oh boy, she means it!'"

WHEN THE FILM was completed, Paramount arranged a test screening in a small theater in the Midwest. The location was as far away from Hollywood as possible, to avoid prying eyes. The Internet was beginning to change how studios did their business; it was no longer possible to have test screenings in Los Angeles for a movie as important as this, which could affect the direction of the studio and even the price of Viacom stock.

"The place we found was so remote that you couldn't fly there commercially," said Lansing, "so we all went in private jets. Two jets came from Los Angeles, carrying the marketing staff and NRG [the market researchers], Tom arrived in his plane with Paula, and I came on another with Jon Dolgen. It was almost comical, seeing this fleet of Gulfstreams parked alongside each other on a small private airstrip in the middle of nowhere."

That evening, the group gathered in a private room near the theater, careful not to be seen by any of the locals who were pouring in for the screening, none of whom had any idea which movie they were about to see. Cruise was kept in another room. NRG's Joe Farrell told the actor he would sneak him into the back of the theater, unobserved, but only once the picture began. It was crucial for the audience not to know there was a superstar in its midst.

"The whole thing felt like a top-secret maneuver," said Lansing.

She settled into her seat and was listening patiently as Farrell came out to introduce the movie. Suddenly, Cruise leaped through the curtains and the crowd went wild. "It's *Mission: Impossible!*" he yelled.

Dolgen grabbed Lansing's hand to prevent her from jumping up.

"I wanted to strangle Tom," she said. "The entire screening was worthless now. Of course everyone was going to like it—the biggest movie star on the planet had come to town just for them." For two hours, she sat seething as the audience whooped and hollered, enjoying the moviegoing experience of a lifetime. "All I could think was, I had the most expensive movie Paramount had ever made, and I had no idea if it actually worked."

When the screening was over and the audience had filed out, she stormed over to Cruise. He smiled bashfully.

"He said: 'I could see the look in your eyes, Sherry. I know you wanted to kill me,'" Lansing recalled. "I said, 'That's an understatement.' He said: 'I'm sorry. I just really wanted them to like it.'"

Throughout, Cruise avoided proselytizing for Scientology, his religion, which would not surface publicly as a force in his life until many years later, when he chose to speak more openly about his beliefs.

Once, after reading a negative article about Scientology, Lansing called him to discuss it. "I said, 'I feel terrible that you're being attacked, and I want to understand this better,'" she remembered. "I didn't want to become a Scientologist, but I respected him and felt I should know more about it." Cruise asked if she was serious, and when she insisted she was, he arranged for her to have dinner at the church's Hollywood headquarters, known as the Celebrity Centre.

"I had a good evening with him and a senior member of the church," said Lansing. "They demonstrated the 'e-meter,' the device they use for measuring your mental state, and asked me some questions to see where I stood. It was very emotional. I left with four books that outlined some of the basic tenets of Scientology, and Tom was very protective of my privacy. He said, 'No one will ever know you went. It's between us.' But I said, 'I don't care. I have nothing to hide.'"

That was one of several Scientology events Lansing would attend over the years, including one with Tom Freston, CEO of Viacom's MTV Networks. His recollection of the evening was less positive.

"I got this invitation to the Scientology ball, this very fancy invitation from Tom, delivered to my house," he noted. "So I called Sherry. [She said], 'Oh, honey, we've got to go to that.' I was mesmerized by the whole thing. [Scientology leader David] Miscavige spoke. They talked about all the great work they'd done at Ground Zero, rehabilitating some people's respiratory systems. There was a lot of self-congratulation. It was fascinating to be there as an outsider. We were given super-VIP treatment and escorted around very carefully everywhere. I had a front-row seat at a pretty bizarre evening. But you couldn't find a more gracious guy than Tom."

Lansing never explored Scientology further, but her affinity for Cruise and some of the other stars she worked with who were adherents made her reluctant to join the critical bandwagon.

"After my visit, no one from the church ever called or solicited anything from me," she said. "I was never pushed to contribute, and it never interfered with my working relationship with Tom or Anne Archer or John Travolta, who were also Scientologists. I didn't see Tom try to convert anybody, and there was never any pressure from him on anyone at the studio."

Only once did Cruise's beliefs affect his professional relationships: during a confrontation with Goldwyn, who had been promoted to president of the film division and as such was the most senior Paramount executive under Lansing. The incident took place shortly after Goldwyn had filed for divorce from his wife, Colleen Camp; he was fighting for custody of his daughter and in his divorce papers allegedly had criticized Camp's commitment to Scientology. There was an added complication: he had recently come out as gay.

"Tom called and said, 'I need to see you and John Goldwyn right away. It's very serious,'" said Lansing. "I called John and said, 'What's happening with Tom?' He said, 'I don't know.'"

Goldwyn stopped by Rosenfelt's office on his way. "John came in and said, 'Tom wants to see Sherry and me. What do you think it's about?'" recalled Rosenfelt. "I said, 'Your divorce.' He said, 'What?' I just knew. And

I knew how Sherry would handle it. She wasn't going to allow business [to be affected by something] personal."

Fifteen minutes later, Lansing was sitting with the two men. The atmosphere was electric. It was clear that Cruise had obtained Goldwyn's divorce papers and was not happy.

"Tom sat down on one couch, and John was on the other one," said Lansing. "Tom said, 'Have I ever treated you disrespectfully?' John said, 'Of course not.' Tom said, 'Have I ever treated anybody disrespectfully?' John said, 'No.' Then Tom said: 'I know you came out, and have I ever said anything negative about your sexuality?' John said, 'Never.' And Tom said, 'So why have you treated me so disrespectfully? Why have you said such bad things about my faith?'"

Goldwyn turned pale. "He said, 'You're right. I should never have done that. I'm sorry,'" Lansing recalled. "Tom said, 'Will you take care of it?' And John said, 'Yes.' And Tom said, 'Then we're fine.'"

IN 2003, AFTER years of success with CW Productions, Lansing learned from a rival studio executive that Cruise was in talks to relocate his company to Warner Bros., where he had just made *The Last Samurai*.

"I called Jon Dolgen," she said. "His take was that the Warner deal must already be done or the executive would never have said anything. I was upset. It was so personal, because Tom was like my younger brother and I really trusted him. We'd had our ups and downs, and disappointments as well as successes, but he was always my partner."

She asked to meet with Wagner. "Paula walked across the lot, and we ended up meeting outside my office. I said, 'I don't understand. You guys are like family.'"

"Sherry got teary-eyed," said Wagner. "She said, 'I want to hear everything you have to say, all your issues, what we can do to change this.' She was very embracing. I said: 'We want more involvement with the studio. Let's develop more things together.' We talked it out. We all had a heart, and everybody realized there was a real, human, personal connection and it transcended business. That was one of the wonderful things about that studio: there was vitality and life, and we aired any grievances we had, and became more collaborative after that meeting."

When Wagner relayed the conversation to Cruise, he put an end to the Warner talks, she recalled: "He said, 'This isn't right. We're staying with Sherry.'"

THE LAST MAJOR picture Cruise and Wagner produced for Lansing was *Mission: Impossible III*, which was planned as Paramount's summer "tent-pole" for July 2005.

That term had only recently come into being to describe the monu-mentally expensive and massively promoted films that could dominate an entire season, sucking up much of a studio's budget and, if all went well, an equivalent portion of the box office.

This latest *Mission* was initially developed by director David Fincher (*Fight Club*), who had in mind a more violent and bloody film than either Paramount or Cruise might have liked, possibly one that would earn an R rating. When he left the project, Joe Carnahan stepped in. A relative new-comer whose rough and rugged second feature, 2002's low-budget *Narc*, had impressed Cruise, he seemed to fit the grittier approach Paramount wanted for this third outing in the series. But after months of work, some-thing was not jelling.

"I was very interested in what I'd pitched him: the punk rock version of that franchise, going more toward where the *Bourne* films were heading and getting some dirt under your nails," said Carnahan. "I wanted it to be less glossy than the De Palma and John Woo versions."

After working with three different writers for more than a year, "The frustrations mounted," he continued. "I was a much younger man, more rash and hotheaded. We just saw very different films. I think I was about a week from being fired when I called Tom. It was a terrifying phone call to make. I actually videotaped myself when I did it. I thought, 'I'm never going to be more terrified than now. If my career is going to crater, why not commemorate it?' So I said to Tom, 'Listen, I'm going to pack my stuff.' He was a total gentleman. He understood. And Sherry was always remarkably supportive."

"I wasn't worried," said Lansing. "I thought, 'This is *Mission: Impossible*. We have Tom Cruise. We'll get any director we want.'"

As expected, agents started calling immediately, telling her that almost every director of stature and commercial worth, including some Oscar winners, wanted to take over the project. Lansing sent a list of candidates to Cruise and Wagner, anticipating a quick reply—"and there was no response," she said.

Never happy living in uncertainty, she left her office and walked the few hundred yards to the CW base to discuss it with Wagner and Cruise, taking a chair at a table beside them in the suite where she had once produced her films.

"We were sitting in Tom's office, at a little table, and Tom said, 'I don't think any of these people are right,'" Lansing recalled. "I said, 'What do you mean?' He said, 'None of them are right.' I said, 'Well, who do you think is?' And he said, 'J. J. Abrams.'"

Abrams at that point was a near-unknown in the film world. But Cruise had been impressed by what he had seen.

"Tom and Paula had met with me about writing a script, and ultimately I was not available because I was going off to direct the pilot for *Lost*," said Abrams. "As Tom was leaving, my assistant gave him the first two seasons of *Alias* on DVD. While I was shooting the pilot, I got a call from Tom, who had watched these two seasons and was very complimentary."

When Abrams got back from the shoot in Hawaii, "We got together and he was talking about his work on *Mission: III* and what they were trying to do," he continued. "But this was never a discussion about my directing that movie—it was just about which stories he was going to tell. If anything, I thought he might want to discuss my working on the script, but that wasn't clear. A couple of months later, I got a call from my agent saying that Tom wanted me to direct."

It was 2004, well before the thirty-seven-year-old had reached the pinnacle of his fame. He had contributed to the *Armageddon* screenplay, spent four years producing the WB's television series *Felicity*, executive-produced *Alias* and now was working on *Lost*. But Lansing struggled to remember who he was.

"Have you seen *Alias?*" asked Cruise. "What about *Lost?*"

Lost had not yet debuted (its pilot would be broadcast in September), and although Lansing would later become an avid consumer of television, she came from a world where it was very separate from film. She brushed the thought aside.

"I said, 'What about this big director who's won two Academy Awards? What about that one who's just been nominated?'" she insisted. "Tom listened, and said, 'They're good. But I don't think they're right.'"

Back and forth they went, dissecting this name and that, and each time Lansing mentioned a strong contender the response was the same: Cruise said no. He was his usual impeccably mannered self, and yet she could not move him. She left the meeting trying to control her frustration.

"My whole year was resting on this picture, and it was meant to start shooting any week," she said. "But I couldn't get him to budge. I went back to my office and called [Disney-ABC chairman] Michael Eisner to see if we could get J.J., and he said, 'He isn't available for eighteen months.' I was relieved. Now I could get one of my choices. So I called Tom and said, 'I'd yield, but he's not free.' And Tom said, 'Then we'll just have to wait.'"

The behemoth that Lansing had envisioned as a lock for summer 2005 was starting to look shaky. "Perhaps I should have thrown myself on his mercy and said, 'I have nothing else,' but I couldn't get those words out of my mouth," she observed. "I was afraid it would sound like he was just a piece of merchandise and this film was another widget we had to get down the production line. So instead I said: 'The franchise will grow old and the audience will get tired of it.' Tom said, 'I don't agree.' Then I pleaded with him, 'Meet some of the other directors.' But he wanted to wait. Finally, I lost it. I said, 'You're going to be too old to do it in two years!' I can't believe I said that. He was only forty-two at the time. But he just smiled and said, 'You think so?'"

Over the following weeks, one meeting took place after another, and each time the pattern would be repeated.

"There was a rhythm," said Lansing. "Tom would look at me and say, 'You seem so depressed.' And I'd say, 'Well, I am.' And he'd take my hand and put his own over it and say, 'Sherry, you're like my sister. Trust me. You know I'd never hurt you,' always very tenderly. Each time we met, the same thing. He'd take my hand and say the same reassuring words. But he'd never give in."

Summer was barreling down on them, and Lansing's movie was failing to fall into place. She felt trapped.

"I was calling every other studio, looking to buy something—anything—to fill the hole on July 4, 2005, when *Mission: Impossible* was meant to open," she said. "I'd ask, 'Does anyone want to co-finance? Does anyone have a big picture where we can jump in and split the rights?' But nobody said yes. We read all these scripts in development, and nothing was close to being ready."

Lansing met with Abrams and Cruise in the latter's home office, hoping she might find a way to pry the director free of his TV deal.

"Tom, to his credit, was clear about why he thought I would do the job that he needed," said Abrams. "It was a very awkward position for all of us. Sherry handled it with this incredible kindness and ultimately agreed that I could do this movie."

"The first thing J.J. said was, 'I'm so sorry I put you in this position,'" she recalled. "He understood that I was being asked to take a leap of faith on him with our biggest franchise. Then he said he wanted to rewrite the screenplay. So not only was I going to have to wait a year and a half before he could shoot, but now he was saying he hated the script."

"It didn't feel like something I could do justice to," said Abrams. "It was very well written, incredibly gritty and cool, and I liked it. But I knew it wasn't the version that I could get inside of."

Three weeks from what should have been the start of production, Lansing realized her tentpole was doomed. Paramount would have no summer blockbuster in 2005. She would have to deal with the fallout, in the press and the industry, and possibly among the shareholders, too.

Days later, her secretary told her Spielberg was on the line.

"He said, 'You know, Tom and I have been working on this project, *War of the Worlds.* We've got a pretty interesting script and I'd like you to read it,'" Lansing remembered. "I said, 'Sure.'"

War of the Worlds was an updated rendering, replete with expensive effects, of H. G. Wells's classic science fiction novel of 1898, an adventure about a widowed father who witnesses an alien attack and fights to save his family. Lansing read it that night, knowing just how hard such an undertaking would be. Spielberg was offering a great joint venture, but it would take forever to make.

"My first thought was, 'This movie will earn a fortune,'" she said, "and my second was, 'It will take three years to complete.'"

She called Spielberg the next day.

"I said, 'Steven, this is great. When will it come out?'"

"July fourth," he replied.

"2006?" she asked.

"No," said Spielberg. "2005."

Lansing could not believe what she was hearing. Suddenly, she had her summer tentpole, and it would pair Cruise with the most successful director in history. The actor had had this in the works even as he was holding her hand, promising everything would be OK.

"Tom must have known all along," she said. "He always denied it, but I was sure he'd been keeping it in his back pocket. I laughed until I cried. When he told me to trust him, he meant it."

CHAPTER 18

Lansing's most important bonds were not just with men like Cruise and Spielberg; she was also drawing closer to some of the industry's notable women.

"For many years, people had pitted women against women, and I'd bought into that," she said. "We thought there was only room for one of us, so there was a guardedness between us. You weren't going to say, 'Oh God, I read the best script,' because you knew that other person might buy it or get the job that might have been yours. But the times had changed, and those feelings didn't exist anymore."

In the mid-1990s, Lansing began to form a bond with the only woman who had ever rivaled her for power, Dawn Steel. The two could not have been more different—one a natural diplomat, the other a brawler.

Born in the Bronx in 1946, the daughter of a semi-professional weight-lifter, Steel had dropped out of Boston University and then become a secretary and sportswriter before running marketing for *Penthouse*. As head of her own marketing company, she subsequently became infamous for selling toilet paper with the Gucci logo. She joined Paramount as a merchandising executive, then switched to production and became president of production in 1985. She knew just as well as Lansing how brutal studio politics could be, and was fired from Paramount while in the hospital, having just given birth to her first child. Later, she joined Columbia Pictures and was forced out with equal bluntness.

In 1995, she and Lansing were invited to the same party and sat to-gether on a couch. For the first time, said Lansing, "we really talked."

Steel, who had turned to producing after leaving Columbia, had mellowed somewhat in the years since, partly because she was happily married to producer Charles Roven, partly because she had become a mother. She was approaching fifty—she was just two years younger than Lansing—and there on the couch, she spoke about her life: how she had enjoyed the success of 1993's *Cool Runnings*, been hurt by the failure of 1995's *Angus* and stung by the public humiliation of losing her job at Columbia.

"She said she felt so smothered by Hollywood she'd taken a few weeks and traveled across the country to clear her head," recalled Lansing. "She had only just got back, and was in a reflective mood. For two hours, we talked about everything except the movies, and especially about her young daughter, Rebecca, and how worried she was that growing up privileged might hurt her growth. I was dealing with a similar situation with Jack and Cedric. The conversation was easy and we just clicked."

Over the next few months, the two women got into a routine of having lunch every third weekend. "We'd meet on Saturday afternoons in our sweats, with our hair tied back, and talk for hours," said Lansing.

The better she got to know Steel, the more she liked her funny, fiery personality. And then, six months into their budding friendship, Steel was diagnosed with brain cancer.

"I called everyone I'd ever met in cancer research about treatment," said Lansing. "I thought Dawn was going to pull through. But she didn't."

Lansing had to face losing Steel just as they were beginning to repair the damage inflicted on them by the industry and their own misconceptions. Watching her friend decline, she witnessed the horror her mother had gone through all over again, her emotions swept up in a vortex that mixed memory and mortality, nostalgia and regret.

"I'd had this feeling ever since the death of my father," she said, "but it was never clearer to me than now: when you die, all you'll remember are the moments of intimacy, the moments of human contact. I visited Dawn near the end of her life when she was very sick. It took all my strength to see such a force of nature so subdued. She could barely speak. She couldn't move. It was horrible. The last thing I said to her was, I was honored she was my friend."

In December 1997, a year and a half after Steel's initial diagnosis, she died at the age of fifty-one. Lansing was one of her pallbearers. Several of the women who had risen alongside them were there, and it struck Lansing as ineffably sad that only now, at this wake, were they meeting as comrades-in-arms.

"In her eulogy, Lucy Fisher spoke about the end, when Dawn was in the hospital and her daughter crawled into her bed," said Lansing. "Her husband was there, too, and Dawn realized that everything she'd been searching for her whole life was in that room."

STEEL'S DEATH FORCED Lansing to look at her life anew.

For such a long time, she had been so immersed in the day-to-day activities of running a business with three thousand employees, extinguishing fires before they could spread, that she'd had little freedom to contemplate her broader goals. But increasingly she was turning toward the outside world. In addition to her work fighting cancer, she had raised money for underprivileged girls to go to college, and had been more active in her efforts to improve education.

When Gray Davis was elected governor of California in late 1998, she asked to be appointed to the University of California's board of regents, the twenty-six-member body that oversaw the ten-campus organization, with its quarter of a million students, five medical centers and three federal laboratories. Davis named her as one of his choices, but that was only the first sally in the battle.

"There are literally thousands of appointments to advisory boards and councils in a state the size and complexity of California," said Barry Munitz, then head of the governor's transition team. "Ironically, the two most desirable slots are on the UC board of regents and the state horse-racing commission. These require confirmation from the Senate, and the hearings are pretty intense."

Lansing prepared obsessively, taking home piles of books and stacks of papers, all heaped on top of her regular pile of scripts. "I had books that went from one end of the room to the other," she said. "I had to steep myself in information. What's the rule on this? How do they handle that? I didn't want anything to catch me by surprise."

In early 1999, she flew to Sacramento and took a seat inside the Senate building, where her confirmation hearing was about to take place, then waited nervously until John Burton, the Democratic leader of the California Senate, entered the room.

"He comes in, looks at a man sitting there, and yells 'What the hell are you doing in my seat?' and storms out," said Lansing. "I was sitting there, ready to read a statement, with a pile of cards in front of me with all the statistics, and he was gone. I thought, 'That's it. I'm collateral damage.'"

Her fears proved unfounded. She won approval from Burton's committee and later the full Senate.

As a regent, she was a consensus builder who drew the respect of friends and opponents alike. Even those who vehemently disagreed with her generally liberal point of view expressed their admiration—among them Ward Connerly, an African American libertarian who had led the fight for Proposition 209, a California ballot initiative passed in 1996 that forbade the use of affirmative action in state-funded institutions, creating problems for those who believed the state should do more to boost higher learning for minorities.

"I frequently found myself sitting next to Sherry at regents' meetings, and we would chat about various issues that were on the agenda," he recalled. "She was a very clear-thinking person, and always had a light-hearted demeanor that greatly impressed me. One of the contentious issues was about providing in-state tuition to what some call 'undocumented' students. Sherry and I talked about that. I voted against it, she voted in favor. But that did not diminish my respect for her in any way."

———

LANSING'S INTEREST IN education dovetailed with her desire to improve how women were portrayed in films.

"She didn't have the luxury of being overtly political or overtly outspoken about the role of women," said CAA's Bryan Lourd, "but in her own very powerful way she handled it by making movies that featured strong women when other people weren't doing that."

Lansing found it strange—even as women were rising through the industry ranks, with two named to run other studios in the late 1990s (Amy Pascal at Sony and Stacey Snider at Universal)—that Hollywood still seemed to keep women at a remove from leading roles. Occasional female-driven pictures would emerge, more by luck than strategy, but no studio had made a practice of initiating movies with women at their core. Instead, executives largely bought into the conventional wisdom that it was men who chose which movies to see, not women, and while women would go with the men, the reverse was not true. Lansing was sure this was wrong.

"Nobody was making movies for women, in particular women over twenty-five," she said. "That group—which included women like me—had almost been forgotten. I kept thinking, 'Why? We still go to the movies.'"

She began to green-light a series of films with this audience in mind. What were known in the industry as "Sherry movies"—pictures that cost anywhere from $12 million to $30 million, often thrillers, always with female leads—became a staple of Paramount's product line. Frequently skewing older (which in Hollywood meant audiences over the age of twenty-five), they included comedies and dramas, and explored such issues as growing up, aging and even interracial relationships.

"I still use the shorthand of 'a Sherry Lansing thriller,'" said Snider, almost two decades later. "*Gone Girl* and *Girl on the Train* [from 2014 and 2016] are part of the continuum that started under Sherry's guidance. They weren't all hers, but she made them part of the film industry's steady diet."

No subject resonated with Lansing more than revenge, partly because it was a plot device that gave her heroines a clear motivation, but also because it tapped into something deeper—a loathing of being seen as a victim, a recollection of how her mother had stood up for herself.

"I never wanted to be a victim, just as my mother didn't," she said. "I wanted to be an equal—an equal with my friends, an equal in my marriage, an equal in my work. I wanted to have an equal voice, and so did every woman."

Lansing's films about women tapped into the deep pool of emotion she had repressed as a child; the anger and fury she had held back so long were unleashed through her heroines.

"There's nobody who understood the animus of the American female better than Sherry Lansing," said Goldwyn, referring to Jung's notion of a masculine inner personality that lies inside a woman (in contrast to the feminine inner personality Jung found within each man). "She gets it. Not the sexuality—the animus."

Lansing was as hands-on with these pictures as she was with Paramount's tentpoles and awards-oriented films, dipping into the casting as well as the scripts, and reserving the right to make the final decision on whoever would star. On 1997's *Kiss the Girls*, a thriller about a woman who has been kidnapped and joins a forensic psychologist (Morgan Freeman) to track down her assailant, she insisted on vetting the actress being considered for the lead, the near-unknown Ashley Judd.

"Who do I have to please to get this part?" Judd asked when they met.

"Me," said Lansing.

Judd's coolness under fire was one of the factors that impressed Lansing enough for her to give the actress the role, and the movie earned a rich $60 million when it opened in October 1997, justifying a sequel, *Along Came a Spider*.

Lansing again cast Judd, by now one of her favorite actresses, in 1999's *Double Jeopardy* after Jodie Foster pulled out because of pregnancy. She was captivated by *Jeopardy*'s premise: if a woman is framed and sentenced to prison for a murder she did not commit, years later she can commit that murder and never be put on trial.

"I loved these films," said Lansing, "because they came from my gut. I knew those women. I knew what they felt like, not being equal. I wanted to be heard, and so did they."

THE FIRST WIVES CLUB was a case in point. Lansing had bought the rights to Olivia Goldsmith's 1992 novel about three middle-aged women bent on revenge against their philandering ex-husbands when she was still a producer, but had trouble getting the script right. When she became studio chief, she handed it over to Scott Rudin.

"Scott said: 'The problem is, you're making it as a drama. We have to make this funny,'" she recalled. "I said, 'Really? But I want its message to be clear.' He said, 'It will be.'"

He was right: there was no doubt where the film stood with regard to its heroines or the foolishness of the men who had ditched them for younger, prettier versions of themselves, and when he had finished developing the screenplay, he and Lansing signed three gifted comediennes to star: Goldie Hawn, Bette Midler and Diane Keaton. And then, days from principal photography, Hawn told Rudin she was quitting.

"Scott said, 'Goldie wants to drop out,'" Lansing remembered. "I couldn't believe it. I called her, and she said she had issues with the script."

Losing Hawn meant Lansing would also likely lose the other leads, who had signed a "favored nations" deal whereby each took the same salary, largely agreeing to do the film because they wanted to work with the other stars. Christmas was looming, the industry would soon shut down for its holiday break, and Lansing was in no mood to risk having one of her highest-profile pictures collapse while everyone was away. She called Hawn.

"I have two words for you," she said bluntly. "Kim Basinger."

Basinger had been sued after withdrawing from the 1993 indie drama *Boxing Helena*, even though no contract had been signed, and a jury had awarded the plaintiffs $8.1 million in a case that pushed Basinger into bankruptcy. There was silence on the other end of the phone.

"There was no question that Paramount was so deep in this movie that they were going to press this legally and make life very unpleasant," said Hawn's agent, Jeff Berg. "Sherry was tough. She wasn't threatening; she was just saying, 'This is what's going to happen. Because if you're not in it, we either have to close down, recast, or delay the film.'"

Twenty-four hours later, the actress agreed to shoot the picture. It opened number one in September 1996.

"Sherry wasn't known to be brutal, so when she was, it had a massive effect," said Rudin. "She was a person of enormous will. It was pretty incredible, really. She got what she wanted."

LANSING WAS KEEN to make movies for younger females as well as those in the older "quadrant" (Hollywood typically categorized audiences as male or female, and above or below age twenty-five). She identified just as much with the heroines of such pictures as 1995's *Clueless* and 2004's *Mean Girls* as with Forrest Gump or *Titanic*'s Rose.

Clueless had been developed as a pilot for Fox by its writer-director, Amy Heckerling, who had based the story on Jane Austen's *Emma*. When Fox decided not to make it ("They were worried about something so female-oriented," said Heckerling), Lansing bought the script, then titled *I Was a Teenage Teenager*, and made it for $9 million. The movie earned $56.6 million in the United States alone.

Mean Girls was one of the few Paramount pictures that flowed without a hitch. It began when writer-actress Tina Fey read Rosalind Wiseman's 2002 self-help book *Queen Bees and Wannabes* and mentioned it to *Saturday Night Live*'s Lorne Michaels, who asked the studio to buy the rights. The resulting script—about an innocent teenager who falls in (and then out) with the mean girls at a public high school—was one of the few Lansing read that required next to no changes.

"We had about ten drafts before we took it to Sherry," said Fey. "She was so trusting and proceeded with confidence. I was a first-time screenwriter, and it's very common in film that you give it to seven other writers, and she didn't do that. She let me do the rewrites, and it helped the movie to have one voice as opposed to a mishmash."

Fey was struck by Lansing's eye for casting. She was convinced Rachel McAdams would be perfect as the leader of the mean girls, even though she was then twenty-four years old and there were discussions about having the younger and tougher Lindsay Lohan in the role. Lohan, seventeen, took the lead instead.

"Sherry and Lorne felt you needed an actress who could [grow from innocent to tough]," said Fey, "and she also felt that, because Rachel was older, Lindsay would be intimidated by her, which was right for the film."

When Harvey Weinstein threatened to sue on the grounds that the movie's title was too close to his upcoming *Jersey Girl*, Lansing never flinched.

"It seemed like it was going to be a real problem," Fey recalled. "But Sherry was so easygoing and gracious about it: 'Oh, honey, I'll handle it.' She was very unflustered, while I was like, '*What's happening?!*'"

Lansing loved both *Mean Girls* and *Clueless* because they tapped into a side of her that others failed to see.

"All of us still have a part of our soul that's twelve years old and insecure," she acknowledged. "That twelve-year-old girl is still in me today. You don't get rid of her, you just control her. There are days when my insecurity is massive, and it doesn't go away, and you remember when you felt most vulnerable and the memories that go with it. If you're in tune with that side of you, the twelve-year-old girl will never die."

AMONG LANSING'S FAVORITE female-oriented films was a low-budget interracial love story that faced rejection at every stage of its production.

Save the Last Dance told the story of a white girl and aspiring dancer whose mother's death leads her to move in with her father and attend an all-black school. She becomes romantically involved with an African American student who teaches her how to dance to hip-hop and helps her get into Juilliard.

"We were at Paramount," said producer Robert Cort, Lansing's former Columbia and Fox colleague, "and we said, 'You know, Paramount has done the dance genre really well, but they haven't done it in a long time.'

We wanted to do an interracial love story, too, so we combined them and that was the basis of the picture. We showed the script to Sherry, and she said, 'I'm making the movie.' She had a lot of notes and a very clear point of view. We had a much rougher movie in mind, and she had a more audience-friendly version in her head."

"It took me back to [1967's] *Guess Who's Coming to Dinner*, with its exploration of an interracial relationship," said Lansing. "It was time for another, and this was wrapped up in a great dance movie. The genre had faded, and I felt it was time to bring it back."

Thomas Carter was hired to direct and a budget was set at $19 million, but when Lansing approached other studios to share the cost, most of them passed. Even Paramount's sister company, the youth-targeting MTV Films, declined. "I heard the same objection everywhere: that young audiences would never accept an interracial romance."

She had seen from her own sons that change was in the air and was emphatic that a social revolution was under way, which the studios had failed to acknowledge. Harvey Weinstein agreed and the Miramax Films chief agreed to split the cost, on one condition—that singer-songwriter Usher play the lead. He told Lansing he had an option on the performer's services, though Lansing doubted that was true.

There was a problem: Julia Stiles and Sean Patrick Thomas not only had been cast but had already begun to rehearse. Lansing was placed in the impossible position of having to choose between a cast in which she believed and the financial safety net that Weinstein offered. Reluctantly, she accepted Weinstein's demands. It was one of the few decisions she truly regretted.

"Usher was brand-new," said Cort. "He had just made his first movie and was very good in it, but then his mother [who served as his manager] wanted like $6 million or $9 million—some insane number. I said, 'Sherry, you don't even know who Usher is, do you?' She said, 'No, not really,' and we laughed about it. So that died."

Without Usher, Weinstein pulled out. "[That] was the only reason we didn't continue on with the project," said Weinstein. "Sherry completely understood and knew it was a big risk."

Lansing went back to her original cast, a pyrrhic victory that left her with a sense of shame as well as relief. "I felt guilty about that young actor and what I'd almost done," she said. "I'm not proud of it."

As shooting commenced, many Paramount executives were skeptical that the movie would ever make money, their doubts reinforced by the recent failure of another interracial story, the 1995 Halle Berry–Jessica Lange drama *Losing Isaiah*.

"I said to [marketing chief] Arthur Cohen, 'We'll make $6 million or $7 million over the opening weekend,'" Cort recalled, predicting a modest number. "He looked at me like it was a rhetorical question, and said, 'The distribution people think it's un-releasable in Texas. They don't even think we'll do $3 million.'"

When the studio tested the movie, nobody wanted to come to the screening. "Joe Farrell, the researcher, actually had to pay people to be there," said Lansing. "He gave them $5 each, and our own marketing people wrote off the picture. They felt a black and white love story couldn't work.'"

Even with MTV finally on board to help market the film, everything looked bleak.

"Four weeks before the movie opens, I get on a plane to India, and I'm certain it's going to be a failure," said Cort. "People were sure the interracial thing was a turnoff."

And then the downward trajectory began to turn around. "Ten days before it opened [in January 2001], Arthur Cohen said, 'I think you can rest easy. It will do $7 million its opening weekend,'" continued Cort. "A few days later, he said, 'It's going to do $10 million.' On the Friday it opened, he said: 'I've never seen something pick up like this. It's going to do between $12 million and $14 million.'"

That weekend, the picture earned $23 million. "It was one of the most profitable ROI [return on investment] movies in the history of Paramount," said Cort. "Sherry was vindicated. It was one of the last examples in my experience of an executive saying, 'I want to do this. I believe in it.'"

———

FEW OF PARAMOUNT'S female-skewing films proved as complicated as 2001's *Lara Croft: Tomb Raider.*

A swashbuckling British aristocrat, the creation of the video game developer Core Design, Croft had debuted in 1996, and names of stars to play her had surfaced almost at once, from Elizabeth Hurley to Catherine Zeta-Jones to Jennifer Lopez, all pure conjecture until Paramount bought the rights in association with producer Lawrence Gordon.

Those rights, however, came with a catch: if the studio did no work on the project for forty-five days, it would lose the option. That forced Paramount to move fast and pushed Lansing into the sort of territory she most disliked, hurtling forward at a breakneck pace, with all the attendant dangers of scripts that would be shoddily written, casts hastily assembled and budgets inadequately vetted.

Concerned about the risk, she supported Dolgen's desire to structure a beneficial deal, one as complex as he had ever negotiated, in which the movie was sold to a German company and then leased back to Paramount. By the time foreign subsidies and tax breaks were factored in, the studio had almost none of its own money at stake in the $94 million tentpole. But it did have its reputation on the line.

One script came in after another, and still there was nothing usable. By mid-1999, the producers had plowed through at least eleven different writers, all struggling to craft a narrative that would engage audiences with a character who hitherto had existed only inside a video game.

While the script was being written, Lansing and Gordon searched for a director and settled on Simon West. He was a craftsman rather than an auteur; his biggest successes had been the 1997 actioner *Con Air* (which, like many Jerry Bruckheimer films, bore the hallmark of its powerful producer just as much as its director) and the 1999 military thriller *The General's Daughter.* But Lansing knew he could bring in a franchise film on time and on budget.

At first West passed. "I didn't necessarily believe it was possible to make a video game into a film, and I'd just done a standard summer blockbuster film with *Con Air* and didn't want to do another [right away]," he said. "Having now done *General's Daughter,* I said, 'I'm interested.'"

The director tried to untangle the thicket of scripts. His attempts infuriated at least one of the writers involved, Steven E. de Souza, the same
man who had been bogged down in the chaos of *Beverly Hills Cop III.*

"He comes in and almost immediately says, 'This script is shit,' even
though it's budget- and schedule-approved," said de Souza. "He hires four
writers to do four or five different drafts. At the end he declares, 'They're
all shit; I'm going to have to write the script,' and insists the studio pay
him a very big number to write it."

"There was a long list of writers that would come and go, and so the
script was in fluidity," said West. "It was very hard for me to prep, because it
was never a stationary target. But that happens on most of those summer
blockbuster movies—there's a long tradition of the draft never [being]
finished. And [in this case] the risk of losing the rights meant there was
no time to stand back and think. The train had left the station, and Sherry
felt the pressure."

While West was rewriting, Lansing turned to who might play Lara. It
was a challenging part to cast, needing an actress sexual enough to resemble the computer creation while accessibly human. The filmmakers
agreed that only one person could pull it off: Angelina Jolie.

It was early 2000, and the twenty-four-year-old was not yet a major
star. She had earned kudos for HBO's *Gia* (1998), in which she played
a real-life model who died of AIDS. She was soon to win an Oscar for
Girl, Interrupted, which would lift her to another level of stardom, but was
plagued by damaging reports about her personal life: she was rumored to
have dabbled in drugs and had an odd relationship with her brother, along
with an even odder one with her soon-to-be-husband, Billy Bob Thorn-
ton, a vial of whose blood she reportedly carried around her neck.

"She definitely had some baggage and something of a dark reputation,"
said West. "Funnily enough, that was one of my selling points: this sort
of troubled and dangerous aspect in her reputation actually helped the
character."

Lansing was concerned, especially when both Jon Voight (Jolie's father) and Jane Fonda (a family friend) called to warn her that the actress

was extremely fragile. "I didn't know if that was true," she said. "But we discussed it, and Larry Gordon got a call like that, too."

With Lansing's blessing, West flew to Mexico to meet Jolie on the set of *Original Sin*, a thriller in which she was starring opposite Antonio Banderas.

"She said, 'Look, I want to do it, but I know what my reputation is, and I'll do anything you want to prove that I'm worthy. I'll be reliable and I'll turn up and I'll work hard,'" recalled West. "She said, 'I don't care if the studio wants to drug-test me every day. Whatever you need, I'll do it.'"

Jolie also sat down with Gordon. "I knew Angelina had some issues, and I met with her and I told her what I knew," he recalled. "I said, 'This is going to be a difficult role, because the British press are so excited about this.' There was a big reward for the first person to get a photo of Lara Croft in costume; there was a bounty. I said: 'The press is going to be vicious. They're going to be looking for you. They're going to know all the things I know. And I just want to tell you: if you do this movie, you're going to have to ride, rope, jump, shoot, learn to fight—you're going to do everything. They have a schedule for you that's just horrendous. You're going to be working your ass off. It's going to be really tough. If you agree to this, and you do these things, I will be your biggest fan and ally for your whole career, as long as you live. If you say you're in and you don't do it, I'll be the biggest enemy you've ever had.' She said, 'I'm in.'"

Lansing met with Jolie before giving her approval. They connected at once.

"I thought she was wonderful," Lansing noted. "She was beyond beautiful—that's the first thing you noticed. She had a perfect face, with perfect lips and eyes. Then she was smart, she was strong, she was very articulate, very together. She talked about how she loved Lara Croft and how we had to protect Lara. She was involved in almost everything from that point on."

Jolie, who signed on for $1 million, was equally taken with Lansing. "What I noticed immediately [was her] empathy," she said. "It was how she achieved the great balance of being tough as nails and equally kind and compassionate. We all wanted Lara to be fun, like the game, but at the heart of it give young girls their Indiana Jones, someone adventurous and strong to look up to. Sherry made that possible."

The actress was drug-tested, regardless.

"We were sufficiently worried that we obliged her to undergo random drug tests, and not just urine tests but also blood tests," said Goldwyn. To everyone's relief, Jolie passed each test.

Even so, the studio and producers were concerned enough to talk about keeping an eye on their star during the shoot.

"There was the notion that we would put a team around her, for two purposes," said a member of the production team. "One really was practical: to get her into great shape for the movie, not only in terms of appearance, but to do what she had to do on-screen. Then there was this notion that we had to give her spiritual and psychological support."

This was when the real problems began. West suggested hiring Bobby Klein, a former photographer and therapist who he believed had the right kind of experience.

"There were issues with the studio and producers being very nervous about Angelina," said West. "There was a discussion with the group: 'We're looking for someone to oversee or keep an eye on her, because we're all making the film.' That guy Bobby Klein came up as somebody who had worked in that world of psychotherapy or drug management or whatever. He was brought in to supervise Angelina."

Relationships that had been tense before became strained to the breaking point now, and Gordon, who had already battled the studio over money and the script and would have further battles while preparing the shoot, bristled at Klein's presence.

"Simon West comes with this guy Bobby Klein," he said. "Who's Bobby Klein? He's dressed all in black. He's a weird-looking guy, a big guy with a white beard and white hair and blue eyes. He's very esoteric and gives me a thing that if you wear it you can't get cancer, or whatever the hell, some bullshit thing. [They said] 'He's going to be a big help and he's going to do all these great things,' and so on and so forth."

As preproduction got under way in England, Klein asked to be placed in charge of Jolie's physical preparation, even though a stunt coordinator was already working with her. When Klein insisted on employing a health expert who had been investigated by Scotland Yard, the production team balked.

"[The expert] wanted her to have milk baths, and started talking about yoga and meditation, and she wanted to be the point person in charge of Angelina's training," said Lloyd Levin, who produced the film with Gordon. "It was just this bullshit. It seemed like spiritual hokum."

When Klein was then accused of sexually harassing West's assistant, among a host of other issues, he left the production.

Gordon was ecstatic. "I said, 'Angelina doesn't want you around, and I never wanted you around, so your ass is gone. You can get your shit and go, or I can get security to throw you off the lot. You decide.' He said, 'I still get my expenses?' I said, 'Unfortunately, yes.'"

WITH KLEIN OUT of the way, Jolie was a dream.

"In the dailies, she was riveting," said Lansing. "She took what might have been a cardboard character and added a layer of mystery and emotion and humanity."

"She trained for months beforehand," noted West. "She worked out physically. She did fight training. She learned how to do bungee ballet. She did everything to make it work. There were a couple of times she was in a rig, where she had to shoot from [several] feet in the air. The rig was hard fiberglass. It was digging into her hips, but she never complained. I did see her go off and have a little weep, to kind of cry out the pain, and then come back on set. She did all these amazing, huge stunts that she was fantastic at."

Only at the end of the long and turbulent shoot did an accident occur, when she fell and damaged her foot.

"It's to be expected," said Jolie. "After all the big stunts, I ended up hurting myself on a smaller stunt. A big jump over a statue, and I landed badly on my ankle. A partial tear, and I came back to work with a cane. Not very Croft. I had physical therapy every morning before work. My goal was to be able to run again by the time we went to Cambodia [one of the picture's locations]. Those dates couldn't move, so I had to make it, no matter. Fortunately, I did."

WEEKS AFTER THE wrap, Lansing saw the edited film.

"Oh my God, it was terrible," she said. "I was in this screening room, and I was so disappointed. It was well shot and well acted, but it was completely disjointed. The story made no sense."

"It was horrible," said Levin. "I thought, 'This can't possibly represent the movie. We've just wasted $100 million.' Sherry got up and faced us [after the screening] and said, 'I'm not going to beat around the bush, but this is a disaster.'"

"It was a very awkward situation," said West. "Sherry and Larry were in the theater, watching it. They weren't really speaking. I had to get my notes separately from them. At that point, Larry said, 'Well, I think it needs a lot more work. I want to bring in another editor.' I said, 'Fine.'"

Lansing authorized a week of reshoots for the ending, and several meetings took place among the filmmakers and the new editor as the finale was revised, the improved ending filmed, and the picture restructured until something coherent emerged.

"We had numerous screenings," said Levin. "We all felt we were moving in the right direction. Sherry was very, very supportive in postproduction. During that process, she had a cool head and was very pragmatic."

Despite the volleys lobbed by the critics, *Lara Croft* made $275 million around the world when it opened in June 2001, enough to warrant a sequel. Lansing had launched a new franchise at minimal cost to the studio and helped turn Jolie into a major star.

And yet the experience left her feeling empty. True, the film had done well, but deep down she knew it was a triumph of marketing over content, of hype over reality.

She had been bothered for some time by her growing awareness that the quality of pictures no longer seemed essential, that clever sales strategies could redeem all but the most abysmal of movies. But never did that sink in as much as in a private conversation with Robert Friedman, her vice chairman and a marketing expert, while they were working on the new edit. When Lansing revealed her fears, he dismissed them with a shrug.

"Don't worry," he said, "we'll be fine."

"What do you mean?" said Lansing. "I don't have a clue what the movie's about."

"I can still sell it," said Friedman. "We're going to open to $40 million or $50 million, and then we'll make two and a half to three times that in total. You can spend all this money to improve the picture, but it won't make the tiniest difference to how much it brings in."

His words proved dead-accurate but left Lansing feeling shaken.

"I can't think like that," she said. "If I did, what would be the point of my job?"

CHAPTER 19

Three months after *Lara Croft* opened, Lansing was lying in bed when Friedkin urgently shook her awake. "Sherry," he said, "America's under attack."

It was the morning of September 11, 2001. They switched on the television and were jolted by the sights and sounds of the two burning towers, and then horrified as they watched one of them collapse.

"We just sat there, frozen," said Lansing. "Then we went downstairs and called our children to make sure they were OK. They were scared and didn't understand. We started calling everyone we knew in New York, and couldn't get through. We didn't know who was alive and who wasn't. We sat mesmerized and scared."

Even after she had gone to the studio and her team had begun to regroup, anxiety permeated every waking moment, and it spread throughout the city.

"Everyone was in a state of shock at Universal along with the rest of the country," said Universal's Ron Meyer. "People weren't sure if they should come to work or stay home. Our emergency personnel, security team and I spent the next three days meeting with large groups in a soundstage to let our employees know we were doing everything possible to ensure a safe environment at work."

Ten days after the attacks, the MPAA's Jack Valenti convened a meeting of the studio heads. In his courtly southern tone, Valenti told them that Attorney General John Ashcroft had warned him, based on terrorist chatter intercepted by the FBI, that the next full-scale attack could well be targeted at a Hollywood studio.

"I had trouble reconciling my responsibilities with my fears," said Lansing. "Every time I heard a loud noise, I jumped. I was telling my staff there was nothing to worry about, even as stanchions were being erected at the gates."

Like Universal and all the major studios, Paramount tightened security, building barricades and adding metal detectors, while Lansing worried that nothing they did would prevent an aerial attack of the kind that had destroyed the World Trade Center.

Kroll, a security firm, was hired to create a new protective system at a cost of millions of dollars. "They analyzed the studio: 'If the bomb hit here, this would happen. If it hit there, that would happen,'" Lansing recalled. "The whole world changed for us. Everyone's car trunk was searched. Our security team used mirrors on long poles to look under each vehicle that entered the lot. We stopped having test screenings there."

Like the tremors that followed large earthquakes, occasional aftershocks would shake even the most confident executives, and the sense of uncertainty continued for months.

"We had watchers on the roofs and across the road," said Dolgen. "Even so, two months after 9/11, some jerk drives into the studio and he's got a case of grenades in his trunk. They were dummies, for a film shoot." Another time, "a guy walked into the parking structure across the street and went to the top floor and was taking pictures of the lot from that vantage point. We grabbed him and called the police, but they told us we had to let him go." Sometime later, the man got into similar trouble in Canada, though there was never proof that he was planning terrorist action.

As a patriotic fervor swept the country, Lansing convened a meeting among the studio chiefs and Karl Rove, then senior adviser and deputy chief of staff to President George W. Bush, who addressed a gathering of film, television and union executives at the Peninsula Hotel in Beverly Hills.

"The heads of all the companies were there," said Lansing. "It wasn't about Republicans and Democrats. It was about what we could do to help the country."

During his presentation, Rove outlined the history of Al Qaeda and its current operations, then opened the floor to questions.

"We discussed what the studios could do," said Lansing. "Content was off the table; there was no suggestion we would produce propaganda. But we did talk about sending DVDs to the troops and making patriotic public service announcements to play in theaters, and later we did all those things."

She drew inspiration from World War II, when the studios had joined forces to make a series of documentaries called *Why We Fight*, as much a case of propaganda as information. "It was a short-lived burst of bipartisan patriotism," she said.

This, of course, assumed there would still be an entertainment industry when the terror died down. Theater attendance had dropped, and none of Hollywood's powers-that-be could predict when audiences would return. They worried that exhibitors would have to introduce extreme security measures that might scare people away for good.

Inevitably, these concerns affected one of Paramount's highest-profile pictures, *The Sum of All Fears*, a movie green-lit before 9/11, which tackled terrorism head-on.

THE FOURTH IN a series of films featuring the character of Jack Ryan created by novelist Tom Clancy, *Sum* followed the CIA analyst's attempts to prevent a group of terrorists from detonating a nuclear device during a football game.

Its subject matter was almost eerily in sync with the times, just as *The China Syndrome* had been more than two decades earlier. Back then, however, Lansing had come away with the lesson that such timeliness did not necessarily help at the box office; now she feared audiences would shun the movie as an unwanted reminder of what had just taken place.

Bringing the picture to the screen had not been easy, especially given Clancy's stubbornness.

"Tom was one of the more difficult people I've known, complicated and unpredictable and all of that," said Lansing. "He hated Harrison Ford and didn't talk to Mace Neufeld, the producer. I guess he had a problem with success. How could you not think Harrison was perfect for the part? How could you not think Mace and Bob Rehme were great producers?"

Early in her run at Paramount, as was her wont, she arranged a meeting between Neufeld and the writer in an attempt to broker a truce.

"She had me fly with her to Maryland to go to a Baltimore Orioles game, because Clancy owned a piece of that team," said Neufeld. "She tried to create a detente between us, and we did start talking again, but it didn't accomplish much. He became very combative in the press. At one point, he said Harrison was too old to play Jack Ryan. We stopped talking after a while, because he just went ballistic over things."

The more successful Clancy became, the more eccentric he seemed. During the making of *Patriot Games*, "we went to visit him at his Chesapeake Bay mansion—me, Mace, Harrison and my daughter, Lucia, who was eleven at the time," recalled Phillip Noyce, the *Sliver* director who also handled the Clancy franchise. "We pulled up, and Clancy came out dressed in military fatigues, and my daughter said, 'I think that's some kind of statement, Dad.'"

The writer invited his guests to go shooting. "We went down to the basement of his house, where he had a safari range, and he was instructing Harrison on how to fire a nine-millimeter pistol," Noyce continued. "I was jet-lagged, and I made the mistake of going to sleep. I slept through his instruction, and that seemed to turn him against me forever."

With three successful Clancy films already released, making a fourth was a priority for Lansing. After several drafts and several writers, the screenplay (credited to Paul Attanasio and Daniel Pyne) was exactly what she wanted. By mid-2000, it was ready to go.

"The script was terrific," she said. "At the end of the second act, a neo-Nazi plants a nuclear bomb in a stadium where the president and the CIA director are watching a football game. What's shocking is that Ryan can't stop the bomb from detonating. I thought that was very realistic. In every movie, the hero saves the day, but not here."

When she sent Ford the script, he didn't agree.

"He came into my office, dressed in jeans and a work shirt," she said. "He was one of the most self-assured actors I'd met, which made it easy to talk to him. He never seemed to doubt what he was saying and never raised his voice. He just said, 'I have a problem with the bomb going off.' I said, 'I think that's the most important thing.' He said, 'There's no movie after that happens.' I said, 'That's one of the reasons I wanted to make it.'"

Faced with losing her star or her script, Lansing made the unusual decision to let Ford go, and replaced him with Ben Affleck, whom she had cast in *School Ties* when he was an unknown.

"I heard Ben was interested, and we went for a walk on the lot," she said. "He asked, 'Why doesn't Harrison want to do this?' I told him, 'He doesn't like the bomb.' That seemed good enough, and he was in. It took a ballsy actor to replace Harrison Ford, but he was willing."

"Sherry wanted to make sure she and I were on the same page," said Affleck. "There was definitely a concern, because Harrison Ford was so iconic and had done such an amazing job. I knew on some level there would be comparisons made, though it was easier because he had replaced Alec Baldwin [in the franchise] and there was already a tradition of people who had come and gone in that role. I hadn't done a movie like that, a big studio blockbuster. It was daunting, but I trusted Paramount was going to get it right."

The actor flew to Maryland to meet Clancy. "You drive to his house and there's a 'tank' sign on the road, and you come around the bend and there's the tank," he recalled. "We had dinner, just the two of us. He was cranky, but he really just wanted to be respected. He wanted his opinion to matter. He didn't like the fact that people had changed his books so substantially when they were adapted to movies. I felt we should have consulted him more, because what made the books so good was his eye for detail. I don't know that he necessarily would have been the right guy to write the screenplay, because he wanted to write thousands of pages."

Phil Alden Robinson (*Field of Dreams*) was hired to direct, an unlikely choice given that he had never made an action film and was best known for more character-driven material. But Lansing liked the blend of thoughtful director and fast-paced thriller.

"When I went to see Sherry, I said, 'Are you nuts? Do you want a nice, sweet, gentle film where people leave and say, "Oh, I felt so good?"'" Robinson recalled. "She laughed and said: 'I don't want *Action Sequel Number Fourteen*. I'd like it to be about the characters and the politics, and be smart and have some humor.' I said, 'If you really mean that, I'd love to do it.'"

The director was advised to steer clear of Clancy, but a few weeks into production, "Sherry called me one night in Montreal and said: 'Tom Clancy hates the script. I told him you'd call, and here's his number.' So I called him. He was critical of any changes to the book, and the book was eight hundred pages. He had a lot of specific notes and sent me a long memo. I had many talks with him during production, and I think that's all he wanted, to have his voice heard. And Sherry did a great thing. He was upset that he hadn't been invited to one of the premieres, and she said: 'In that case, we're going to have our premiere in Washington and you're going to sit next to me.' And that's exactly what she did."

Later, Robinson even offered to record a DVD commentary with Clancy, in which the writer would have free rein to say anything he wanted, no matter how disparaging. "I didn't know if Sherry would let us do it, but she did," said the director. "It's the frankest DVD commentary you'll hear."

NOW, MONTHS AFTER that conversation, the film was shot and edited, and the marketing campaign was about to get under way.

"On the morning of September 11, I was [meant to be] doing a sound mix, getting ready to show Sherry and Goldwyn the film," said Robinson. Then the attacks took place, and for twenty-four hours everything froze. "We delayed a day, and on the thirteenth we went in. There was a lot of security; there were police cars at the front gate—I never knew if they were props or real police cars. We went into the screening knowing everybody was nervous, but when the lights came up at the end, there was this audible sigh of relief, and I remember Sherry saying, 'This film is so positive and life-affirming, we could release it today.'"

"There were still very real concerns about the bomb," Lansing acknowledged. "The marketing people felt it was too scary to put in the commercials, and the initial TV spots had nothing to indicate it goes off. I thought that was a mistake. It's what made the movie unique."

She asked to have the explosion put back in the commercials, and the campaign worked. No matter how jolting it must have been for audiences to see a bomb going off in every two-minute trailer and thirty-second ad, the movie was nothing if not topical.

In May 2002, *Sum* opened to mixed reviews but strong box office. Many saw it as a reaction to 9/11, ignoring the fact that filming had wrapped weeks before the terrorist attacks and the most contemporary parts of the picture had been put in place more than a year earlier. Despite her concerns, Lansing remained steadfast.

"We delayed the test screenings by a week or two, but that's the only concession we made to 9/11," said Robinson. "We did not make changes for content. Sherry was not afraid. She said, 'Let's just put our best foot forward.'"

THE SUM OF ALL FEARS marked a turning point for Paramount and its chairman. After almost a decade of success, it was the studio's only release of 2002 to earn more than $100 million at the domestic box office.

Whereas previous years had been flush with hits, 2002 and 2003 witnessed a succession of flops. True, there were exceptions (among them *We Were Soldiers, The Wild Thornberrys Movie* and *Changing Lanes*), but for the first time since Lansing came to Paramount, the studio barely eked out a profit, and the failure of such pictures as *The Four Feathers* and *K-19: The Widowmaker* (a thriller that brought Harrison Ford back to the Paramount fold, directed by Kathryn Bigelow) hurt her personally as well as professionally.

"The film division wasn't doing well," said Biondi, the former Viacom president. "They were making their numbers, largely because of their TV business, but there was a lot of talk about how Paramount was playing low-risk baseball, and how they weren't taking any creative chances. Jon Dolgen's contention was, 'I'm not in the awards business. That's a talent issue. We're in the moneymaking business.'"

The desire to make bigger and more profitable films was leading each studio away from the risky and original, and Lansing realized that thinking was beginning to color her, too. Hollywood was transitioning away from the artistic landscape she had loved, and she was torn about how much to transition with it.

"Sherry started to be unhappy," said Friedkin, who was experiencing a career rebirth in the worlds of opera and independent film, even as his wife was struggling. "She was unhappy for a long time."

Interesting movies were still being released, but fewer were emerging from the majors. Independents such as Miramax were stealing the studios' thunder as mainstream Hollywood filmmaking shifted away from the dramas Lansing had always favored and toward mega-productions that wolfed down all the resources that might have been available for other endeavors.

Split rights, foreign sales, tax breaks and local subsidies became the lingua franca of the day as studios hurried to find outside financing, reflecting the epidemic of fear that was spreading through the industry— partly because the gushing stream of revenue from DVD and television that had ballooned since the early 1980s was drying up, and partly because the corporations were ever trying to squeeze out more profit.

"That was the beginning of a difficult time with these content companies, when the quarter-to-quarter existence really started to emerge," said Bryan Lourd. "Sherry went from being able just to say yes to [having to] qualify yes with 'if we get a partner.'"

"All of us were protecting our downside," said Lansing. "Films about people, emotions, society—they were on the way out. It was all about the tentpole now. Every generation creates the films it needs, and I understood that and accepted it. But these films were different from the ones I'd loved and they weren't the ones I wanted to make. I was no longer in the zeitgeist and I knew it."

By the early 2000s, the studios no longer seemed like the creative hubs they had once been. Rather, they had become corporate machines hungry for the franchises they needed to survive—from *Harry Potter* to *Batman* to *Spider-Man* to Paramount's own *Mission: Impossible*. The importance of compelling marketing, the hidden force that had propelled *Lara Croft* to box office victory, ran like a subterranean stream through all of Paramount's conversations. It seemed impossible to think of a film without considering that. More often than not, the product was ceding ground to the way it was sold.

"When I started in the business, you made a movie and put it out, and marketing was relatively minor in the scheme of things," said Lansing. "But at some point during my time at Paramount, marketing became as important as the movie. And then marketing became even more important."

The summer of 2001 showed how much things had changed, when one expensive blockbuster tumbled out after another, all sequels to previous films. These were not so much movies as brands, each sold to their audiences with the same methods and media that were used to sell soap or breakfast cereal. It hardly seemed to matter whether the pictures were good. From *Jurassic Park III* to *Dr. Doolittle 2* to *Scary Movie 2* to *Rush Hour 2* to *American Pie 2*—each released in the prime summer window between Memorial Day and Labor Day—they dominated the box office.

"The business was changing," said Goldwyn. "Everybody was feeling tyrannized and anxious."

Lansing could not avoid the discomfiting truth that she was part of an increasingly industrialized complex. She could learn how to function in this environment, but the movies Hollywood was making were not in her blood.

"If your values are changing, if your interests start to be somewhere else, and you see that in yourself, you know it's time to go," she said. "You say, 'I'm the establishment, and I don't mind being the establishment. I'm not young, and I don't mind not being young.' I started to want other things—to be at the regents' meetings or listening to scientists talk about their latest advances or even just traveling. The passion I'd had was shifting to something else."

The same disillusionment that had washed over her was dampening the spirits of her staff. Many had been at her side for more than a decade; some had lingered in these executive offices from their twenties into their forties.

"What Sherry wouldn't do was look at the things bubbling up in the culture that needed to be paid attention to, in terms of movies," said Rudin. "And she didn't have a staff that had a handle on that."

"As a group, we'd become stale," said Rosenfelt, the executive to whom Lansing had grown closest. "We'd been together too long. It was harder and harder for us. There's a shelf life on those jobs."

"What was coming through development was very, very slight," said Dolgen, "and when that happens, other things happen. It makes you want to sell off more of the pictures. It makes people nervous. People get tired, and because they get tired, the output suffers. Shame on us, probably, for keeping people too long. Shame on us all."

BATTLES WERE BEING waged at ever greater personal cost, victories won only after blood had been spilled on the tracks—none as much as with *The Hours*.

Its producer, Rudin, had assembled a top-notch cast (Meryl Streep, Julianne Moore, Nicole Kidman), along with one of Britain's leading theater directors, Stephen Daldry, to make the $21 million period piece based on Michael Cunningham's 1998 novel about three women in different eras, their stories linked by Virginia Woolf's 1925 novel *Mrs. Dalloway*.

Paramount, increasingly entrenched and wary of risk, had partnered with Harvey Weinstein, who had fallen out with Rudin over 2001's *Iris*. The two men were a study in contrasts: each terrified (and terrorized) many of those who knew him, but Rudin could be as refined as Weinstein was rough. Their talent, intelligence and sheer rage were balanced, if not complementary. One magazine called them "The Id Couple."

Once shooting began, the two men fought like pit bulls, particularly over Kidman's look in the movie. Rudin, like Lansing, wanted her to wear a prosthetic nose to better resemble her real-life counterpart, Woolf; Weinstein hated the idea. When the Miramax executive insisted on seeing makeup tests, Rudin refused, and even had one of Weinstein's emissaries barred from the set.

"He was coming to tell Nicole not to wear the nose," said Rudin. "I hired security guards to keep him away."

When Weinstein forced Paramount to pull the movie out of the Venice Film Festival and openly criticized the Philip Glass score, Rudin called him, outraged. "You skunked me," he said. "It's despicable that you pulled this stunt and damaged my movie in front of the press. I don't think I could ever trust you again." He sent a crateload of cigarettes to the chain-smoking Weinstein, with a note: "Thanks as always for your help."

"We both bring strong viewpoints to every project we work on," said Weinstein, "and like any good producer[s] we are passionate about our opinions. Sherry understood that."

Then she, too, fell victim to Rudin's wrath.

"He complained that we weren't mounting a proper Oscar campaign, although we were flooding the trade papers with ads," she said. "I confronted him, but his response was irrational. He kept calling Rob Friedman and yelling at him that Paramount wasn't spending enough. But it was a bottomless pit."

Their clashes grew even more intense once *The Hours* received nine Oscar nominations in February 2003. "Scott smelled he could get Best Picture, Best Actress, best this and that," said Lansing. "We were spending so much money I cannot tell you. But he wanted us to spend more. How did the Oscars become this monstrosity where people are spending zillions and having parties and slipping things here and there? What happened to the camaraderie?"

Rudin insisted Paramount was in the wrong. "They really ditched the Academy campaign," he argued. "Harvey said, 'I'm not spending money on the Academy,' because he was chasing [the Oscar for] *Chicago*. Sherry got very dogmatic about it. She didn't want to take him on because she didn't think [*The Hours*] was going to win. But the movie was a real player; it had won the Golden Globe. When you're in a situation where you are very clearly right, and you're getting stonewalled by the person who is meant to be your partner, that's not fun."

By the time of the 75th Academy Awards in March, it was clear *The Hours* would lose to *Chicago*, and Rudin skipped the ceremony.

"Losing is a very hard thing," said Lansing. "You're going to sit there at the Academy Awards; you know you're not going to win, and you want it so much that you can't handle it. You think success is going to fill you up, but you can only fill yourself up."

The Oscars might have been the end of the matter, but Lansing's relationship with Rudin further deteriorated when he lashed out at her in an interview with *Esquire*.

"He said I 'blew it' by not spending enough, and accused Jon and me of not caring about our movies," said Lansing. "At the time, we were working on the budget for *Lemony Snicket's A Series of Unfortunate Events*, which Scott was producing. Scott claimed I'd lied about it."

"I found the amount of energy being poured into this circle jerk frustrating and debilitating," he told the magazine. "These people can give you a lot of pain when they're trying to make a movie with you. Imagine what they can do when they're just trying to give you pain."

The article infuriated Lansing. "I remember getting it and just breathing a sigh of 'wow' and putting it down," she said. "It really hurt me, and when you're hurt you get angry. He'd violated my trust. It's one thing fighting; it's another going public. I said: 'After all we've done, after all the years of support, you've turned against us. We were your best friends. You broke the code.' It was profoundly painful. Scott was like a difficult brother, but an artist-producer to whom I'd become incredibly close. I felt betrayed and hurt."

Once she might have laughed off such a spat, but not now.

"It was one fight too many," she said. "I was plain burned out."

CHAPTER 20

In January 2003, in the midst of her battle with Rudin, Lansing fled Los Angeles for the sanctuary of Atlanta, telling only her husband and none of her staff.

Hollywood was in its post-Christmas lull, and the rest of the world was holding its breath in anticipation of the March 20 invasion of Iraq. Dark shadows were looming on the horizon and a palpable anxiety had pierced even the sealed bubble of Hollywood. In the sixteen months since 9/11, the film business had seemed increasingly disengaged from the world around it, just as Lansing had felt disengaged from its movies. She ached for something more meaningful.

Three years earlier, she had told Dolgen she was thinking of resigning and entering the nonprofit world, only for him to scoff at the notion. Even her lawyer, a veteran hardened by too many Hollywood skirmishes, had persuaded her to stay on when her contract was up for renewal.

But her dissatisfaction was growing. She thought of other men and women who had embarked on different lives, even at a point when their careers had reached a peak, and wondered whether she could do the same. None had done so as impressively as President Carter, who had created an institute devoted to global peace after his humiliating loss to Ronald Reagan in the 1980 election. When a friend asked Lansing if she would like to meet him, she leaped at the chance.

"He was an idol of mine," she said. "After the presidency, he'd used his life to change the world, devoting himself to everything from global health to building homes for the poor. I felt he'd lived a pure life in the years since he'd left the White House."

Now she was heading to see him.

As her car pulled out of Paramount and onto Melrose Avenue, she glanced up at the giant images plastered on the studio's outer walls, touting such coming attractions as *How to Lose a Guy in 10 Days* and *Rugrats Go Wild*, both movies she liked, neither one of which would be remembered for long. They were her last glimpse of the studio before the traffic swallowed her up.

She sat in silence as her car wound along the anonymous streets and then onto the choked freeway, until her driver deposited her at LAX. As she passed through security, she hoped no one would spot her. What would people think if they recognized her, she wondered? Should she unburden herself and admit the truth? And if not, what else could she say?

It was cold when she landed in Atlanta. As she left the airport and drove into the city, she looked out at the men and women wandering past her along the frosted streets, some languid, some laughing, all locked in their own private concerns just as she was in hers.

Suddenly she felt anxious. She remembered being face-to-face with another of her heroes, Nelson Mandela, and being so tongue-tied she could barely speak. "I was so awed by him, I was like a babbling idiot," she said. "I just kept saying, 'It's so nice to meet you, it's so nice to meet you,' and left."

That thought consumed her as she checked into her hotel and went to her room. Alone, she called Friedkin.

"This is the dumbest thing I've ever done," she said. "I've flown across the country just to see Jimmy Carter and I'll probably be with him for all of four minutes."

"Ask about Camp David," he said. "Ask about the Middle East, then you'll be fine."

"The Middle East?" she laughed. "How am I going to find out everything I need to know about the Middle East between now and tomorrow morning?"

The next day, she rose early and gathered her things. After a workout and breakfast, she set out to meet the president.

"I spent four and a half hours with him," she recalled. "I had lunch with him and his wife, Rosalynn, and met the staff that worked at the Carter Center, which did so much to promote human rights around the world. He seemed so happy, as if he'd found a new purpose in life, and that outer-directed purpose gave him an inner peace."

Carter pointed out his library and museum, set amid acres of parkland filled with trees, and spoke about his endeavors since creating the center in 1982.

"We talked primarily about the work of the Carter Center, that appealed to her," he said. "The Carter Center goes wherever people don't want to go, and we negotiate with leaders who are responsible for unnecessary wars or human rights abuse. We also discussed the plight of the poorest people on earth, in particular women and girls, whose basic human rights are violated grossly. We were exploring a way to address this issue on a global basis."

They discussed health care, too, one of the issues that most concerned Lansing, and Carter's success in fighting diseases that had ravaged the lives of millions but were now in abeyance. In particular, he spoke of his efforts to end Guinea worm, a tropical parasite that can infect humans and then grow inside them until meter-long worms crawl out of the skin, causing agonizing pain.

"He was dealing with things that nobody else would touch," said Lansing. "Guinea worm, river blindness—he helped lead the world in the fight to eradicate them."

Above all, Carter addressed the one matter that weighed on her so much: how to move to the next stage of her life. He had done so himself, without choice, when he was just a few years shy of Lansing's age. Nothing was better proof of his success than the Nobel Peace Prize he had received six weeks earlier.

Carter believed Lansing could do anything she set her mind to. He believed in the possibilities of change, and held a mirror to a future full of hope.

"He encouraged me to follow my instincts," said Lansing. "He showed me there was a whole world that could open up, if I just took the next step."

LANSING RETURNED TO Los Angeles vowing to leave Paramount.

But events were moving faster than her. The pressures coming from above were intense, and she knew that Dolgen, her friend, might not last without a new team around him. Now—perhaps too late—she tried to shore up their regime. Marketing chief Arthur Cohen was edged aside in September, and two months later so was Goldwyn.

After thirteen years at Paramount and a lifetime on Hollywood's center court, Goldwyn had seen the best and the worst the business had to offer. His grandfather, Sam, one of the greatest of all producers, had come to America from Warsaw in 1898 and gone on to make classics such as 1946's *The Best Years of Our Lives* and 1955's *Guys and Dolls*; his father, Sam junior, had cautioned his son against the duplicity of the studios, only to see him reach the summit of one of the very institutions he despised. This third-generation member of the Hollywood Goldwyns had survived his recent divorce, his conflict with Cruise, and even coming out as gay. But his work had suffered, as he was only too aware.

"My last tour of duty, I knew I was about to head into really rocky periods, personally," he said. "Scott Rudin was at a very crazy place at that time. He was furious, and everyone was furious, and he wrote a vicious letter about me, copied to everybody. He said I was a liar and I should be fired."

When Dolgen summoned him to go over Paramount's upcoming film slate, the two had a blowup. "He just went crazy," said Goldwyn. "He said, 'You call this a schedule? You call these titles?' I thought, 'I'm done. I'm not going to sit here and be yelled at by Jon, not after being here for three Academy Awards and establishing two franchises. Really, after all that, this is how I'm talked to?'"

That weekend, he and Lansing agreed to go their separate ways. If Goldwyn had hoped his boss might persuade him to stay, he was wrong.

"Could I have fought for my job?" he asked. "Probably. But it wasn't worth it to me. It just wasn't worth it. The door was held open for me [to leave]."

THREE THOUSAND MILES away, in Viacom's corporate offices, another door was being held open.

Mel Karmazin, Viacom's president and CEO, had always been an odd fit with his boss Redstone—the latter as mercurial as he was cerebral, the former a bluff salesman type who had headed CBS before Viacom bought it in 1999. Many thought Karmazin had only ever agreed to be Redstone's deputy in the belief the older man would soon retire, leaving him in charge of the media empire Redstone had built. But he had misjudged the Viacom chairman's tenacity, forgotten this was the same fighter who had clung to a burning balcony as the flames licked at him and the flesh was seared from his hands. Over the course of five years they had tried to work together but had only grown further apart. Now they despised each other.

"Mel had his own narrative of what went wrong that was different from Sumner's," said Dolgen. "And Sumner's included a fair amount of blame for Mel."

Within months of Goldwyn's departure, their relationship ruptured, and over Memorial Day weekend 2004, Lansing learned Karmazin was out.

"Mel had enough, and Sumner kind of punched his ticket," said Tom Freston, then the head of MTV Networks, who was unable to explain the precise trigger that led Karmazin to leave. "He really was not happy working for Sumner, and Sumner didn't feel Mel showed him the proper respect."

As the news swept through the upper reaches of Viacom, Redstone scrambled to regroup while his other executives waited to learn their fate. Someone would be the victor in the battle to replace Karmazin, and someone else would be the loser, and the ripples from that struggle inevitably would trickle down through the company.

Before the weekend was over, without consulting anyone, Redstone offered Karmazin's job to Freston.

"Sumner pulled me into the Carlyle Hotel [where he lived] and sat me down," said Freston. "I said, 'You know, this is a big decision. Let me talk this over with my wife. Give me twenty-four hours.'"

Incensed that his subordinate had not jumped at his generous offer, Redstone chose not to wait. Without telling Freston that he was rescinding the promotion, he instead gave the job to Leslie Moonves, the ambitious and charismatic chairman of CBS TV, who took it at once. The next day, Freston called to accept.

"Too late," said Redstone. "I've already offered it to Les."

"Jesus Christ!" said Freston. "You said you were going to give me a day."

That weekend, he met with Moonves and Redstone, along with a handful of other top executives in Viacom's headquarters.

"We were trying to figure out what to do," said Freston. "We were going to carve the company into two pieces. Sumner was going to become the CEO. [He said] 'You guys are going to run this thing together.' Then there was a meeting about who was going to run what, and how the announcement was going to be teed up for the following morning."

The men brokered a deal: Freston and Moonves would ascend in tandem as Redstone's seconds-in-command, but there would be a shake-up outside their circle. There was no room for Dolgen, they concluded. None of them had been close to him, and they disliked his penny-pinching ways, regardless how much Viacom had benefited from them.

"Dolgen and Freston always had a bad relationship," said Rudin. "Dolgen felt the movie division of MTV [which Freston had run] was a disaster. There was a massive amount of conflict there."

Redstone said he would deliver the news to Dolgen himself.

"Sumner called me," said Dolgen. "I didn't know anything was coming. He told me there were changes, and that was it. He didn't say anything about [firing] me."

Unaware of Redstone's intention, and failing to realize he had gotten cold feet, Dolgen carried on as usual over Memorial Day, and it was only the following day, when he was shown a press release announcing the Viacom restructuring, that he realized what it meant. The document mentioned that Lansing was being given new duties, but said nothing about him. He called Freston to demand an explanation.

"I was [stunned]," said Freston. "I thought Sumner had talked to him about, 'You're going to be leaving the company, we're going to honor your contract,' all of that type of stuff. But he had not. He did not step up to the plate. Jon says, 'I'm reading this press release. What does this mean for me?' I basically had to tell [him] the decision had been made over my head. It was really uncomfortable."

After years of hoarding the company's money as if it were his own, of working nonstop, of finding elaborate and arcane ways to maximize Viacom's profit, Dolgen had to learn of his firing by default. Not one of the company's top officers had the decency to tell him.

In the early afternoon of June 1, shortly after his conversation with Freston, Dolgen called Lansing to break the news. She was having lunch with a reporter in the studio commissary when a phone was brought to her table. Breaking away, she hurried to her friend's office.

"Jon told me he was leaving," she recalled. "I said, 'Well, I will, too.' But he said: 'Don't do that. I'll be fine. You have people to protect.' He wasn't bitter. He was philosophical. He said, 'If [MCA-Universal chairman] Lew Wasserman could end up out of a job, someday it had to end for me.'"

Lansing was shaken. "Jon was my partner, my best friend, my brother," she said. Perhaps she should have resigned there and then, but she vacillated, either lacking the conviction to quit or clinging to the hope she could still turn Paramount around.

"Sherry was a success at a time when the business was run on instinct," said Rudin. "When Jon left, it was very hard for her. The guys I loved in the business were buccaneers, and she was one of them. She never cared about the P&Ls [profit-and-loss statements]. She could have doubled down, but she'd reached a point where she wasn't interested anymore."

"That's when I saw her depressed for the first time," said producer Lynda Obst. "That era, that period—she knew it was over."

————

LANSING WAS LEFT to run the studio alone.

"They gave me Jon's job, which I never wanted," she said. "They literally said to me, 'You'll do this job.' Because I was in charge of the budget, I couldn't escape meetings after fifteen minutes, as I did when Jon was there. I was dealing with home video and worrying about how many DVDs were shipped and things like that. I thought, 'I've truly become a suit.'"

Contracts, negotiations and corporate bureaucracy began to dominate Lansing's life, while creative encounters, and the thrill of listening to new ideas, began to recede—all summed up in her dealings with America's biggest retailer, Wal-Mart.

"Wal-Mart had become the largest seller of DVDs in the country," she said. "I met with Lee Scott, its CEO, and flew to their headquarters in Bentonville, Arkansas, to meet with a group of employees." There she tried to summon whatever joy she could as she watched the employees begin their shifts with the Wal-Mart cheer: "Give me a W! Give me an A! Give me an L! Give me a squiggly!"

She did everything to persuade herself this was all good fun. "I wanted to be responsive," she said. "But my heart wasn't in it."

"We talked about [her leaving] for five years before it happened," said CAA's Lourd. "Sherry was always very forthcoming about, 'This will last as long as it does and then I will leave. With any luck I will leave on my own terms.'"

Her spirit had fled the enterprise, and it was only a matter of time before the rest of her followed. When Freston suggested she should fire her remaining staff and bring in fresh blood, she could not take it anymore.

"If I'd waited for the perfect moment, I'd never have left," she said. "The job had become a way of life, and I'd found a rhythm that worked well over twelve years. But if I didn't start doing the other things that really mattered to me, I'd never get to do them at all. There were so many times when I'd said to Billy, 'I'm going to quit,' it was almost anticlimactic when I finally did."

"She decided when she was going to step down," said Lourd, "and plotted it and left elegantly and graciously."

In fall 2004, Lansing called Redstone. "I told him I was going to leave when my contract was up at the end of 2005, or earlier if he could find a successor," she said. "He asked me to stay, and then made me sign something saying I wouldn't go to a rival company. He told me he was sad, but not surprised."

Freston was "dumbfounded" when he found out, he said. "But she bowed out with total class."

Lansing's planned exit was kept under wraps and hidden from all but the key players, even as Freston and Redstone worked on finding a replacement, until on November 2, 2004, the *Los Angeles Times* broke the news.

In a story headlined "Hollywood Pioneer Lansing Is Poised to Exit Paramount," reporter Claudia Eller wrote: "Sherry Lansing, a Hollywood pioneer who for three decades has been one of the most powerful figures in the movie business, plans to step down as chairwoman of Paramount Pictures when her contract expires at the end of next year. According to a source familiar with the situation, Lansing will stay long enough to help choose her successor and to aid in the transition."

Word tore through the industry, and a generation of executives that had grown up with Lansing as their role model collectively gasped in amazement.

Rosenfelt was on an exercise bicycle at the gym when she saw the news on KTLA TV. "It was the last thing I expected," she said. "I was like, 'What?' I was stunned." Part of her was heartbroken that Lansing was leaving, and part of her thrilled at the way her friend had orchestrated everything. She was convinced, like all of Lansing's colleagues, that their boss had leaked the story, leaving her firmly in control of her destiny.

"The way Sherry left was like an incredibly produced movie," said Manning. "We all looked at it and thought, 'Oh my God! That's brilliant.'"

ON FEBRUARY 16, 2005, a crowd gathered outside Grauman's Chinese Theatre, the very first place Lansing had visited when she arrived in Los

Angeles four decades earlier, to watch as her hand- and footprints were embedded in concrete. Diane Keaton and Sidney Poitier were there, and so were dozens of others. It was Lansing's last day as studio chairman, and her friends had joined the celebration en masse.

"There were crowds upon crowds," said Lansing. "Anyone from the studio was allowed to come. They gave speeches, and so did I."

That evening, Paramount hosted a farewell party on the lot. She arrived at the studio with Friedkin after darkness had enveloped the buildings, and nobody could be seen. A momentary pang went through her that her exit had come to this.

"I said, 'Why's it dark? Has everybody gone home?'" she recalled. She glanced up to see a handful of men and women emerging from the darkness, strolling toward one of the soundstages. Then a dozen more appeared. Then hundreds were walking to the stage where the party was being held. "Everyone came—every waitress, every assistant," she said. "I saw a mass of people pouring in, streaming from all over the studio."

Inside the cavernous building, huge posters lined the walls, showcasing many of the movies Lansing had green-lit, which had since become classics—*Titanic, Forrest Gump, Saving Private Ryan, Braveheart*—with her face and Friedkin's printed in place of the stars'. That evening, it was announced that her favorite studio theater—the Little Theatre, where she had spent so many hours—was being named after her.

"That's all I could have asked for," she said. "Because that's where I'd spent so much of my life, watching the dailies, seeing the movies over and over again. That's where I saw *Fatal Attraction*. That's where I saw *The Accused*. That's where I saw *Forrest Gump* and almost every single one of the two hundred movies we'd made while I was running the studio, many not just once but dozens of times."

After Redstone spoke (as did President Carter via video), Morgan Freeman delivered a toast, and hordes of employees milled around Lansing in disbelief that this woman who had been their leader for so long—who had broken every barrier, who had defined an era—would soon be gone.

As the chitchat wound down, a handful asked to have their pictures taken with her; then others joined in, and an impromptu line began to form. Soon everyone was standing there. "People stood waiting to take a picture with me," said Lansing. "Every policeman that worked there, every guard. They stayed until two in the morning. I'll never forget it."

When the last shots had been snapped and the final champagne glasses clinked, she took her leave of the stragglers and stepped out into the cool of the night. There had been rain these past few weeks, and a thin oily coating covered the sidewalk. She could see her reflection in the puddles that had formed.

She walked around the deserted studio one last time, lost in silence. The buildings were bathed in a half-light, empty and abandoned at this unholy hour; a few generators buzzed, but otherwise all was still.

"I didn't feel nostalgic," she said. "I just wanted to say one last goodbye."

CHAPTER 21

On February 17, 2005, Lansing stepped into the world newborn. "All of a sudden I had to recreate my life," she said. "But I was like a kid, giddy after graduating from college. Life is an evolution. It's about choices, about chapters. And this was the chapter I wanted to experience now."

After decades of accommodating moguls and movie stars, of balancing budgets and dissecting scripts, she felt liberated, as if she had shed one skin and grown another. She was eager to do the work she loved, spend time with friends and even go on vacation without feeling guilty if she lingered too long.

"I used to think, sometimes I'd just like to go shopping on a Friday, but I realized that wasn't in my DNA," she said. "I was incapable of not working. Some gene pushed me, made me want to say at the end of each week, 'What did I accomplish?' That's why I never cared for the word 'retired.' I preferred 'rewired.'"

While her peers who had left their jobs—more often than not with no choice—spoke wistfully of the corporate jets, the lackeys and the limousines that had once been at their beck and call, she missed none of those things. The perks of her old position seemed minor compared to the restrictions that had hemmed her in.

Still, she acknowledged moments of trepidation. "My greatest fear was that I wouldn't have enough to do," she said. "I was apprehensive. I even wondered if I should move away from Los Angeles, and worried about feeling marginalized once I left the film business. But I enjoyed the city more than ever. I ate in the same restaurants, got together with the same friends. I could even go to a concert without having to hold a script in my lap. And it was wonderful to be learning new things."

Her immediate priority was to find offices for the Sherry Lansing Foundation, a nonprofit she had established as the umbrella for her activities, with a focus on education, cancer research and the aging workforce, the areas to which she was most drawn. Cancer had been a prime concern ever since her mother's death; education since her involvement with Big Sisters (now reconstituted as Big Brothers Big Sisters); and, having turned sixty, she wanted others to have the same opportunities for change.

When a real estate agent tried to steer her toward the kind of squat, prewar building that mirrored Paramount's architecture, she demurred, opting for a Century City high-rise far removed from the denizens of show business, well before the area had become an entertainment industry hub. She wanted to embrace the future, not the past. So it was ironic that when she moved into her new offices and gazed out the window, she found herself looking down at the very Fox lot where she had begun her march to fame. It gave her a sense of coming full circle.

After recruiting an executive to run the foundation and finding two assistants, Lansing at last was ready to give herself over to her new adventure. She wished to be active rather than reactive, to play offense rather than defense. "I didn't just want to raise money and give out grants," she said. "I wanted to get my hands dirty. I wanted to be at the center of things."

Her biggest challenge lay in adapting to the often languid pace of the nonprofit world. She was used to returning calls within minutes and having her own calls returned just as fast, but no such code of conduct applied here. Early in her post-Paramount years, she was working on En-Corps, a program she had created to retrain workers with a background in math and science to become teachers in underserved Los Angeles schools. When she called a dozen school principals to discuss it, not one called her back.

SHE TRIED TO adjust to this alternative universe and slowed her tempo as much as she could, until Eli Broad, a billionaire philanthropist, set her straight. "Why should you put up with it?" he asked, advising her to do as he did and expect others to raise their standards. Emboldened, she discovered that a dose of impatience helped rather than hurt. Being gracious was all well and good, but force and conviction were necessary, too. History, she knew, was littered with well-meaning souls, but only zealots moved mountains.

"I thought, 'Why should we tolerate different standards? There's an urgency to what we're doing,'" she said.

EnCorps was one of two programs she spearheaded to help older people reenter the workplace or find meaningful activities related to education. Redefining aging, as she put it, was of enormous importance to her. The other program was PrimeTime LAUSD, which helped volunteers go into Los Angeles schools and offer their services in various ways. Neither program was established without resistance.

When Lansing told California governor Arnold Schwarzenegger about EnCorps and asked for his support in getting corporations to cover the $15,000 it would cost per employee, he was skeptical—until Qualcomm, IBM, Bank of America and other giants stepped up. That convinced Lansing she was on the right track.

"Philanthropy isn't about money, it's about good ideas," she said. "If you have a good idea, you'll find a way to execute it."

She believed everything in her past had led to this, that her experiences as an actress, producer and executive had all prepared her for the third act of her life. "Creating a nonprofit is like producing a movie," she said. "You have to have passion for an idea. You have to get others to share it. And you have to find the funding to bring it to life. You can never give up, you can never give in. You need to use every drop of talent you've been given to make things work. And that's what I intended to do."

She did not have billions to lavish, unlike some leading philanthropists, but she had something of her own. "I had a voice," she said, "and that voice could be heard."

WEEKS BEFORE LEAVING Paramount, she had been contacted by Steve Westly, California's state controller and chief financial officer. Assuming he was seeking her endorsement, like so many politicians (including a Senate hopeful named Barack Obama), she diverted the call to corporate communications.

In fact, he was reaching out to tell her she was on his short list to join a new board that would oversee billions of dollars that California voters had just authorized for the burgeoning field of embryonic stem cell research. If he selected her, Lansing would be one of the board's patient advocates, representing those with cancer.

Defying conventional wisdom, the state had voted in favor of Proposition 71, a 2004 ballot measure approving the sale of $3 billion in bonds to fund stem cell research, federal funding for which had been restricted by the George W. Bush administration on the grounds that human embryos would be destroyed.

"Parts of the Christian right were saying, 'Oh my gosh, maybe the U.S. shouldn't even be allowed to do research in this area,'" recalled Westly. "The basic thrust was, not only should California lead the way to try and find cures for diabetes, blindness and heart disease, but this was also a huge job [creator] and stimulus for the California economy."

Only a few years earlier, scientists had reported a breakthrough in culturing embryonic stem cells—cells in the embryo that possess an almost magical ability to grow into other types of cells. Their work offered untold hope for regenerating damaged limbs and curing diseases, though it also left Lansing with a pang of sorrow when she thought how it might have saved her mother. Over lunch, she urged Westly to name her to the board.

"It was humbling to have to audition," she said. "I told Billy, 'I'll never get it, but it's a good experience.'"

She was "a no-brainer," said Westly, "an obvious first pick. She was brilliant, she was driven, she got things done. I was interested in people with high EQs [emotional quotients] who could navigate very difficult situations and get to winning."

Two weeks after their lunch, he appointed her to the Independent Citizens' Oversight Committee (ICOC), the freshman board overseeing the newly created California Institute for Regenerative Medicine (CIRM).

In December 2004, Lansing was sworn in. She was as nervous that day as she had been on her first day at Fox. Gathered at the San Francisco swearing-in were some of the most brilliant minds in the country, all members of the stem cell committee.

"I wasn't used to sitting at government tables, with the flag and the state seal," she said. "I was used to being in meetings where everybody was always screaming. I had to dress a certain way and behave a certain way. I told myself, 'You're not in Hollywood anymore.'"

After the board secretary introduced David Baltimore, the president of Caltech and a Nobel Prize winner for medicine, and David Kessler, the former commissioner of the Food and Drug Administration, it was Lansing's turn. "I thought, 'If he introduces me as 'movie executive Sherry Lansing,' I'm just going to crawl under the table,'" she said. Instead, she was introduced as the chairman of Stop Cancer.

Wittingly or not, her post-Hollywood career had begun.

SHE WAS IMMEDIATELY flung into a court battle as Prop 71's opponents tried to have it declared illegal.

The opposition, led by the Life Legal Defense Foundation, chose to attack the legality of the board itself, rather than the ethics of embryonic stem cell research.

"Our lawsuit focused on a feature of Prop 71 that many people, from all points of view, had noted, commented on and criticized," said its vice president for legal affairs, Catherine Short. "This feature was that the governing board of CIRM, the semi-appointed, semi-ex-officio body that was going to be handing out $3 billion in taxpayer money, was riddled with conflicts of interest and, once established, was outside the 'exclusive management and control of the State,' as constitutionally required."

Two lawsuits were filed in California courts, arguing that the proposition was unconstitutional, each likely to wend through the system for years. (Later, they were merged into one.)

"The board members of the initiative didn't think there would be litigation," said Bob Klein, a real estate developer who had spent millions backing the initiative, "but I was convinced that there would be, because of the extreme positions taken during the initiative. With the kind of rhetoric that had been used during the campaign, it was pretty clear. Since they had already tried court battles to block us, they would continue. My concern was how long this would take. I looked at [another ballot measure favoring] early childhood education. That was tied up in court for years."

"The brilliance of the opposition was just to wear everyone down," said Lansing. "We were only allowed to take out a tiny amount of money for overhead, and they knew if they kept the lawsuits going, we'd have to shut our doors."

Many of her fellow board members had family members who were sick or had health issues themselves, and they clung to the research as their last best hope. The patient advocates often had the disease they represented, whether Parkinson's or AIDS, and one was terminally ill, which made her fierce commitment all the more heartbreaking as far as Lansing was concerned.

Knowing the fight could last years, she met with Klein, and the two came up with a plan to generate millions of dollars to keep the board going, even as the courts froze state funding until the legal battle could be resolved. They began to call everybody they knew, with Lansing flying from one city to another to win over wealthy donors.

"I remember being on a plane with [entrepreneurs] Richard Blum and John Moores, coming back from the Carter Center," she said. "I was on the phone, begging for help—'We're running out of money!'—when they overheard me, and each one wrote a check for $1 million, then and there. It's one of the most generous things I ever saw."

Her efforts took place even as critics griped about the board's ineffectiveness, unaware of the counteroffensive being waged behind the scenes.

"The September 9, 2005, meeting of the California Institute for Regenerative Medicine (CIRM) governing board had the markings of a Hollywood script—but whether it was one written by Frank Capra or Samuel Beckett remains to be seen," noted *The Sacramento News & Review*. "On that day, the lead actors in California's $3 billion stem-cell enterprise announced the first grants of $40 million to 16 research universities and institutes. The plot twist was that they didn't actually have a single cent to hand out, as the monies remain tied down by lawsuits challenging the constitutionality of the venture."

Lansing was summoned to give a deposition. Meeting the plaintiffs' lawyers, she found a pleasant young woman preparing to depose her. The other side was just as sincere as hers, she realized, however misguided she might consider them.

"This beautiful, freckled girl took my testimony," she recalled. "I looked at her and thought, 'How can you hate stem cell research? It might save you one day.'"

After weeks of fundraising, she and Klein cobbled together enough money to keep the board functioning. They explored ways to raise more.

One of the political insiders Lansing had gotten to know suggested a path through an arcane procedure that was perfectly legal but would need Schwarzenegger's approval. If the governor consented, he could sign off on a $150 million loan.

"With the money we'd raised," said Klein, "the governor was in a position where he could make a bold move and say, 'Look, these are civic leaders from throughout the state and from every major business community, and the state needs to stand behind the people.' He could make a $150 million gap loan to us after we placed the initial bonds and got through the court of appeals. The question was, who was going to convince him to take this critical step? The pivotal person was Sherry."

Knowing that Schwarzenegger had broken ranks with his party to support Prop 71, Lansing did everything to persuade him. It worked.

In November 2006, CIRM announced: "It will have $181 million available by the end of the year to fund research, training, and facilities development grants. The funding comes through a $150 million General Fund loan, ordered by California Governor Arnold Schwarzenegger earlier this year, and $31 million from the sale of bond anticipation notes (BANs) to private individuals and philanthropic foundations. The funds will support stem cell research in California, until litigation challenging the voters' right to fund it through general obligation bonds concludes."

Lansing was so grateful that she subsequently hosted a fundraiser for Schwarzenegger, giving him cover among Hollywood's liberal contingent when he ran for reelection.

The legal assault, said Klein, was overwhelming—though from Short's point of view, her organization was handicapped by having far less money than his. "We had very little," she said.

In December 2005, the plaintiffs "unloaded on us 150 or 200 'interrogatories,' asking for every document that had ever seen the light of day from the beginning of the initiative," said Klein. "This was ten days before Christmas and we had to have it all in by January 10. The staff worked through Christmas, through New Year's, and all 150 interrogatories and all the discovery motions were fully filed, much to their shock."

In an initial ruling in April 2006, Alameda County Superior Court judge Bonnie Sabraw decided in the board's favor, rejecting the argument that Prop 71 was unconstitutional.

An appellate court supported that decision, leaving only one hurdle: the California Supreme Court. Lansing knew the lawsuit would have to end there, because there was no constitutional issue that would merit taking it further. "This was a states' rights issue," said Klein. "That was the case under the constitutional laws."

On May 16, 2007, the California Supreme Court announced it would not review *People's Advocate and National Tax Limitation Foundation v. Independent Citizens Oversight Committee*, meaning that the appellate court ruling stood.

"This is the end of the road," Dana Cody, Life Legal Defense Foundation's executive director, told the *Los Angeles Times*.

Days later, the bond sale moved forward, and the board started its real work. "Overnight," said Westly, "résumés came in from the best universities in the world—Oxford, Cambridge, Tsinghua. Every major scientist on the planet was sending their résumé to UCLA, Stanford, USC, saying, 'I want to do research in your state.'"

"I was ecstatic," said Lansing. "It was a validation of everything I'd hoped for but was afraid to believe."

THAT BATTLE MARKED the beginning of a wholesale reconfiguration of her life as she waded waist-deep into the world of philanthropy. If her fights at Paramount had been with individuals, her struggles now were with the establishment itself.

"It wasn't so much an [individual] opponent," said her friend Barry Munitz, the man who had overseen her appointment as a regent while running Governor Davis's transition team. "It was that the system was slow, conservative. There's an old saying about change in academic life: it's like dancing a ballet in molasses."

One would never have known that from her schedule, as she crisscrossed California for regents' meetings; maintained her activities on the boards of Stop Cancer, the Lasker Foundation and the Carter Center, among others; and even went to Benin with the Red Cross and to Myanmar with the former president. Much of this came to her through happenstance rather than planning. "You don't find the cause," she said, "the cause finds you."

She became one of the leaders in the effort to open the Martin Luther King Jr. Community Hospital, the only major hospital to serve South Central Los Angeles. That hospital replaced the notorious King/Drew Hospital, which had closed years earlier when federal funding was withdrawn. Rallying the forces needed to open the institution was a gargantuan endeavor that involved mobilizing the UC regents, having the University of California agree to supply a permanent staff of doctors, and bringing in outsiders who would fund the hundreds of millions in operational and building costs. The new hospital opened in July 2015, eight years after the old one had closed. It was among Lansing's proudest achievements.

As her life changed, so did Friedkin's. In 1999, he had directed his first opera, Alban Berg's *Wozzeck*, to much acclaim. Now he began to travel for different productions, and Lansing frequently accompanied him.

"Billy did operas in Turin, Vienna, Tel Aviv, Munich and Florence," she said. "We'd rent a one- or two-bedroom apartment, and we'd wake up whenever we wanted, like newlyweds. Billy would fix breakfast, and then I'd have these simple, existential days. I'd go out and speak to anyone who could understand me. I'd make local friends, and have lunch or coffee or visit a museum, and then have dinner with Billy in the evening. These were some of the happiest times in my life, when it was just the two of us."

There was only one blot on those halcyon days: when she learned that the two men she had groomed to be her successors at Paramount, Robert Friedman and Donald De Line, were being pushed aside by Redstone. But that was counterbalanced by the blockbuster returns of her last major pictures, *War of the Worlds* and *Mission: Impossible III*.

"Robbie and Donald both went on to do well," said Lansing. "They were living their own lives and I was living mine."

NO ASPECT OF Lansing's new life proved more daunting than the fight over tuition costs at the University of California, which affected hundreds of thousands of students each year.

Costs had skyrocketed at the UC campuses, with undergraduate fees rising 90 percent in the six years prior to 2007, according to the *Los Angeles Times*. When the Great Recession struck in 2008 and the State of California slashed the university system's budget, the regents felt they had no choice but to charge students even more.

"We were almost $1 billion behind [what was needed to fund the UC system], because of the cuts," said UC president Mark Yudof. "On top of that, we had to put in around $1 billion a year to make sure our retirement system would be viable. Tuition had to be increased, because there are only so many places you can go."

The timing was terrible. Everyone in the state was suffering, and many people were without jobs. Opponents argued that the regents should slash the salaries of the highest-paid faculty, and the regents themselves were divided. But Lansing insisted that cutting salaries would make the UC less competitive in the long run, damaging its resources and reputation, even though she viscerally disliked the idea of tuition hikes.

"Sherry did not want to see tuition go up, or at least go up more than it had to," said Jerry Brown, who became governor of California in January 2007. "She was very helpful in keeping tuition down. [I wanted] to keep the tuition down in the short term but would argue for lowering the cost structure of UC so the tuition could stay down for a very long time. Of course, that's very challenging for the board, for the president of the university and for the entire structure of UC. You're talking about a level of transformation that's not easy."

More than most regents, Lansing knew from personal experience what a burden this would be. Some of the young men and women she had befriended through Big Brothers Big Sisters had to plead with their families to go to school; it was inconceivable that these families would assume thousands of dollars in debt when they could barely pay the rent.

And it was not just the poor who felt squeezed. Lansing also had middle-class friends, including skilled technicians who had worked on her films, who came to her for advice, desperate because they had to choose between paying their mortgages and supporting their kids through college.

When the regents raised tuition by a massive 32 percent in November 2009, student anger boiled over.

"During two days of protests at UCLA, where the UC regents met to vote on the fee increase, about 2,000 students from the 10-campus system confronted riot police, shouted slogans and blocked building exits," *Time* reported. "Like a scene out of the angry 1960s, students surged against barricades and briefly seized a building near the main campus quad; police used taser guns on several protesters, and arrested nearly 20. All the while, police helicopters hovered overhead, TV vans with high antennas stood ready and students played drums and strummed guitars."

California Highway Patrol officers in riot gear swept through the university but were powerless to stop the students, who headed for the regents' meeting place.

"They surrounded the building," said Yudof. "We were trapped. There were officers that had guns with rubber bullets. Some people went out in disguise, but I couldn't because everyone knew my face."

"They held us hostage," said Lansing. "The cops said, 'You have to stay here until the mob dies down.' I said, 'That's ridiculous. They're not going to hurt us. They're college kids.'"

She gathered her things and started to leave. "I said, naively, 'I'll pretend I'm a student. They won't recognize me,'" she recalled. "I told one of the staff members, 'We'll carry our notebooks in front of us, just like the kids, and we'll walk out.'"

Ignoring objections, Lansing left the conference room once her meeting was over, stepped out of the building, and plunged into the crowd. Looking down at her notebook in an attempt to hide her face, she wove through the mass of people with their clenched fists and banners held high, comically imagining no one would notice her.

She almost got away with it, when a young woman spotted her. "Regent!" she screamed. The crowd turned as one.

"That's when I first knew physical fear," said Lansing. "I was caught. I thought they'd attack me because 'crowd fever' was in the air and there were thousands of them packed in."

A police officer pried her loose and she started to run.

"I was in my little high heels, with my book bag, waving around the notebook in one hand," she said. "Some of the students followed me, and a reporter chased after me with his camera, and it was all over the evening news. But I managed to get away."

The protests continued deep into 2011, inflamed by the Occupy movement that was spreading across the country. At one point a police officer pulled a gun on a student, while another pepper-sprayed peaceful demonstrators. At UC Riverside, a student hurled himself at the regents and had to be torn off them, said Lansing, who by this time had been elected chairman of the regents, and who may well have been spared worse because she had reached out to hear the students' point of view.

"She met personally with students, which is something none of the other regents did," noted Larry Gordon, then a higher-education reporter for the *Los Angeles Times*. "[That] was a nice touch."

There seemed to be no way out until Brown advocated the passage of a new ballot measure, Proposition 30, which would raise personal income taxes and the state sales tax in order to defray education cuts. Lansing agreed to back it on one condition: that the governor commit $100 million for UC tuition. She knew he would need all the student support he could get if he were to have a hope of passing the measure, and this seemed a fair trade-off.

"If not," she argued, "why would the kids lend it their support?"

Brown gave his tacit approval, and Lansing began to tour the university's campuses in an attempt to win the students over. Sitting in cluttered offices and tiny dorm rooms, she begged them to back the proposition.

"I said, 'I know you think we're all evil and we're monsters, but we're not,'" she recalled. "I told them we had no choice but to raise tuition because the state kept cutting our budget. But I assured them, 'The governor will support us if you back Prop 30. This has to be our strategy.'"

The students reached out to friends and families and alumni, while Lansing worked behind the scenes to persuade her fellow regents to endorse the ballot measure. They could vote against it as individuals, she said, but it was essential the board give Brown its organizational backing. "I knew we could horse-trade," she said, "because I'd been doing that for years at Paramount."

"She [was] a good advocate for UC," said Brown. "It helped push public opinion in a positive direction and gave us the ultimate victory we had."

In November 2012, Prop 30 was approved by a resounding 55 percent of the voters; Brown gave the UC more money; the regents froze tuition. The fight was over, at least for now.

———

EARLY IN THE tuition battle, Lansing was shaken to learn that her husband would have to undergo a triple bypass, surprising given how physically fit he was.

While the operation went well, things took a serious turn for the worse when Friedkin discovered he had an infection caused by the bacteria Serratia, a hospital-borne infection highly resistant to antibiotics that he had picked up during his bypass. It had spread from his bloodstream into his sternum, the bone protecting the heart. Lansing was consumed with fear, especially when she found out that another operation was needed and there was a real chance the sternum would have to be replaced, an extremely serious procedure with no guarantee of success.

"He had this terrible infection," she said. "The operation had a 50 percent mortality rate. It was horrible, just horrible."

Friedkin was still in the hospital when he was told this. By now, he had lost all confidence in the doctor who had operated on him and insisted on moving to another institution.

"The first hospital claimed I was cured and there was no problem," he said. "You see liquid coming out of your chest, and the guy says there's nothing wrong. I said, 'I've got to get out of here.' Sherry did the impossible and got me moved."

The day of the operation, Lansing watched with growing anxiety as doctors at UCLA Medical Center—the hospital where she had taken Friedkin—wheeled him into the operating room. With hours of uncertainty ahead of her, she found refuge in the university chapel.

"I was terrified," she said. "I was afraid he was going to die. I remember crying. I prayed to God, 'I'll do anything you want, just save him.'"

For eight hours, she waited while Friedkin remained in the operating room, not knowing whether he was going to live or die. At last, one of the surgeons came out. The operation had gone well, he told her, and the sternum did not have to be removed, but there was still the possibility that something could go wrong.

"They reconstructed it," said Lansing. "It was the most painful thing in the world. It took two months for him to get better, but we knew he was going to make it."

He emerged stronger than before and went on to direct his most acclaimed film in years, 2011's *Killer Joe*, as well as resume his peripatetic opera career. The change of doctors and his wife's forcefulness were crucial, he believed.

"I wouldn't have survived otherwise," he said. "She saved my life."

FRIEDKIN'S ILLNESS AND the protracted tuition battle took place even as Lansing was preoccupied with the most important mission of her life: the creation of Stand Up to Cancer.

Over lunch with one of her friends, Ellen Ziffren, shortly after leaving Paramount, she had discussed the idea of doing something bigger and bolder in the fight against cancer. But what? A documentary? A fundraiser? The women were not sure.

To formulate a plan, they approached Lisa Paulsen and Kathleen Lobb, executives with the Entertainment Industry Foundation, a nonprofit group used to raising millions of dollars for a multitude of causes. These women in turn recruited Katie Couric, the *Today* show host who was soon to be named anchor of the *CBS Evening News* and who had lost her husband to colon cancer.

"I had my very personal experience with my husband, and my sister Emily died of pancreatic cancer," said Couric. "Everybody has been touched by this disease."

In conversations that began in late 2005 and stretched into 2007, the women settled on a plan: they would create a telethon, an hour-long televised fundraiser sprinkled with some of Hollywood's biggest names. Lansing was convinced that stars, producers and executives alike would rally to the cause. Cancer affected everyone, she argued; there was not a man or woman in America who did not have a friend, a relative or even a child who had the disease.

"We had all dealt with cancer in our lives, in our families," she said. "We were raw, even angry, because advances had not developed as fast as we might have hoped, given the billions of dollars that had been invested in research."

The project became more pressing when Lansing heard that an old acquaintance, Laura Ziskin, was working on a similar idea.

Then in her mid-fifties, Ziskin was at the peak of an impressive career that had seen her produce such movies as 1987's *No Way Out* and 2002's *Spider-Man*, run a division of 20th Century Fox, and executive-produce two Academy Awards telecasts. But she had recently been treated for stage three breast cancer. After going through radiation, chemotherapy, a mastectomy and a stem-cell transplant, she felt she had a new lease on life, only for the cancer to strike again. She knew it might be fatal, but would not succumb until she had fought it with everything she had—including her skills as a producer. Joining three other women to create a television special specifically focused on breast cancer (the others were marketing executives Rusty Robertson and Sue Schwartz, and producer Noreen Fraser, also a breast cancer survivor), she was moving ahead with her plans when Lansing called.

"Let's work together," she said.

Of the nine women, many did not know each other at all; many had never worked on a project this large; and many were new to the non-profit world. But all had been impacted by cancer. Two were survivors; the others had mothers, sisters, brothers, cousins, spouses, colleagues and friends who had fought the disease.

"Whenever you do something new, it's difficult," noted Lansing. "There are hundreds of hurdles you have to get over, and as soon as you get past those there are even bigger ones. We were trying to create something dynamic and full of sizzle, but also scientifically solid. We said, 'We're all mightier together than separately.'"

Things got off to a shaky start at a breakfast meeting when two of the women questioned whether some of the others had the ability to handle an operation like this. "They said, 'We don't think you guys can do this on your own,'" remembered Schwartz. "'You have no infrastructure. You have no capacity. Why should we put our faith in you?'" Later, the tension was resolved, but other conflicts simmered.

One meeting, said Schwartz, "was very contentious. Sherry said, 'Just apologize.' I said, 'But I didn't do anything wrong.' She said, 'Look, I've apologized so much in my life, I don't even know what I'm apologizing for anymore. Don't ever let ego stand in the way of the result.'" Schwartz took her advice. "I wrote this mea culpa, hated every minute of doing it, but the issue was put to bed."

In another meeting, "I was feeling really bad energy," said Robertson. "And Sherry stood up. She walked over to me and hugged me in front of everybody, and she goes, 'You are going to do great, and I'm here to help you in any way.' She's the tie that bound us together, the tie that binds."

That binding almost snapped when questions were raised about whether Ziskin or Fraser should be the lead producer. As the women settled into Lansing's office to discuss it, the conversation became heated and tears spilled over.

"When people are passionate, emotions run high," said Schwartz. "Because this was a shotgun marriage, there were some bumps in the road."

Couric had persuaded NBC to air the show. But even as the women went back and forth resolving their issues, their ambition was growing. What if every network agreed to run it, the women wondered? That would create a media "roadblock" and a sensation.

Lansing began to reach out to the other network chiefs, helped by Ziffren's husband, Ken, a leading entertainment lawyer.

"We didn't just double-team them," said Couric. "We triple- and quadruple-teamed them to embrace this unprecedented effort."

Only Fox declined, because News Corp. president Peter Chernin favored devoting resources to his own preferred cause, malaria. In the end, ABC, NBC and CBS all pledged to air a one-hour, commercial-free, prime-time benefit. A date was set for Friday, September 5, 2008.

Problems remained. One was raising money (a secret of the telethon world was that most of it had to be raised ahead of time, through sponsorships and the like). The other was getting a scientific seal of approval.

"This was nine Hollywood women with absolutely no credentials, with one who was battling cancer, but who was our conscience and in front of us every day," said Lansing. "We had to get credibility. Someone said, 'Get Phil Sharp and everyone will flow your way.'"

Phillip Sharp was a Nobel Prize–winning geneticist whose services were as coveted as any movie star's. Lansing knew how unlikely he would be to commit. This would take more than a few letters and phone calls; it would require a whirlwind campaign to convince him. When they learned that he would soon be attending a cancer-related conference, the women set out in force.

"In the midst of this meeting, Sherry Lansing approaches me," Sharp recalled. "At her side were Laura Ziskin and the others. And she walked up and introduced herself and basically said, 'I want you to help us start Stand Up to Cancer,' then in a much more articulate and elaborate way talked about what they were trying to do to transform cancer research to make it more collaborative, to translate it far more to patients' benefit, to really change the culture. I knew these ladies were going to have an enormous impact. I thought, 'If I have any spare time left in my life, I should be helping them,' and I decided to do it almost instantaneously."

"The minute he said yes," said Lansing, "he got every scientist he wanted on the advisory committee—and suddenly we had credibility."

The women—all amateurs, all enthusiasts—convened a series of meetings with Sharp and the other scientists, forging the guidelines of their fundraiser: who would handle what, where the money would go, how applicants for funding should apply, and how the eventual recipients would be determined.

Some of the women favored spending the money on advocacy, others on whatever form of cancer had attacked them or their families.

"As everything fell into place with the final network commitments," recalled Lobb, "we said to the scientists: 'We feel confident that we can raise a lot of money. Tell us what should be done differently in terms of cancer research.'"

The scientists suggested creating "dream teams," bringing together groups of researchers and medical specialists across different institutions and even different countries—as few as 54 and as many as 111 scientists on any one team—who had not collaborated before. It was a bold idea that would require convincing the scientists to overcome their ingrained competitiveness and reluctance to share data.

"That hadn't been done before, certainly not in the nonprofit world in [that] way," said Sharp. "We've changed philosophies: a surgeon re-moving a pancreas in Philadelphia is sending the tissue immediately to basic scientists in San Diego and Princeton—and it's that integration that's been so productive. You have to develop a culture in which people collaborate and share, and we've been able to do that in very successful ways."

"If you've ever been struck by cancer, you know how frustrating it is," said Lansing. "Often, one hospital doesn't communicate with another. We wanted to bring down the barriers between the scientists, so that they would all work together."

She was convinced the idea could succeed because she had seen it work with the stem cell endeavors. "The thing that board did so well was to break down the silos and make it a group effort," said Lansing. "It be-came all about sharing information. No scientist was allowed to keep his research to himself, and the information had to be made public."

Lansing met with Ziskin to finalize their plans. "I remember sitting with Laura, who was the soul of this and gave it her whole life, and asking her, 'How do we make this work?'" she recalled. "Laura said, 'You need to give them a whole lot of money. Not $10,000. Not $100,000. Not even $1 million—but $10 million. If you have that much money to give out, they'll find a way to get along.'"

Raising such an enormous sum—not just $10 million, but multiples of that, if several projects were to be funded—was all but unimaginable.

"We established a goal of raising $100 million," said Paulsen. "It was sheer will. We didn't really have a rhyme or reason. I said, 'We don't have any idea how much will be raised in a proactive telethon. They've mainly been reactive—like after 9/11, after the 2004 tsunami, after Hurricane Ka-trina.'"

Lansing embarked on the fundraising and discovered just how diffi-cult it could be. "You can go all the way to Texas or New York, and have a wonderful meeting," she said, "and the person will say, 'Great. Here's $5,000'"—a fraction of what she was after. "Time and again, you get used to hearing the word no."

Donations began to trickle in, but they were paltry, and Lansing knew it was vital to secure at least one gargantuan commitment in order to leverage others' support. When their best hope, Chicago Bulls and White Sox owner Jerry Reinsdorf, turned them down, she was crushed. Then, almost in passing, Reinsdorf mentioned someone who might help: Bud Selig.

"You guys have to talk to him," he said. "He's coming to town."

The commissioner of Major League Baseball and his wife were due in Los Angeles that weekend. Calls were hastily placed, schedules scrambled and rearranged, as the women dropped everything to meet him at his hotel.

"We sat down, and Sherry and Laura did the pitch," said Ziffren. "Laura talked about her battles [with cancer]. She talked about the television special. She talked about the science. She talked about the importance of this and why we had to do it now. I held my breath for a full two minutes, and then Sherry put her hand on Bud and said, 'We want MLB [Major League Baseball] to be our first $10 million donor.' None of us could believe she really said that: $10 million."

"I'd never asked anyone for $10 million in my life," Lansing acknowledged. "If I ask for $1,000 and they say yes, I'm thrilled. If someone gives me $25,000, I think I'm going to pass out. But I did it just like I was asking him to pass me the salt. Underneath, I was going, '$10 million! What the hell am I saying?'"

"We were coming from our home in Phoenix to a baseball scouts' dinner that we go to every year," explained Selig. "And we went up to our room, and there were these women. I must tell you, I've had a lot of presentations made to me over the years, but this was as impressive and emotional and sensitive a presentation as I have ever heard. You could tell how strongly Sherry felt about it and how well conceived the whole plan was."

"Well—" he began.

His wife cut in. "She said, 'Come on, Buddy, what are you waiting for?'" recalled Lansing. "And she gave him this nudge on the arm. I call it the nudge that was heard around the world. And he burst out laughing."

"My wife gave me a poke in the ribs," confirmed Selig. "And we said yes."

The meeting had lasted all of fifteen minutes. As the women got up to leave, several started to cry, but Lansing would have none of it. Crying implied doubt; doubt implied the possibility of failure; failure was not an option.

"I said: 'Never cry,'" she recalled. "'Never cry again.'"

At 8:00 p.m. (EST) on September 5, 2008, the first ever *Stand Up to Cancer* special kicked off with a message from Sidney Poitier.

"We used to have such wild dreams, the kind that brought us together, made us a movement," he said, before a virtual galaxy of stars appeared onstage in Los Angeles' Kodak Theatre, where the telethon was taking place. "To those who say, 'Impossible, can't happen, won't happen,' [we say] 'We didn't hear a word.'"

That broadcast led to pledges of $101 million—$23 million of it coming from the telethon alone, the rest raised beforehand—and led the women to make it a regular event, broadcast on each network and many cable channels.

By the end of 2016, they had obtained almost $500 million for multiple dream teams spread across the world. That money paid for everything from 160 separate clinical trials involving 1,100 scientists in 131 institutions to research that changed the life of David Gobin, a retired Baltimore K9 cop with lung cancer.

"If those nine ladies hadn't started Stand Up to Cancer," he said, "I honestly don't know if I'd be here today."

More than anything, the women had proved they could work as one.

"It's like any recipe," said Schwartz. "You take a lot of spices and think, 'Oh, this is going to be really difficult to stomach,' but the spices end up making a broth that's really palatable. All of us, with our different disciplines, helped create a structure that was completely unique. Laura was a phenomenal producer; Katie was a great journalist; Lisa understood the nonprofit world; Ellen had important contacts; Rusty and I had marketing and branding capabilities; Kathleen was excellent at crisis management; and Sherry was Sherry."

ONLY ONE OF Lansing's Stand Up to Cancer friends was not at her side as the organization kept growing: Ziskin, who died in June 2011.

She was sixty-one, six years younger than Lansing. Like the latter, she had started as a reader before becoming a producer and executive; like her friend, she had laid siege to the barricades of a male world and largely succeeded; and also like her, she had experienced her greatest glory in her middle years, when all the struggles she had experienced paled beside the success of the *Spider-Man* franchise. If she had never quite burned with Lansing's incandescence, she, too, had lit a path for women, and without her the path seemed darker.

Once these women had been rivals, fighting for their careers. Then they had become allies, fighting for their cause. Now Ziskin was gone.

On June 28, 2011, Lansing, along with hundreds of others, pulled into the Sony Pictures parking lot to attend Ziskin's memorial service. It was a virtual who's who of Hollywood over the past thirty years, an empire of men and women who had shaped the culture.

As Lansing headed toward the stage where the service was taking place, she took in the studio around her. This was the former headquarters of MGM, the grandest of all the motion picture fiefdoms, home to as many stars as there were in heaven until the lot was sold to Sony in 1989.

It was here that Lansing had first worked with Daniel Melnick, in an office filled with his artwork, piled high with scripts and readers' notes, one of the happiest times of her life. More than three decades had passed since then, and many of the men and women with whom she had toiled shoulder to shoulder were dead, often barely remembered, least of all by the generation that now ruled the kingdom that once was theirs.

Melnick had died two years earlier, after years of drug abuse had exerted their toll and forced him to sell his exquisite home and the paintings he loved so much. At the end, he bore little resemblance to the dynamic executive Lansing had admired.

She thought of him and the other towering figures who had accompanied her on her journey. Hawks, her *Rio Lobo* director, had died in 1977, weeks after her arrival at Columbia, embittered by his inability to make another film, consigned to the shelf of former greats. She had spoken to him one final time, weeks before his death, when she called to say how happy she was in her new post at Columbia. "You'd have been a better actress," he grunted.

James Aubrey, one of her mentors, the man called "the Smiling Cobra" by many but never by Lansing herself, had passed away in 1994 at the age of seventy-five, lamented by few, forgotten by most. And Dawn Steel, pushed out of the safety of the studios and into the murky waters of independent producing, had been dead for fourteen years. She had hardly gotten her second act under way, let alone commenced her third.

These were giants all, their ghosts permeating the offices and stages where Lansing walked now. It saddened her how fast their names had faded, how quickly their achievements had been bleached out by time.

Her father Norton was dead, too, having succumbed to dementia in his later years, even as he and Lansing had become ever closer, his gruffness replaced by a sweetness none would have expected of the man in his prime. He named her his executor, and his death hit her hard.

She thought of him, but above all, she thought of her mother. What would Margot think of her daughter now? Would she be proud of everything Sherry Lee had accomplished? Would she admire the woman she'd become? Would she at last feel free to reveal those secret scrapbooks she had kept through the years, and perhaps enjoy them at her daughter's side? Lansing thought of the terrible irony that her failure to save her mother had led her to help save so many others. She thought of Margot's struggle at the end, and then she thought back to one of her favorite memories: when she sat beside her mother as they watched the Academy Awards, having begged to stay up late for the broadcast.

She remembered the pain and the passion she had felt, the longing and the hurt: how she had ached to be onstage like Susan Hayward, so elegant in her black dress and white gloves, when James Cagney and Kim Novak presented her with an Oscar for *I Want to Live!*, whose title could almost be Lansing's motto.

Did her mother ever imagine her daughter would have such success?

Did she ever think a day would come when Lansing would take her place on that Oscar stage, too?

EIGHT MONTHS BEFORE the *Stand Up* special, Lansing received a call from Sid Ganis, her former Paramount colleague and now the president of the Academy of Motion Picture Arts and Sciences, informing her that the board of governors had named her that year's recipient of the Jean Hersholt Humanitarian Award—an honorary Oscar.

Lansing was overwhelmed, not just by the extraordinary recognition, but by the fact that it came for the work that mattered to her even more than film, in the nonprofit field.

On the evening of February 25, 2007, the police were out in force, as was their wont on the biggest night of the show business year. Hundreds of officers, detectives, and security guards swarmed through the streets of Hollywood, milling among the fire engines, the ambulances and the armada of television news vans that jostled for space at the 79th Academy Awards. As thousands of fans swarmed to get a good view of the stragglers who walked down the red carpet and disappeared inside the Kodak Theatre, those who were seated waited for the show to begin.

A few rows from the front, Lansing sat squeezed beside her husband and sons, trying to calm her nerves. She was not new to this: she had been nominated for *Fatal Attraction* and had attended countless award shows during her time as a studio head. But she felt naked now.

"I was nervous," she said. "I'd been to too many parties, and sat through too many award shows, listening to people snipe about the winners and criticize their speeches. I didn't want to embarrass myself."

Before the ceremony, she had asked for her friend Poitier's advice. "He told me he couldn't sleep for weeks in the lead-up to the Oscars," she recalled. "He said, 'We set such high standards for ourselves. We expect nothing less than perfection.'"

She glanced at the men and women who filled the seats around her, the very locus of everyone who was anyone in Hollywood. There was Leonardo DiCaprio, the actor whose casting she had secretly questioned until she met him, soaking wet and gorgeous, on the set of *Titanic*. There was Tom Hanks, who had made two of her favorite movies, *Forrest Gump* and *Saving Private Ryan*, and who had been stoic in both, even though he had given up half his salary on the former and endured discomfort on the latter. And there was Steven Spielberg, the filmmaker she had come to admire so much as she watched him move effortlessly from *Ryan* to *War of the Worlds*, the picture that had rescued her just when she thought her summer was doomed.

Thanks to a previous rehearsal, she knew exactly when she would go onstage, how much her Oscar weighed (eight and a half pounds), and how long she would speak—two minutes in all out of a five-minute segment. Afterward, she would be led through a warren of backstage rooms, where she would be interrogated by the reporters cloistered there—print journalists in one room, radio in the next, TV in the third—all eager to ask about her storied life. Few knew the mixture of strength and suppleness it had taken to get to the top, the resilience, the adamantine will.

Other women had risen to power in her wake, but none had done so with quite her élan or left anything like her imprint. Even a decade after her departure from Paramount, she remained the gold standard for what an executive should be, an icon in a world with too few.

"She paved the way for the tsunami of women who now fill the executive ranks of our industry," said Meryl Streep. "[She was] the pioneer who made 'female head of studio' no longer an oxymoron, by virtue of her smarts, her determination, her capacity for tough decisions, and not insignificantly, her charm, her calm and her kindness."

"She was tough, but she had a lot of grace in her toughness," said Jane Fonda. "It was a combination you didn't find that often, and for a woman it was a really important thing."

Lansing was the first woman to reign in this man's world and still the one who had done it the best. She had not so much knocked obstacles aside as ignored them altogether, allowing other women to follow in her footsteps while never bothering to look at the footprints she had left behind.

She was a paradox: a feminist icon who was not especially active as a feminist; a revolutionary more at ease with the establishment than with other rebels; a groundbreaker who seemed oblivious to the ground she had broken.

She had remade herself at each stage of her career and even now was in the midst of remaking herself once more, as if only by cracking her old shell could she be free to grow a new one.

She valued the future over the past, action over reflection, optimism over pessimism. She had created a remarkable career, only to abandon it for a quite different one. This evening, for the first time, these two careers were coming together.

After the obligatory opening monologue, the Oscar host, Ellen DeGeneres, guided the audience through a panoply of awards before reaching the middle of the show. Lansing took a deep breath as a smiling Tom Cruise materialized onstage.

He spoke about her distinguished work, and the many lives she had lived, inside and outside the studio. "She is an uncommon individual, a singular woman," he said. "She is the very personification of what this significant award represents."

Then Lansing stepped out, and the audience rose to its feet.

Alone at the podium, she did not address her roots as an actress, nor her résumé as a producer, nor even her twelve years as a studio chairman. As always, she was less focused on the past than the present, more intent on what she was doing now than what she had done before.

"Through my work, I have met research scientists who struggle every day to find cures for diseases," she said. "They do so quietly, without glamour or attention, but always with passion and conviction. I have met schoolteachers who are battling against insurmountable odds, and yet they never stop trying to reach our children. To me, they are the real heroes, and tonight I share this honor with all of them. A special thank-you to the members of the Academy for this extraordinary honor. I promise to spend the rest of my life trying to live up to it."

ACKNOWLEDGMENTS

When I began work on this book in late 2012, my biggest challenge lay in finding out about Margot Heimann's life in Germany. Then I stumbled on John Burland, a former airline executive living in Mainz and the best researcher I've ever met. I'm deeply indebted to him and the half-dozen men and women who spoke to me about their memories of Margot and Mainz: Werner Heimann, Charlotte Hölz, John Keller, Fritz and Lotte Kramer and Elsbeth Lewin.

I'd also like to thank my gracious editor, Amanda Patten, and the team at Crown Archetype, along with my agent, ICM Partners' Jennifer Joel, and her colleague John DeLaney, who worked assiduously to make this book happen.

I have benefited from the counsel of my colleagues at the *Hollywood Reporter*, most notably its chief creative officer, Janice Min, who has taught me more about journalism than she will ever know, along with Matthew Belloni and Kim Masters. I also appreciate the great contribution of photo editor Audrey Landreth Viola.

I wish to thank my friends and family for putting up with (or possibly enjoying) my absences, and in particular my parents, Norman Galloway and Janine Webber, for their love and support.

Many biographers develop mixed feelings about their subjects the more time they spend with them. I had the opposite experience. After countless hours of interviews with Sherry Lansing, I have come to admire her more than I ever thought possible. I owe her my gratitude for taking a risk on this book and sticking with it, even when it caused her pain. Her input has been invaluable, but this is very much my work and I take full responsibility for it.

Hundreds of other people gave many hours of their time. I'd like to thank the following:

J. J. Abrams, Ben Affleck, Kirstie Alley, Anne Archer, Harold Becker, Richard Benjamin, Robert Benton, Jeff Berg, Albert Berger, Rick Berman, Frank Biondi Jr., Lorenzo di Bonaventura, Robert Bookman, Richard Brander, Richard Breitman, Dan Bronson, Jerry Brown, Michael Brownstein, Patricia Burke, J. C. Calciano, James Cameron, Don Carmody, Joe Carnahan, Jimmy Carter, Peter Chernin, Glenn Close, Jay Cocks, Arthur Cohen, Joan Cohen, Rob Cohen, Megan Colligan, Douglas Collins, Ward Connerly, Robert Cort, Katie Couric, David Crane, Peter Cury, Bruce Davey, John Davis, Donald De Line, James Dearden, Peter Desberg, Jonathan Dolgen, Michael Douglas, Donna Dubrow, Barbara Duhl, Frank Duhl, Dale Dye, Michael Eisner, Jack Engelhard, Robert Evans, Sharon Farrell, Tina Fey, Wendy Finerman, Gary Fleder, Jane Fonda, Jodie Foster, Margaret Foti, Marc Freedman, Morgan Freeman, Tom Freston, William Friedkin, Michael Friedman, Robert G. Friedman, Fred Gallo, Sid Ganis, Dee Gardner, Alex Gartner, Judith Gasson, Mel Gibson, Bruce Gilbert, Mark Gill, David Gobin, Gary Goddard, John Goldwyn, Lawrence Gordon, Mark Gordon, Don Granger, Linda Gray, Colin Greene, Paul Greenfield, Winston Groom, Jean Guerin, Marc Gurvitz, Bill Haber, Bruce Halev, Tom Hanks, Roz Heller, Alan J. Hirschfield, Amy Holden Jones, Toni Howard, Jeffrey Jaffe, Jill Jaffe, Leonard Jaffe, Max Jaffe, Stanley Jaffe, Jon Jashni, Mark Johnson, Angelina Jolie, Ashley Judd, Doris Kaiser, Jonathan Kaplan, Pete Keeley, Jordan Kerner, Pat Kingsley, Bob Klein, Steve Kloves, David Koepp, Judith Kovler, Norman Kurland, Alan Ladd Jr., Jon Landau, Dick Lansing, Jack Larson, Martha Lauzen, Lloyd Levin, Gary Levinsohn, Miriam Lewin, Kathleen Lobb, Bryan Lourd, Martha Luttrell, Adrian Lyne, Leonard Maltin, Frank Mancuso, Michelle Manning, Andrea Markin, Frank Marshall, Laurie Marshall, Bill Mechanic, Richard Meier, Susan Merzbach, Nicholas Meyer, Ron Meyer, Lorne Michaels, Chris

Mitchum, Leslie Moonves, Pat Morin, Barry Munitz, Larry Nagler, Marcia Nasatir, Mace Neufeld, Rick Nicita, David Niven Jr., Edward Norton, Phillip Noyce, Lynda Obst, Jennifer O'Neill, Suzanne O'Neill, Dan O'Rourke, Michael Ovitz, Sharon Owsley, Paula Parisi, Alan Parker, Walter Parkes, Amy Pascal, Lisa Paulsen, Alexander Payne, Sung Poblete, Claire Pomeroy, Terry Press, Frank Price, David Puttnam, Jack Rapke, Sumner Redstone, Robert Rehme, Bonnie Reiss, Burt Reynolds, Mark Ridley-Thomas, Dan Rissner, Rusty Robertson, Phil Alden Robinson, Robert Rodat, Wayne Rogers, Karen Rosenfelt, Eric Roth, Max Rothschild, Scott Rudin, George Schlatter, Sue Schwartz, Andrew Sehler, Marsha Sehler, Bud Selig, Judy Blattberg Shapiro, Phillip Sharp, Catherine Short, Ellen Sigal, Casey Silver, Myra Silverman, Stacey Snider, Steven E. de Souza, Steven Spielberg, Dennis Stanfill, Steve Starkey, Gloria Stern, John Stiefel, Jack Stobo, Sharon Stone, Meryl Streep, Michael Tadross, Michael Tolkin, Robert Towne, Sebastian Twardosz, Stephen G. Ujlaki, Giovanni Volpi, Paula Wagner, Ray Wagner, Mark Wahlberg, Randall Wallace, Arlene Washington, Harvey Weinstein, Paula Weinstein, Simon West, Steve Westly, Annabelle Weston, Patrick Whitesell, Pam Williams, Irwin Winkler, John Woo, Markus Würz, Ron Yerxa, Mark Yudof, Steven Zaillian, Robert Zemeckis and Ellen Ziffren.

NOTES

CHAPTER 1

2   **Both were careful not to repeat:** Gary Baum, "Why Century City Ranks Among the Worst Real Estate Deals in Hollywood History," *Hollywood Reporter*, October 4, 2013.

4   **"There've been those that have tested her":** Author interview with Michael Douglas.

4   **"More times than I care to admit":** Robert Evans, email message to author, January 28, 2015.

5   **They included the brassy Dawn Steel:** Wolf Schneider and Pat Troise, "The Hollywood 10 Step," *Movieline*, April 1998, 76–81.

CHAPTER 2

8   **Six decades before Lansing's trip:** Personal recollections of Mainz in 1938 and of the teenage Margot Heimann come from the following schoolmates, neighbors and contemporaries: Werner Heimann, John Keller, Freddy and Lotte Kramer, Charlotte Hölz and Elsbeth Lewin. I am also grateful to Dr. Richard Breitman of American University for helping me retrace Margot's journey to America.

8   **It was in the cinemas:** These were among the films advertised locally in the first week of May. See *Mainzer Anzeiger*, May 3, 1938. For a brief account of Hollywood policy toward the Nazis, see Ben Urwand, "The Chilling History of How Hollywood Helped Hitler," *Hollywood Reporter*, August 9, 2013.

9   **Fritz had never achieved as much:** Max's clothing store, M. Hyman & Sons (the name spelled differently from the family name, Heimann), had a brush with fame during the 1984 presidential race when the Rev. Jesse

Jackson caused an uproar for using the word "Hymie." "There's a place down off Maxwell Street called 'Jewtown,'" he later explained. "Understand? 'Jewtown is where Hymie gets you if you can't negotiate them suits down,' you understand? That's not meant as anti-Semitic. . . . You go down to Jewtown . . . and you start negotiating . . . and if Hyman and Sons show up, they're called Hymie. There's no insult even to them." See Sydney H. Schanberg, "Jackson as Polarizer," *New York Times*, April 10, 1984.

10   **One of Fritz's secrets:** Minna's family believed she died in childbirth, but the date on her tombstone in Mainz's New Jewish Cemetery indicates that she survived nine days beyond that.

10   **On May 17 she boarded the SS *Washington*:** Ancestry.com. New York, Passenger Lists, 1820–1957.

10   **The ship was enormous:** *Shipping Wonders of the World*, Part 22, July 7, 1936, accessed July 5, 2016, *www.shippingwondersoftheworld.com/manhattan.html*.

10   **It had its own orchestra:** Dozens of Holocaust survivors describe the journey in testimonials at the USC Shoah Foundation. Many were so seasick they were unable to leave their cabins.

11   **Weeks earlier, a banner headline:** "Seize 3; Expose U.S. Spy Ring," *Chicago Tribune*, February 27, 1938.

11   **A serial killer had just been caught:** Charles Leavelle, "Brick Slayer Is Likened to Jungle Beast," *Chicago Sunday Tribune*, June 5, 1938.

11   **At nineteen, Margot became engaged:** "The engagement of Miss Margot Heimann to Alan Joseph of Michigan City was announced recently by her parents, Mr. and Mrs. Fritz Heimann of 7609 South Essex Ave.," the *Chicago Tribune* informed readers on February 25, 1940. Lansing only learned of her mother's engagement during the research phase for this book.

12   **But he was an artist by nature:** Information about David Duhl comes from author interviews with Leonard Jaffe, Max Jaffe, Doris Kaiser and Max Rothschild.

18   **"Sherry, this is Mr. Norton Lansing":** Norton's father had changed the family name from Lansky to avoid any association with a slum landlord of that name. Author interview with Richard (Dick) Lansing.

19   **"My father was very narcissistic":** Author interview with Andrea Lansing Markin.

21   **She fell in love with the school:** In 2011 the school named a 250-seat theater in Lansing's honor. She also contributed $5 million toward its fundraising campaign.

21   **In this pre-feminist, "pre-revolution" world:** Author interview with Laurie Marshall.

23   **"He was very, very intelligent":** Author interview with John Stiefel.

23   **"Even then, she was kind of a prize":** Author interview with Michael Brownstein.

CHAPTER 3

26   **Here she was soon to be discovered:** Figures cited are for the City of Los Angeles. The population was 1,970,358 in 1950 and grew to 2,186,061 in 1970, according to the U.S. Census Bureau. "Historical Resident Population City and County of Los Angeles, 1850–2010," Los Angeles Almanac, Historical Resident Population, *www.laalmanac.com/population/po02.htm.*

28   **Lyndon B. Johnson had escalated:** John Whiteclay Chambers II, ed., *The Oxford Companion to American Military History* (New York: Oxford University Press, 1999), 757.

30   **"The city burning is Los Angeles' deepest image of itself":** Joan Didion, *We Tell Ourselves Stories in Order to Live: Collected Nonfiction* (New York: Alfred A. Knopf, 2006), 164.

31   **"I was going to be an intern at Cedars":** Author interview with Michael Brownstein.

32   **"I remember—this isn't nice":** Ibid.

34   **"We were thrown into rejection":** Author interview with Linda Gray.

35   **"She was very intellectual":** Author interview with Richard Brander.

35   **The gentleman was producer Walter Wanger:** In 1951, believing his wife, actress Joan Bennett, was having an affair with agent Jennings Lang, Wanger shot Lang in the thigh and groin. He subsequently pleaded temporary insanity and received a four-month sentence. "Joan Bennett Sees Mate Shoot Agent—'Thought He Was Breaking Up My Home,' Says Wanger—Jennings Lang Hit by Two Bullets; Actress Denies Any Romance," *Los Angeles Times*, December 14, 1951.

36   **With his rough-hewn manner:** Sharon Farrell, *"Hollywood Princess" from Sioux City, Iowa* (Topanga, CA: Sharon Farrell, 2013), 181.

36   **"It was very mysterious":** Author interview with Annabelle Weston.

37   **"Sherry was so outstanding that I just had to go backstage":** James Bacon, *Los Angeles Herald-Examiner*, February 2, 1969.

37   **That in turn heralded an outpouring:** "It's a whole different business now," says William Holden in Wilder's penultimate film, 1978's *Fedora*. "The kids with beards have taken over."

38   **Their works were not the distant gunfire:** Garth Jowett, *Film: The Democratic Art* (Boston: Little, Brown, 1976), 482.

38   **The two top box office hits of 1966:** *The Bible* earned $34.9 million, according to TheNumbers.com. *Hawaii* made $34.6 million. Both figures are North American (domestic) box office.

38   **"What paid studio bills in the mid-1960s":** Mark Harris, *Pictures at a Revolution: Five Movies and the Birth of the New Hollywood* (New York: Penguin, 2008), 3.

39 **"Each week we'd throw a cocktail party":** Author interview with George Schlatter.

39 **"It took us almost three weeks to shoot that":** Author interview with Dee Gardner.

40 **"She was very good":** Author interview with Ray Wagner.

40 **Lansing was thrilled when the *Hollywood Reporter* described her:** John Mahoney, "Columbia's 'Loving' Strong B.O. Attraction; 'Brilliant,'" *Hollywood Reporter*, February 19, 1970.

40 ***Variety* praised her:** A. D. Murphy ("Murf"), "'Loving,'" *Variety*, February 18, 1970.

41 **"It was a very tearful parting":** Author interview with Michael Brownstein.

42 **Halfway through Michael's tour of duty:** Ibid.

42 **"We're getting a divorce by attrition":** Ibid.

CHAPTER 4

44 **"Many people are conveniently called enigmas":** Todd McCarthy, *Howard Hawks: The Grey Fox of Hollywood* (New York: Grove Press, 1997), 4.

45 **He had never liked his women:** Ibid., 643.

46 **Polly Platt, a production designer:** Rachel Abramowitz, *Is That a Gun in Your Pocket? Women's Experience of Power in Hollywood* (New York: Random House, 2000), 21.

46 **"She was absolutely terrified":** Author interview with Chris Mitchum.

47 **She did not know that the sixty-three-year-old actor:** Scott Eyman, *John Wayne: The Life and Legend* (New York: Simon & Schuster, 2014), 427–28.

48 **Early in the shoot, Wayne left:** McCarthy, *Howard Hawks*, 636.

48 **When the studio dragged its feet:** Mitchum had no recollection of that, but Hawks confirmed the story. "The stand-off was resolved only when Hawks fulfilled his threat to shut down production in Mexico, which he did for two days, until Mitchum arrived," writes Todd McCarthy. "'I just asked if they wanted to go on their record or mine,' Hawks said. 'Chris was on the next plane.'" Ibid, 632.

48 **O'Neill recalled meeting him:** Author interview with Jennifer O'Neill.

50 **When *Rio Lobo* opened in December 1970:** Kevin Thomas, "Wayne in Hawks' 'Rio Lobo,'" *Los Angeles Times*, December 30, 1970.

50 **"However charitable one might care to be":** McCarthy, *Howard Hawks*, 640.

51 **"Her heart wasn't in it":** Author interview with Burt Reynolds.

CHAPTER 5

54 **"I said, 'Why don't you come and be a reader?'":** Author interview with Ray Wagner.

54   "She kept a little wire-bound book": Ibid.

55   "It was one of the most interesting ways to begin a career": Author interview with Jeff Berg.

56   Wagner watched with delight: Author interview with Ray Wagner.

57   Even his office was filled with artwork: Author interview with Robert Cort.

57   "A lot of studio executives ride the fence": Douglas Martin, "Daniel Melnick, Hollywood Producer, Dies at 77," *New York Times*, October 16, 2009.

58   Average weekly attendance had tumbled: Garth Jowett, *Film: The Democratic Art* (Boston: Little, Brown, 1976), 475.

59   The corporate owners brought in "a new age of greed": Author interview with Leonard Maltin.

60   "She walked in wearing a green miniskirt": Author interview with Susan Merzbach.

63   "[One of the men] said": Haber believed it was a lunch, not a dinner, and that he and Rosenfeld flew the two women to Catalina Island. Author interview with Bill Haber.

64   These were Lansing's happiest years: Author interview with Susan Merzbach.

65   "He was at his best when he was angry": Dave Itzkoff, *Mad as Hell: The Making of 'Network' and the Fateful Vision of the Angriest Man in Movies* (New York: Times Books, 2014), 1.

65   Lansing read the 160-page black comedy: MGM script synopsis dated July 21, 1975, provided by Merzbach.

65   "It was one of the most astonishing things I'd ever read": Author interview with Susan Merzbach.

66   "Sherry Lansing was a most attractive girl": Don Siegel, *A Siegel Film: An Autobiography* (London: Faber and Faber, 1996), 420.

CHAPTER 6

69   "There was no feminism in Hollywood": Author interview with Paula Weinstein.

70   De Havilland took Warners to court: Until de Havilland successfully sued, studios made it a practice of adding all the days an actor had not worked to the end of his or her contract, including weekends and vacations. This allowed them to extend contracts ad infinitum. In 1943, de Havilland sued and a California court found in her favor, ruling that a seven-year contract could last no more than seven years from the date when services began. California Labor Code Section 2855 is known informally as the de Havilland Law.

70   "Sexism doesn't have to be about making a pass": Author interview with Marcia Nasatir.

71   **It would earn a spectacular $300 million:** *Star Wars* made $307.3 million following its initial May 25, 1977, release in North America, while *Close Encounters of the Third Kind* made $116.4 million following its November 16, 1977, release in North America and a total of $303.8 million worldwide; boxofficemojo.com.

72   **A drama starring Jane Fonda:** For a definitive account of the making of *The China Syndrome*, see Aaron Latham, "Hollywood vs. Harrisburg: The Story Behind the Race to Finish *The China Syndrome* Before the Inevitable Real-Life Accident," *Esquire*, May 22, 1979, 77–86.

73   **"We didn't know anything about a woman named Sherry":** Author interview with Michael Douglas.

73   **"I was the young punk with one credit":** Author interview with Bruce Gilbert.

74   **Douglas found an ally in her:** Budget and salaries come from the Columbia Pictures archive, Picture Budget Recap, January 13, 1978. The movie's budget later rose to $6.1 million. See Robert Gutwillig, "The Worst Thing You Can Do in Hollywood Is Harm a Star," *Look*, April 30, 1979, 43.

75   **Among the alternative titles were:** These titles are included in a one-page document preserved by Merzbach. Other suggestions: *This Is Kimberly Wells Live, Film at 11, The Silent Syndrome, Contract: Earth, Broken Trust, Killer Watt, The System Works, The Sanest Man* and *Responsibility*.

75   **At various times on location:** Patricia Bosworth, *Jane Fonda: The Private Life of a Public Woman* (Boston: Houghton Mifflin Harcourt, 2011), 435.

76   **"I was wearing very elevated espadrilles":** Author interview with Jane Fonda.

76   **"He was an enormous protector of hers":** Author interview with Robert Cort.

76   **Known as "the Smiling Cobra":** "The face Aubrey presented to the world was that of the controlled tactician, the master of cool," writes Peter Bart in *Fade Out: The Calamitous Final Days of MGM* (New York: William Morrow, 1990), 33–34. "The after-hours Aubrey was a whole different animal—hard-drinking and feral . . . the fabled 'Jungle Jim.'"

78   **"We were really scared":** Author interview with Martha Luttrell.

80   **"The film falsely suggests":** George F. Will, "A Film About Greed," *Newsweek*, April 2, 1979.

80   **On the morning of March 28, a valve malfunctioned:** Among other accounts of the incident, see "Backgrounder on the Three Mile Island Accident," United States Nuclear Regulatory Commission, *www.nrc.gov/reading-rm/doc-collections/fact-sheets/3mile-isle.html*, accessed July 1, 2016.

81   **Fonda was shooting *The Electric Horseman*:** Author interview with Jane Fonda.

81 **"The world has never known a day quite like today":** "Meltdown at Three Mile Island," *American Experience*, first broadcast on PBS February 22, 1979.

81 **"No interviews—this whole thing is too serious":** Excerpt from Bridges's diary, March 28, 1979.

82 **The film did well:** Boxofficemojo.com.

83 **"Truffaut and I were friends":** Author interview with Robert Benton.

84 **Some studio executives felt Streep:** Details of the salaries and budget come from the Columbia Pictures archive: Analysis Detail Listing for *Kramer vs. Kramer*, October 18, 1980; Studio Daily Progress Report, December 12, 1978.

84 **"I was a young actress, for the most part unknown":** Meryl Streep, email message to author, June 23, 2014.

84 **"He felt we were rushing":** Author interview with Stanley Jaffe.

85 **The film opened on December 19, 1979:** Boxofficemojo.com.

86 **"It was obviously a tremendous trauma for everyone":** Author interview with Alan J. Hirschfield.

86 **It would not be long before the full extent of his misdeeds:** See David McClintick, *Indecent Exposure: A True Story of Hollywood and Wall Street* (New York: William Morrow, 1982).

86 **After wooing but failing to hire:** Aljean Harmetz, "Melnick Named President of Columbia Pictures," *New York Times*, June 2, 1978.

87 **"I knew he was doing drugs, but barely":** Author interview with Alan J. Hirschfield.

88 **"In the field I operated in":** Author interview with Frank Price.

88 **Price longed for the glamour of film:** Aljean Harmetz, "Frank Price Named to Head MCA's Universal Film Studio," *New York Times*, November 12, 1983.

88 **"It was generally known that there was chaos at Columbia":** Author interview with Frank Price.

89 **But when Price took up his post:** Ibid.

89 **"It was very hard work getting Danny":** Author interview with Alan J. Hirschfield.

89 **"When I make a mistake, it's a beaut":** Aljean Harmetz, "What Price Glory at Columbia?" *New York Times*, October 5, 1980.

90 **With Price promoted to president:** "Frank Price Seen Assuming Vacant Col Presidency," *Hollywood Reporter*, March 5, 1979.

90 **Only eight months earlier, she had told *Life*:** Jim Watters, "The New Hollywood Hotshots," *Life*, April 1979.

91 **"John was a difficult character":** Author interview with Frank Price.

92 **"Dennis and I just didn't agree on anything":** Author interview with Alan Ladd Jr.

93   **News reports at the time claimed:** "Now This Is What We Call Star Wars," *Los Angeles Magazine*, September 1979.

93   **"I had a couple of very good friends":** Author interview with Alan J. Hirschfield.

93   **He could not help thinking of Melnick's demands:** Ibid.

94   **"It was the first time a woman [would be] in a top role":** Author interview with Dennis Stanfill.

94   **"She was really worried about losing control":** Author interview with Martha Luttrell.

95   **"When Sherry makes a decision":** Ibid.

96   **On January 2, 1980, the front page of the *New York Times*:** Aljean Harmetz, "Sherry Lansing, Former Model, Named Head of Fox Productions," *New York Times*, January 2, 1980.

96   **"There were magazine profiles and news analyses":** Budd Schulberg, "What Makes Hollywood Run?" *New York Times Magazine*, April 27, 1980.

96   *Us* **used her name as an answer:** *Us*, March 4, 1980.

97   **The *Los Angeles Times* headlined its story:** Charles Schreger, "A Movie Mogul Eats Her Words," *Los Angeles Times*, January 4, 1980.

CHAPTER 7

99   **"Those were hard days for a woman to come in":** Author interview with Alan J. Hirschfield.

99   **Fox had deep pockets:** *Newsweek*, January 14, 1980, 69.

100   **It was a mistake that one of Lansing's colleagues:** Author interview with Robert Cort.

100   **and one that became even costlier:** James Rainey, "Disney's 'Star Wars' Merchandise Gives the Force to Younger Generation," *Variety*, December 1, 2015.

100   **"When big corporations saw the kind of money":** Author interview with Amy Pascal.

100   **"We were starting from zero":** Author interview with Alan J. Hirschfield.

102   **"the ultimate WASP":** Author interview with Robert Cort.

106   **A second meeting did not go so well:** Excerpt from Bridges's diary, February 22, 1981.

106   **The filmmaker was especially taken aback:** Author interview with Jack Larson.

107   **"I ask him how much [shit] will he eat?":** Excerpt from Bridges's diary, August 26, 1981.

107   **"Robert Redford has been booted out of *The Verdict*":** Marilyn Beck, "Without Redford, Verdict's Out," *Palm Beach Post*, September 3, 1981.

108   **She considered asking Fonda to star:** Lumet alludes to the problems with Redford, but doesn't name him, in *Making Movies* (New York: Alfred A.

Knopf, 1995), 39: "They did five additional rewrites [with a third writer]. By now there was a million dollars in script charges on the picture. The scripts kept getting worse.... The star kept eliminating the unpleasant side of the character, trying to make him more lovable so that the audience would 'identify' with him." "I just found the character unrelatable to me at that time," Redford told his biographer. Michael Feeney Callan, *Robert Redford: The Biography* (New York: Alfred A. Knopf, 2011), 362.

108   **"a man of appetites":** Author interview with Susan Merzbach.

109   **"There were a few 'conditions precedent'":** Author interview with David Puttnam.

111   *National Lampoon's Animal House:* Boxofficemojo.com.

111   **Reluctantly, Levy agreed to give the picture a trial run:** Author interview with Don Carmody.

111   **The picture opened across the nation:** Boxofficemojo.com.

112   **"I was in Norman's office":** "Norman didn't believe that from me," said Hirschfield. "I knew Sherry would never stand for that, and Norman would have been the wrong person for the job." Author interview with Alan J. Hirschfield.

113   **"It was a sea of dysfunction":** Author interview with John Davis.

113   **But Davis was nothing if not shrewd:** Alex Ben Block, *Outfoxed: Marvin Davis, Barry Diller, Rupert Murdoch and the Inside Story of America's Fourth Television Network* (New York: St. Martin's Press, 1990), 25.

114   **A six-foot-four, three-hundred-pound Denver oilman:** Harry Anderson et al., "From Oil to Films: A Giant Step," *Los Angeles Times,* August 2, 1981.

115   **"A guy was suing Marvin":** Author interview with Wayne Rogers.

117   **When a publicity release of July 1982 announced:** Aljean Harmetz, "Melnick Is Leaving Fox Before End of Contract," *New York Times,* July 29, 1982.

117   **"The day before he died":** Aljean Harmetz, "How a Hollywood Rumor Was Born," *New York Times,* December 12, 1982.

117   **"We thought he had it all":** Ibid.

118   **"An inquiry by the Los Angeles District Attorney":** Jeff Gerth, "Studio Investigation Centers on Contract of Producer at Fox," *New York Times,* October 11, 1982.

118   **Even the usually circumspect trade press:** "Melnick Denies Fund Misuse, Connection to Lawyer's Death," *Hollywood Reporter,* September 29, 1982.

118   **When the *Hollywood Reporter* printed Melnick's denials:** Harmetz, "How a Hollywood Rumor Was Born."

118   **"The uglier the rumor":** Ibid.

118   **"Watch for this story":** Ibid.

118   **"It was so fantastic":** Ibid.

119   "We have found no evidence": Ibid.

120   "[It is] one of the most arid": For Ebert's review, see *www.rogerebert.com/reviews/the-king-of-comedy-1983*.

120   The country was going through: Richard X. Auxier, "Reagan's Recession," Pew Research Center, December 14, 2010.

121   The director was appalled: Peter Biskind, *Easy Riders, Raging Bulls: How the Sex-Drugs-and-Rock-'n'-Roll Generation Saved Hollywood* (New York, Simon & Schuster, 1998), 406.

121   "Ultimately, what did it mean?": Author interview with Susan Merzbach.

121   "We hadn't been really successful": Author interview with Alan J. Hirschfield.

121   "My dad loved Sherry": Author interview with John Davis.

122   "Sherry never really felt he needed her": Author interview with confidential source.

122   "I said, 'If we're partners, we're partners'": Author interview with Stanley Jaffe.

CHAPTER 8

124   "Stanley was very direct": Author interview with Karen Rosenfelt.

125   "Paramount has figured out, better than any other studio": Tony Schwartz, "Hollywood's Hottest Stars," *New York Magazine*, July 30, 1984, 24.

126   On January 4, 1983, the industry's trade publications: Stephen J. Sansweet, "Sherry Lansing Joins 'Kramer' Producer to Start Film Firm with Paramount Link," *Wall Street Journal*, January 4, 1983.

127   "I believed in them and believed they would do great": Author interview with Michael Eisner.

128   "Things got very strained": Author interview with Richard Benjamin.

130   "I remember going to a preview": Author interview with Stanley Jaffe.

131   The movie tanked: Boxofficemojo.com.

131   Even though Eisner maintained: Author interview with Michael Eisner.

131   "Paramount didn't hire us": Author interview with Stanley Jaffe.

132   To Jaffe, that was more than manageable: Ibid.

132   In February 1983, on his way home from a trip: William G. Blair, "Charles G. Bluhdorn, the Head of Gulf and Western, Dies at 56," *New York Times*, February 20, 1983.

132   Bluhdorn's deputy, Martin Davis: Bryan Burrough, "The Siege of Paramount," *Vanity Fair*, November 6, 2007.

132   Once, when Katzenberg dropped by: James B. Stewart, *Disney War* (New York: Simon & Schuster, 2005), 38.

133 **"Marty Davis was elected year-in":** Author interview with Michael Eisner.

133 **Over at Fox, Marvin Davis:** Thomas M. Pryor, "Stanfill's 'High Noon' at Fox," *Variety*, July 1, 1981.

133 **"Barry had his opportunity at Fox":** Author interview with Michael Eisner.

133 **No matter how much Frank Mancuso:** Author interview with Frank Mancuso.

138 **"She was emotional, emotional, emotional":** Author interview with Martha Luttrell.

139 **"Yes," said Gasson:** Author interview with Judith Gasson.

140 **"My goal as an agent":** Author interview with Michael Ovitz.

141 **"You have to realize":** Ibid.

142 **"I think I'm going to cut my throat":** Author interview with Stanley Jaffe.

CHAPTER 9

143 *Fatal Attraction* **was based on a short film:** Author interview with Stanley Jaffe.

144 **"I'm not going to say [the story] was autobiographical":** Author interview with James Dearden.

144 **The short came only a few years:** Joyce Wadler, "Harris Found Guilty of Murder," *Washington Post*, February 25, 1981.

145 **She resumed work with Dearden in Los Angeles:** Author interview with James Dearden.

146 **Later the name Sean was changed to Alex:** Ibid.

146 **"It was the perfect what-if":** Author interview with Michael Douglas.

148 **"We even had a Halloween scene":** Author interview with James Dearden.

149 **"I went and woke my wife up":** Author interview with Adrian Lyne.

149 **"This could be the shortest meeting":** Author interview with Stanley Jaffe.

150 **"There was a debate about her sexiness":** Author interview with Michael Douglas.

151 **"My hair was long and I didn't know what to do with it":** Author interview with Glenn Close.

151 **"She just knocked it out of the park":** Author interview with Michael Douglas.

151 **In fall 1986, shooting got under way:** Paramount Pictures Budget Summary, September 24, 1986. The document notes: "This budget figure does not include allocation of $1.6 million for Jaffe-Lansing term-deal overhead which will be added to the negative cost of the picture upon completion."

151 **"Stanley's got a good shit detector":** Author interview with Michael Douglas.

151 **"We tried to take its innards out to make it real":** Author interview with Adrian Lyne.

151 **Lyne urged Douglas to make his character believably flawed:** Author interview with Michael Douglas.

152 **"There's a scene where they're arguing":** Author interview with Adrian Lyne.

153 **"We were on hour thirteen":** Author interview with Stanley Jaffe.

154 **"I thought, in the words of *The Mikado*":** Author interview with Nicholas Meyer.

154 **Finally he'd agreed to work on the movie:** Ibid.

155 **"I burst into tears":** Author interview with Anne Archer.

155 **"I had to pretend it was a great idea":** Author interview with James Dearden.

156 **"I had a big talk to her about the theater":** Author interview with Michael Douglas.

156 **Close rejected that out of hand:** Author interview with Glenn Close.

156 ***Fatal Attraction* opened on September 18, 1987:** Boxofficemojo.com.

156 ***Time* put Douglas and Close on its cover:** "The Thriller Is Back," *Time*, November 16, 1987.

157 **"It's about men seeing feminists as witches":** Pauline Kael, "The Current Cinema: The Feminine Mystique," *New Yorker*, October 19, 1987, 106–11.

CHAPTER 10

158 ***Reckless Endangerment*—which later became *The Accused*—:** Initial reports indicated that the bar's patrons had cheered on the rape. Later reports undermined that assertion. See Jonathan Friendly, "The New Bedford Rape Case: Confusion over Accounts of Cheering at Bar," *New York Times*, April 11, 1984.

160 **"I read these drafts and said":** Author interview with Jonathan Kaplan.

161 **Lansing had a somewhat different recollection:** Topor did not respond to requests for comment.

161 **Steel was willing to green-light the picture:** Paramount Pictures Budget Summary, April 23, 1987, notes a budget of $8.4 million, plus $1.6 million in overhead.

161 **"Dawn didn't have quite enough power":** Author interview with Jonathan Kaplan.

162 **"They thought I was still this child":** Author interview with Jodie Foster.

162 **"Our biggest problem was the boys' club":** Author interview with Jonathan Kaplan.

163 **"I was scared to prepare":** Author interview with Jodie Foster.

163 **"[Marketing executive] Sid Ganis comes up":** Author interview with Jonathan Kaplan.

164 **"Out of twenty women in the focus group":** Ibid.

165 **"I felt terrible about it," she said:** Author interview with Jodie Foster.

165 **The actress' life had been thrown into upheaval:** Howell Raines, "Reagan Wounded in Chest by Gunman; Outlook 'Good' After 2-Hour Surgery; Aide and 2 Guards Shot; Suspect Held," *New York Times*, March 31, 1981.

165 **"It was a serious concern," said Kaplan:** Author interview with Jonathan Kaplan.

166 **In a November 1988 *People* magazine cover story:** Kelly McGillis, "Memoir of a Brief Time in Hell," *People*, November 14, 1988.

167 **The revelation of McGillis's ordeal:** Boxofficemojo.com.

167 **In February 1989, Foster was nominated:** Author interview with Jodie Foster.

167 **"There are very few things":** Academy Awards Acceptance Speech Database, *http://aaspeechesdb.oscars.org/link/061-3*.

168 **"When we got to Japan":** Author interview with Michael Douglas.

168 **"We were hysterical," said Jaffe:** Author interview with Stanley Jaffe.

169 **"Sherry and Stanley had this amazing partnership":** Author interview with Jonathan Kaplan.

169 **"I was in New York in March 1991":** Michael Cieply, "Stanley Jaffe Named Paramount President: The Veteran Producer May Help Boost the Firm's Sagging Film Operation," *Los Angeles Times*, March 19, 1991.

169 **"The day I told her was one of the hardest":** Author interview with Stanley Jaffe.

172 **"Unlike the novel":** The changes rankled Engelhard, who saw his work as an exploration of cultural differences. "The husband's a Jewish speechwriter and the wife is a Grace Kelly type," he said. "So the novel, obviously, has many layers, political, religious, cultural, that Hollywood won't touch." Author interview with Engelhard.

172 **"It didn't read as well as *Fatal*":** Author interview with Adrian Lyne.

172 **Lyne wanted to make some script changes:** Holden Jones was incensed to learn that Goldman's name was on the shooting script and not hers. "I'd spent two and a half years on it, but it looked fancier with his name," she said. The Writers Guild eventually awarded her sole credit. Holden Jones also resented changes to her script. Lyne, she said, was "under the thumb of Redford. The first two acts were almost the same, but from the point where the couple splits up, Adrian made it more sympathetic to the rich man. In my version, [Demi Moore] leaves Redford. He doesn't heroically give her up." Author interview with Holden Jones.

172 **"I remember meeting him in a large":** Author interview with Adrian Lyne.

173 **"Tom, Adrian, Sherry and I sat with Goldman":** Author interview with Alex Gartner.

173 **His arguments with Lansing became so passionate:** Lansing's relationship with Lyne alternated between affection and frustration. At one point during the shoot, she recalled: "I said, 'You're impossible!' and something came out of my mouth. And he said, 'Did you just spit at me?' I looked at him, shocked, and said, 'Did I? This is crazy!'"

174 **"Redford received $5 million":** Author interview with confidential source.

174 **"Adrian is a great admirer of beautiful actresses":** Author interview with Alex Gartner.

174 **Three weeks before *Indecent* was due:** In a suit filed April 28, 1992, the film's backers, MGM and Pathé, alleged that "sudden success has caused Harrelson to attempt to take advantage of his new popularity by disregarding his existing obligations [to MGM] in favor of improperly taking on another motion picture project he now considers more favorable." The suit was amended June 4 to add conspiracy charges against Paramount, Lansing and Lyne.

175 **"I said, 'Fine, we'll let you leave":** Author interview with Alan Ladd Jr.

175 **"It was a huge moment":** Author interview with Bryan Lourd.

177 **To everyone's surprise, Redford:** Author interview with Michael Tadross.

178 **"We would test it on the Paramount lot":** Author interview with Alex Gartner.

178 **While they were editing:** Elizabeth Kaye, "The Sexes: This Proposal Is for Status Quo," *New York Times*, April 18, 1993.

178 **"The most astonishing aspect of this picture":** Ibid.

179 **When *Indecent* debuted in April 1993:** Boxofficemojo.com.

179 **"[That] was a whole reconnect for him":** Author interview with Bryan Lourd.

CHAPTER 11

180 **"Studio executives, at that particular time":** Author interview with Wayne Rogers.

181 **It was a small affair by Hollywood standards:** Luttrell believed she and Lansing were two of the party's organizers. Lansing remembered it differently.

182 **He had once raced a car through the streets:** William Friedkin, *The Friedkin Connection* (New York: HarperCollins, 2013), 179.

182 **On another occasion, after winning:** Ibid., 207.

182 **He had worked with many of the same people:** Author interview with William Friedkin.

182   **"We drove to the Rockridge market":** Ibid.

183   **Many were skeptical, said John Goldwyn:** Author interview with John Goldwyn.

186   **Jaffe had been at Paramount Communications:** Alan Citron and Nina Easton, "Tartikoff Takes On a Challenge at Paramount," *Los Angeles Times,* May 2, 1991.

186   **"He would have these crazy ideas":** Author interview with Michelle Manning.

187   **More than anything, his work was hindered:** Bill Carter, "Tartikoff Is Injured in Car Crash," *New York Times,* January 3, 1991.

187   **"I remember coming to his office one day":** Author interview with Stanley Jaffe.

187   **"Brandon said, 'Oh, we just need some clips'":** Author interview with Michelle Manning.

187   **Jaffe and his boss, Martin Davis, conferred:** Author interview with Stanley Jaffe.

188   **"I remember the two of us meeting with [Jaffe]":** Author interview with William Friedkin.

188   **Jaffe said yes to both demands:** Johnnie L. Roberts, "Paramount Names Sherry Lansing Chairman of Motion Picture Operations," *Wall Street Journal,* November 5, 1992.

CHAPTER 12

189   **Women were still nowhere near equal:** Jaclyn Fierman, "Why Women Still Don't Hit the Top," *Fortune,* June 30, 1990.

189   **In the entertainment industry, several women:** "The Employment of Executive Women in Film and Television: 1991," cited by Claudia Puig, "Hollywood's 'Glass Ceiling' Cracking?" *Los Angeles Times,* August 13, 1991.

190   **Indications that a tectonic shift was under way:** Martha Lauzen, executive director of San Diego State University's Center for the Study of Women in Television and Film, questioned this. "The mention of a few high-profile women in positions of power can skew and distort our perceptions of reality," she said. "The blatant sexism of the fifties, sixties and seventies was giving way to the subtler sexism of the eighties, nineties and [later]. The attitudes about what women could and could not achieve were still present; they just went underground." Author interview with Lauzen.

190   **"It didn't feel that things were utterly impossible":** Author interview with Stacey Snider.

190   **The promise that rippled through Hollywood:** Stacy L. Smith, Marc Choueiti, Elizabeth Scofield and Katherine Pieper, "Gender Inequality in 500 Popular Films: Examining On-Screen Portrayals and Behind-the-

Scenes Employment Patterns in Motion Pictures Released Between 2007–2012," Annenberg School for Communication and Journalism, University of Southern California, 2013.

191 **"It wasn't that Brandon had left bad stuff":** About a week into the job, said Lansing, "I called up Stanley and I said, 'Stanley? You forgot to tell me something.' He said, 'What?' I said, 'You got titles—you ain't got scripts!' He said, 'You didn't want me to tell you everything.'" Robert W. Welkos, "Every Day Was High Noon," *Los Angeles Times*, August 22, 1993.

192 **She was the only one who did not know Lansing:** Author interview with Michelle Manning.

192 **It was crucial to get at least one franchise film:** Tartikoff wanted the sequel, but hit a stumbling block, Goldwyn recalled. "Lorne Michaels said, 'Brandon, this is how you do your job. Give Mike and Dana [Carvey] a check for $1 million each and then say to Mike, "I want the next one in nine months."'" Tartikoff did just that while on a plane with Myers. "[He said] 'What would you like to do next, Mike?' Mike said, 'I would like to do my version of Fellini's *Satyricon*.' They got off the plane and there was no *Wayne's World 2*." Author interview with John Goldwyn.

192 **Mike Myers's debut feature, *Wayne's World*:** Boxofficemojo.com.

192 **On-screen, Myers was an endearing personality:** Kim Masters, "Ganging Up on Mike," *Vanity Fair*, October 2000.

193 **"Mike had always wanted to do *Passport to Pimlico*":** Author interview with Lorne Michaels.

193 **"Going into that meeting was like the Bataan Death March":** Author interview with confidential source.

193 **"Mike came in wearing a T-shirt":** Author interview with confidential source.

194 **"She made up this fabulous story":** Author interview with John Goldwyn.

194 **Lansing turned to Myers:** Author interview with confidential source.

194 **It did well enough to cover its cost:** The film made $48.2 million in North America; Boxofficemojo.com.

194 **"The first in the series":** Boxofficemojo.com.

194 **Jaffe had refused to give the series' original producers:** When Frank Mancuso suggested they return $9 million of their salary for *Days of Thunder* in order to make up for its disappointing performance, "we told them to get fucked," said Simpson. "We said, 'We made you $1.6 billion. You people are cheap.'" Rod Lurie, "Are They Killing Paramount?" *Los Angeles Magazine*, July 1993.

194 **"At the eleventh hour, a memo comes in":** Author interview with Steven E. de Souza.

195 **"Sherry's the greatest diplomat in the world":** Author interview with Robert Rehme.

195   **"It wasn't particularly the kind of script I liked"**: Author interview with Mace Neufeld.

195   **The movie resumed several weeks later:** *"Cop 3* was a very strange experience," director John Landis told the website Collider in September 2005. "The script wasn't any good, but I figured, 'So what? I'll make it funny with Eddie.' [But] when I started giving Eddie some shtick, he said, 'You know, John . . . Axel Foley is an adult now. He's not a wiseass anymore.' . . . I had this strange experience where he was very professional, but he just wasn't funny." Steve "Frosty" Weintraub, "The Collider Interview: John Landis, Part II," Collider.com, September 2, 2005.

196   **"A third stumbling feature"**: For Evans's account see Robert Evans, *The Kid Stays in the Picture* (Beverly Hills: New Millennium Press, 2002), 408–16.

197   **"Bob would say things like"**: Author interview with Sharon Stone.

197   **Three weeks into Lansing's tenure:** Author interview with Phillip Noyce.

197   **The director was in Los Angeles:** Patricia Apodaca, "Cameraman Stars in Volcano Ordeal," *Los Angeles Times,* November 25, 1992.

198   **Lansing waited on tenterhooks:** Author interview with Sharon Stone.

198   **Noyce, who had been battling:** Ingo Petzke, *Phillip Noyce: Backroads to Hollywood* (Sydney: Pan Macmillan Australia, 2004), 229.

198   **"Bob at one point asked for an editing room"**: Author interview with Stanley Jaffe.

198   **Meanwhile, the production was thrown into turmoil:** Stone also had issues with Eszterhas. When he and Noyce went to persuade her to make the film, "Joe agreed to be massaged by Sharon," said Noyce. "He got down on the floor and Sharon was sitting astride him. He was moaning. There was nothing sexual about what they were doing. It was all about control. When he allowed himself to be subservient to her power, that's when she agreed to play the role." Author interview with Phillip Noyce.

198   **"My engagement with Bill MacDonald"**: Author interview with Sharon Stone.

199   **"Fuck 'em!" he said:** Lurie, "Are They Killing Paramount?"

200   **The filmmakers moved forward with the changes:** Author interview with Phillip Noyce.

200   **"a prolonged recession"**: "Labor Force Realignment and Jobless Recoveries," FiveThirtyEight.com, July 25, 2010.

200   **"The studio bought new $100,000 Mercedes-Benz"**: Bernard Weinraub, "The Talk of Hollywood: Good Job! Here's Your Mercedes!" *New York Times,* July 12, 1993.

201   **"merge with Viacom"**: Burrough, "The Siege of Paramount."

202   **"All the way back, when Sumner just had a few drive-ins"**: Author interview with Frank Biondi Jr.

202 **"We were coming back from [the NBC talks]":** Ibid.

202 **The two parties entered into secret talks:** Geraldine Fabrikant, "Viacom to Announce Deal to Acquire Paramount," *New York Times*, September 12, 1993.

202 **It was "an act of destiny":** Jonathan Weber, "Viacom, Paramount See Smooth Merger: Chiefs Say They Expect No Competing Bid to Be Made for the Latter," *Los Angeles Times*, September 14, 1993.

203 **Davis, sniffing the danger "Killer Diller" posed:** Burrough, "The Siege of Paramount."

203 **A week after Viacom went public:** Kathryn Harris and John Lippman, "Diller Seeks to Outbid Viacom for Paramount," *Los Angeles Times*, September 21, 1993.

204 **"You'd be on the phone with an agent":** Author interview with Michelle Manning.

204 **"Sumner said, basically, 'I'm doing it'":** Author interview with Frank Biondi Jr.

204 **"Our current position demands brevity":** Ian Johnson, "Viacom Captures Paramount," *Baltimore Sun*, February 16, 1994.

205 **"She was very vulnerable":** Author interview with John Goldwyn.

205 **Martin Davis was edged aside:** Jaffe subsequently sued for $20 million, but lost. See Geraldine Fabrikant, "Ex-President of Paramount Sues over Stock Options," *New York Times*, April 15, 1994.

205 **"There was a house-of-cards theory":** Author interview with Karen Rosenfelt.

205 **"He said, 'I'm going to prove that synergy works'":** Author interview with John Goldwyn.

CHAPTER 13

209 **"The book had its charms":** Author interview with Eric Roth.

209 *Forrest* **had been developed by Warners:** Kristen O'Neill, "Gumption," *Premiere*, April 1995, 102.

209 **One of Lansing's top priorities:** Other actors including Robin Williams, Michael Keaton and Bill Murray had all passed. Author interview with Wendy Finerman.

210 **"The script went around to any number of directors":** Author interview with Tom Hanks.

210 **"I remember reading the script on an airplane":** Author interview with Robert Zemeckis.

211 **It was still unclear whether Sonnenfeld:** Finerman was having dinner with Zemeckis when she heard Marshall was back in. "Ovitz calls and says, 'Penny is having second thoughts,'" she recalled. "I said, 'Oh my God! You can't do this! This is my project. This is my future.'" After

"a bit of a struggle, Penny went away." Author interview with Wendy Finerman.

211   **"I had just done [1993's] *Philadelphia*":** Author interview with Tom Hanks.

212   **Goldwyn had given her a warning:** Author interview with John Goldwyn.

213   **"It was a pretty nice day":** Author interview with Jack Rapke.

214   **"We were forty-eight hours from turning on the camera":** Author interview with Robert Zemeckis.

214   **"I said, 'There's only one reason to continue' ":** Author interview with Jack Rapke.

214   **"There was a donnybrook going on":** Author interview with Tom Hanks.

215   **After days of talks, both sides:** Author interview with confidential source.

215   **At the same time, Lansing persuaded Jaffe:** Starkey, one of the producers, had a different recollection of the sequence of events. "There were two different renegotiations," he said. "Renegotiation number one was getting the movie started when we were in South Carolina for the first day of principal photography. There was a second renegotiation that occurred when we got back to Los Angeles." Author interview with Steve Starkey.

215   **"I was alone":** Author interview with Tom Hanks.

216   **"We shot on Sundays with a splinter unit":** Author interview with Robert Zemeckis.

216   **"We worked twenty-seven straight days in a row":** Author interview with Tom Hanks.

216   **"Bob finds me there and drags me out":** Author interview with Michelle Manning.

217   **"Everybody at the studio was pissed off":** Author interview with Robert Zemeckis.

217   **"It was very, very tense":** Author interview with John Goldwyn.

217   **"Bob was adamant the audience shouldn't fill out":** Starkey believed it was he who clashed with Lansing. "I was up at the front saying, 'You guys, you can pass the preview cards back,'" he said. "Sherry's yelling, 'Send them out!' Bob did not say one word. Bob was sitting in the back, horrified." Author interview with Steve Starkey.

217   **"He shouted: 'I don't know what your problem is' ":** Author interview with John Goldwyn.

217   **"*Forrest Gump* is one of those movies":** Frank Rich, "The Gump from Hope," *New York Times*, July 21, 1994.

218   **The picture became one of the highest-grossing movies:** Boxofficemojo.com.

218   **"They were all so hungover that Bob":** Author interview with Michelle Manning.

218   **"It was rough":** Author interview with Robert Zemeckis.

CHAPTER 14

219 **The same was not true for Biondi:** Ken Auletta, "That's Entertainment," *New Yorker*, February 12, 1996.

220 **"Boy, he could blister people":** Author interview with Frank Biondi Jr.

221 **Back in Los Angeles, she gave detailed notes:** Author interview with Frank Marshall.

221 **A critical drubbing did not sink the film:** Boxofficemojo.com.

221 **"Sherry understood how to deal with complicated men":** Author interview with John Goldwyn.

222 **"He could be ferocious":** Ibid.

224 **"I knew nothing of my genealogy":** Author interview with Randall Wallace.

224 **"I decided to pass":** Author interview with Mel Gibson.

224 **After finishing 1994's *Maverick*:** Ibid.

225 **"I thought, directing this thing is going to be a big, epic deal":** Ibid.

225 **"I said, 'The fates are saying you've got to play the part'":** Author interview with Alan Ladd Jr.

226 **Gibson came to the studio to negotiate a deal:** Author interview with Bill Bernstein.

226 **"He felt he wasn't being respected":** Author interview with Jeff Berg. Bruce Davey also confirmed the incident.

226 **"We were right up to the moment of [shooting]":** Author interview with Mel Gibson.

226 **A week later, Gibson and Davey accepted:** Rachel Abramowitz, "Dressed to Kilt," *Premiere*, May 1995, 77.

226 **Production got under way in Scotland:** Author interview with Bruce Davey.

227 **She looked on in wonder as epic scenes unfolded:** Ray Bennett, "A Kind of Hell," *Hollywood Reporter*, March 5, 1998, S12–S14. Where different sources report different numbers, I have gone with the Paramount Pictures production notes for *Braveheart*.

227 **"It took everything I had":** Author interview with Mel Gibson.

228 **"Some of the stuff was way over the top":** Ibid.

228 **"Sherry is probably the smartest executive I've seen":** Author interview with Bruce Davey.

229 **"It was extreme":** Author interview with Randall Wallace.

229 **"It's two in the morning":** Ibid.

229 **"Steve and I had the film down to three hours":** Author interview with Mel Gibson.

230 ***Braveheart* opened May 24, 1995:** Boxofficemojo.com.

CHAPTER 15

233   **She was particularly disturbed:** Terry Pristin, "Friedkin Signing Keeps 'Jade' in Lansing Family," *Los Angeles Times*, April 18, 1994.

233   **She had bought the project, based on a Joe Eszterhas story:** Andy Marx, "'Jade' Deal a $2.5 Mil Gem," *Variety*, November 8, 1992.

234   **Jaffe said he and Lansing discussed the matter:** Author interview with Stanley Jaffe.

234   **"Sherry was the head of the studio":** Author interview with William Friedkin.

235   **They did not always see things:** Ibid.

235   **Goldwyn had been to a recent exhibition:** Author interview with John Goldwyn.

236   **But Lansing knew it was contending:** Richard Natale, "'Waterworld' Sails to No. 1," *Los Angeles Times*, July 31, 1995.

236   **Costner had almost died along the way:** Shelley Levitt, "Kevin Costner's Hawaii Uh-Oh," *People*, May 29, 1995.

237   **"[Universal's] Casey Silver couldn't run away fast enough":** Author interview with Bill Mechanic.

237   **"They were all calling, saying, 'We had such a good thing'":** Ibid.

237   **"I told Peter that finding a partner was his problem":** James Cameron, email to author, February 16, 2015.

238   **Lansing sent Bernstein, her chief of business affairs:** Author interview with Bill Bernstein.

238   **He found an operation:** For a detailed account of the physical challenges, see Paula Parisi, *"Titanic" and the Making of James Cameron* (New York: Newmarket Press, 1998).

239   **"Cameron wanted real wallpaper":** Author interview with Fred Gallo.

239   **"He said, 'Your budget's running way over!'":** Author interview with Bill Mechanic.

239   **Dolgen said Paramount would only stick to the deal:** Author interview with Bill Bernstein.

240   **"This proved later to be an enormous source of animosity":** Cameron email to author.

240   **Nor did the tension ease when Redstone bragged:** Author interview with John Goldwyn.

241   **"Everyone thought they were going to lose money":** Cameron email to author.

241   **"Peter was hiding his head in the sand":** Author interview with Bill Mechanic.

242   **Then, during the shoot, Winslet chipped a bone:** Christopher Godwin,

"James Cameron: From 'Titanic' to 'Avatar,'" *The Times* (London), January 9, 2010.

242 **As word leaked about the nightmare shoot:** Godwin, "James Cameron."

242 ***Newsweek* headlined a story:** "A Sinking Sensation," *Newsweek*, November 24, 1996.

243 **while *Time* wrote:** Kim Masters, "Glub, Glub, Glub . . . ," *Time*, November 25, 1996.

243 **"She was very excited that the raw footage captured":** Cameron email to author.

243 **"Chernin said, 'Jon, I need relief' ":** Author interview with John Goldwyn.

243 **"We were carrying the movie on our books":** Author interview with Peter Chernin.

244 **"We got a call from Robbie Friedman":** Cameron email to author.

244 **"Harrison Ford angrily warned studio executives":** Bernard Weinraub, "As Problems Delay *Titanic*, Hollywood Sighs in Relief," *New York Times*, May 29, 1997.

244 **"Tensions between the two studios":** Bernard Weinraub, "As *Titanic* Hits No. 1, Perils Lurk in Its Future," *New York Times*, December 22, 1997.

244 **Cameron wanted to go even later:** "The reality of getting the film done at the necessary level of visual quality was becoming almost impossible," wrote Cameron in an email to the author. "The film was simply too long and the visual effects too unprecedented. . . . I said if we could establish a foothold with a good opening right before Christmas, then audiences had the relatively quiet months of January and February to find the film, and it would create an opportunity for repeat viewing. It was a radical hypothesis, with no real-world precedent."

245 **"She had a very emotional reaction":** Ibid.

246 **Contrary to industry expectations:** Boxofficemojo.com.

246 **"The picture went 'clean' ":** Author interview with Bill Bernstein.

247 **"She sent over the photo in a silver frame":** Author interview with Jon Landau.

CHAPTER 16

248 **"She was tough when she needed to be tough":** Author interview with Bryan Lourd.

248 **"She would do her reading on a Friday":** Author interview with Karen Rosenfelt.

249 **Lansing would buzz each executive directly:** Author interview with Michelle Manning.

249 **"Sherry was a really hard worker":** Author interview with Scott Rudin.

249 **When Jordan Kerner, a producer:** Author interview with Jordan Kerner.

250 **Many of these producers considered Lansing a friend:** Author interview with Michelle Manning.

251 **"To my dismay, she now said she wanted changes":** Alexander Payne, email message to author, September 11, 2015.

251 **Lansing leveled a finger at him:** Author interview with John Goldwyn.

251 **Lansing's irritation welled up:** Rebecca Traister, "Ed Norton to Paramount's Sherry Lansing: Burn This!" *New York Observer*, September 30, 2002.

252 **When Fox cast him in 1997's** *Fight Club*: Ibid.

252 **"Did he have a deal?":** This is Lansing's recollection. Wahlberg confirmed the essence of their conversation. Author interview with Mark Wahlberg.

252 **"It wasn't a film I had much interest in":** Edward Norton, email message to author, June 19, 2016.

252 **"Sherry said, 'We're going to force his hand'":** Author interview with Mark Wahlberg.

253 **"I was informed, again, that Paramount would sue me":** Edward Norton, email message to author.

253 **Faced with the real possibility:** "I don't know where this story about me bringing a cameraman comes from," said Norton. "That's hyperbole." He explained: "My assistant at the time and I used to shoot little behind-the-scenes photos and movies on every film." Ibid.

253 **"It was surreal":** Author interview with Donald De Line.

253 **His tantrums were legendary:** Amy Wallace, "The Hottest Seats in Hollywood," *Los Angeles Times*, August 14, 2000.

254 **Paramount had paid $1.5 million:** Benedict Carver, "Truman Suit Retort," *Variety*, June 22, 1998. The $1.5 million included Niccol's directing fee, although he subsequently did not direct.

254 **"I got a call very early in the morning":** Author interview with Michelle Manning.

254 **"Crazy idea":** Author interview with Scott Rudin.

254 **"He was blowing up my phone":** Author interview with Michelle Manning.

257 **"Sherry had a specific method":** Author interview with Don Granger.

258 **The** *Star Trek* **franchise, which had been launched:** Designer-entrepreneur Gary Goddard expressed frustration when Jaffe turned down the possibility of creating a full-size Starship Enterprise in downtown Las Vegas, where the $150 million cost would have been covered by the city's redevelopment committee. He said Lansing supported the project, but she had no recollection of it when interviewed for this book. Later, Goddard and Paramount worked on a more minor-scale attrac-

tion in Las Vegas. See Gary Goddard, "Now It Can Be Told: The 'Star Trek' Attraction That Almost Came to Life in 1992," posted April 5, 2012, *www.thegoddardgroup.com/blog/index.php/now-it-can-be-told-the-star-trek -attraction-that-almost-came-to-life-in-1992*.

258   **"When I brought it to Leonard"**: Author interview with Rick Berman.

261   **Rodat had been mesmerized**: Author interview with Robert Rodat.

261   **He knew of the five Sullivan brothers**: See Dan Kurzman, *Left to Die: The Tragedy of the USS Juneau* (New York: Pocket Books, 1994).

261   **Rodat took his idea to Gordon**: Author interview with Mark Gordon.

262   **"You can't seriously"**: Author interview with Rob Cohen.

262   **"The screenplay first came to me through my agents"**: Steven Spielberg, email message to author, July 23, 2015.

263   **"Steven said, 'Look, with the technology that now exists'"**: Author interview with Tom Hanks.

263   **"The budget was set at"**: Author interview with confidential source. The budget may initially have been somewhat lower. See Peter Bart, *The Gross: The Hits, the Flops—The Summer That Ate Hollywood* (New York: St. Martin's Griffin, 2000), 155.

263   **"[She] was a great team leader"**: Spielberg, email message to author.

264   **"I got there early"**: Author interview with Robert Rodat.

264   **"It was five days"**: In addition to *Saving Private Ryan* and *Amistad*, Spielberg was working on another co-production with Paramount, 1998's *Deep Impact*. "So concerned was Spielberg about *Deep Impact*—a screening of the film at Paramount, which was coproducing the movie, had been so disastrous that executives walked out mumbling 'straight to video'—that he was taking footage home at night and coming back in the next morning with notes for [director Mimi] Leder." Nicole LaPorte, *The Men Who Would Be King: An Almost Epic Tale of Moguls, Movies, and a Company Called Dream-Works* (Boston: Houghton Mifflin Harcourt, 2010), 162.

264   **"This was the beginning"**: "I asked for ten days of training," said Dye, a retired Marine Corps captain who had served in Vietnam. "It was reduced to eight. Then it got reduced to about five. We went from the crack of dawn until long after dark, consistently trying to give them the basic infantry skills they needed. I purposely pushed hard." Author interview with Dale Dye.

266   **"I'll never forget it"**: Author interview with Terry Press.

266   **"I discussed the rating at length with Sherry"**: Spielberg, email message to author.

266   **Despite its near-three-hour length**: Boxofficemojo.com.

266   **"Here Spielberg, the creator of *Schindler's List*"**: Richard Schickel, "Reel War," *Time*, July 27, 1998.

267 **"Somebody told me that Harvey had hired":** Author interview with Terry Press.

268 **"I remember feeling flushed":** Ibid.

268 **Spielberg was relatively stoic:** Others said Spielberg was angry. "Spielberg politely smiled and clapped, but he was furious at having lost by what he considered dirty means, and when the ceremony was over and it came time to head backstage and do press, an act that would mean following Harvey and his procession, Spielberg refused to go." LaPorte, *The Men Who Would Be King*, 202.

CHAPTER 17

269 **The actor was in the middle:** Andy Marx, "Cruise Team Inks Par Deal," *Variety*, November 3, 1992.

270 **"The goal was to make a couple":** Author interview with Paula Wagner.

270 **"The mandate from Sherry and John Goldwyn":** Ibid.

271 **Her relationship with De Palma:** Author interview with John Goldwyn.

271 **"When Brian called asking for help":** Jay Cocks, email message to author, August 18, 2015.

271 **"Jay is a phenomenal film historian":** Author interview with Paula Wagner.

272 **"Brian wanted it to be done with sleight of hand":** Ibid.

272 **"I suggested making [him] the major villain":** Cocks, email message to author.

272 **"We'd done a bunch of research":** Author interview with David Koepp.

273 **"She said, 'OK, kids, here are your rules'":** Author interview with Paula Wagner.

274 **Cruise, in fact, had been given some stern counsel:** Author interview with confidential source.

274 **Wagner, a newcomer to the production realm:** Author interview with Paula Wagner.

274 **Lansing sent Don Granger, her production executive:** Author interview with Don Granger.

274 **At one point, a crew member noted:** Author interview with confidential source.

275 **Cruise was as committed to producing as acting:** Author interview with Paula Wagner.

275 **"Brian saw the enormity of Tom's star power":** Author interview with Rick Nicita.

275 **"He got a lot of interference":** Author interview with confidential source.

276 *Mission*'s **success, with earnings of $458 million:** Boxofficemojo.com.

276   **"It was like these two immovable mountains"**: Author interview with confidential source.

277   **"We thought we were cursed"**: Author interview with John Woo.

277   **"We start hearing these things"**: The hailstorm was the most expensive natural disaster in Sydney's history, costing more than A$1.7 billion and damaging some 35,000 buildings. Cassie Crofts, "Sydney's Apocalyptic Hailstorm," *National Geographic*, April 14, 2016.

277   **"I said, 'Sherry's really mad'"**: Author interview with Paula Wagner.

278   **Throughout, Cruise avoided proselytizing**: Stephen Galloway, "Pat Kingsley Finally Talks: Tom Cruise, Scientology and What She's Doing Now," *Hollywood Reporter*, December 20, 2013.

279   **"I got this invitation to the Scientology ball"**: Author interview with Tom Freston.

279   **Goldwyn stopped by Rosenfelt's office on his way**: Author interview with Karen Rosenfelt.

280   **Fifteen minutes later, Lansing was sitting with the two men**: Kim Masters, "The Passion of Tom Cruise," *Radar*, September 2005.

280   **Goldwyn turned pale**: Goldwyn declined to discuss the matter.

280   **"Sherry got teary-eyed"**: Author interview with Paula Wagner.

281   **"I was very interested in what I'd pitched him"**: Author interview with Joe Carnahan.

282   **"Tom and Paula had met with me"**: Author interview with J. J. Abrams.

284   **"It didn't feel like something I could do justice to"**: Ibid.

CHAPTER 18

286   **Born in the Bronx in 1946**: See Dawn Steel, *They Can Kill You but They Can't Eat You: Lessons from the Front* (New York: Pocket Books, 1993).

288   **In December 1997**: Bernard Weinraub, "Dawn Steel, Studio Chief and Producer, Dies at 51," *New York Times*, December 22, 1997.

288   **"There are literally thousands of appointments"**: Author interview with Barry Munitz.

289   **"I frequently found myself sitting next to Sherry"**: Author interview with Ward Connerly.

290   **"She didn't have the luxury of being overtly political"**: Author interview with Bryan Lourd.

290   **"I still use the shorthand of 'a Sherry Lansing thriller'"**: Author interview with Stacey Snider.

291   **"There's nobody who understood the animus"**: Author interview with John Goldwyn.

291   **Judd's coolness under fire**: Judd was impressed by Lansing's granular attention to detail, right down to her makeup and hair. When Lansing asked

her to change her hairstyle, Judd replied that the dowdy style fit the time and place. "Honey," said Lansing, "you're a movie star." Author interview with Ashley Judd.

291 **and the movie earned a rich $60 million:** Boxofficemojo.com.

292 **"I have two words for you":** Others reported that Lansing warned, "I'll take your house"—the same threat she had used with Mike Myers. See Kim Masters, "Hollywood's Best Revenge," *Time*, October 7, 1996.

292 **Basinger had been sued:** The $8.1 million award was later voided. See Judy Brennan and Edward J. Boyer, "Damages Against Kim Basinger in Film Suit Voided," *Los Angeles Times*, September 23, 1994.

292 **"There was no question that Paramount":** Author interview with Jeff Berg.

293 **"Sherry wasn't known to be brutal":** Author interview with Scott Rudin.

293 **When Fox decided not to make it:** Author interview with Amy Heckerling.

293 **The movie earned $56.6 million:** Boxofficemojo.com.

293 **"We had about ten drafts before we took it to Sherry":** Author interview with Tina Fey.

294 **"We were at Paramount":** Author interview with Robert Cort.

295 **"Usher was brand-new":** Ibid.

295 **Without Usher, Weinstein pulled out:** Harvey Weinstein, email message to author, July 9, 2015.

296 **"I said to [marketing chief] Arthur Cohen":** Author interview with Robert Cort.

296 **That weekend, the picture earned $23 million:** Ibid.

297 **Those rights, however, came with a catch:** Edward Jay Epstein, "How to Finance a Hollywood Blockbuster," *Slate*, April 25, 2005.

297 **One script came in after another:** David Hughes, *Tales from Development Hell: The Greatest Movies Never Made?* (London: Titan Books, 2003), 212–35.

297 **At first West passed:** Author interview with Simon West.

298 **"He comes in and almost immediately says":** Author interview with Steven E. de Souza.

298 **"There was a long list of writers":** Author interview with Simon West.

298 **"She definitely had some baggage":** Ibid.

299 **"She said, 'Look, I want to do it'":** Ibid.

299 **"What I noticed immediately":** Angelina Jolie, email message to author, June 18, 2015.

300 **The actress was drug-tested, regardless:** Author interview with John Goldwyn.

300 **"There was the notion that we would put a team around her":** Author interview with confidential source.

300 **West suggested hiring Bobby Klein:** Christine Spines, "Tomb with a View," *Premiere*, July 2001.

300 **Relationships that had been tense before:** Gordon blamed Paramount for cutting $9 million from the budget at the last minute. "If you ask a lot of people, you'll find this out: he's difficult," he acknowledged. "You know what difficult means? Difficult means you say, 'No, I can't do that.' They want you to fall over your back and do what they tell you, not even knowing what they're asking. I'm one of these people that says no." While prepping the film in London, tensions escalated and he was stripped of his full rights as producer, he added. "I had to eat shit for the whole movie, because all my creative rights were gone. Simon West was the boss of the movie, so Simon West got to make the movie he wanted to make. I lost my teeth." Later, he said, his full rights were restored. Author interview with Lawrence Gordon.

300 **"Simon West comes with this guy Bobby Klein":** Ibid.

300 **As preproduction got under way in England:** Ibid.

301 **"[The expert] wanted her to have milk baths":** Author interview with Lloyd Levin.

301 **When Klein was then accused:** Spines, "Tomb with a View."

301 **Gordon was ecstatic:** Author interview with Lawrence Gordon.

301 **"She trained for months beforehand":** Author interview with Simon West.

301 **"It's to be expected":** Jolie email to author.

302 **"It was horrible":** Author interview with Lloyd Levin.

302 **"It was a very awkward situation":** Author interview with Simon West.

302 **"We had numerous screenings":** Author interview with Lloyd Levin.

302 **Despite the volleys lobbed by the critics:** Boxofficemojo.com.

CHAPTER 19

304 **"Everyone was in a state of shock":** Author interview with Ron Meyer.

304 **Ten days after the attacks:** Sallie Hofmeister and James Bates, "Movie Studios React to FBI Warning," *Los Angeles Times*, September 21, 2001.

305 **"We had watchers on the roofs and across the road":** Author interview with Jonathan Dolgen.

305 **As a patriotic fervor swept the country:** Rick Lyman, "A Nation Challenged: The Entertainment Industry; Hollywood Discusses Role in War Effort," *New York Times*, November 12, 2001.

307 **"She had me fly with her to Maryland":** Author interview with Mace Neufeld.

307 **During the making of *Patriot Games*:** Author interview with Phillip Noyce.

307 **After several drafts and several writers:** Akiva Goldsman (*A Beautiful Mind*) was among the other writers who worked on it.

308   **"Sherry wanted to make sure she and I were on the same page"**: Author interview with Ben Affleck.

309   **"When I went to see Sherry"**: Author interview with Phil Alden Robinson.

309   **"On the morning of September 11"**: Ibid.

310   **In May 2002, *Sum* opened to mixed reviews**: The movie earned $194 million globally; boxofficemojo.com.

310   **Many saw it as a reaction to 9/11**: See "The Sum of All Fears Controversy," Fox News, June 3, 2002.

310   **"We delayed the test screenings by a week or two"**: Author interview with Phil Alden Robinson.

310   **"The film division wasn't doing well"**: Author interview with Frank Biondi Jr.

311   **"That was the beginning of a difficult time"**: Author interview with Bryan Lourd.

312   **"The business was changing"**: Author interview with John Goldwyn.

313   **"What Sherry wouldn't do was look at the things"**: Author interview with Scott Rudin.

313   **"As a group, we'd become stale"**: Author interview with Karen Rosenfelt.

313   **"What was coming through development"**: Author interview with Jonathan Dolgen.

313   **One magazine called them**: Anne Thompson, "The Id Couple," *New York Magazine*, November 4, 2002.

314   **"He was coming to tell Nicole not to wear the nose"**: Author interview with Scott Rudin.

314   **When Weinstein forced Paramount to pull the movie**: Writer Ken Auletta described being present with Weinstein as he wrestled over what to do and mused, "Do I be the good Harvey or the bad Harvey?" See Auletta, "Beauty and the Beast," *New Yorker*, December 16, 2002.

314   **Rudin called him, outraged**: Thompson, "The Id Couple."

314   **"We both bring strong viewpoints"**: Harvey Weinstein, email message to author, July 9, 2015.

314   **Rudin insisted Paramount was in the wrong**: Author interview with Scott Rudin.

315   **"I found the amount of energy"**: Kim Masters, "Can This Marriage Be Saved?" *Esquire*, May 2003.

CHAPTER 20

318   **"We talked primarily about the work of the Carter Center"**: Author interview with Jimmy Carter.

319   **Marketing chief Arthur Cohen was edged aside in September**: Claudia Eller, "Paramount Marketing Exec Resigning After 14 Years," *Los Angeles Times*, September 10, 2003.

319   **and two months later so was Goldwyn:** Dave McNary, "Paramount Prexy Is Stepping Aside," *Variety*, November 24, 2003.

319   **"My last tour of duty":** Author interview with John Goldwyn.

320   **"Could I have fought for my job?":** Ibid.

320   **Mel Karmazin, Viacom's president and CEO:** Lawrie Mifflin, "Making a Media Giant: Viacom to Buy CBS, Forming 2d Largest Media Company," *New York Times*, September 8, 1999.

320   **"Mel had his own narrative of what went wrong":** Author interview with Jonathan Dolgen.

320   **"Mel had enough, and Sumner kind of punched his ticket":** Author interview with Tom Freston.

321   **"Sumner pulled me into the Carlyle Hotel":** Ibid.

321   **"We were trying to figure out what to do":** Ibid. CBS chairman Leslie Moonves declined to comment. Mel Karmazin did not respond to requests for comment.

321   **"Dolgen and Freston always had a bad relationship":** Author interview with Scott Rudin.

321   **"Sumner called me":** Author interview with Jonathan Dolgen.

322   **"I was [stunned]":** Author interview with Tom Freston.

322   **"Sherry was a success at a time when the business":** Author interview with Scott Rudin.

322   **"That's when I saw her depressed for the first time":** Author interview with Lynda Obst.

323   **"We talked about [her leaving] for five years":** Author interview with Bryan Lourd.

323   **Her spirit had fled the enterprise:** The recollection is Lansing's. "That's not my style," said Freston. Author interview with Tom Freston.

324   **Freston was "dumbfounded" when he found out:** Ibid.

324   **In a story headlined:** Claudia Eller, "Hollywood Pioneer Lansing Is Poised to Exit Paramount," *Los Angeles Times*, November 2, 2004.

324   **Rosenfelt was on an exercise bicycle at the gym:** Author interview with Karen Rosenfelt.

324   **"The way Sherry left was like an incredibly produced movie":** Author interview with Michelle Manning.

CHAPTER 21

330   **In fact, he was reaching out to tell her:** Megan Garvey, "State Bets on the Promise of Stem Cell Research," *Los Angeles Times*, November 4, 2004.

330   **"Parts of the Christian right were saying":** Author interview with Steve Westly.

331   **She was "a no-brainer":** Author interview with Steve Westly.

331   **"Our lawsuit focused on a feature of Prop 71"**: Author interview with Catherine Short.

332   **Two lawsuits were filed in California courts:** Lee Romney, "Court Asked to Expedite Stem Cell Research Suits," *Los Angeles Times*, June 15, 2006.

332   **"The board members of the initiative didn't think"**: Author interview with Bob Klein.

332   **"The brilliance of the opposition was just to wear everyone down"**: "Our goal was to win, not to drag things out," said Short. "Our goal was to have Prop. 71 declared unconstitutional pursuant to Article XVI, section 3, of the state constitution." Author interview with Catherine Short.

333   **"The September 9, 2005, meeting"**: Ralph Brave, "Stem-Cell Wonderland," *Sacramento News and Review*, October 20, 2005.

333   **"With the money we'd raised"**: Author interview with Bob Klein.

334   **In November 2006, CIRM announced:** CIRM, "$181 Million Headed for Stem Cell Institute: California Philanthropists Extend Support to Stem Cell Research, as $150 Million Loan Clears Last Hurdle," posted November 20, 2006. *www.cirm.ca.gov/about-cirm/newsroom/press-releases/11202006 /181-million-headed-stem-cell-institute-california*.

334   **"We had very little"**: Author interview with Catherine Short.

334   **In December 2005, the plaintiffs:** Author interview with Bob Klein.

334   **In an initial ruling in April 2006:** Lee Romney, "Judge Upholds Stem Cell Initiative," *Los Angeles Times*, April 22, 2006.

334   **"This was a states' rights issue"**: Author interview with Bob Klein.

334   **On May 16, 2007:** *California Family Bioethics Council v. California Institute for Regenerative Medicine*, 147 Cal. App. 4th 1319 (2007).

335   **"This is the end of the road"**: Mary Engel, "Hurdle to Stem Cell Funds Cleared," *Los Angeles Times*, May 17, 2007.

335   **Days later, the bond sale moved forward:** Author interview with Steve Westly.

335   **"It wasn't so much an [individual] opponent"**: Author interview with Barry Munitz.

335   **She became one of the leaders:** Jennifer Steinhauer, "Deal Will Turn a Los Angeles Hospital Private," *New York Times*, November 20, 2009.

336   **There was only one blot on those halcyon days:** Dave McNary, "Par's Grey Area," *Variety*, July 12, 2005.

336   **But that was counterbalanced by the blockbuster returns:** *War of the Worlds* earned $592 million, while *Mission: Impossible III* made $398 million (both are worldwide numbers); boxofficemojo.com.

336   **Costs had skyrocketed at the UC campuses:** Richard C. Paddock, "Less to Bank On at State Universities," *Los Angeles Times*, October 7, 2007.

336   **"We were almost $1 billion behind"**: Author interview with Mark Yudof.

337   **"Sherry did not want to see tuition go up"**: Author interview with Jerry Brown.

337   **"During two days of protests at UCLA"**: Kevin O'Leary, "Tuition Hikes, Protests in California and Elsewhere," *Time*, November 21, 2009.

338   **"They surrounded the building"**: Author interview with Mark Yudof.

338   **The protests continued deep into 2011**: Chris O'Brien, "How One Student's Pepper Spray Photo Became an Internet Meme," *San Jose Mercury News*, November 23, 2011.

339   **"She met personally with students"**: Author interview with Larry Gordon.

339   **"She [was] a good advocate for UC"**: Author interview with Jerry Brown.

340   **"The first hospital claimed I was cured"**: Author interview with William Friedkin.

341   **"I had my very personal experience with my husband"**: Author interview with Katie Couric.

342   **Joining three other women to create a television special**: Fraser, alone among the women, did not respond to requests for comment.

342   **Things got off to a shaky start at a breakfast meeting**: Author interview with Sue Schwartz.

343   **In another meeting, "I was feeling really bad energy"**: Author interview with Rusty Robertson.

343   **"We didn't just double-team them"**: Author interview with Katie Couric.

344   **"In the midst of this meeting, Sherry Lansing approaches me"**: Author interview with Phillip Sharp.

344   **"As everything fell into place with the final network commitments"**: Author interview with Kathleen Lobb.

344   **"That hadn't been done before"**: Author interview with Phillip Sharp.

345   **"We established a goal of raising $100 million"**: Author interview with Lisa Paulsen.

346   **"We sat down, and Sherry and Laura did the pitch"**: Author interview with Ellen Ziffren.

346   **"We were coming from our home in Phoenix"**: Author interview with Bud Selig.

347   **"We used to have such wild dreams"**: "2008 Stand Up to Cancer Telecast," YouTube, posted November 2, 2010, *https://youtu.be/0biMPOMFcoA*.

347   **That broadcast led to pledges of $101 million**: Author interview with Kathleen Lobb.

347   **By the end of 2016, they had obtained almost $500 million**: Ibid.

347   **"If those nine ladies hadn't started Stand Up to Cancer"**: Author interview with David Gobin.

347   **"It's like any recipe"**: Author interview with Sue Schwartz.

348   **Only one of Lansing's Stand Up to Cancer friends:** Aljean Harmetz, "Laura Ziskin, Producer of 'Spider-Man' and 'Pretty Woman,' Dies at 61," *New York Times*, June 13, 2011.

348   **On June 28, 2011:** Gregg Kilday, "Tobey Maguire, Sally Field Pay Tribute to Laura Ziskin at Memorial Service," *Hollywood Reporter*, June 29, 2011.

348   **Melnick had died two years earlier:** Douglas Martin, "Daniel Melnick, Hollywood Producer, Dies at 77," *New York Times*, October 16, 2009.

349   **James Aubrey, one of her mentors:** Burt A. Folkart, "James Aubrey Jr., Former Head of CBS and MGM, Dies," *Los Angeles Times*, September 11, 1994.

351   **"She paved the way for the tsunami of women":** Meryl Streep, email message to author, June 23, 2014.

351   **"She was tough, but she had a lot of grace in her toughness":** Author interview with Jane Fonda.

352   **He spoke about her distinguished work:** "Sherry Lansing Receiving the Jean Hersholt Humanitarian Award," YouTube, posted February 4, 2016, *https://youtu.be/bTpfh38kvdQ*.

PHOTO CREDITS

p. 3: *(top)*, BEI/BEI/Shutterstock; *(center)*, Courtesy of Lightstorm Entertainment; *(bottom)*, Kevin Winter/Getty Images Entertainment/Getty

p. 4: *(top)*, Kevin Winter/Getty Images Entertainment/Getty; *(center)*, Evan Agostini/Getty Images Entertainment/Getty; *(bottom)*, Stephen Shugerman/Getty Images Entertainment/Getty

p. 5: *(top)*, Courtesy of Vince Bucci Photography; *(bottom)*, Courtesy of ABC Photography

p. 6: *(top)*, Berliner Archives/Rex by Shutterstock; *(bottom)*, Alexandra Wyman/WireImage/Getty

p. 7: *(bottom)*, AP Photo/Chris Carlson

p. 8: *(top)*, Berliner Archives/Rex by Shutterstock; *(bottom)*, Lester Cohen/WireImage/Getty

All other images courtesy of the Sherry Lansing archives.

INDEX

ABOUT THE AUTHOR

STEPHEN GALLOWAY is a senior editor with the *Hollywood Reporter*. He was named Entertainment Journalist of the Year in 2013.